Thomas Eakins

Thomas Eakins (1844-1916)

General Editor: John Wilmerding

and the Heart of American Life

Sponsored by **BRITISH AIRWAYS**

National Portrait Gallery, London

Published for the exhibition at the National Portrait
Gallery, London from 8 October 1993 to 23 January
1994

Published by the National Portrait Gallery,
2 St Martin's Place, London WC2H 0HE, England,
1993

ISBN 1 85514 095 0

A catalogue record for this book is available from the
British Library

House editor: Gillian Forrester
Assistant editor: Katie Bent
Designer: Derek Birdsall RDI
Indexer: Helen Baz

Phototypeset in Monophoto Walbaum by August
Filmsetting Limited, Haydock, St Helens, England

Printed and bound in Italy by Amilcare Pizzi, Milan

Photographic acknowledgements: the publishers
would like to thank the following for making
copyright photographs available: The Conway
Library (fig.2b); The Courtauld Institute of Art
(fig.17); The Mansell Collection (fig.44a); The Witt
Library (figs.27–31, 36–38). Photographers: Henry
Nelson (no. 33); Lee Stalsworth (nos. 1, 5–6, 28, 35,
37, 40). All other photographs were supplied by the
owners of the works of art reproduced or the sources
given in the text.

Extracts from manuscripts in Charles Bregler's
Thomas Eakins Collection are reproduced with kind
permission of the Pennsylvania Academy of the Fine Arts.

Front cover: *Amelia Van Buren*, *c*.1891 (detail of no.
27). Reproduced by permission of the Phillips
Collection, Washington, DC

Back cover: *Self-portrait*, 1902 (no. 41). Reproduced
by permission of the National Academy of Design,
New York

Contents

Sponsor's Foreword

As the world's largest international airline, and one aiming to become the first global airline, it is proper to be supporting the National Portrait Gallery's winter exhibition of the work of Thomas Eakins. This is our major corporate sponsorship of the year for which we are both transporting the paintings to Britain and providing financial backing.

But why should British Airways sponsor an art exhibition? The reason is that we are a British company with recognised responsibilities to the wider community – responsibilities that we take seriously. As such, one of our corporate goals includes 'being a good neighbour'.

This exhibition of Thomas Eakins's work is the first ever seen in Europe. Arguably America's most distinguished portrait painter, he lived and worked around Philadelphia, an area in which our business is fast growing following our recent alliance with the American airline USAir.

Eakins painted the high flyers of his time from all walks of American society – generals and bishops, sportsmen and academics. The exhibition captures the spirit of nineteenth-century Philadelphia in all its facets in the progressive decades following the Civil War, and brings to Europe some fifty of his best portraits loaned by museums and galleries from all across the United States.

We are proud to be involved with Eakins's work which I am sure you will enjoy.

ROBERT AYLING
Group Managing Director, British Airways

Patrons

Under the distinguished patronage of:

H.E. The Honorable Raymond G.H. Seitz,
Ambassador of the United States of America

H.E. Sir Robin Renwick KCMG,
Her Majesty's Ambassador to the United States of America

Support for production of the catalogue was generously provided by:

The E. Rhodes and Leona B. Carpenter Foundation

The Wyeth Endowment for American Art,
established to support scholarship in American art.

Support for the Symposium was generously provided by:

The Dietrich Foundation

The Wyeth Endowment for American Art,
established to support scholarship in American art.

The National Portrait Gallery is also grateful to Paul Mellon KBE for his support.

List of Lenders

Foreword

When I first travelled in the United States as a Commonwealth Fund Fellow more than thirty years ago, I had the good fortune to be able to visit forty-four states of the Union. It was an extraordinary educational experience, akin to a latter day Grand Tour. As a former student of the Courtauld Institute, taught primarily to appreciate Italian art, and with interests centred on the European field, I was astonished by the quality of much American nineteenth century painting. Not unexpectedly, I was deeply impressed by the vigour, brilliance and freshness of Winslow Homer's paintings of the New England coast; but I was arrested most of all by the work of the great Philadelphian artist and teacher, Thomas Eakins, a dour and uncompromising Realist, whom Walt Whitman so memorably described as a force rather than a painter. Eakins's portraits seemed to me to have a presence and insight wholly comparable to the great nineteenth century French masters whose styles and careers were at the core of every art history course in Britain.

In those far-off days one found very few books on British art on the shelves of American university libraries; but there was an even greater ignorance in Britain about American art. As far as British art in the United States is concerned, this situation has been remedied, largely through the enthusiasm of Paul Mellon and his establishment of the British Art Center at Yale, to which he gave the comprehensive collection of British paintings, drawings and illustrated books he had brought together since 1959 at his home in Virginia. But historic American painting is still very little known or regarded in this country, or indeed in Europe. There is only one Eakins portrait in the whole of the European continent, that of Clara Mather in the Musée d'Orsay in Paris. Yet for decades now Eakins has been acclaimed by American scholars as one of the truly great masters of the late nineteenth century; John Wilmerding has rightly declared, in the essay which follows, that he was 'one of the towering humane visions in the history of art'.

Over the last twenty years or so, the National Portrait Gallery has devoted exhibitions to a number of painters who were leading exponents of portraiture in this country, from Van Dyck to Ramsay and Zoffany, from Sir Thomas Lawrence to Sargent and Augustus John. We have never sought to mount a special exhibition of the work of G.F. Watts, whose ideals were synonymous with those for which the Gallery was founded in 1856, for the obvious reason that the Gallery already contains most of the portraits which Watts painted as his pantheon of Victorian endeavour. But it is fascinating that in Philadelphia Eakins was pursuing a similar course, painting all those mainly professional people who were contributing to a revival of civilized life in the newly confirmed United States after the horrors and deprivations of the Civil War. Few of these portraits were commissioned; like Watts, Eakins sought his sitters out. It is this generation of distinguished scientists, surgeons, writers, teachers, musicians and sportsmen, celebrated by Eakins, that we, too, seek to celebrate in the present exhibition, the first we have devoted to a great foreign artist who did not practise in (indeed never visited) this country. It is particularly fitting that we should be honouring a great American master at precisely the moment that Mrs Drue Heinz's munificent benefaction to the Gallery, the splendidly rehoused Archive and Library which bears her name, is being opened. Coincidentally, the fine portrait of Admiral Melville which members of the Heinz family have recently presented to the National Gallery of Art in Washington is one of the masterpieces in the exhibition.

When I first considered organizing an Eakins exhibition in London, I sounded out the directors and curators of a number of American museums, approaching them with some diffidence; I was deeply relieved to discover that, without exception, they were enthusiastic about the idea of Eakins being presented on this side of the Atlantic. The way was led by Carter Brown, then Director of the National Gallery of Art, and his colleague, Nicolai Cikovsky, Jr., Curator of American Painting. Anne d'Harnancourt, Director, and Darrel Sewell, Curator of American Painting, at the Philadelphia Museum of Art, to whom I am particularly grateful, have been a constant source of help throughout. At the Metropolitan, Philippe de Montebello, Director, John K. Howat, Head of the American Wing, and H. Barbara Weinberg, Curator of American Painting, were all encouraging. As I sought specific loans, Phyllis Rosenzweig kindly showed me the wonderful sketches owned by the Hirshhorn Museum in Washington; Susan Danly and her colleagues at the Pennsylvania Academy of the Fine Arts allowed me to examine the wealth of material which had been acquired from the widow of Charles Bregler, one of Eakins's students, and which later formed the subject of an exhibition at the Academy; and Commander and Mrs William Bagbey kindly took me to see the collections owned by the descendants of Mrs Eakins living in Roanoke. Helen Cooper, Curator of American Painting at the Yale University Art Gallery, and Jock Reynolds, the Director of the Addison Gallery of American Art at Andover, were both welcoming. All the great American museums, but most especially Philadelphia, which has lent no fewer than fourteen works from its remarkable Eakins collection, have been exceptionally generous with important loans, and the Trustees and I are very deeply grateful to them all.

My most important debt, however, is to John Wilmerding, who, in spite of many other calls on his time, kindly agreed to act as Academic Consultant, advising me on the selection and taking on the major task of coordinating the catalogue. It was his idea that the catalogue entries should be contributed by a large number of scholars, representing different aspects of Eakins scholarship; he also arranged an Eakins seminar at Princeton to coincide with the exhibition, so that he could involve graduate students in the catalogue writing, a teaching

practice he introduced at the Metropolitan Museum, where he is consultant in the Department of American Painting. Without John Wilmerding's infectious enthusiasm and energy and his typically rapid responses to all sorts of questions, the exhibition could hardly have got off the ground. It has been a very refreshing and stimulating experience for me, and indeed for all of us at the Gallery concerned with the exhibition, to work with so remarkable an American scholar. At the same time, we would like to thank Susan Lehre, Professor Wilmerding's assistant, with whom we have been constantly in touch.

John Wilmerding has also been instrumental in securing for us two special grants. The Wyeth Endowment for American Art, concerned especially with the support of scholarship in American art, has given financial support for the production of the catalogue; the Wyeth Foundation, together with the Dietrich Foundation, also provided funding for the Symposium to be held in London during the course of the exhibition. The E. Rhodes and Leona B. Carpenter Foundation has also supported the production of the catalogue. We are extremely grateful to these charitable organizations for their help.

It is almost impossible nowadays to mount an exhibition on the scale of the present one, in this case involving transatlantic loans in its entirety, without very substantial financial assistance. I was very grateful, therefore, to Robert Ayling, now Managing Director of British Airways, for his warm and positive response when I first approached him about *Eakins*. Not only has British Airways provided the air transport for the loans from the United States, it has also funded the land transport, the installation of the exhibition, and the publicity. We are enormously indebted to British Airways for its enlightened and most generous sponsorship.

Raymond Seitz, the American Ambassador in London, and Sir Robin Renwick, HM Ambassador in Washington, kindly agreed to act as Patrons of the exhibition, and have been of generous practical help in our

attempts to secure vital loans. Ed McBride, Cultural Attaché at the American Embassy, and Gordon Tindale and Kathy Culpin at the British Embassy in Washington, have all been very supportive in this regard. I gratefully acknowledge, too, the assistance of Charles Moyer, Chairman of the International Arts Council in Philadelphia, who has been indefatigable on our behalf.

The exhibition has been designed and installed by Barry Mazur, who has brought his innate sensitivity to a particular theme to his concept of the space and his choice of colours and materials. Derek Birdsall has given very particular care to the design and layout of this catalogue, and I am extremely grateful to him for the handsome production which has resulted. It is a great privilege to curate an exhibition in the company of two such distinguished (and imperturbable) professionals.

As always, many of the Gallery staff have been involved in one way or another with the exhibition, and I am grateful to them all for their professional contribution to its success. Principally I am indebted to Kathleen Soriano, who has masterminded the complexities of the transport with her usual skill, and Gillian Forrester, who, as editor of the catalogue, has performed a mammoth task liaising across the Atlantic with all the many contributors. She has been ably assisted by Katie Bent.

Finally, I am particularly delighted that Paul Mellon, KBE, has wished to be associated with the exhibition. I hope that *Eakins* will go some way towards fostering a greater appreciation of historic American art in this country, a wish that he expressed in his recently published *Autobiography*.

JOHN HAYES
Director,
National Portrait Gallery, London
6 August 1993

Acknowledgements

The National Portrait Gallery would also like to thank the following who contributed in many different ways to the organization of the exhibition and preparation of the catalogue:

Dita Amory
Mark Aronson
August Filmsetting
Linda Bantel
Ada Bartoluzzi
Helen Baz
Julie S. Berkowitz
Lorena A. Boylan
John Buchanan
Elizabeth Colman
Luci Collings
Barbara Dayer Gallati
Margaret Dong
Maureen I. Donovan
Cecilia M. Esposito
Suzannah Fabing
Kathleen Flynn
Mary Gardner Neill
Ann V. Gunn
Donna J. Hassler
Joseph Holbach
William Innes Homer
Denise J.H. Johnson
John Juson
Elyssa Kane
Peter M. Kenny
Louise Laplante
Martin Lee
Richard Lees
Roger Mandle
Lisa E. Marian
Anne-Louise Marquis
Marceline McKee
Ignacio Moreno
Barbara Odevseff
Caroline B. Padiva
Charles Parkhurst
Roy Pateman
Michele Peplin
Stephen B. Phillips
Joan-Elizabeth Reid
Allen Rosenbaum
Susan E. Strickler
Colin Thomson
Nancy S. Quaile
Novelene Ross
Julie A. Solz
Douglas Winterich
The Witt Library
Inez S. Wolins

List of Contributors

Contributors to the catalogue section
are identified by the initials given in
parentheses

Fred B. Adelson (FBA)
Rowan College of New Jersey

Brian T. Allen (BTA)
Yale University

Britt Steen Beedenbender (BSB)
Rutgers University

Martin A. Berger (MAB)
Yale University

Julie S. Berkowitz (JSB)
Thomas Jefferson University

Maria Chamberlin-Hellman (MC-H)
Marymount College

Nicolai Cikovsky, Jr. (NC Jr.)
National Gallery of Art, Washington

Laurie V. Dahlberg (LVD)
Princeton University

Susan Danly
Mead Art Museum, Amherst College

Julia M. Einspruch (JME)
Princeton University

Kathleen A. Foster (KAF)
Indiana University Art Museum

Michael Fried (MF)
Johns Hopkins University

Jennifer Hardin
Princeton University

John Hayes
National Portrait Gallery, London

William Innes Homer (WIH)
University of Delaware

William Patterson Hong (WPH)
Princeton University

Elizabeth Johns (EJ)
University of Pennsylvania

Franklin Kelly (FK) National Gallery of Art,
Washington and University of Maryland

David M. Lubin (DML)
Colby College

Sally Mills (SM)
Princeton University

Elizabeth Milroy (EM)
Wesleyan University

Paul Paret (PP)
Princeton University

Jules David Prown (JDP)
Yale University

Darrel Sewell (DS)
Philadelphia Museum of Art

Daniel J. Strong (DJS)
Princeton University

Margaret Rose Vendryes (MRV)
Princeton University

H. Barbara Weinberg (HBW)
The Metropolitan Museum of Art, New York

Amy B. Werbel
Yale University

John Wilmerding
Princeton University

Bryan Wolf (BJW)
Yale University

Catalogue Note

The paintings and drawings in the catalogue section are arranged in broad chronological order. The photographs in the exhibition (nos. 50–9), which are all from Charles Bregler's Thomas Eakins Collection, Pennsylvania Academy of the Fine Arts, do not have individual catalogue entries, but are discussed and illustrated in *Thomas Eakins and the Art of Photography* (pp. 180–91). Sizes of works are given in centimetres (height before width) with the size in inches shown in parentheses. All works are by Thomas Eakins unless otherwise stated.

Bibliographical references in the catalogue entries and endnotes are abbreviated, and cite the author's surname and year of publication. References are listed chronologically. In the case of works without known authors, full titles are cited. Where more than one work by the same author is cited, references are listed chronologically by date of publication. Where more than one work by the same author and published in the same year is cited, references are differentiated by numbers in parentheses after the date. Full references are given in the Bibliography (pp. 200–203).

References to exhibitions in the catalogue entries and endnotes are abbreviated, and cite the location and opening year of the exhibition. Exhibitions are listed chronologically. Where more than one exhibition took place in the same location and the same year, references are differentiated by numbers in parentheses after the date. Full references are given in the List of Exhibitions (pp. 204–206).

The Tensions of Biography and Art in Thomas Eakins

John Wilmerding

Viewed along with Winslow Homer as one of the greatest artists America has produced, Thomas Eakins shared in creating on one level a penetrating image of American life and character, and on another level one of the towering humane visions in the history of art. That by the end of his life he was both honoured and misunderstood provides a clue to the opposing and sometimes balanced tensions that ran throughout his turbulent career. Perhaps because Homer's greatest expression was as a landscape painter, he has generally seemed a more accessible and national figure to Americans, who have so identified nature and geography with the country's history and destiny. Although Eakins was just as much a consummate realist, also a trait continually admired in the American tradition, his unrelenting and acute observations of people, especially in his later portraits, revealed truths his Victorian sitters no less than subsequent viewers often found difficult to accept.

Ill and near the end of his life, Eakins addressed his students and in effect posterity: 'If America is to produce great painters and if young art students wish to assume a place in the history of the art of their country, their first desire should be to remain in America to peer deeper into the heart of American life'.[1] He went on to assert this priority over the superficial emulation of multiple European artistic examples. Yet as a young man, he spent some of his crucial formative years abroad, defining an approach to drawing and painting indelibly shaped by the modern French painters with whom he studied in Paris and by the seventeenth-century Spanish masters whom he enthusiastically discovered in Madrid and Seville.

What most of his biographers have emphasized is Eakins's early training as a draughtsman, first at the Pennsylvania Academy of the Fine Arts in Philadelphia during the early 1860s and then under Jean-Léon Gérôme in Paris later in the decade. They have stressed his earliest school work in science and mathematics, including practice in perspective drawing, subsequently reinforced by Gérôme's teaching of the essentials of line, as elements ultimately suited to an American temperament preferring practical and cleanly defined forms. The art historian Barbara Novak in particular has placed Eakins in what she has argued is a conceptually-based American tradition of linearism and technical clarity, extending from John Singleton Copley's American work in the eighteenth century through the luminist landscape painters of the mid-nineteenth to the minimalism of the twentieth.[2]

Yet, American as Eakins was in his reliance on a firm structure of line and space for his pictures, his art is in fact a complex fusion of linear and planar clarification with a fluid and textured European painterliness. Although he was to pass his entire mature career, after returning from Paris in 1870, in his native Philadelphia, Eakins would pursue an active artistic dialogue between American and European styles of painting. Even as he scrupulously situated his figures within the closures of rooms, from the first home scenes of the early 1870s to the starkly mortal subjects of his late portraits after the turn of the century, he swathed them with expressive brushwork, energetic textures, and mysterious chiaroscuros of lighting. Throughout, he held his drawing lessons at the Pennsylvania Academy and under Gérôme in equilibrium with the bravura pigments of Ribera, Velázquez, and Rembrandt.

Interestingly, Eakins's biographers have by and large tended to formulate their discussions around either his life or his art. While all art historians will have an interest in the place of art in an artist's life, and correspondingly, in how a life is expressed in one's art, many of the major writers about Eakins have been drawn to the separated concerns of his biography versus his painting. Characteristic of those writing primarily about the artist's life are Lloyd Goodrich, Gordon Hendricks, and most recently, William Innes Homer,[3] in contrast to others who have attended to the almost independent life of his art, like Sylvan Schendler, Michael Fried, and David Lubin.[4] Again, this tension that appears to exist between the person and his painting is not so easily unravelled, for it is equally true that many of the critical turning points in Eakins's life – his firing from the Pennsylvania Academy in 1886 and later from the Drexel Institute in 1895, the deaths of his favourite sister Margaret in 1882 and of his father in 1899 along with the suicide of his niece Ella Crowell in 1897 – occasioned some of his most forceful works, just as his critical fortunes or misfortunes found vivid expression in the faces who sat or stood before him, mirroring his own emotional and spiritual state.

Two of the major and most familiar paired elements in Eakins's career were his dual allegiances to art and science. Well known is his extensive early training both in design at the Pennsylvania Academy and in anatomical study at the Jefferson Medical College. These complementary practices led not just to the sequences of drawings of machine parts, perspective renderings, and bone and muscle studies; they also underlay the artist's recur-

ring imagery of medical portraits, whose subjects so often pose in operating amphitheatres or classrooms like inspired painters or sculptors, wielding scalpels instead of brushes or palette knives. For that matter, he treated many of his later sitters, who were concert singers, musicians, art students or painters, as professionals akin to his scientists or physicians. Together, they all relied on the sensitive co-ordination of intelligence and action, of mind and body, of brain and hands. From his earliest rowers and piano players to his latest surgeons and cello players, the human conduct Eakins most admired and celebrated was that which combined the poetry and creativity of art with the precision and control of science. Ultimately, artist and scientist were one in joining passion and intelligence, the emotional and the physical, mystery and clarity.

There are other polarities of imagery and representation which appear to inform the rhythms of Eakins's artistic chronology, for example, the oppositions of outside and inside, physical and human nature, society and self, male and female, past and present, clear illumination and impenetrable dark, action and stillness, narrative and silence, performance and meditation. While he held some of these contrasting states in balance throughout his work, we may argue that his art generally shifted as it proceeded from the outer world to the inner, from social context to individual isolation, from sunlight to brooding shadow, from the stopping of the moment to the suspension of time, and from the working of the hand to that of the mind. Another characteristic of his artistic process was the painting of the subjects in series, which tended to evolve in paired or contrasting sequences. For example, in the early seventies he painted side by side the home interiors with women and the rowing landscapes dominated by men; in the eighties the arcadian pictures, alternatively with women and with men, some dressed, others naked; and around the turn of the century artists and boxers, singers and clergymen.

Often we sense within these groups a methodical internal exploration of not only variations on a theme but the contrapuntal play of differing realms, as if examining two sides of a coin, alternate aspects of human nature, or sexual distinctions. This treatment of parallel and complementary subjects is evident from the beginning of Eakins's mature career, notably in the suites of piano and sculling pictures from around 1870 to 1875. In the former – *Frances Eakins* (fig. 15b), *Home Scene* (no. 7) and *Elizabeth at the Piano* (no. 15) – principally his sisters sit at the piano, absorbed in the passing moments of sound or private reveries.

Fig.1
At the Piano (Frances and Margaret Eakins)
*c.*1871
Oil on canvas, 55.9 × 45.7 (22 × 18)
Archer M. Huntington Art Gallery,
The University of Texas at Austin.
Gift of Caroline Crowell, MD, 1964

Occasionally, a second subordinate figure appears, such as his younger sister Caroline playing on the floor, pondering the life of written marks on a slate in opposition to her older sister's proximity to the notes of music above, in *Home Scene*. We sense in these an individual consciousness, amplified in some by the second presence, hinting at another state of mind, age, or self-awareness. They are all situated in darkened, ambiguous corners of rooms, in which light plays a crucial role of illuminating telling details, unifying the major forms, and making palpable the unseen energies of passion, familial intimacy, and creativity. The death of Eakins's mother in 1872 may have given special poignance to the quiet force and intensity of this group, as family bonds and separations were to reverberate powerfully throughout the rest of the artist's life.

In these works the source and direction of the light are clear enough, but Eakins modulates its intensity, selectively highlighting important edges or surfaces. On one level the illumination is rational and optical as it models, even caresses, forms such as cheeks and fingers, while on another we come to realize that it also defines the emotional content of these paintings. Thus, he carefully draws together the interrelated elements – triangulates as it were, in both composition and meaning – with light falling strongest across the side of a face, the open music sheets, and fingers lifting from the piano keys. Subtly, we enter a co-ordinated world of physical and mental activity (fig.1).

Also beginning in the early 1870s, Eakins completed his first acknowledged rowing masterpiece, *The Champion Single Sculls* (*Max Schmitt in a Single Scull*) (fig.2), where the co-ordination of hand and eye, figure and environment, were equally evident. After the American Civil War, sculling was one of the sporting and leisure activities that gained in popularity, with the changes in the working week, vacation hours, and belief in the therapy of exercise.[5] The artist joined his male friends in regular rowing and sailing outings along the Schuylkill River in Philadelphia and nearby

Fig.2
The Champion Single Sculls
(*Max Schmitt in a Single Scull*)
1871
Oil on canvas, 81.9 × 117.5 ($32\frac{1}{4}$ × $46\frac{1}{4}$)
The Metropolitan Museum of Art.
Purchase 1934, Alfred N. Punnett Fund
and Gift of George D. Pratt

Delaware Bay. Paralleling the home scenes, he painted over the next few years several boating pictures – *The Pair-Oared Shell* (fig.9a), *The Biglin Brothers Racing* (National Gallery of Art, Washington, DC), *The Biglin Brothers Turning the Stake* (The Cleveland Museum of Art), *Starting Out After Rail* (fig.3), and *Sailboats (Hikers) Racing on the Delaware* (no. 11) – all set on expansive planes of sunlit water.

Eakins not only paints this outdoor world as a male environment. His strong, hard light here is also masculine, one might argue, indeed rational and scientific in its ordered clarification and control (in contrast to the muted ambience of feeling and sentiment in the domestic scenes). It is directly and centrally into this construct that Eakins places himself for the first time: as the rower in the right middle distance beyond Max Schmitt, with his signature literally inscribed on the sternboard of his shell. Michael Fried has written about the significance of the artist's training as a draughtsman and calligrapher; Eakins learned the latter craft from his father.[6] Within these lean spatial envelopes Eakins seems almost to have placed his oarsmen like written markings on the glassy slates of water. But these works rely on more than just his practice in perspective rendering; they equally draw upon his study of anatomy, both in his full understanding of organic human form and in the coherent interrelationship of his figures within their surrounding space.

The rowing and sailing paintings appear to be more photographic than their interior counterparts, due to their overall sharpness of definition and conscious sense of observation. But all of these early series focus on aspects of the momentary and transitional, especially in hands poised over piano keys, or in the midst of rowing strokes. What is haunting about them all is that Eakins calls attention both to the power of the immediate and the tenderness of time's transcendent passage. Altogether, Eakins's mastery of expressive gesture and glance, light and space, in his paintings from the first half of this decade would find shape in his style thereafter, with increasing eloquence and economy.

In the mid-seventies, having renewed his associations with colleagues at Jefferson Medical College, Eakins took up the subject of anatomy and the human form in another way, with the undertaking of several impressive medical portraits. Although unresolved in certain sections, and selective in its degree of finish, *Professor Benjamin Howard Rand* of 1874 (no. 12) was the first of these, a sensitive rendering of the doctor concentrating on his books, surrounded at his desk by medical instruments, papers, and pet cat. With incandescent touches of colour and isolated highlights of brightness illuminating different textures in the enveloping darkness, this presents at once a private world of suggestive sensuality and mental concentration.

Fig.3
Starting Out After Rail
1874
Oil on canvas, 60.9 × 50.8 (24 × 20)
Museum of Fine Arts, Boston.
Charles Henry Hayden Fund

Detail of no.11

Following this in 1875 came the *Portrait of Dr Gross* (*The Gross Clinic*) (fig.4), later critically and popularly perceived as the artist's greatest accomplishment. Perhaps so, though this perception has unfortunately shadowed judgements of the balance of his career by somehow implying that he never achieved this level of power again and that the late portraits in particular were relative failures. Certainly, this was his largest and most ambitious canvas to date, and it is also true that at the end of his career he turned away from complex, multiple-figure compositions, in favour of immobilized single sitters. But *The Gross Clinic* belongs to a different, earlier age both for Eakins and for America. It represents many efforts combined on his part: a synthetic tribute to the paint handling and compositional mastery of his Paris teachers, Bonnat and Gérôme, and to the chiaroscuro drama of the baroque, most obviously Rembrandt's *Anatomy Lessons* (see fig.5). At the same time that this summarizes Eakins's artistic apprenticeship abroad, it also fervently addresses the American present, in the realms of science and art. Foremost, of course, it is an anatomy lesson about the living and not the dead; Eakins paints not the dissection of a cadaver but a new, medically advanced operation on a patient's thigh. With its stark lighting and dense monochromatic palette, the picture takes on the resonance of a life-and-death drama, but primarily to elevate the modern professionalism and wisdom of a senior surgeon to a heroic stature.

Where we might see Eakins's previous paintings as contemplations of familial and collegial connections, this image addresses the individual in relation to humanity. Dr Gross stands before his associates, assistants, and students, at once performing and explicating the operation underway. He is both doer and thinker, as the dual emphasis on head and hand testifies. As before, strong lighting triangulates Gross's prominent brow, scalpel held in his fingers, and active work on the open incision, linking within the picture's centre knowledge and practice. In counterpoise are the standing form of Gross and the seated colleagues nearby, each representing differing levels of attention and participation. Such balancing of the single self and democratic society calls to mind the poetic stance of Walt Whitman, America's most original poet of the age and soon to become a sympathetic friend to Eakins. Whitman's writing also invoked the living present with his liberated free verse and all-embracing cosmos. First published in 1855, his celebrated and celebratory *Leaves of Grass* began with the famous opening lines, which

Fig.4
Portrait of Dr Gross (The Gross Clinic)
1875
Oil on canvas, 243.8 × 198 (96 × 78)
Jefferson Medical College of Thomas Jefferson
University, Philadelphia

Whitman recast in 1867 and 1871:

One's-Self I sing, a simple separate person,
Yet utter the word Democratic, the word En-Masse.

Of the physiology from top to toe I sing,
Not physiognomy alone nor brain alone is worthy
  for the
  Muse, I say the Form complete is worthier far,
The Female equally with the Male I sing.

Of Life immense in passion, pulse, and power,
Cheerful, for freest action form'd under the laws
  divine
The Modern Man I sing.[7]

Eakins painted one other full-scale seated portrait in this first medical group, that of *Dr John H. Brinton* of 1876 (fig.25a). He would return to this subject and format in later years, but meanwhile turned to other themes, as if to amplify ideas embodied in *The Gross Clinic*. That picture, after all, had been undertaken as a submission for display at the Philadelphia Exhibition, marking the nation's centennial in 1876. Rejected for inclusion in the art building because of its perceived raw brutality of realism, it had to hang with the medical displays, and occasioned the first extensive criticism Eakins was to receive. His disappointment no doubt prompted him to shift his artistic focus. At the same time, preparations for the Fair and the concurrent opening of the new Pennsylvania Academy building stimulated fresh attention to the history and practice of the arts in America. Eakins now began a highly productive and influential ten-year period of teaching at the Academy, and the creativity of the artist was on his mind as much in his own work as in his classroom.

Implicit in *The Gross Clinic* was the image of a technically accomplished creative spirit who inspires those around him, and Eakins no doubt had in his consciousness the precedents of Velázquez he had seen a few years before in Spain. It appears no accident that Dr Gross stands before us and his operation much as the artist does next to his monumental canvas within his famous *Las Meninas* (fig.6).[8] Eakins elaborated on this idea in several closely related paintings in the year or so immediately following the completion and criticism of his clinic picture. One response was to turn inward, and his next paintings were smaller in scale, darker and more constrained compositions, and devoted to fewer figures in private settings. A major theme for him was that of old age; which he had examined with Dr Gross and also associated with his own father, the central figure in a small painting of 1876, *The Chess Players* (fig.44). Here two of Benjamin Eakins's elderly friends concentrate over a chess table in a darkened room; the game itself

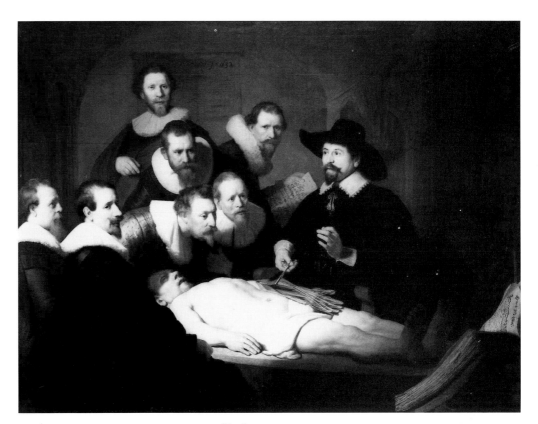

Fig.5
Rembrandt van Rijn, *The Anatomy Lesson of Dr Tulp*
1632
Oil on canvas, 50 × 63.5 (18½ × 25)
Mauritshuis, The Hague

Fig.6
Diego Rodríguez de Silva y Velázquez,
Las Meninas (The Maids of Honour)
1656
Oil on canvas, 318 × 276 (125 × 109)
Prado Museum, Madrid

is measured and cerebral, the hushed setting closes out the bright activity of the outside world, and all within is fragile and distilled in time. Out of intelligence and experience these individuals emblematically still make their marks and plot the course of their later years.

By contrast, another painting of the same date, *Baby at Play* (no. 14), obviously depicts the concentrations of childhood. Jules Prown has convincingly argued that this image, with its strongly illuminated forehead and glance linked with active hand, is a conceptual pendant to Samuel Gross: one addressing the beginnings of experience and learning, the other life's culmination of wisdom and understanding.[9] Yet a third important work in this cycle is *William Rush Carving His Allegorical Figure of the Schuylkill River* (no. 17), in which Eakins explicitly depicted an artist in his studio, here the early colonial wood sculptor in Philadelphia, who like Eakins had suffered certain critical rejection in his time. But the scene of the artist carving with the object of his attention nearby is in one sense a reworking of the medical amphitheatre into a comparably creative individual's place of work. Thus, the power and pain of art are fused undercurrents in much of Eakins's output generated by *The Gross Clinic*.

More broadly, the Centennial Fair marked a powerfully resonant national anniversary, and in its wake developed the pervasive colonial revival in all of the American arts, from architecture to furniture and visual imagery in painting. The interest in Rush was part of this, as was the Chippendale copy chair shown in the painting and a variety of artefacts from earlier times appearing in a new sequence of canvases from the late 1870s and early 1880s. These include *In Grandmother's Time*, 1876 (fig.18b), *Seventy Years Ago*, 1877 (The Art Museum, Princeton University, New Jersey), *Young Girl Meditating*, or *Fifty Years Ago*, 1877 (The Metropolitan Museum of Art, New York), *The Spinner*, c.1878 (no. 18), *The Courtship*, c.1878 (Fine Arts Museums of San Francisco), *Retrospection*, 1880 (Yale University Art Gallery), and *Homespun*, 1881 (fig.7). Their very titles are indices, on one level, of the wave of nostalgia and reverie sweeping America at this time, and on another, of perhaps Eakins's own impulses towards escapism and introspection. That several of these works were watercolours, a relatively new medium for the artist, also indicates he had reached a fresh stage of originality and experimentation in his career. During the next few years he would take up work in plaster and bronze as well as photography, and his subjects would show new concern with forms in motion, *plein air* motifs,

Left: Detail of no.14

Fig.7
Homespun
1881
Watercolour, 35.6 × 27.6 (14 × 10$\frac{7}{8}$)
The Metropolitan Museum of Art.
Fletcher Fund, 1925

carefully posed models, and anatomical studies.

At the outset of the decade Eakins essayed his one major religious subject, *The Crucifixion*, 1880 (fig.45), as much a depiction of organic human form as an expression of emotional content, and soon thereafter a series of arcadian themes in both paintings and photographs with clothed and naked males as well as females. The early eighties, too, saw the production of a few pure landscapes. These visual currents culminate with *The Swimming Hole* of 1883 (fig.8), a scene of Eakins and his male students skinny-dipping in an idyllic rural landscape. Its sense of portraiture and frozen poses derives from preparatory photographic studies made on the spot, at the same time that its solid triangular composition of rhythmically arranged male nudes alludes to the casts Eakins knew of ancient sculpture, friezes, and pedimental fragments. Yet its celebration of freely expressed sexuality and the benign

Fig.8
The Swimming Hole
c.1883–1885
Oil on canvas, 69.4 × 92.2 (27$\frac{5}{16}$ × 36$\frac{5}{16}$)
Amon Carter Museum, Fort Worth, Texas

sunlit landscape were to have an elegiac finality. The variety and growth in his artistic expression of this period partially reflected his confidence as an innovative teacher as well as his rapid mastery of new techniques and media.

But the ferment in his art of the mid-eighties was also due to increasing frustration and turbulence in his professional life at the Pennsylvania Academy. On top of the personal loss of his favourite sister Margaret, who died in 1882, Eakins was facing rising criticism for his liberated methods. Insisting on the fundamental lessons of working directly from the live model, especially as a means of grasping and rendering the truths of human anatomy correctly, he removed the loin cloth from a male model in a class that included female students. This offended conservative Victorian society in Philadelphia, and ultimately led to Eakins's forced removal from the Academy in 1886. Something of the pain and distress in his life may be seen in the portrait he painted the year before of his new wife, Susan Macdowell Eakins, known as *The Artist's Wife and His Setter Dog* or *Lady with a Setter Dog* (no. 22). One of his best students, she set aside her active painting career during his lifetime, but later resumed an active and accomplished professional life of her own. More relaxed in pose and casually arranged than most of his portraits, it reflects the new familial intimacy of marriage and the private spaces of the artist's home. Although centrally placed, Susan's figure is a gentle diagonal sliding across the picture. Nothing is rigidly aligned: the chair on the rectangle of the carpet, the rug's angle in relation to the picture plane, the sitter against the angled walls behind. An oil study and portion of a plaster in the background testify to the artist at work, and even the central contrast of the two alert faces of Susan and their setter dog Harry below hint of an underlying irony. Yet the head held forward and eyes circled in red suggest some sad tension beneath the surface, evidence again that Eakins could not help but project self into his works of most intense feeling.

Detail of no. 22

To escape the strain and conflict, Eakins travelled west to the Dakota territories in 1887, and the one last landscape he painted then, *Cowboys in the Bad Lands* (Private Collection), is of a mood altogether different from *The Swimming Hole* of four years earlier. Now the greens of his palette are drained and thin, the space is empty and desolate, the figures starkly silhouetted and isolated. Although this trip was intended to revitalize himself, we nonetheless feel Eakins's mood of gravity. There were mixed gains in the years that followed. Although his productivity fell off during the later eighties, he did meet and consolidate his friendship with Walt Whitman after his return. This led to the powerful close-up portrait of the poet in the last years of the bard's life (no. 23), and in 1889 Eakins received the major commission to paint a portrait of *Dr*

Fig.9
The Bohemian (Franklin L. Schenck)
*c.*1890
Oil on canvas, 60.6 × 50.2 (23⅞ × 19¾)
Philadelphia Museum of Art.
Gift of Mrs Thomas Eakins and
Miss Mary Adeline Williams

D. Hayes Agnew (no. 36). This evolved into his second full-scale clinic picture (fig.36a), the artist's largest canvas. Historians have noted that the white robes indicate the advances in antiseptic medicine since the time of *The Gross Clinic* over a decade earlier. This later work has often been viewed as a less original and integrated treatment of the theme, with its clearer separation of surgeon, observers, and operation. Yet there is arguably greater psychological and sexual complexity in this painting, with its male participants pressing in on the female patient undergoing a mastectomy, the strong visual form of the nurse balancing Agnew's figure, and the observing artist himself painted by his wife at the centre right-hand edge of the canvas.[10] In part because he maintained the bluntness of his methods in teaching as well as in representation, Eakins's life and work continued in tension with the society around him. Having given up the outdoor landscape, he now turned away as well from the large group portrait.[11]

The last decade of the century represents a new phase in the painter's late maturity. In portraits mostly of single individuals, he focused his attention on personal strengths and idiosyncrasies, usually with his characteristic uncompromising intensity of observation. By selecting for most of his subjects fellow-professionals, friends, and associates, he was able to paint with a sympathy and sensitivity some of the finest works of his career. While some of his biographers have lamented the seeming repetitiveness of format in these later portraits,[12] the works in fact demonstrate subtle variety and penetrating insight.[13] It is perhaps too easy to explain this period as a pulling back from formerly ambitious compositions, and important to see the patterns of exploration that did engage him during the nineties. For example, he undertook sequences of portraits which were clearly typological images: students, professors, doctors, critics, musicians, and painters. Some by their very titles or subtitles reveal Eakins's intentional balancing of generic type and explicit physiognomy: *The Veteran, The Bohemian* (fig.9), *The Singer, The Cello Player*. Like himself, these subjects, too, possessed a creative spirit or technical expertise, authority or accomplishment.

Among his memorable achievements of the early nineties are *Professor Henry A. Rowland* (no. 31), *Amelia Van Buren* (no. 27), and *The Concert Singer* (no. 26). The first gives us a scientist, diffraction grating in hand, pondering the vision of numbers and of measures inscribed in Eakins's hand-made frame around him. Within an otherwise largely monochromatic environment, Rowland occupies the centre in sharpest precision and brightest lighting (on his face, right hand, and instrument), holding the one focal burst of colour. The assistant nearby appears more preoccupied with doing than thinking, as Eakins again makes us aware of degrees of cerebration and the delicate interdependence of mental and physical exertion. Amelia Van Buren is also caught up in her thoughts, contained as well by the chair back, arms, and the fan on her lap, which frame her torso, and make all the more radiant her determined, pensive glance out beyond the picture frame. *The Concert Singer* is also a study of human isolation, in this instance a performer caught in the midst of her aria. We almost sense the delicate musical notes reverberating in the abstracted empty space surrounding her. Indeed, the austerity of this composition and spatial ambiguity suggest a new level of abstraction in Eakins's late work. With its flattened design, cropped details of palm leaves and conductor's hand, and the low angle of vision, one thinks of the parallel constructions of Edgar Degas's dance and orchestra subjects of the same period.

The imagery of art and of the artist was never far from Eakins's mind and at the end of the decade he returned to portraits of painters. Two of the strongest were respectively of *William Merritt Chase*, *c*.1899 (no. 35), and *Henry O. Tanner*, 1902 (no. 39). These are contrasts in pose, despite the limitations of the head-and-shoulders format and character. The former captures in profile the cosmopolitan elegance of a painter quite different from Eakins, who nonetheless befriended and supported him, while the latter's downward glance captures something of the brooding visionary Tanner had become as an artist. To each we feel Eakins has brought a mixture of respect and affection, as much for the established colleague as for the accomplished student.

Detail of no.26

At the turn of the century Eakins turned once again, for a final time, to a sporting subject, that of men boxing or wrestling in an arena. In four large canvases, all of stilled indoor scenes, he posed virile figures generally pausing during or after the action (fig.10). These are Eakins's last celebrations of the male nude, and encapsulate his multiple interests from a decade before – photography, anatomy, and arcadian idealism. The three major boxing pictures (see no. 34) contain different-sized crowds in the background, reminders of the observers in his earlier clinic compositions. Conceptually, too, he implies that a sporting contest also relies on perfected physical coordination, and engages the onlooker with another type of performance. (In this light, perhaps not surprisingly, a couple of years later Eakins returned as well to reprise the theme of his *William Rush*, the artist at work in his studio.) Of the several works in this boxing suite, the most moving and thoughtful is *Between Rounds*, 1899 (no. 34). Here we see a subtle range of controlled action and immobility in the three principal figures, from the standing trainer to the boxer at rest and timekeeper below, all visually linked by the echoed play on concentrating faces and outstretched arms. In keeping with the mood of his later art, these images seem most to present a private, mental world, one that would dominate his last working decade.

For further indiscretions in his teaching practices, Eakins lost his position at the Drexel Institute in 1895, and a number of female sitters in these years reported uncomfortable sexual advances or posing demands, once more tempering his successes with a sense of frustration, failure, and rejection. One familiar response was to take up portraits of himself and family members. Throughout the nineties he painted various canvases of his father-in-law, William H. Macdowell (see no. 28), and in 1899 a final portrait of his father Benjamin, who was to die at the end of the year, as well as one of Mrs Eakins (no. 37), followed in 1902 by his own self-portrait (no. 41). All of these focus on the strongly lit face and upper torso otherwise surrounded by impenetrable dark. For himself and his wife, as for a few others, he chose the almost painfully direct glance and positioning of close-up frontality.

Fig.10
Taking the Count
Oil on canvas, 244.6 × 214 (96$\frac{5}{16}$ × 84$\frac{5}{16}$)
Yale University Art Gallery, Whitney Collections of Sporting Art, given in memory of Harry Payne Whitney, BA 1894, and Payne Whitney, BA 1898 by Francis P. Garvan, BA 1897

Detail of no.28

Fig.11
The Old Fashioned Dress (Miss Helen Parker)
*c.*1908
Oil on canvas, 153.4 × 102.2 (60⅜ × 40¼)
Philadelphia Museum of Art.
Gift of Mrs Thomas Eakins and
Miss Mary Adeline Williams

Around the turn of the century Eakins's painting acquired a new gravity and intensity. Although generally limiting himself to the single figure, he continued to exploit the expressive possibilities of varied formats, one of which was the full-length portrait. Some subjects in this series were academics, others friends, several (as indicated by their titles) universalized types: *The Dean's Role Call* (*Professor James W. Holland*), 1899 (Museum of Fine Arts, Boston), *The Thinker* (*Louis Kenton*), 1900 (no. 38), *Professor Leslie Miller*, 1901 (fig.47), *Professor William Smith Forbes*, 1905 (Thomas Jefferson University), and *The Old Fashioned Dress* (*Miss Helen Parker*), 1908 (fig.11). For the most part with plain backgrounds and subdued colouring, these works depict self-absorbed individuals almost detached from the physical present, despite the materiality of their clothes and weight of their standing figures. More than just burdened with thought, they suggest an air of retrospection, in various ways. For example, the abstracted background for Kenton reprises Eakins's abiding feeling for Velázquez's portraiture, while the old-fashioned dress once belonging to her grandmother that Helen Parker wears recalls the nostalgic themes of the Centennial period. It also sets up an evocative juxtaposition between youth and age, the present and the past, no doubt partially on Eakins's mind as he advanced in years himself. The solid stiff-backed chair with its turned poles and finials, next to which the young girl stands, suggests solidity in contrast to fragility, a chiselled beauty fighting against time, character past in tension with character to be.

During the first years of the new century Eakins also produced some of his most sympathetic as well as unsympathetic character studies. When confronted with patrons whose professions seemed spiritually devoid of the creative spark and accomplishment he found in science and the arts, he could be devastating. Bankers and businessmen appear desiccated, vain, or heartless, as in the portraits of *Charles Percival Buck*, 1904 (The Art Museum, Princeton University), *John B. Gest*, 1905 (Private Collection), and *A.W. Lee* (Reynolda House, Winston-Salem, North Carolina). In two of his largest single portraits of the period, *Mrs William D. Frishmuth*, 1900 (fig.12), and *The Actress* (*Suzanne Santje*), 1903 (fig.13), he painted compelling embodiments respectively of commanding will, determination, and magisterial authority in the one, and a paradoxical mix of langour and passion in the other. Sometimes Eakins had the disquieting ability to paint individuals looking older than they were, to show the effects of ageing and

Fig.12
Mrs William D. Frishmuth
1900
Oil on canvas, 246.4 × 184.2 (97 × 72½)
Philadelphia Museum of Art.
Gift of Mrs Thomas Eakins and
Miss Mary Adeline Williams

Fig.13
The Actress (Suzanne Santje)
1903
Oil on canvas, 203.2 × 152.4 (80 × 60)
Philadelphia Museum of Art.
Gift of Mrs Thomas Eakins and
Miss Mary Adeline Williams

the inevitability of loss and transition. Other paintings in these later years remained unfinished – *A Singer (Mrs W.H. Bowden)*, c.1906 (no. 46), is an example – variously because a sitter was upset or dissatisfied, and did not or could not return for further posing. Yet there are equally moments when we feel he went as far as he intended, bringing to intense completion the head, face, and eyes especially of an individual, while leaving portions of the torso or background barely brushed in, as sufficient evidence of inner character, moral force, or psychological presence as all that counted.

One of the most haunting and poignant of all Eakins's works is the simple head-and-shoulders portrait of *Edith Mahon*, 1904 (no. 44), another singer seen past her prime. Now the Victorian chair which held or framed or set off so many previous subjects, including Kathrin Crowell (no. 8), Amelia Van Buren (no. 27), and Helen Parker (fig.11), exists here as a nearly disembodied fragment floating in the dark penumbra to the right of Mahon's head. The physical world has literally and conceptually receded behind the strongly lit presence of spirit and intelligence embodied in this saddened but not self-pitying expression. Her watery eyes and fleshy neck are characteristic of the unflattering but telling details that Eakins frequently recorded in his late portraits, reminders of pain just beneath the surface of things or the inevitable pressures as our lives advance. Eakins's own frustrations and critical misunderstandings through his later life almost seem to whisper in the shadows. Yet, despite the wear and tear that comes with ageing, he found in Mrs Mahon's eyes a self-acceptance and resolve, a sense of basic humanity as profound as anything he painted, and worthy of comparison with Rembrandt.

Two important groups of pictures are at the heart of Eakins's last active decade of work, one new in theme, the other old but made new: the series of portraits of Catholic clerics at the Overbrook Seminary outside Philadelphia and the late versions of William Rush in his studio. In the former he found a heightened spiritual and contemplative power, while in the latter he intensified his own identification with the image of an embattled artist struggling to liberate the truth in his art. Possibly his Quaker background gave him a particular sympathy for the discipline and purity of thought he sensed in these men of the church hierarchy. At the same time, we have seen that much of his later career was moving towards explorations of the interior life. In more than a dozen portraits of differing formats – head-and-shoulders; half- and full-length; frontal, three-quarter view; and profile; seated and standing

– he considered the moral strengths and other worldliness of the priestly calling. Among the most impressive results were the canvases of *Monsignor James P. Turner*, 1900 (St Charles Borromeo Seminary, Overbrook, Pennsylvania), *Sebastiano Cardinal Martinelli*, 1902 (fig.48a), *Monsignor James F. Loughlin*, 1902 (no. 47), *Archbishop William Henry Elder*, 1903 (fig.46), *Archbishop Diomede Falconio*, 1905 (no. 48), and *Monsignor James P. Turner*, c.1906 (fig.49a). This last was a *tour de force* of pallid face set above a column of incandescent raspberry red vestments, conveying fervent passion in check with serene meditation, and temporality in balance with transcendence.

Although the Rush subject nominally returned Eakins to an early preoccupation of the mid-1870s, the versions he painted in full studies and final compositions during 1908 represent a new amplification and personalization of the imagery. Again, this was a reflection of past art history as well as recent personal history, as the artist labours in his studio, with the unclothed female model nearby, who stands as the source of his inspiration and of his embattled reputation. Art and life are mirrored, as the carved nymph of the Schuylkill and the posing nude face each other across the floor. But the forward position of the model and strong lighting of her flesh indicate that she brings to the present moment his lifelong concerns with issues of anatomy, nudity, and sexuality. In the most familiar canvas of the group (fig.14) the model stands with her back to us, but significantly, in two other full-scale works (National Museum of American Art, Washington, DC, and the Honolulu Academy of Arts, Hawaii), both unfinished, Eakins finally showed the woman in full-frontal nudity. Scholars have pointedly noted that in these last versions the artist has painted his own features in the figure of Rush, thus joining genre and autobiography. Even more, the Honolulu picture of *William Rush and His Model* (fig.17c) shows the artist taking the model's hand as he assists her stepping down from the modelling stand at the end of the session. The narrative has moved from the past and recent life in the studio to the active present: the gesture of the male is almost that of taking a dance partner, or even a bride. Although the glances of both are averted from us within their private realm, Rush/Eakins is also unapologetically presenting one of the central elements of his art, uninhibited nudity and sexuality, to his audience, then and now.

Where does Eakins's art end up? Our first realization must be that the significance and place of his late work, literally in the twentieth century, mark neither decline nor advance

from the apotheosis of his iconic *Gross Clinic*. Rather, the often difficult, impenetrable, coarse works of his culminating maturity belong to a different world, as different as the two centuries which his life connected. In part, he had moved, like the pre-eminent American intellectual of the age, Henry Adams, from a world of relative order and absolutes to one of unsettled change or in Adams's words, 'chance' and 'chaos'.[14] Where the sciences in the age of Eakins's youth primarily sought to clarify objective facts, the sciences of the new century at the time of his death were newly exploring the subjective world of the psyche and the subconscious. At least two central aspects of his late work, the heightened abstraction of pictorial space and the intensified psychological content, place Eakins within the larger cultural developments of the modern age, whether the parallel currents of post-impressionism in Europe or other intellectual advances of the early twentieth century.

More to the point, in the very years of Eakins's most probing and abstracted last works came the announcement of some of the new century's most significant scientific discoveries and theories, notably the revelations of Sigmund Freud, Albert Einstein, and Marie Curie. In 1897 Freud defined his concept of the 'Oedipus complex', and two years later, in the year of Benjamin Eakins's death, Freud published his *Interpretation of Dreams*, suggesting the psychological role of our inner reveries. The discoverer of polonium and radium, Curie in 1898 announced the term 'radioactivity', which led to the awarding of two Nobel prizes to her in 1903 and 1911. In this connection, it is worth noting that the related discovery of X-rays in 1895 was also honoured in 1901, while only a few years later Picasso and Braque would undertake the artistic penetration of forms with Cubism. Just as figure and ground were becoming interchangeable, and as psychoanalysis was revealing our interior selves, Einstein proposed in 1905 in his famous equation $E = MC^2$ the theory of relativity, defining for the modern century the fluidity of solid and space and the unnerving instability of the physical universe.[15] Against this background perhaps we can better understand the indeterminate picture spaces to be found at this time in the late landscapes of Winslow Homer or Claude Monet, the dissolutions of form occurring with the post-impressionists, and the disturbing insights into private truths confronting us in Eakins's portraits.

Part of the originality of Henry Adams's *Education* is that in writing about himself in the third person, he ingeniously combined objectivity and subjectivity. Written in 1905 and first published privately the following year, the book sought to grasp the nature of the modern age. Aware of Mme Curie's discoveries, Adams referred to 'the metaphysical bomb she called radium', and pondered 'the Energy of modern science', which society believed 'to be as real as X-rays'.[16] Arriving at a theory in layman's terms close in spirit to Einstein, he defined 'this problem in dynamics' as one in which history 'could study only motion, direction, attraction, relation', for 'motion is the ultimate object of science'.[17] For Eakins as for Adams this was an uncertainty of the self as much as of society, and brings us back again to the mystery and ambiguity shrouding the late portraits. Adams might have also spoken for the painter when he wrote about the 'evidence of growing complexity, and multiplicity, and even contradiction, in life', and that 'the new American would need to think in contradictions'.[18] Certainly, the historian could join his colleagues in science and art when he claimed, 'in 1900, his historical neck [was] broken by the sudden irruption of forces totally new'. 'In 1901 the world had altogether changed'.[19]

Possibly, most poignant was the anxiety Henry Adams shared with Thomas Eakins of confronting human nature, and in particular oneself: 'Of all studies, the one he would rather have avoided was that of his own mind. He knew no tragedy so heartrending as introspection'.[20] The tensions of Eakins's life and art were ultimately those of our time, and one measure of his greatness was that he did not avoid them.

1. *Philadelphia Press*, 22 February 1914.
2. Novak 1969, chapter 11, 'Thomas Eakins: Science and Sight', pp.191–210.
3. Goodrich 1982; Hendricks 1974; and Homer 1992.
4. Schendler 1967; Fried 1987; and Lubin 1985.
5. The most thorough discussion of the social history and context of this subject is Johns 1983 (1), chapter 2, '*Max Schmitt in a Single Scull* or *The Champion Single Sculls*', pp.19–45.
6. See Fried op. cit., *passim.*
7. Whitman 1982, p.165.
8. See Johns op. cit., pp.13, 75; she links *The Gross Clinic* also to Velázquez's *Martinez Montanes*, 1656 (Prado Museum, Madrid).
9. Prown 1985, pp.121–7.
10. See the discussion of this work in Lubin 1985, pp.27–82.
11. See the discussion of this turning point towards the concentrated portraits of few figures and single individuals in Cikovsky, Jr., 'Thomas Eakins: *The Art Student (Portrait of an Artist)*, c.1890', in Cikovsky, Kelly and Shaw 1989, pp.126–30.
12 See Goodrich op.cit., vol.II, pp.215–20.
13. See Wilmerding 1991, pp.224–63.
14. See Adams (Sentry ed.) 1961, pp.284–8, 381–3.
15. See Urdang 1981, pp.259–83.
16. Adams op. cit., pp.452, 479.
17. Ibid., pp.378, 383, 489.
18. Ibid., pp.397, 497.
19. Ibid., pp.382, 404.
20. Ibid., pp.432.

Fig.14
William Rush Carving His Allegorical Figure of the Schuylkill River
1908
Oil on canvas, 92.6 × 123.1 ($36\frac{7}{16} \times 48\frac{7}{16}$)
The Brooklyn Museum. Dick S. Ramsay Fund

Thomas Eakins and his European Contemporaries

John Hayes

Fig.15
Thomas Couture, *Antoine Etex*
Oil on canvas, 117.2 × 85.4 (46¼ × 33⅝)
Birmingham City Museum and Art Gallery

Thomas Eakins arrived in Paris in October 1866. He stayed there for three years painfully perfecting his craft, visited Switzerland, Italy, Germany and Belgium, spent a final six months in Spain, and then returned to Philadelphia, never to set foot in Europe again. His subsequent painting career in the United States spanned the whole of one of the most remarkable periods in American history: an age that witnessed an industrial, commercial and professional revolution that in scale and impact far surpassed anything that had taken place, or was taking place, in Europe or elsewhere in the world; and as a patriot Eakins was deeply proud of the achievements of his native land. But if Eakins seemed to require no further stimulus from European art and culture, it is no less true that Paris in the late 1860s had been peculiarly suited to his youthful needs, both as an art student and as a thoughtful individual with a wide range of mainly practical interests.

Paris in the last years of the Second Empire has been characterized in many different ways. Society in its upper echelons was no doubt frivolous and decadent; the régime, in spite of liberalization, remained repressive; and the city itself had been utterly changed, socially and geographically, by Haussmann's great boulevards. But the prevailing ethos, as elsewhere in Europe at the time, was scientific. When Zola defended his *Thérèse Raquin*, 1867, a novel recounting a 'ferocious sexual relationship', bitterly attacked as pornographic, he wrote that he had given himself up entirely to 'precise analysis of the mechanism of the human being'. This scientific state of mind found expression that same year, 1867, in the Exposition Universelle, where Eakins, who had made neat perspective drawings of workshop apparatus when he was still at high school, was spellbound by the power of the heavy machinery on display.

Thinking people in the mid nineteenth century had an immense faith – to a large extent supplanting religious belief – in the capacity of science to unravel the secrets of the universe through ever-increasing and ever more accurately tested factual knowledge. Renan's critical *Life of Jesus* created a sensation when it appeared in 1863. Hippolyte Taine, a brilliant expositor who had succeeded Viollet-le-Duc as professor of aesthetics and the history of art at the Ecole des Beaux-Arts when Eakins was there, followed Auguste Comte and John Stuart Mill in propounding that scientific method should be extended to every form of human activity; in other words, it could be as valid when applied to art as it was to botany. Niebuhr, Ranke, Mommsen and others had

already pioneered its application to history; but as a positivist, Taine went further than the new scientific historians, and attempted to deduce general laws from the knowledge of a myriad of individual facts. The accumulation of detail, he argued, would lead to the discovery of what he called *la faculté maîtresse* which was the essence of whatever was under scrutiny; by definition great works of art reflected the essential qualities of their period and represented its characteristic types – *le personnage régnant* – whether it were the nude athlete of the Greeks, or Faust and Werther in the romantic age. The essence of the mid nineteenth century was, of course, that very pursuit of facts accepted then as synonymous with the search for truth – in a word, as far as art and literature were concerned, Realism. Taine's ideas, vigorously and fluently expressed, must have reinforced Eakins's scientific and rational leanings, in particular his view that figure painting depended upon a thorough mastery of anatomy through dissection and composition upon the logic of one-point perspective. Artistic truth required the most exact method. Eakins held to these principles throughout his life, in spite of the stiltedness that was apt to result in some of his finished work.

Taine's ideas were important for Eakins in two other respects. He popularized for a French audience Herbert Spencer's concept of the survival of the fittest – the individual who stood out from the mass – and, as a concomitant of his belief in art as realism, preached Courbet's doctrine that painting should be concerned with contemporary and indeed ordinary life: 'to record the manners, ideas and aspects of the age as I myself saw them ... that is my aim', Courbet had famously declared in 1855. Eakins had been brought up in a democratic milieu at Philadelphia's egalitarian but high-flying Central High School. He respected and admired people in any walk of life who aspired to do things supremely well, and had no time for those who did not. Taine (and Spencer) taught that in this he was scientifically correct; and it was achievers, the creators of modern Philadelphia, who were to be the principal subject of Eakins's painting.

Portrait painting was not, however, a genre that Eakins pursued in Europe. In mid nineteenth century Paris, art school teaching and academic painting centred on the nude. Eakins regarded the female body as the most beautiful of nature's creations, and he was appalled by the way in which contemporary French painters could successfully exhibit at the Paris Salon meretricious paintings of 'naked women, standing sitting lying down flying dancing doing nothing which they call Phrynes,

Venuses, nymphs...'. William Bouguereau, one of the main culprits, was a Salon juror, and taught at the Académie Julian to which (because of his influence in the art world) foreign as well as French students flocked; his pictures were extremely popular with American collectors. Ironically, in view of his obvious concern with surface qualities, Bouguereau declared it as his aim in portraiture to capture the intellectual character of his sitters. Gérôme, Eakins's teacher, was an altogether more substantial personality, and Eakins owed him a profound debt for his patient and perceptive encouragement of his student work. He, too, was immensely popular with American collectors, but for very different kinds of picture: his skilful and meticulously delineated genre scenes set in exotic lands. Gérôme's precise, colourful, jewel-like style was never one Eakins sought to emulate but his thorough research into his subject matter and his archaeological exactitude, part and parcel of Gérôme's integrity, were methods Eakins did absorb, applying them, for example, to his paintings of William Rush (see no. 17) and Frank Hamilton Cushing (fig.30a).

Towards the end of his time in Paris Eakins studied briefly at Léon Bonnat's Academy, where Velázquez (fig.6) and Ribera rather than Ingres were the models. Interest in the great seventeenth-century Spanish masters had been revived some years before by Champfleury (the critic who first acclaimed Courbet) as part of his attack on romanticism and promotion of the new realism; and the influence of their style was widespread in the second half of the nineteenth century. Manet and Whistler were among great artists profoundly affected. For Eakins the sheer power of Spanish painting, what he called its bigness, was a revelation, and this experience was decisive for him: breadth, the more painterly handling he had first discovered in the work of Thomas Couture (fig.15), and a predilection for subdued tones, became the cornerstones of his maturing and very personal realist style. It is curious, however, considering how Eakins was developing, that there is not a single mention either of Courbet or of Manet, painters one feels he could not have failed to admire, in the whole of his very descriptive and self-revelatory correspondence home.

A young French artist who preceded Eakins to Spain, and who made copies there of works by Murillo and Velázquez, was Carolus-Duran (later the teacher of Sargent). Carolus-Duran secured his reputation at the Salon in 1869 with his striking portrait of his wife, *La Dame au Gant* (fig.16), and, together with Bonnat (fig.19) and Henri Fantin-Latour, became the

Fig.16
E.A. Carolus-Duran, *La Dame au Gant* (*Madame Carolus-Duran*)
1869
Oil on canvas, 228 × 164 ($89\frac{3}{4}$ × $64\frac{1}{2}$)
Musée d'Orsay, Paris

leading fashionable portraitist in Paris in the 1870s and 1880s, working in the realist tradition with its dark Spanish tones and penchant for descriptive detail. Indeed, both Bonnat (who had settled in to a kind of academic realism by the 1870s) and, to an even greater degree, the shy and withdrawn Fantin-Latour, executed at any rate their more formal portraits with the clarity and sharpness of focus of the photograph. Degas also achieved greater naturalism through the use of photography, but, in his case, the naturalism was compositional; a fascination with unconventional designs and unexpected *placements*, poses and gestures, reflecting the instaneity and randomness of the snapshot. Impressionist instaneity – expressed through similar apparently accidental compositions, blurring at the edges of the field of vision, broken high-keyed colour, and a dexterous, direct handling of paint – represented the ultimate of which the Realist vision was capable. This was not a direction which Eakins took. He probably knew more about the possibilities of photography than any other painter of his day, but he used it principally and most originally for a scientific study of motion, germane, for example, to his painting of *The Fairman Rogers Four-in-Hand* (no. 19). As a composer he was classically inclined; informal designs derived from photographs, in which figures might be unceremoniously cut by the edges of the canvas, as in the *Wrestlers* (Columbus Museum of Art, Ohio), are exceedingly rare. Like Degas, he was concerned with descriptive outline rather than with atmospheric perspective, and his river scenes, in particular *Max Schmitt in a Single Scull* (fig.2), have more the precision and poise of Gérôme than

Fig.17
Frank Holl, *Lord Overstone*
1881
Oil on canvas, 127 × 101.6 (50 × 40)
The Loyd Collection, Lockinge

Fig.18
Sir Hubert von Herkomer, *John Couch Adams*
1888
Oil on canvas, 59.7 × 39.4 ($23\frac{1}{2}$ × $15\frac{1}{2}$)
National Portrait Gallery, London

the instaneity and atmosphere of an Impressionist.

Eakins never visited England, where the demand for portraiture had always been greater than anywhere else in Europe, and where both demand and the prestige of portraiture as an art form increased very considerably in the halcyon decades up to 1914. Following hard on the Pre-Raphaelite aesthetic, the realist tradition was predominant, as in France, from the 1860s to the 1880s. Frank Holl, much admired and respected for his honesty of purpose, was the most searching and unflattering professional portrait painter of this period in his scrutiny of individual physiognomy (fig.17); former Pre-Raphaelite (Sir) John Everett Millais, the most sought after portraitist of his day, and comparable in many ways with Bonnat, produced commanding likenesses, firmly drawn and solidly modelled (fig.20); (Sir) Luke Fildes, like so many other contemporary portraitists, had an eye for fashion and accessories; and (Sir) Hubert von Herkomer, best known, as Fildes was, for the realism of his sentimental genre paintings, was photographic but painterly, using the strong lighting favoured by Holl and the solid modelling characteristic of Millais (fig.18). A younger generation of artists who had studied in Paris were converted to French *plein air* naturalism, and the ideals of this movement informed the portraiture of painters like Henry La Thangue and Stanhope Forbes, who discovered their Brittany in Cornwall. It is symptomatic of this trend that the New English Art Club, founded in 1886 as a breakaway movement from the Royal Academy, was to have been called the Society of Anglo-French Painters.

Fig.20
Sir John Everett Millais, *Mrs Bischoffsheim*
1873
Oil on canvas, 130.8 × 90 (51½ × 35½)
Tate Gallery, London

Fig.19
Léon Bonnat, *Mary Sears (later Mrs Francis Shaw)*
1878
Oil on canvas, 126.5 × 75 (49¾ × 29½)
Museum of Fine Arts, Boston, Gift of Miss Clara Endicott Sears, 1930

Fig.21
Franz von Lenbach, *Prince Regent Leopold of Bavaria*
1902
Oil on cardboard, 76.2 × 61.6 (30 × 24¼)
The Metropolitan Museum of Art, New York.
Bequest of Jacob Ruppert, 1939

Fig.22
Wilhelm Trübner, *Carl Schuch*
1876
Oil on canvas, 147.5 × 117.5 (58 × 46¼)
Nationalgalerie, Berlin

Fig.23
Wilhelm Leibl, *Frau Gedon*
1868–1869
Oil on canvas, 119.5 × 95.7 (47 × 37¹¹⁄₁₆)
Neue Pinakothek, Munich

Fig.24
Ludwig Knaus, *Franz Damian Leiden*
*c.*1868
Oil on canvas, 94 × 70 (37 × 27½)
Wallraf-Richartz-Museum, Cologne

Fig.25
Max Liebermann, *Bürgermeister Heinrich Burchard*
1911
Oil on canvas, 200 × 151 (78¾ × 59½)
Kunsthalle, Hamburg

Fig.26
Heinrich von Angeli, *Count Arthur Mensdorff*
1900
Oil on canvas, 69 × 54 (27⅛ × 21¼)
Royal Collection, Osborne House
By gracious permission of Her Majesty The Queen

At the time Eakins was working in Paris many of his fellow Americans were choosing to study in Germany, mainly at the Munich Academy. William Merritt Chase (see no.35) and Frank Duveneck were both there in the early 1870s, and Duveneck returned to the city in 1878 to found a school of his own. The leading Bavarian portraitists of this period, Franz von Lenbach (fig.21), Wilhelm Leibl (fig.23) and Wilhelm Trübner (fig.22), all indebted to Dutch seventeenth-century portraiture, notably Hals, were the founders of the Munich tradition of painterly realism, and the Munich

style, which favoured spontaneity and expressive brushwork, was to pervade American portraiture in the decades following. After the establishment in 1870 of the Hohenzollern Empire most of the more prominent German artists tended to gravitate to Berlin. The immensely popular Ludwig Knaus (fig.24), mainly a genre painter in the Dutch manner, moved from Düsseldorf to Berlin in 1874, Max Liebermann settled there in 1884, Lovis Corinth in 1900, and Max Slevogt in 1901. The last three painters, all of whom had been associated with Leibl and Trübner, became known

as the German Impressionists, and developed an even more vigorous style of painting than prevailed in Munich. Liebermann it was who dominated the Berlin art world, from his positions as professor at the Berlin Academy and president of the Berlin Sezession, posts which he occupied from 1889 and 1899 respectively (fig.25); all three artists were still active in Berlin after 1918.

Berlin had, however, been a centre for a more sober kind of realist painting since the romantic age, and perhaps the most distinguished German painter (and graphic artist) of

Fig.27
Ivan Kramskoi, *Mikhail J. Saltykov-Stschedrin*
1879
Oil on canvas, 88 × 68 (34⅝ × 26¾)
State Tretyakov Gallery, Moscow

Fig.28
Ilya Repin, *A. Ignatiev*
1902
Oil on canvas, 89 × 62.5 (35 × 24¼)
State Russian Museum, St Petersburg

the middle and later years of the nineteenth century, Adolf von Menzel, spent most of his long life working in the city. Menzel had a passion for factual veracity approaching that of Zola; any object, however trivial, was found worthy of his brush (Moltke's binoculars are a celebrated example, and it was as record – documentation rather than glorification – that Menzel envisaged the huge history paintings he executed to celebrate the ceremonies and triumphs of the first Wilhelmine era. Even Heinrich von Angeli, the international court painter of the age, was primarily a realist (fig.26), in contrast to the seductive glamour purveyed by his idolized predecessor, Franz Xaver Winterhalter, who was still living in Paris, but in semi-retirement, during Eakins's sojourn in the French capital.

The Russian painter Ilya Repin's study of piled up accoutrements is very close in character to Moltke's binoculars. Realism was a more powerful force in Russia than elsewhere, because it was closely associated with the feeling of social responsibility among the intelligentsia following the emancipation of the serfs in 1861. Artists wanted to paint scenes from everyday rural life in an unsentimental manner; to do this they left the cities, and a movement known as the *peredvizhniki* or wanderers came into being which included the finest painters of the day, Nikolai Ge, Ivan Kramskoi and Repin (the more sentimentally anecdotal Vasily Perov formally joined the group in 1870). As portraitists, all these artists were capable of painting vigorous and direct character studies (fig.28); in his larger scale pictures Kramskoi could be close in mood to Millais and Carolus-Duran, and there was an element of photographic realism in his work (fig.27). Alexander III, who ruled from 1881 to 1894, wanted to encourage a national school of painting; what amounted to a national gallery was in fact formed by the Muscovite industrialist, Pavel Tretyakov (fig.29), who presented his huge collection to the city in 1892.

Tretyakov commissioned Russian portraitists to paint a number of illustrious contemporaries for his gallery, Perov's *Dostoevsky* (fig.30), Repin's *Mussorgsky* and Ge's *Tolstoy* (fig.31) being among the best known. In England G.F. Watts had already conceived a similar idea, a series of portraits of eminent Victorians, as early as the 1850s. The subjects were to be chosen by himself, and he destined his Hall of Fame for the National Portrait Gallery (founded in 1856). Watts mostly used a head-and-shoulders format so that he could concentrate on character (fig.32), and the results were searching, uncompromising, and often disturbing. Josephine Butler might have

Fig.29
Ilya Repin, *Pavel Mikhailovich Tretyakov*
1883
Oil on canvas, 98 × 76 ($38\frac{1}{2}$ × 30)
State Tretyakov Gallery, Moscow

Fig.30
Vasily Perov, *Feodor Mikhailovich Dostoevsky*
1872
Oil on canvas, 99 × 80.5 (39 × 31$\frac{11}{16}$)
State Tretyakov Gallery, Moscow

Fig.31
Nikolai Ge, *Count Leo Tolstoy*
1884
Oil on canvas, 96 × 71 (37$\frac{3}{4}$ × 28)
State Russian Museum, St Petersburg

been describing a work by Eakins doomed for
the attic or retention in the artist's studio when
she wrote to her son about Watts's portrait of
her: 'It is rather terrible . . . not at all pretty and
the jaw and head are strong and gaunt. I don't
think my friends will like it. But then he is not
doing it for us, but for posterity; and no doubt it
will convey an idea of my life's work'. Eakins,
too, was thinking of posterity, but he had no
notion of keeping his pictures together as a
series.

Herkomer, who must have met Eakins
when he was in Philadelphia, was another
leading artist of the late Victorian age
interested in portraying great men; and he
requested national heroes like Kitchener and
Baden-Powell to sit for him. Eakins, like
Watts, was concerned with painting a much
wider range of personalities than Herkomer,
many of them, however, though undeniably
remarkable in character, not strictly speaking
of great eminence; and, until the latter part of
his career, when he came closer to Watts in his
concentration on the inner life of his sitters, his
preferred method of revealing the soul or summing up a life's work was quite different from
the intentions of either. Eakins liked to select a
very definite, perhaps critical, moment which
would heighten the potency, and increase the
realism, of his image: the surgeon (a true
personnage régnant of the late nineteenth century) turning to explain to his students what he
has just performed, the sculler in the very
middle of his stroke, the singer projecting a
specific phrase – and he painted it with
absolute precision. The only comparison is
with Degas. Degas studied physiognomy, gesture and muscular movement so assiduously
that he could depict a very particular action
with similar exactitude, whether it were a
prostitute waiting disconsolately for custom, or
a laundress with her iron; a dancer adjusting
her shoe or poised in arabesque; a woman
combing her hair or drying herself after a bath.
His was the realism of everyday Parisian life,
notably that of the world of entertainment.
The subjects of his portraits were caught
momentarily, too, but many of them seem to
regard us defensively, as though they were
trapped by the tensions and circumstances of
their lives (fig.33). Eakins's sitters tend to rise
above events. Where Degas was apprehensive
about life, Eakins was normally robust. In the
last resort it was temperament which separated the two great masters.

Soon after he was ousted from his teaching
post at the Pennsylvania Academy in 1886,
Eakins was already being regarded in America
as rather old-fashioned. His work was dour and
it bore little relationship to the Munich style

Fig.32
George Frederic Watts, *Matthew Arnold*
1880
Oil on canvas, 66 × 52.1 (26 × 20½)
National Portrait Gallery, London

Fig.33
Edgar Degas, *Edmond and Thérèse Morbilli*
c.1865
Oil on canvas, 116.5 × 88.3 (45⅞ × 34¾)
Museum of Fine Arts, Boston.
Gift of Robert Treat Paine, 2nd, 1931

associated with society portraiture. Moreover, in Europe there were new currents. George Heard Hamilton dates the demise of Realism from 1886, the year of the last Impressionist exhibition, which signified the break-up of Impressionism as a coherent movement: and he describes the reaction against the conventions of naturalism as part of a broader stirring of disenchantment with rationalism and with science as the mid-Victorians understood it. That same year 1886 was also the date of Jean Moréas's Symbolist manifesto in *Le Figaro*, which announced that it was the business of poets and painters to discover forms which described an idea, rather than to derive formal relationships from observation of the natural world. Gauguin showed us that shapes and colours made an emotional appeal to the spectator irrespective of representation. The Swiss artist, Ferdinand Hodler, who was one of the leaders of the Symbolist movement, had begun to develop his personal imaginative style in Paris in the early 1880s (fig.34), and the young Edvard Munch was already breaking away from the naturalist formulae of his talented friends and mentors in Oslo by the middle of that decade. Whistler, who had been greatly influenced by Courbet, was denouncing 'ce damné Réalisme' as early as 1867. Both the Symbolist and the Aesthetic movements, the latter carrying the banner of art for art's sake, soon had many adherents in New York if not in Philadelphia.

During the thirty years or so prior to 1914 the pace of change in artistic style was increasingly rapid – Synthetism and Neo-Impressionism were soon followed by the Nabis, the Fauves, Cubism and the Blaue Reiter – and exhibiting bodies more or less radical in which portraiture played a significant role proliferated in defiance of the conventional and the academic. In England the New English Art Club was followed by the International Society (1898) and the Camden Town Group (1911). Both the Munich and Berlin Sezessions were founded in 1892, and the Berlin Neue Sezession, a revolt against the German Impressionists, in 1910; the more illustrious Vienna Sezession, led by Gustav Klimt, in which symbolism and art nouveau were the formative influences, dates from 1897. Formerly realist portraitists like Trübner developed a Sezession intensity in their later work; though, of course, there were also artists like the beguiling Danish painter, August Jerndorff, who continued to pursue photographic naturalism in their portraiture until the end of the century, even if sometimes to heighten complex and mysterious emotions.

The newly wealthy in this age of unprecedented economic expansion stood in need of status and reassurance. For them (as for the eighteenth-century patrons of Thomas Hudson or Sir Joshua Reynolds) a portrait was more a social than a private image, and the requirement from the painter was the provision of a public persona, idealization not scrutiny. Even Liebermann diluted his modern style in the 1900s to paint 'boardroom' portraits in which bankers and businessmen were elevated by an imperious pose or tilt of the head. In England, during the Edwardian age, (Sir) William Orpen was the most successful purveyor of this kind of portrait. But society portraiture in the last decades of the nineteenth century was characterized also by a new rhetoric and panache reflecting the opulence of these years. Especially was this true of portraits of society women. Giovanni Boldini, who had settled in Paris in 1872, developed his unmistakable personal manner, with its brash and spectacular brushwork, at about the time of the last Impressionist exhibition; and fashionable Parisian society found his style irresistible. Antonio de la Gandara, no less popular in the 1890s, specialized in rather pert beauties in couture dresses painted at full-length with a Whistlerian narrow format and plain background. However, the master of bravura, and the most acclaimed painter of the age was, of course, John Singer Sargent. With his dazzling facture, original and arresting designs, and innate feeling for *hauteur*, Sargent expressed with incomparable felicity the glamour and self-regard of *la belle époque* (fig.35). Much imitated in Edwardian England, his influence was international and affected leading painters in their respective countries such as G.D. Mirea, onetime pupil of Carolus-Duran, who worked in far-off Romania. Apart from the brilliant Spanish painter, Joaquin Sorolla, who also acquired an international reputation, the most distinguished and original of those who painted with a similar panache and fluency was Valentin Serov (fig.36), who portrayed the fashionable and intellectual society of St Petersburg in the aesthetically stifling reign of Nicholas II, the last of the Tsars. Daring and angular compositions, dramatic poses, vivid characterization, sensitivity to the nuances of class, and lively, colourful brushwork which by 1910 embraced Fauvism, give Serov a place at least equal to the Frenchman Jacques-Emile Blanche, the German Liebermann and the American Chase, in the annals of contemporary society portraiture (fig.37).

Fig.34
Ferdinand Hodler, *Helene Weiglé*
c.1889
Oil on canvas, 80 × 61 (31½ × 24)
Kunsthaus, Zurich,
Gottfried Keller Foundation

Realism had given way to Symbolism, the Victorian solidity of Bonnat and Millais had been succeeded in popularity by the grandiloquence of Boldini and Sargent, and avant-garde artists of many different persuasions and groupings – painters such as Cézanne, Van Gogh, Munch, Kirchner, Matisse and Picasso – had invested portraiture with a new meaning, while Eakins continued to work in Philadelphia. Eakins remained a realist; indeed he was resented by many of his later patrons for making them look even more aged and crumpled than they were. He was not religious, and he had no interest in the mystical; nor was he innovative. What he was, however, was powerful. Walt Whitman, in 1887, called him a force not a painter. Of course, he did not have the explosive force of a Van Gogh, and his low-keyed tonality was at the opposite end of the spectrum from post-impressionist colour. But some of his later images seem to represent an idea as much as a person – *The Thinker* (no. 38) is an obvious example – and possess a haunting hyper-reality, in large part due to the intensity of the gaze, close in character to Symbolist painting as exemplified by Hodler (who also painted types), or at least to portraits with a certain visionary and introspective quality like the earlier works, dependent on Puvis de Chavannes, of the Russian painter, Mikhail Nesterov (fig.38), who was at this period of his long life primarily a religious artist; and such connections link Eakins's later work in portraiture with the ideals of the new age.

Fig.35
John Singer Sargent, *The Acheson Sisters*
1902
Oil on canvas, 269.2 × 198 (106 × 78)
Devonshire Collection, Chatsworth.
By permission of the Chatsworth Settlement Trustees

Fig.36
Valentin Serov, *Princess O.K.Orlova*
1911
Oil on canvas, 235 × 156 ($92\frac{1}{2}$ × $61\frac{3}{8}$)
State Russian Museum, St Petersburg

Note
In the preparation of this brief and very general essay I have been indebted primarily to the immense resources of the Witt Library; but also to the work of many scholars, principally Linda Nochlin for her wide-ranging study of Realism, an intellectual *tour de force*, Elizabeth Johns for her equally brilliant book on Eakins, *The Heroism of Modern Life*, and William Homer, for his recent monograph on Eakins.

Fig.38
Mikhail Nesterov, *Ekaterina Nesterova*
1905
Oil on canvas, 142.5 × 107.8 (56⅛ × 42½)
State Tretyakov Gallery, Moscow

Fig.37
Valentin Serov, *M.N. Ermolova*
1905
Oil on canvas, 224 × 120 (88 × 47¼)
State Tretyakov Gallery, Moscow

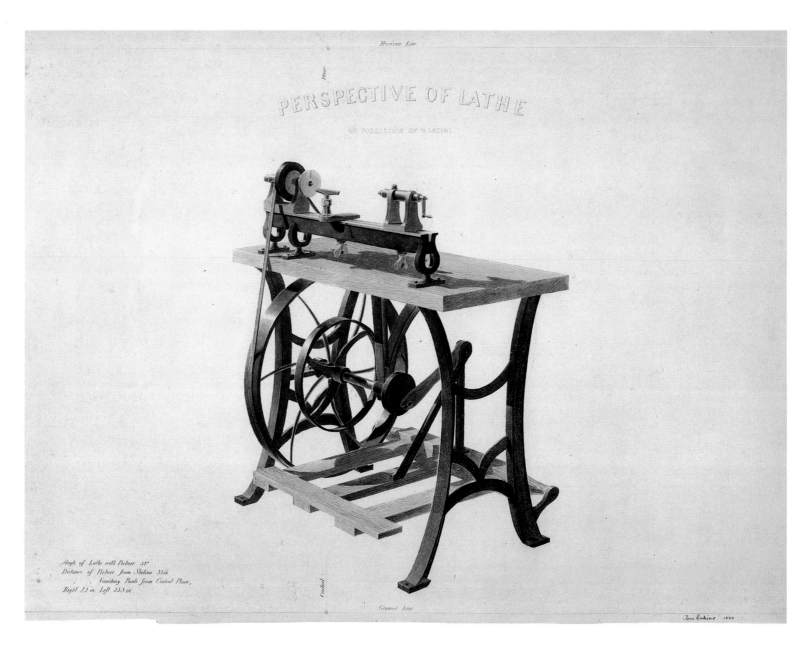

1

Perspective of a Lathe

1860

Pen, ink and watercolour on paper,

41.4 × 55.9 (16$\frac{5}{16}$ × 22)

Signed and dated l.r. in ink: *Tom Eakins 1860*

Inscribed at top by artist: *PERSPECTIVE
OF LATHE/IN POSSESSION OF
B. EAKINS.*

Other perspective notations within work.

Hirshhorn Museum and Sculpture Garden,
Smithsonian Institution. Gift of Joseph H.
Hirshhorn, 1966 (HMSG 1966.1554)

One may question the rationale for the inclusion of a high school mechanical drawing in an exhibition of the mature work of Thomas Eakins. Is there a significant connection between this early exercise in penmanship and perspective, and the later art of the American realist? What can we learn from Eakins's *Perspective of a Lathe*?

In fact, this drawing, and others of its type, present us with quite a range of interesting information about the artist, his background, and his approach to art.[1] On one level, the drawing is a fine example of the young Eakins's abilities as a mechanical draughtsman. On another, it is an indicator of an important part of his artistic training within an educational system that valued the mastery of such industrial arts exercises as evidence of disciplined thought and clear vision.

Perhaps of greatest interest to those familiar with Eakins's later works is the fact that the drawing foretells the artist's continuing and enthusiastic involvement with the preparatory work – ground plans, perspective drawings, oil sketches, photographs, and other preliminary studies – that he considered necessary for the planning and execution of successful works. Thus, as a youthful drawing, as an educational benchmark, and as an indicator of the philosophical and practical foundations of Eakins's art, the *Lathe* is worthy of examination.

Thomas Eakins executed the *Perspective of a Lathe* in 1860, when he was in his last year at Philadelphia's Central High School, a progressive public institution with a liberal arts curriculum established in 1836.[2] The drawing and writing (or penmanship) curriculum there had been established in 1840 by Rembrandt Peale, an educator and member of a prominent Philadelphia family of artists. As a student in the late 1850s and early 1860s, Eakins studied under Professor Alexander Jay MacNeill, a former pupil of Peale's who shared his educational philosophy and methodology.

In the course of his four years at Central High School, Thomas Eakins worked his way through eight semesters of the combined disciplines of writing and drawing. A carefully-planned sequence of classes guided students through the analysis and execution of simple lines and curves, two-dimensional patterns and three-dimensional objects. Students were introduced to lettering and drawing tools, principles of geometry, categories of line and form, projection and perspective systems, and light and shadow. Peale's manual *Graphics* as well as other handbooks and treatises shaped the lessons.[3] During the last two years of study, advanced mechanical and perspective drawing, ornamental writing, and design were pursued. These were subjects Eakins could also practise at home with his father, Benjamin Eakins, a professional writing master.

The *Perspective of a Lathe*, a finished ink and watercolour drawing of a machine owned by his father, demonstrates Eakins's mastery of his drawing and writing lessons.[4] In its meticulous draughtsmanship, its organization of complex geometrical forms in space, its painstaking exploration of light and shadow on grained wooden planks, smooth metal wheels, gears and spindles, its crisp, ornamental outline and copperplate lettering, and its overall design, the drawing indicates Eakins's skill in the graphic presentation of a three-dimensional object. It does not show artistic genius or spontaneity, nor was it intended to do so. It does show that the young Eakins had mastered the methods and practices of his drawing and writing programme.

Yet, one cannot help but wonder why such industrial arts exercises, the end products of

lessons quite different from those pursued in art academies, were deemed appropriate for Eakins and his peers. In fact, the drawing curriculum at Philadelphia's Central High School reflected a nineteenth-century movement in universal education that came to be known as the 'art crusade'.[5] Advocates of this pedagogy believed that widespread, systematic instruction in the principles and practices of drawing and writing would produce perceptive, diligent citizens capable of clear vision and disciplined thinking. To many idealistic educators the potential intellectual and aesthetic benefits of this system of instruction for the American public were immense.

For Thomas Eakins the results of this education were quite significant; from it he received much of the practical and philosophical bases of his art.[6] It seems clear that the artist's devotion to working out his compositions using a logical sequential method, and his systematic exploration of the world around him came from his early education. It provided a framework for his remarkable quest for knowledge about his subjects, which included the exploration of underlying structures as well as superficial ones, and his desire to share both the knowledge and the methods by which it could be acquired through his teaching and his art.

The *Perspective of a Lathe*, then, exemplifies Thomas Eakins's lifelong commitment to the logical acquisition, assimilation and application of knowable facts about his subjects, whether they be complicated mechanical devices investigated during his student years or complex human beings painted in his maturity. As an accomplished youthful drawing, as a symbol of an educational philosophy, and as a premonition of his continuing acceptance and advocacy of the philosophy and method that shaped his early education, Thomas Eakins's *Lathe* merits careful consideration.

MC–H

1. Other mechanical and perspective drawings from Eakins's Central High School years are known today. *A Drawing of Gears* (1860) is in the Hirshhorn Museum and Sculpture Garden; see Rosenzweig 1977, p.27. Nine others (*Icosaedron* [1859], *Icosaedron; Two Winches* [1859], *Column with Crosspiece* [1859], *Geometric Solids* [1859–60], *Geometric Form* [1859–60], *Gears* [1860–61], *Steam Engine; Hexagon and Cube* [1860–61], *Governor Mechanism* [1860–61], and *Three Spirals* [1860–61]) are part of Charles Bregler's Thomas Eakins Collection, Pennsylvania Academy of the Fine Arts; see Foster forthcoming 1994, nos. 5–13. These high school drawings were initially saved by Eakins and his wife. Later they passed into the hands of Charles Bregler, a devoted former student and friend who organized and labelled them as part of his efforts to document the life and work of his master. Bregler sold the Hirshhorn drawings in the 1940s; the Pennsylvania Academy works were acquired from his widow in 1984.
2. On the history of the school, see Edmonds 1902; and Johns 1980, pp.139–49.
3. Peale 1834. See Johns op. cit., *passim*, for a detailed analysis of the curriculum and lists of recommended handbooks. For another interpretation of the effect of the curriculum on Eakins, see Fried 1985, pp.33–104.
4. The lathe remained in the possession of the Eakins family for some time. It is probably the same one that Thomas Eakins later kept in his studio and used to make wooden teaching devices for his students in the 1880s; see A. Albright as told to E. Stuart, 'Memories of Thomas Eakins', *Harper's Bazaar*, vol.81, no.2828, August 1947, p.139.
5. See Johns op. cit., pp.139–44; and Marzio 1976.
6. See Johns op. cit., pp.139–49, for the complete presentation of this thesis, and specific examples of the relationship between Eakins's mature art and his early drawing instruction. Johns's thesis has been confirmed by examination of related material in Charles Bregler's Thomas Eakins Collection, Pennsylvania Academy of the Fine Arts; see Foster op. cit., chapter 1.

Provenance: Charles Bregler, Philadelphia; Joseph Katz, Baltimore, 1940s; M. Knoedler & Co., 1961; Joseph H. Hirshhorn, New York, 1966; Hirshhorn Museum and Sculpture Garden, 1966.

Exhibitions: Philadelphia, Museum of Art, 1944, no cat. no.; Minneapolis, Minneapolis Institute of Arts, 1976, no. 150; Washington, DC, Hirshhorn Museum and Sculpture Garden, 1977, no. 5; Philadelphia, Museum of Art, 1982 (1), no. 2.

Literature: Schendler 1967, p.13, ill. p.14 (fig.1); Hendricks 1974, p.10, ill. (fig.14); Stebbins 1976, p.187, ill. p.188 (fig.150); Rosenzweig 1977, p.26, ill. p.26 (fig.5); Chamberlin-Hellman 1981, pp.51–2, ill. p.571 (fig.1); Goodrich 1982, vol.I, p.5, ill. p.6 (fig.3); Johns 1983 (2), pp.2–3; Sewell 1982, pp.3–4, ill. p.6 (fig.2); Milroy 1986, pp.42–3, ill. p.367 (fig.6); Homer 1992, p.15, ill. p.14 (fig.9); Foster forthcoming 1994, nos. 5–13.

2
Study of a Standing Nude Woman
Charcoal and black crayon on pink laid paper,
61.6 × 47.6 (24¼ × 18¾)
Unsigned and undated

Philadelphia Museum of Art.
Gift of Mrs Thomas Eakins and
Miss Mary Adeline Williams (29.184.43)

Thomas Eakins's drawings of nudes, more specifically his studies of female nudes, have received a considerable amount of scholarly attention. Among the reasons for this is the relative scarcity of such drawings in American art before the last quarter of the nineteenth century, when the European academic practice of making life drawings from nude models was reluctantly accepted into American art academies' curricula. Such drawings, as well as the studies that preceded them in the training of young artists, indicate the nature of academic practice in America.

The rather large number of Eakins's life drawings available today is also a point of interest. While a number of drawings, including nos. 2 and 3, have been known for a long time, many new drawings by Eakins have come to light only recently as a result of the acquisition of a significant collection of Eakins material by the Pennsylvania Academy of the Fine Arts.[1] Thus, there is now a more comprehensive body of the artist's youthful works, including copies of picturesque prints, perspective and mechanical drawings, cast drawings, drawings of everyday objects in notes and letters, dissection, anatomical and life drawings. These works have proven irresistible to scholars hoping to determine the specific interests, capabilities and artistic growth of a young man still in his formative years.

In fact, differing assessments of Eakins's charcoal life drawings of whole figures have produced three schools of thought on the dating and circumstances surrounding the creation of these studies. One group believes that the Philadelphia Museum drawings and related works were created in the period 1863 to 1866 when Eakins was studying in the life classes at the Pennsylvania Academy; others hold the opinion that many of the charcoal life drawings were executed between 1866 and 1869 when Eakins was studying in Paris; and yet another group contends that the drawings demonstrate Eakins's work as a young artist and life class instructor between 1874 and 1876, several years after his return from study abroad.[2] The sheer diversity of opinion on this issue has been remarkable. However, with the evaluation of the new material at the Pennsylvania Academy, the case for the dating of these life drawings to Eakins's student years at the Academy has been strengthened considerably.

No matter what one's opinion on the dating of the life drawings is, the studies are of great interest for a more encompassing reason: they indicate the future direction of Eakins's art and life, with his remarkable devotion to the study of the human figure. As a student, as a practising artist, and as a teacher, he continuously strove to acquire and share with others his knowledge and skill in the representation of the human figure. This ultimately proved to be quite controversial, for Eakins's views on the limits for appropriate study of the nude were different from those held by most of his contemporaries. Eventually his reputation as a teacher and as a person suffered, most spectacularly when he was forced to resign his position as Director of the Schools at the Pennsylvania Academy in 1886 for supposed improprieties, some of which involved nude models. It is hard to look at Eakins's drawings of nudes and not think ahead to the impact his devotion to such studies had on his art and life.

Thus, the charcoal studies of nude women embody many of the significant elements of Eakins's artistic career. The drawings are interesting for themselves, as well as for what they indicate about Eakins's artistic education, his approach to the human figure and his future as an artist and teacher.

In spite of the controversies over the time and place of the execution of the life studies, their position within the prescribed sequence of an academic education in art is secure. They represent a stage in the academic training of an artist after the mastery of drawing from prints and other two-dimensional works, followed by simple, three-dimensional objects, i.e., plaster casts of classical sculpture fragments, and finally more complex works, plaster casts of whole antique statues. In their study of the antique, art students were supposed to translate smooth, chilly, colourless and motionless casts into drawings sharing the same qualities, and simultaneously appreciate the fine points of exemplary works from the past. For Eakins the study of the antique was problematic; he spent five months at it in Philadelphia and avoided it as much as possible in Paris. Yet, he did learn from his study of ancient sculpture. Assessments of his later paintings, sculptures, photographs, and teaching methods have revealed much familiarity and borrowing from the antique, in spite of his professed antipathy to extended elementary study from it.[3]

As a Pennsylvania Academy student in the early 1860s, Thomas Eakins was anxious to move on to academic life study, the reward for capable draughtsmen. The switch from antique to life study was even more startling than had been the move from high school mechanical drawing with its sharp pencils, clean lines and ideal geometries to Academy cast drawing with its messy charcoal, smudgy shadows, and irregular forms. With life study the subjects suddenly had individual shapes, warmth, colour and the potential of movement. The enthusiastic Eakins found the work challenging.

Various characteristics and qualities of the Philadelphia Museum charcoal life drawings seem to place them at the stage of Thomas Eakins's development after he moved from antique to life study in 1863. Reasons for this include points of correspondence between the setting and props depicted in the drawings and what was in use at the old Academy then; knowledge of the treatment and perception of female models in Philadelphia; objective analysis of the materials used; and consideration of the patterns of retention of studies by Eakins and his family. Stylistic analysis of the drawings themselves, clearly a subjective undertaking, should also be considered in this placement.

Eakins's *Study of a Seated Nude Woman* and *Study of a Standing Nude Woman* are unusual for life studies of the time in that they include specific details about their settings: studio space with the props of wrinkled background cloths and a painted block upon which one model sits. From the distribution of shadows, it is also possible to assume the overhead placement of artificial light in this space. Unlike most other artists, Eakins has made no attempt to disguise or minimize the fact that the interior is obviously a studio; in fact, the props define the space occupied by the figures and emphasize their dimensionality.

The actual setting in these drawings appears to be much like the Academy basement life studio (fig.2a), a room illustrated in a letter sent to Eakins while he was abroad by his old friend and classmate Charles Fussell.[4] In this reminder of 'our old sanctum', Fussell depicted a nude female model reclining under a hanging lamp with reflectors while a group of male students toiled at their boards. It is interesting to note that in Fussell's illustration and in the exhibited drawing of the nude seen from the back by Eakins, the faces of the female models are not covered, while in his frontal representation of the seated model, the figure is masked. This is a feature that strikes modern viewers as quite strange, although it would not have been perceived as such in the 1860s or 1870s. The masking of female models was a continuing, although not consistent, practice at the Pennsylvania Academy and other American art schools during much of the nineteenth century.[5] The reasons for this practice were the public's belief that the exhibition of the female body for payment was far from respectable, and the Academy's notion that the identity of the models must be safeguarded, both to protect their reputations and to encourage women to apply for work.

In fact, professional models were frequently in short supply in Philadelphia. Willing workers were recruited from all walks of life. As Eakins later wrote of his attempts to upgrade the recruitment of female models at the Academy:

The old plan was for the students or officers to visit low houses of prostitution & bargain with the inmates. This course was degrading & would be unworthy of the present academy & its result was models coarse, flabby, ill formed & unfit in every way for the requirements of a school....[6]

In the quest to establish a chronology for Eakins's life drawings, nos. 2 and 3 have been linked since they are on identically sized and watermarked paper. Analysis of the handmade paper has indicated French manufacture, but information about artist's materials used in America at this time reveals that such papers were readily available in Philadelphia in the 1860s and later.[7]

It is interesting to consider whether or not the retention of these life drawings by Eakins and his family can assist in their assessment. Clearly the individuals in question were dedicated savers. Thanks to their urge to preserve, there exists today a wealth of Eakins material: preparatory studies and finished works, but also notebooks, sketchbooks, expense journals, letters to each other, and drawings of various types. Charcoal life drawings are just one category amid many. It seems likely that these studies, like the high school perspective and mechanical drawings, would have been kept in a group as examples of the artist's work during a particular phase of his training after he had moved on to the next. Uneven in quality and degree of finish, the life charcoals do not seem sufficiently accomplished for him to have brought them back as samples of his student work in Paris, where he started to do life studies in oil, his preferred medium from then on. They also bear little resemblance to his dated works of the mid-1870s.

When taken together, all of these reasons make a compelling case for the placement of the large charcoal life studies in the period between 1863 and 1866. Yet the arguments are strongly suggestive, rather than definitive, and are likely to remain so.

The drawings themselves, no matter what their dating may be, have much to offer. Both are obvious classroom life studies, not studies of posed figures planned for insertion into other compositions, a frequent preparatory practice of academic artists and one used by Eakins later on.

In the creation of these nudes, Eakins used a soft charcoal stick to establish the major forms of figure and surroundings. He then smudged and cleaned areas with stumps to blend and modulate the darks and lights, and subsequently added fine, dark accents with a pointed piece of charcoal. As has been oft noted, his use of the medium is quite painterly. The figures have been established with shaded volumes, patches of light and shadow. The reliance on linear description is minimal. As a result, the full-bodied nudes appear quite sculptural and weighty, in fact, what might be termed 'Rubensian'.

In both drawings there are some curious anomalies and awkward passages. It is not hard to pick out areas of limited attention by the artist, for example, hands and feet. Eakins has drawn only one hand, and that quite minimally; the roughly blocked feet do not seem to have captured much of his interest, either. Such areas contrast with the developed volumes of the rest of the figures. Of course, life models, unlike antique statues, posed for limited times only. Perhaps the young artist simply ran short of time for these secondary parts.

The *Standing Nude Woman* is the more conventional life drawing of the exhibited pair. Here a full-figured, dark-haired woman with her right foot in front of her left leans away from the viewer at a slight angle. Posing before a wrinkled back cloth, she seems to be leaning on a raised horizontal prop, although there is little indication of the actual support for her right arm and bowed head. Eakins, like earlier artists who drew ample female nudes from the back, was clearly interested in the contrapostal shifts in the pelvis and shoulders and the differences between the weight-bearing and relaxed legs. The play of soft lights and velvety darks over and around the figures makes Eakins's study intriguing. Dark pools of shadow in the lower part of the drawing and an oblique shadow cast by the figure on the right indicate the presence of overhead lighting on the figure's left. The barely modelled back and left arm are softly illuminated while the buttocks and legs are bathed in shadow. In a number of areas, but especially along the figure's right contour, the shadows have been emphasized with overlaid fine charcoal lines.

The *Standing Nude Woman* seen from the back differs in a variety of significant ways from the frontal *Seated Nude Woman Wearing a Mask*. In the latter, the model has assumed a twisted pose with her left ankle tucked under her right thigh at the front edge of the painted rectangular box on which she sits. Her right leg extends below the mass of the rest of the figure. At first glance, the woman appears to be a uniformly substantial one. Yet, upon closer scrutiny, it appears that certain parts — her right arm, left thigh, pendulous breasts and large feet — are fleshier than others. Certainly she is unusually proportioned as represented here by Eakins.

The masked head facing in the direction of the overhead light is arresting. Even with knowledge of the reasons for its presence, the mask seems to make the otherwise exposed woman more vulnerable and more remote at the same time. It confounds the viewer by blanking out an area that would normally be expressively modelled. As Kenneth Clark has written in *The Nude*, 'how determinant in any conception of the nude body is the character of the head that surmounts it. We look first at the face. It is through facial expression that every intimacy begins'.[8] In Eakins's drawing the mask effectively thwarts the intimacy suggested by the uncovered full body. The mask and the other dark rectangle in the piece, the block, form the apex and base of a tipped pyramidal composition. Between those dark areas is the woman. The seated woman is made up of shaded, sloping, rhythmically connected volumes that give the figure a sensual presence. She sits slumped to one side, with her head turned to the other. Her thighs are splayed and flattened as they push against other parts of her body. Her arms brace her torso. Tension is produced by the lateral shifts of the body and the completely different profiles of its two sides. On the left, a long undulating line separates the illuminated figure from its darker background; on the right, some parts of the body are lighter than their background, some darker and some enveloped in deep shadow.

There is a strong sculptural quality to this figure. While it is not evocative of ideally proportioned, gracefully posed classical female nudes, it is reminiscent of another sculptural tradition, the Hellenistic. With its lack of idealization, its twisting pose, its splayed limbs, and its delineation of the effects of age and condition on the body, it actually recalls a Hellenistic work owned by the Academy in the 1860s. Eakins's *Seated Nude Woman Wearing a Mask* and *Crouching Aphrodite* (fig. 2b) both have ample, seemingly fruitful, bodies with large breasts and thighs, sloping shoulders, twisted poses, legs bent at the knee to fold back on themselves, and heads sharply turned to one side. The cast of the well-known work was in a basement gallery near the life classroom where Eakins had studied.[9] There is no doubt that he knew the work.

While these points of correspondence are interesting in a truly academic way, it is not easy to assess their actual implications. After all, Eakins did not necessarily select the model or set the pose. Yet, his familiarity with the cast might have had a role in the creation of the drawing. Perhaps his earlier academic education provided him with an internalized vocabulary of form that surfaced in his study. Perhaps Eakins, like Rubens in Clark's analysis, 'drew from the antique... till certain ideals of formal completeness were absolutely fixed in his mind; then when he drew from nature he instinctively subordinated the observed facts to the pattern established in his imagination'.[10] Perhaps Eakins's study of the masked woman is both a drawing from nature and the memory of antique form, the study of a paid model sitting in a studio, but also an interpretation of a crouching goddess.

Whether or not one accepts the notion of Eakins confronting the living model and bringing forth his knowledge of the antique, or the suggestion that these large charcoal life drawings were made during the artist's student years at the Pennsylvania Academy, one must admire Eakins's drawings of the female nudes. Impressive in the handling of the masses of the human body, the play of light and shadow, and the context of the studio, the studies demonstrate Eakins's ability to create powerful, individual forms within the formal discipline of academic life drawing. As exemplars of Eakins's study of the human figure within the academic context, they are symbolic of his art as a whole.

MC–H

Fig.2b
Crouching Aphrodite
Copy of an original of the 3rd century BC
Marble
Louvre, Paris

1. On the major collections of Eakins's drawings and their histories, see Siegl 1978, pp.7–9, *passim*; Rosenzweig 1977, pp.11–15, *passim*; and Foster forthcoming 1994, *passim*.
2. On the dating of these life drawings from 1863 to 1866, see Foster op. cit., chapter 1; Chamberlin-Hellman 1981, pp.59–63; and Goodrich 1982, vol.I, pp.10–13. For the proposed dating of 1866 to 1869, see Hendricks 1974, p.28. For the proposed dating of 1874 to 1876, see Siegl op. cit., pp.60–1; and Homer 1992, pp.155–6.
3. See Simpson 1987, pp.71–95.
4. Letter of December 1866 in Hirshhorn Museum and Sculpture Garden; see Rosenzweig op. cit., pp.38–41.
5. On the history of masking, see Chamberlin-Hellman op. cit., pp.61–2, no. 171.
6. Letter to Committee on Instruction, January 1877 [incorrectly dated January 1876], Pennsylvania Academy of the Fine Arts, archives.
7. See Siegl op. cit., pp.62, 171; and Foster op. cit., chapter 1.
8. Clark 1956, p.205.
9. See *Catalogue of the Forty-First Annual Exhibition of the Pennsylvania Academy of the Fine Arts*, 1864, p.25. I am grateful to my friend Cheryl Leibold, Archivist at the Pennsylvania Academy of the Fine Arts, for confirming this information.
10. Clark op. cit., p.201. I am grateful to my friends David Holt and Ephraim Rubenstein for discussing this aspect of life drawing with me.

Provenance (nos. 2 and 3): Given by the artist's widow, Susan Macdowell Eakins, and Mary Adeline Williams, 1929.

Exhibitions (no. 2): Philadelphia, Pennsylvania Museum of Art, 1930, no. 1; Philadelphia, Museum of Art, 1944, no. 2; Philadelphia, Museum of Art, 1953, no. 44; New York, Cooper Union Museum, 1954, no. 32; Philadelphia, Museum of Art, 1962, no. 3; New York, Whitney Museum of American Art, 1970, no. 2.

Exhibitions (no. 3): Philadelphia, Museum of Art, 1944, no. 1; Philadelphia, Museum of Art, 1950, no. 98; Philadelphia, Museum of Art, 1953, no. 42; Philadelphia, Museum of Art, 1962, no. 2; New York, Whitney Museum of American Art, 1970, no. 1; New York, Whitney Museum of American Art, 1976, no. 151; Philadelphia, Museum of Art, 1976 (1), no. 328; Philadelphia, Museum of Art, 1982 (1), no. 5.

Literature (no. 2): Burroughs 1923 (2), pp.302–23, ill. p.306; Hendricks 1974, p.338, ill. no. 227; Siegl 1978, p.61, ill. pl.16; Goodrich 1982, vol.I, pp.10–12, ill. pl.6.

Literature (no. 3): Burroughs 1923 (2), pp.302–23, p.307; McKinney 1942, ill. p.46; Canaday 1959, p.312; Porter 1959, ill. pl.1; Canaday 1964, pp.88–105, ill. p.95; Rennie 1968, ill. p.21; Novak 1969, pp.205–7, ill. pl.11–17; Gerdts 1974, pp.6–14, ill. p.119; Hendricks 1974, pp.29, 338, ill. fig.33; Williams 1975, pp.56–61, ill. f.p. 57; Sellin 1976, p.30, ill. pl.8; Siegl 1978, pp.60–1, ill. pl.15; Goodrich 1982, vol.I, pp.10–12, ill. pl.5; Homer 1992, p.155, ill. pl.150.

3
Study of a Seated Nude Woman
Wearing a Mask
Charcoal and black crayon on pink laid
paper, 61.6 × 47.3 ($24\frac{1}{4} \times 18\frac{5}{8}$)
Unsigned; inscribed l.r. by Mrs Eakins: *T.E.*

Philadelphia Museum of Art.
Gift of Mrs Thomas Eakins and
Miss Mary Adeline Williams (29.184.49)

4

Study of a Girl's Head
*c.*1868–1869
Oil on canvas, 44.6 × 36.4 (17$\frac{9}{16}$ × 14$\frac{5}{16}$)
Unsigned and undated

Philadelphia Museum of Art.
Gift of Mrs Thomas Eakins and
Miss Mary Adeline Williams (29.184.8)

After an ocean voyage fraught with sea-sickness and a navigation of the French bureaucracy that proved equally stressful, Thomas Eakins wrote to his father on 26 October 1866, giving a translation of the letter of introduction which he had secured from the man whom he hoped would be his mentor during his stay in France:

Paris the 15th Oct. 1866
Mr. the Director [Count Alfred-Emelien de Nieuwerkerke, Superintendent of the Ecole des Beaux-Arts],
I have the honor to introduce to you Mr. Thomas Eakins who presents himself to work in my studio. I pray you will receive him as one of my scholars. Accept the expression of my most particular sentiments.
J.L. Gerome[1]

Eakins must have taken considerable pride in translating the words of the French master for the benefit of Benjamin Eakins, himself a distinguished teacher of calligraphy and amateur painter in Philadelphia. Being accepted into the Ecole Nationale des Beaux-Arts under the tuition of Jean-Léon Gérôme – one of the most respected and influential artists of Second Empire France – was the first great success of Thomas Eakins's career, a credit to the ingenuity of the artist and the loyal support of his family. It was his father's promise of financial assistance that had enabled Eakins to go abroad at all, and which freed him to explore the opportunities available in Paris at a time of great artistic experimentation and debate. Because he was destined for a career in America, he was unburdened by the constraints of the rigid salon system, harsh critics and institutionalized traditions which sought to stifle the innovation of young French artists. Eakins was able to assimilate techniques from numerous sources into his nascent philosophy of uncompromising truth to nature, and thereby forged a style as both artist and academician that would be critical to the development of American modernism in the twentieth century.

Although Eakins entered Gérôme's studio in October 1866, it is known from his letters that he was not given permission to take up a brush until the March of the following year. Eakins's first months in Paris were spent in a similar way to his time at the Pennsylvania Academy of the Fine Arts, sketching in charcoal from plaster casts (which he disliked) and from the live model. Eakins continued this practice of drawing from life when he began painting, and the majority of oil studies that survive from his European trip are of the human figure. They are brief sketches never intended to be brought to a 'finish', in keeping with the tradition of student exercises in the Paris studios.[2] Nonetheless, they record Eakins's first essays in the manipulation of light and colour, and an examination of the artistic considerations they reveal sheds light on the diverse influences which might have inspired them.

Eakins's first attempts at painting under Gérôme's supervision were 'beastly' by his own account. In September 1867, when he had rented his own studio to allow him to practice away from supervision, he wrote to his father, 'I have been only 4 months at the brush and can't do it yet'. In spite of this difficulty he expressed hope that he would be able to paint a life study before the following summer 'as well as anybody in the class'.[3] Such reports suggest that neither no. 4 nor no. 5 was painted before 1868. Until that time, at the suggestion of Gérôme, Eakins was concentrating on the modelling of brightly coloured objects, including some of his instructor's 'Eastern stuffs'. Of these exercises, Eakins wrote in the same letter, 'I am learning something from them, faster than I could from the life studies'.

Eakins's education was characterized by the expected fits and starts of a beginner, but some of the distractions were less of an artistic than a peripatetic nature. In July and August 1867 he travelled to eastern France and Switzerland; in the July of the following year he travelled more extensively through Europe with his father and sister, Frances, who were visiting from Philadelphia. Yet it was in January 1868 that travel caused the most serious disruption of his studies, when Gérôme left Paris on a trip to Egypt that lasted until mid-April.

During this time the studio was left in the hands of Gustave Boulanger, an academic painter in the style of Cabanel and Bouguereau. Eakins seems never to have mentioned Boulanger in his letters home, yet in one dated 6 March 1868, in the midst of Boulanger's tenure, he expressed a philosophy that not only rejected Boulanger's brand of history painting, but seemed to hint at a turning-point in his own relationship to Gérôme. Ostensibly reacting to a debate his father was having with friends in Philadelphia regarding the role of an artist, Eakins's comments steered towards issues that had begun to trouble the French Academy with the appearance of Courbet and Manet, and which would intensify in the 1870s with the advent of the Impressionists. He wrote to his father using words that expressed the frustration of a new generation of artists:

...the professors as they are called read Greek poetry for inspiration & talk classic & give out classic subjects & make a fellow draw antique... I love sunlight & children & beautiful women &

5
Study of a Girl's Head
*c.*1868–1869
Oil on canvas, 51 × 40.9 (20⅛ × 16⅛)
Incised u.l. in paint by Charles Bregler:
study by/Thomas Eakins

Hirshhorn Museum and Sculpture Garden, Smithsonian Institution.
Gift of Joseph H. Hirshhorn, 1966
(HMSG 1966.1501)

men their heads & hands & most everything I see & some day I expect to paint them as I see them and even paint some that I remember or imagine [or] make up from old memories of love & light & warmth &c &c. but if I went to Greece to live there twenty years I could not paint a Greek subject for my head would be full of classics the nasty besmeared wooden hard gloomy tragic figures of the great French school of the last few centuries & Ingres & the Greek letters I learned at the High School....[4]

Given that Boulanger typified this very type of academic classicism, and Gérôme was on a tour of the kind described, it should have come as no surprise that Eakins began exploring other opportunities in Paris during the first months of 1868. At the end of his letter, Eakins reported that he had been accepted into the studio of the sculptor, Augustin-Alexandre Dumont, for the purposes of 'model[ing] in clay every once in a while'. Eakins was clearly tired of studying plaster casts, and his desire to work in three dimensions from life might be considered as a development of his early anatomical studies at Philadelphia's Jefferson Medical College, which he had undertaken as an antidote to the Pennsylvania Academy's penchant for plaster cast study. In Paris as in Philadelphia, working from casts of antique ideals could not substitute for a living model.

The convincing depiction of a three-dimensional figure was at the heart of Eakins's early essays, as can be seen from the Paris studies that survive. Sculpture proved beneficial to Eakins, as did the techniques used by Thomas Couture, whose book, *Methode et Entretiens d'Atelier* (published in America in 1879 as *Conversations on Art Methods*), Eakins had read by February 1868. Just two weeks after the opinionated letter about the classics, Eakins wrote to his father that he had purchased not only Couture's book, but a photograph of him as well. Given Couture's antagonism to the Academy, Eakins's attention to the artist's writings marked his most dramatic departure from the academic system in which he had immersed himself, even if he read Couture's book more out of curiosity than dissent. He wrote to his sister, Frances, in April 1869:

Gerome always makes me think of Couture they are so different ... I saw four little things by Couture here lately ... What a grand talent. He is the Phidias of painting & drawing ... His art & Gerome's can hardly be compared. They are giants & children each to the other, & they are at the very head of all art.[5]

In the second sentence of the preface to his book, Couture stated unequivocally, 'it has been impossible for me to learn by academic means'.[6] Such an admission from a successful painter and instructor must have been comforting to Eakins, who was encountering great difficulty in the studio, and was currently without a teacher whom he found sympathetic. Similarly, Eakins presumably thought that his reservations about academic instruction were vindicated by Couture's declaration that 'to teach from the antique is impossible'.[7] These highly suggestive remarks were accompanied by step-by-step instructions in such exercises as the capturing of light effects and the application of colour, both aspects of painting which had eluded Eakins; the studies he saved from his time in Paris show his early essays in light and colour.

Nos. 4 and 5, two of these studies, make an interesting comparison, for while they have almost identical subjects, their treatments are significantly different. The Philadelphia study (no. 4) shows a contour of charcoal filled in with thin washes of pigment, describing only lights and shadows with little detail in facial features. In contrast, no. 5, while still spare of detail, shows evidence of filling in the values between the extremes, seeking to express the full three-dimensionality of the figure from the back of the neck, to the roundness of the cheekbone and the complicated recesses of the nose. Reading both as studies of the formal qualities of light, they have much in common with Couture's method of isolating the 'dominants' of light and shade, which in turn guide the search for the values that lie between them. Couture emphasized the importance of speed when laying in these first tones as well as the expressive potential of the brushwork, two qualities in evidence particularly in the Hirshhorn study.

At some point after Gérôme's return to Paris and Eakins's summer travels with his family in 1868, the two artists seem to have come to the same conclusion: that Eakins's career on his return to America would necessarily follow a different path from the one Gérôme had chosen. Eakins was still a long way from attempting a finished picture, but he already knew that the pictures he saw at the Paris salons, 'Phrynes, Venuses, nymphs, hermaphrodites, houris & Greek proper names', as he disdainfully referred to them, would not please the naturalistic tastes of Philadelphians. He wrote to his father in May 1868, 'I can conceive of few circumstances wherein I would have to make a woman naked'. Still, the mutual respect between Eakins and Gérôme flourished, and while Eakins was sceptical about ever painting 'poetical subjects & compositions like Raphael', he cited Gérôme's dictum that, whatever one ultimately chose as subject matter, 'the trade part must be learned first'.[8]

Fig.4a
Léon Bonnat, *Portrait of a Man*
1868
Oil on canvas, 81.3 × 65.3 (32 × 25 11/16)
The Cleveland Museum of Art.
Bequest of Noah L. Butkin

Probably due to their diverging interests, in the summer of 1869 Gérôme encouraged Eakins to seek the guidance of Léon Bonnat, an artist running one of the private studios that operated outside the Ecole but adhered to its general principles. The two teachers were friends – Bonnat had accompanied Gérôme on the 1868 trip to the Middle East – but held different aesthetic viewpoints. Bonnat put greater emphasis on naturalistic depiction of the human figure, as exhibited in his religious history scenes and particularly in his portraiture (fig.4a). He encouraged his students to depict the figure as defined by light and shadow, exercising what was called value painting. In the late 1880s, long after Bonnat had won Eakins's admiration, a critic wrote of Bonnat's modelling as 'the science which Bonnat commands for his brush, making of it a sculptor's tool.'[9] Such fidelity to the human figure, coupled with subject matter drawn from modern life, was more along the lines of what Eakins was trying to achieve, and would enhance his appeal to potential patrons back home.

The few months Eakins stayed in Bonnat's studio were cut short by the instructor's departure from Paris in the early autumn of 1869. Gérôme too had left the city on another trip, and sensing that his student days were over, Eakins himself decided to make a trip to Spain. He had already recognized that he would not make his career painting like Jean-Léon Gérôme (fig.4b), and this view was confirmed by his revelatory exposure to Ribera and Velazquez, whose works he described as what he 'always knew was possible in painting' but had not yet seen. They confirmed for him the importance of the example of Bonnat, who had encouraged the study of Spanish art, and had influenced Eakins to the extent that he wrote in his notebook that he must decide never to paint in the manner of the master, meaning Gérôme. Of the Spanish painters, he wrote, '[T]his is clearly the manner of Bonnat and Fortuny [another French academic and friend of Gérôme], and it is always toward this that my own instincts carried me.'[10]

Eakins left Europe in June 1870, never to return. In attempting to identify the influences on him, one wants to ask where he stood in relation to the more famous controversies shaking the foundations of the art world in Paris at the end of the 1860s. Unfortunately, Eakins's letters are perhaps most remarkable for what they do not mention. He criticized the academic trend toward classicized history scenes and the plethora of 'Phrynes, Venuses, nymphs, hermaphrodites' at the annual salons, but did not discuss the assault being waged

against them by the followers of Corot, Millet, and Courbet; he expressed interest in Couture's theories, but did not acknowledge Couture's most famous student, Edouard Manet. Both Manet and Courbet mounted major private retrospectives concurrently with the 1867 Exposition, yet Eakins seems to have been more enrapt by the achievements of the Industrial Revolution on display, lauding the primacy of the American sewing machine over its European competition. His appreciation for Manet and Courbet would come later in his career, by which time the influence of these artists could not go unnoticed in either Europe or America.

It is possible that Eakins was so firmly directed towards an academic education that he saw the artistic battles in Paris as not his to engage. His apolitical stance throughout his stay in Paris – of which he reassured his father in one letter[11] – may have kept him out of the fray, even as he was forging his own means of mediating academic practice with modern sensibility. These studies from his student years are the first examples of his desire to bridge the two, exhibiting qualities that Eakins would develop more thoroughly and to which he would remain faithful throughout his career. This might indicate why he saved these studies all his life. Whether they were executed with Gérôme or Bonnat in mind, or Couture's book in hand, they succeeded in breathing life and psychological presence into the traditions of the French academy.

DJS

1. Letter to Benjamin Eakins, 26–27 October 1866, Pennsylvania Academy of the Fine Arts.
2. For a thorough examination of academic training in nineteenth-century France, see Boime 1971.
3. Quoted in Goodrich 1982, vol.I, p.23.
4. Letter to Benjamin Eakins, 6 March 1868, Pennsylvania Academy of the Fine Arts.
5. As transcribed in Goodrich op. cit., vol.I, pp.46–7.
6. Couture 1879.
7. Ibid., p.2.
8. Letter to Benjamin Eakins, 29 October 1868, Pennsylvania Academy of the Fine Arts.
9. Quoted in Weinberg 1991, p.159.
10. Goodrich op. cit., vol.I, p.62.
11. Letter to Benjamin Eakins, n.d. [c.30 December 1866 or January 1867], Pennsylvania Academy of the Fine Arts.

Provenance (no. 4): Collection of Mrs Eakins; given by her, 1929.

Provenance (no. 5): Collection of Mrs Eakins; given to Charles Bregler; sold to Joseph Katz, Baltimore; to M. Knoedler & Co., New York, 1961; purchased by Joseph H. Hirshhorn, 1966; given by him, 1966.

Exhibitions (no. 4): Philadelphia, Pennsylvania Museum of Art, 1930, no. 2; Philadelphia, Museum of Art, 1944, no. 9; Washington, DC, National Gallery of Art, 1961, no. 1; New York, Art Students' League, 1967, no cat. no.

Exhibitions (no. 5): Philadelphia, Museum of Art, 1944, no. 8a; New York, M. Knoedler & Co., 1944, no. 1; Pittsburgh, Carnegie Institute, 1945, no. 29.

Literature (nos. 4 and 5): Rosenzweig 1977, pp.42–3, ill.42; Siegl 1978, p.50, ill. p.50; Goodrich 1982, vol.I, pp.17–49, ill. p.24; Foster and Leibold 1989, pp.40–60; Homer 1992, pp.23–49, ill. pp.34, 39.

Fig.4b
Jean-Léon Gérôme, *Portrait of a Lady*
1851
Oil on canvas, 92.6 × 73.7 (36½ × 29)
The Art Institute of Chicago. Silvain and Arma Wyler Foundation, Restricted Gift

6

Margaret

*c.*1871

Oil on canvas, 46.5 × 38 (18⅜ × 15)

Unsigned

Hirshhorn Museum and Sculpture Garden,
Smithsonian Institution. Gift of Joseph H.
Hirshhorn, 1966 (HMSG 1966.1504)

Born in 1853, Margaret Eakins (1853–1882), affectionately called Maggie by family and friends, was nine years the artist's junior. Margaret admired her brother, and patiently modelled for several of his early home-life scenes. He painted her in five oils and at least two watercolours, and at the artist's insistence, she took spinning lessons to add historical authenticity to the watercolour paintings.[1] Many casual family snapshots exist, and represent telling traces of Margaret Eakins's life.

This small study of Eakins's favourite sister at around the age of eighteen dates from shortly after his return from Europe. It is a testament to the challenge of working with colour placed before him. A consummate draughtsman, he was frank about his struggle to reconcile what he saw with what he could reproduce with paint on a two-dimensional surface. More than one letter from his years of study abroad attest to the artist's serious attitude towards making studies.[2] The loose brush strokes in this painting with their sculptural qualities leave the impression of a quick yet deliberate rendering of the familiar face before him. Eakins had assured his father and convinced himself that he could 'paint heads good enough to make a living anywhere in America',[3] and it is the face of Margaret which received his attention here, her dress and the background given only as abbreviations. The left shoulder appears to be strangely foreshortened, but on close examination, reality has been strictly rendered. The painting is an accurate representation of the sitter sinking into a pillow resting behind her. Eakins portrayed her pose accurately using casually placed broad strokes in areas around the face. The artist has carefully directed and reworked the paint with a small detail brush, adding pattern to the fabric of the pillow and texture to the frill around its edge. This unsigned practice-piece, as well as all the small canvases of home scenes, which are generally unsigned, remained in the Mount Vernon Street house until after the artist's death. They offer an intimate glimpse into the gas-lit, multi-textured atmosphere of a late nineteenth-century, middle-class drawing-room.

The majority of the images of Margaret Eakins, both painted and photographed, portray her as brooding and introspective. Her austere expression in this painting was perhaps not so much a reflection of her personality as an indication of the pain endured in the Eakins house during the tragedy of her mother's mental illness. The Eakins children cared for Caroline Cowperthwaite Eakins in the home for several months. Mrs Eakins died in June 1872. She succumbed to 'exhaustion from mania' leaving her three daughters to care for their widowed father, Benjamin, and the bachelor, Thomas.[4] Frances, the eldest, married William Crowell later that summer. Subsequently, the young Crowell family left Philadelphia in 1877 to make their home in Avondale, Pennsylvania.

The twenty-four-year-old Margaret remained as matriarch in the Eakins household. She was already acting as something of a manager for her brother, by keeping a ledger of Eakins's exhibitions and of his professional expenses. Margaret does not appear to have played the role of the typical eligible Victorian young lady during a period in her life when marriage would have been generally considered paramount. Society judged whether a young woman was attractive and fit to be a wife by her passivity and feminine deportment. The overall air of informality of the Eakins household, as suggested in several straightforward family photographs, did not appear to foster such traits in Margaret. Living among intellectuals who prized the integrity of the mind over appearances, she had a seriousness and wore understated attire that made her comfortable in her intimate family circle but left her outside the more conventional society, with its opportunities for marriage.

Margaret Eakins's interest in outdoor sports contributed to her bronzed complexion and strong, fine figure. She was accomplished at ice skating, rowing, sailing, and swimming. It is not surprising that one admirer remembered her as carrying herself 'like an animal'.[5] Eakins painted a splendid portrait of Margaret in her corduroy skating jacket in the same year as this study (fig.6a). The extraordinary representation of texture shown in the handling of her garment almost overpowers the full face of his sibling. This painting reveals, more than any other, the striking resemblance which Margaret bore to the artist.

Candid, outdoor photographs are perhaps more telling than any of the paintings which include Margaret, however. She appears at ease in nature, self-assured and able. A smile, captured in a photograph taken while on vacation (fig.6b), remains the single image of Margaret as the fun-loving aunt and generally 'grand person' her sister's children remembered so fondly.[6]

In December 1882, Margaret uncharacteristically declined her father's invitation to travel to Canada.[7] This was a sign of oncoming illness. Within days of her father's departure, she became feverish. The family learned that she had contracted typhoid, a disease which scientists had recently discovered was transmitted through the contaminated drinking water of Philadelphia. Margaret Eakins, despite her healthy attitude towards life, never recovered. She died a few days before Christmas at the age of twenty-nine.
MRV

1. Hoopes 1971, p.62.
2. Eakins wrote in 1869 that 'an attractive study is made from experience and calculations ... the study maker must keep many of his landmarks entirely in his head ... so that a wonderful study is an accomplishment'. (Quoted in Hendricks 1974, p.55).
3. Goodrich 1982, vol.I, p.50.
4. Ibid., vol.I, p.79.
5. Ibid., vol.I, p.220.
6. McHenry 1946, p.95.
7. Goodrich op.cit., vol.I, p.220.

Provenance: Susan Macdowell Eakins, Philadelphia; Mrs Francis W. Schaefer, New Milford, Connecticut; Joseph Katz, Baltimore; M. Knoedler & Co., New York, 1961; Joseph H. Hirshhorn, New York, 1966; given by him, 1966.

Exhibitions: Philadelphia, Pennsylvania Academy of the Fine Arts, 1917, no. 32; New York, Whitney Museum of American Art, 1970, no.7; Washington, DC, Hirshhorn Museum and Sculpture Garden, 1975, no.15.

Literature: Marceau 1930, no. 10; Goodrich 1933, pp.38–9, no. 40; McHenry 1946, p.21; Schendler 1967, pp.23, ill. p.29; Hoopes 1971; Hendricks 1974, ill. p.319; Rosenzweig 1977, pp.46–7; Goodrich 1982, vol.I, p.67; Homer 1992, pp.53–5.

Fig.6a
Margaret in Skating Costume
1871
Oil on canvas, 61 × 52 (24 × 20½)
Philadelphia Museum of Art. Gift of Mrs Thomas Eakins and Miss Mary Adeline Williams

Fig.6b
Margaret Eakins, at the Beach with Thomas Eakins's Setter Dog, Harry
c.1880
Albumen print, 10.5 × 8 (4⅛ × 3⅛)
The Pennsylvania Academy of the Fine Arts, Philadelphia. Purchased with funds donated by the Pennsylvania Academy Women's Committee

7

Home Scene

*c.*late 1870–1871
Oil on canvas, 55 × 45.8 ($21\frac{11}{16} \times 18\frac{1}{16}$)
Signed l.r.: *Eakins*

The Brooklyn Museum, Gift of George
A. Hearn, Frederick Loeser Art Fund,
Dick S. Ramsay Fund, Gift of Charles
A. Schieren (50.115)

Intimate interiors provided the settings for almost all of Eakins's depictions of women during the 1870s. These women were most often shown reading, playing a musical instrument, or absorbed with animals or children. In Eakins's early art men tended to be physically engaged out of doors, while women were mentally active inside. *Home Scene* portrays Eakins's six-year-old sister Caroline (1865–1889) and his eighteen-year-old sister Margaret (1853–1882; see no. 6) in a genre scene typical of the artist's work during this period.

Caroline lies on richly patterned carpeting; with her left hand she props up her head and with the other draws on a small slate. Margaret sits directly behind the child, on a piano stool. With her head also propped, Margaret turns away from her musical score and piano apparently to play with a kitten on her shoulder. Just behind the child's head Eakins has placed a cat and on the piano's music stand we see a small orange. The two sisters are compositionally linked by the large triangle that they form, with Caroline at the base and Margaret's head at the apex. A strong light streams in from the left of the picture highlighting portions of each sister's hands and face as they cast shadows against the tiny slate, piano and sheet music.[1]

The canvas illustrates the potential for many different kinds of 'play'. Caroline, whether writing or drawing, actively plays with her slate, Margaret plays with the kitten, and the piano alludes to the potential of musical play. Each figure, positioned with a hand on her head, hints at the necessary connections between mind and physical activity. On the blank slate before her, Caroline is free to create images and words which please her; with no script to dictate her activity, she works on a *tabula rasa*.[2] Margaret, who sits before a piece of commercially printed sheet music, has the option of interpreting the music, but the black notes on the page denote the creativity of another. While Caroline imagines her drawings, Margaret appears to have been following her music. Placed in opposite corners of the composition, the black slate with its white markings will provide a telling contrast with the white sheet and its black notes; these emblems of creation are formal and symbolic 'reversals' of each other, marking the divide between imagination and replication.

The Eakins children may present an opposition between imaginative and replicative pursuits, but they must also be seen as being on the same continuum of female development. Eakins's representation of his sisters begins to tell the story of play as a pedagogical tool for socializing American women in the nineteenth century. An 1868 compilation of graduation addresses given at a prominent woman's school provides insights into the schooling of middle-class women in America during the last century. In one such address the school's principal reminded the graduating class:

How long a course of training has been required to prepare you for this day! From your first rude attempts to form letters with a pen, from your first imperfect efforts to express thoughts in writing... And how long and laborious has been your application to the science of music, to prepare you to perform with skill and execution the most difficult pieces of the greatest masters of the science of harmony.[3]

Moving from basic writing skills to the mastery of complicated piano pieces, her students went from unformed girls to educated women. The orator makes clear the purpose of all of these hours of labour when she admonishes students not to 'expect in this place to hear much upon the *rights of women*, while her *duties* will claim most of our attention'.[4]

Caroline may begin by drawing and writing her name on the slate, but in time she will be expected to progress to the piano that her sister now sits at. Caroline creates, but she is poised on the brink of committing herself to replicate the works of other 'masters'. The canvas, however, offers us more than a mere reflection of Victorian norms. Whether playing with the kitten or gazing wistfully at her sister, Margaret turns away from her sheet music, neglecting the replicative potential of her piano, while Caroline ignores both her sister and the cat in order to pursue the imaginative possibilities of her chalk board.

Because Eakins, as a realist, is thought to be a replicator of reality, we might expect him to associate more closely with the activity of his older sister. But in addition to downplaying Margaret's art, Eakins also provides subtle links between himself and his younger sister. Not only does Caroline draw, but her framed rectangular slate, oriented vertically, echoes the shape and orientation of Eakins's framed canvas. In the lower right corner of the painting, directly across from Caroline's chalk board, Eakins has scratched his name in white letters, almost as if his sister had reached across and scribbled it with her small chalk. For Eakins, realism seemed compatible with Caroline's imaginative work; for as he himself stated, a great painter paints objects 'he once saw or which he imagines from old memories or parts of memories'.[5]

By creating visual links between himself and Caroline, Eakins's work blurs the traditional continuum of female development. If Caroline's development towards copying offers the 'normal' route, her continued interest in creating might here be proffered as another possibility. The artist's identification with Caroline seems fitting, given the fact that his life was dedicated to the kinds of imaginings which Caroline presently enjoys, even as she seems culturally destined to forsake them.
MAB

1. Caroline's placement and activity link her closely with Ella Crowell as depicted in *Baby at Play* (no. 14).
2. Just as the slate is framed, so must Caroline's discourse be circumscribed by the language and customs of society. She remains, however, free to create within the societal bounds which constrain us all.
3. Phelps 1868, pp.332–3.
4. Ibid., pp.31–2.
5. Letter from Thomas Eakins to Benjamin Eakins, 6 March 1868, Pennsylvania Academy of the Fine Arts, Charles Bregler's Thomas Eakins Collection.

Provenance: Mrs Thomas Eakins, M. Knoedler & Co.; purchased, 1950.

Exhibitions: Philadelphia, Museum of Art, 1944, no. 11a; New York, M. Knoedler & Co., 1944, no. 4; Wilmington, The Wilmington Society of Fine Arts, 1944, no. 4; Pittsburgh, Carnegie Institute, 1945, no. 22; Colorado Springs, Fine Arts Center, 1947, no. 5; Fort Worth, Art Association, 1949, no. 22; New York, American Academy of Arts and Letters, 1958, no. 21; New York, The Arts Students' League, no. 5; Baltimore, Museum of Art, 1968, no. 63; New York, The Whitney Museum of American Art, 1970, no. 6; Houston, Meredith Long & Co., 1980, no. 24; Philadelphia, Museum of Art, 1982(1), no. 10; Southampton, The Parish Art Museum, 1990 and Buffalo, Albright-Knox Art Gallery, 1992, no cat. no.

Literature: Hendricks 1974, pp.66, 67, 333, ill. pl.7; Goodrich 1982, vol.I, pp.67, 75, 220, ill. pl.16; Johns 1983 (1), pp.116, 117, ill. fig.77; The Brooklyn Museum 1987, checklist no. 4; Fried 1987, pp.22, 42, 45, 53, ill. fig.15; Dayer Gallati 1990; Homer 1992, pp.53–5, ill. pl.44.

8

Kathrin

1872

Oil on canvas, 159.4 × 122.6 (62¾ × 48¼)

Signed l.r.: *Thomas Eakins/1872*

Yale University Art Gallery. Bequest of
Stephen Carlton Clark, BA 1903 (1961.18.7)

Eakins became engaged to Kathrin Crowell
(1851–1879), the sister of his best friend William J. ('Billy') Crowell, two years after this
portrait was painted.[1] At the time of the portrait Eakins was twenty-eight and Kathrin was
twenty-one. The painted image of Kathrin,
Eakins's first large full-length, is consistent
with a later recollection of her by a friend,
Sallie Shaw, as

small, with medium brown hair, not a tomboy . . .
enjoying fun though not creating much fun, and
rather exclusive, 'not associating with many'. She
was not artistic; she played the piano, but 'nothing
special'; 'just a good decent girl'.

Sallie Shaw believed that Eakins's father
'engineered the engagement to Kathrin.
Rumor had it that it was her younger sister,
Elizabeth, vivacious as well as pretty, whom he
loved'.[2] A small group of 'gentle but condes-
cending' letters from Eakins to Kathrin,
known as Kate or Katie, written between 1873
and 1877, have recently surfaced in the Bregler
collection. They 'have little intellectual or
artistic content and dwell mostly on weather,
health, and travel plans'; they suggest that
'seven years younger than Eakins, less educated and less well traveled, [Kathrin] was
easily dominated by him'. Eakins and Kathrin
were still engaged when she died of meningitis
in April 1879.[3]

The portrait depicts Kathrin seated in a
turned armchair upholstered in red plush that
has an elaborately carved crest, a chair which
appears repeatedly in Eakins's portraits.[4] A
large cupboard and bookcase looms behind the
chair. Kathrin wears a filmy white dress, a red
bow of ribbon pinned with a silver brooch at
her neck, a fine silver chain necklace, and a red
fillet in her pulled-back hair; one buckled
black shoe with white stockings is visible. She
holds an unfolded red and brown fan in her
right hand. The bookcase doors, one of which is
open above her head, have metallic diamond-
shaped grilles and dust curtains. Kathrin's left
foot rests on an upholstered footstool with her
right leg bent so that the foot is tucked beneath
her left knee, forming a pocket in which an
indistinctly drawn kitten lies on its back, a paw

raised in response to her teasing fingers. Floral
carpeting covers the floor.

The room is illuminated from the upper
left. Rectangular reflections on the ball ter-
minals of the chair arms suggest that daylight
enters through an outside window. The left
side of Kathrin's face is lit, casting her features
into shadow. The highlit frame of the open
bookcase door initiates a strong vertical axis
descending through the bright side of her face,
the bow, the necklace and the side of her left
leg and foot, to the shoe and protruding corner
of the footstool at the bottom. Immediately
adjacent to it, a dark vertical band is created by
the dimly perceived books, the shadowed side
of Kathrin's face, the kitten, and the unlit side
of her leg. The crest rail of the chair and the
ledge dividing the cupboard and bookcase
establish firm intersecting horizontal lines at
eye level, hers and ours.

The gauze-like texture of the dress and the
open fan suggest that it is warm, perhaps
summertime. The ponderous furniture and
abundance of heavy fabrics — carpet, upholstered footstool, plush upholstery and cur-
tained cupboard doors enclosing leather-bound
books — provide an oppressive environment
that seems dusty and musty. The predominant
warm shades of brown and red evoke the
atmosphere of what Louis Mumford called
'the Brown Decades'. Kathrin manifests no
interest in the shadowed realm of books — an
allusion to the life of the mind — behind her
head; her attention is completely directed
towards the playful kitten. A small person, she
seems dominated by as well as contained
within the rectangular forms of the stool, chair,
bookcase and the room itself, powerful material presences suggestive of domestic (paren-
tal) authority. Yet Kathrin is not completely
docile. Although her legs and arms echo the
diagonal placement of the enframing chair,
bookcase and footstool, her upper body twists
forward in a gentle counter movement. There
is some identification between Kathrin and the
kitten, encased in her body as she is embedded
in the furnished interior, soft and alive, com-
pliant yet able to scratch. The spatial construction resembles nested boxes — the kitten in the
lap of Kathrin who is seated in a chair dominated by the bookcase within a claustrophobic
room — *and* a spiral slowly turning coun-
terclockwise as it descends from the bookcase
to the chair to Kathrin to the footstool with her
foot turned towards the viewer as if she were
about to step down and out.[5]

The artist's position, and therefore that of
the viewer, is as if seated to the right and at
Kathrin's eye level. 'Thomas Eakins/1872' is

inscribed in cursive script in perspective on the
floor in the lower right, subordinate to and
facing towards the figure of Kathrin. The portrait is not flattering; Kathrin's large nose and
mouth, and bony fingers, are not attractive.
The surprising lack of any sense of physical
appeal in Eakins's portrayal of his future fian-
ceé contrasts with the almost explicitly sexual
iconography of the furry kitten, often, as in
Manet's *Olympia* of 1863, a sign of female sexuality, here specifically placed in the area of
the genitalia.[6] Eakins's attitude towards his
future fiancée as manifested subliminally in
this depiction is perplexing. The enigma of the
human relationship is echoed in the obscure
unfinished patch to the right of the footstool.
JDP

1. The Yale University Art Gallery possesses a
study drawing for the painting, pencil on paper,
35.5 × 26 centimetres (13¹⁵⁄₁₆ × 10¼ inches). In
August 1872, the year of Kathrin's portrait,
Eakins's sister Frances married Billy Crowell,
and the newlyweds lived in the Eakins's Mount
Vernon Street home.
2. Goodrich 1982, vol.I, p.79. Elizabeth seems
more attractive than Kathrin in Eakins's portraits
of her, *Elizabeth Crowell and Her Dog* (San Diego
Museum of Art, early 1870s) and *Elizabeth at the
Piano* (Addison Gallery of American Art, Phillips
Academy, 1875; no. 15). Eakins kept the latter
portrait throughout his life.
3. Foster and Leibold 1989, pp.64–6, 131, 154,
400.
4. And which also turned up in the Bregler
collection (ibid., p.64).
5. As in Eakins's much later *William Rush and
His Model* (fig.17c).
6. Echoing the vulgar term 'pussy'. Eakins
undoubtedly became aware of *Olympia* when
he was in Paris between 1866 and 1870.

Provenance: Mrs Thomas Eakins; Stephen Carlton
Clark (by late 1920s).

Exhibitions: New York, Metropolitan Museum of
Art, 1917, no. 2; Philadelphia, Pennsylvania
Academy of the Fine Arts, 1917, no. 77; New York,
National Academy of Design, 1939, no cat. no.;
Philadelphia, Museum of Art, 1944, no. 14; New
Haven, Yale University Art Gallery, 1960, no. 38;
New York, Center for Inter-American Relations,
1967; New York, Whitney Museum of American
Art, 1970, no. 8.

Literature: Goodrich 1933, pp.45, 163; McKinney
1942, p.83 (ill.); McHenry 1946, pp.21, 29; Porter
1959, ill. pl.9; Schendler 1967, pp.23, 27, 30 (ill.),
33, 87, 124; Hendricks 1974, p.67, ill. pl.9;
Goodrich 1982, vol.I, pp.79–80, and vol.II, p.280;
Foster and Leibold 1989, pp.24–6, 131, 154, 400;
Homer 1992, pp.51–2, 99, 124, 263.

9
Perspective drawing for
The Pair-Oared Shell (II)
1872
Graphite, ink and watercolour on paper,
80.8×120.8 $(31\frac{13}{16} \times 47\frac{9}{16})$
Inscribed l.r. in black ink by Mrs Eakins:
Thomas Eakins/Perspective of picture painted
before 1876

Philadelphia Museum of Art. Purchased:
Thomas Skelton Harrison Fund (44.45.1)

Eakins enjoyed many sports: swimming, sailing, skating, wrestling, boxing, hunting, riding – the full repertory of wholesome outdoor pastimes recommended in his day by the ever-popular handbook, *Walker's Manly Exercises*. Beginning with his second edition; published in 1834, Walker commenced his list of suitable activities with rowing, a sport established early in the century by collegiate competition in England, and soon taken up in the USA. By the 1850s the boats were lighter and faster, and American rowing clubs had formed to promote competition and offer access to shared equipment. Both the new boats and the new clubs opened the sport to middle-class amateurs like Eakins, who seems to have taken up rowing in the early 1860s, at the time when local interest in sculling increased. His friend and high-school classmate, Max Schmitt, was a great oarsman whose victory on the Schuylkill on 5 October 1870 was commemorated in the first major exhibition painting Eakins completed upon his return from Paris: *The Champion Single Sculls*, also known as *Max Schmitt in a Single Scull* (fig.2). This painting, which includes a self-portrait sculling in the distance, expressed Eakins's own expertise, his pride in his friend's triumph, and his characteristic commitment to novel, contemporary subjects.[1]

The portrait of Schmitt was the first in a series of six finished oils and five watercolours of rowers made between 1870 and 1874, exploring all the possibilities of the subject: single scullers, pair-oared shells and four-man barges, seen at rest or while racing, at sunset or at midday, enclosed by the arch of a bridge or set against open water. Such persistence may have been fuelled by his own love for the sport, but Eakins also relished a subject featuring semi-nude figures. His academic training had focused on figure painting, but he found opportunities for nude subjects rare in American life; the muscular rowers let him demonstrate his skills as a figure painter while proving the vitality of antique themes of athletic prowess and beauty.[2]

The brothers John and Barney Biglin fit this heroic mould well. Professional oarsmen, they were champions like Max Schmitt, models of mental and physical discipline for the modern age. 'They are both in their prime, and have made the art of rowing a study most of their lives', reported the *Philadelphia Press* when the Biglins came to town for the historic occasion of the first pair-oared race in the USA, held on the Schuylkill river on 20 May 1872.[3] Their victory that day inspired Eakins to compose four paintings, including *The Biglin Brothers Racing* (National Gallery of Art, Washington, DC), and the greatest of his rowing pictures, *The Biglin Brothers Turning the Stake Boat* (Cleveland Museum of Art). His first painting in this series, *The Pair-Oared Shell* (fig. 9a), does not depict the race, however, but shows instead an early evening practice run. Here, no cheering crowds line the bank, and a spirit of calm teamwork reigns as the brothers pull under the shadow of the old Columbia Bridge.[4] The mood is contemplative, while the boldness of the composition, with its figures suspended between broad horizontal and vertical bands, offers perpetual visual tension.

Two full-scale preparatory drawings for *The Pair-Oared Shell* survive to tell us of another source of appeal within this subject that kept Eakins engaged for five years: perspective. Overall, ten such drawings for the rowing paintings remain to demonstrate the intensity of his fascination. He would rely on such planning drawings throughout his career, but the sustained energy seen in the series of rowing perspectives was never repeated. Such density of effort signals many layers of meaning. First, these drawings are an expression of his academic training and his methodical habits of mind. His assiduous display of hard work and professionalism seems appropriate to a young man anxious to justify his long and expensive education and make a good first impression. It also shows respect for the methods of his teacher, Gérôme, and asserts a mature mastery of its own. But Gérôme probably would have hired a draughtsman to prepare his perspective schemes, while Eakins, even if he could have afforded this practice (or have found a draughtsman more skilled than himself), surely would have chosen to undertake this work personally. His delight in perspective, first seen in his high school work (see no. 1), is the second message of these drawings. Eakins enjoyed linking mathematics, geometry, and the arts. The orderliness and precision of mathematical systems appealed to him, and in his search for a scientific way to control and express the chaotic three-dimensional visual world on a two-dimensional surface, the exactness of linear perspective held more than just a mechanical utility, it promised 'truth'. He preached the gospel of linear perspective to his students annually, and his own drawing manual, based on these lectures, was largely dedicated to its beauties.[5]

Fig.9a
The Pair-Oared Shell
1872
Oil on canvas, 61 × 91.4 (24 × 36)
Philadelphia Museum of Art. Gift of Mrs Thomas Eakins and Miss Mary Adeline Williams

Eakins's affection for perspective reveals itself in a comparison between no. 9 and another one of the same size that preceded it (Philadelphia Museum of Art). This first drawing, mostly in graphite, plots the location of the empty Biglin shell in space and on the surface of the composition; probably it was derived from a gridded plan of the river and the bridge pier, and a very detailed plan of the shell itself. This drawing tells us the exact dimensions of the boat, the specific location on the river, the configuration of the bridge, the distance of all objects from the viewer, and the position of the sun, which allowed one scholar to deduce that the time depicted is 7.20 p.m., probably in early June 1872.[6]

The second drawing, no. 9, recapitulates the basic facts of the first in order to plan the reflections. This job could have been overlaid on the first drawing, but Eakins would not allow the muddying of his work. On the fresh page, the figures are set within the boat in pale, broad, but exacting washes. The confident and abstracted style of the figures suggests that they were copied from pre-existing studies, probably in oil, such as no. 10; they show no more detail than necessary to establish the principal masses for the reflections, which are constructed on the checkerboard grid of the water's surface according to Eakins's own system. This method, explained in the draft of his projected drawing manual, reduced the curved and impossibly varying wave surfaces to three simple facets — two sloping sides and a flat 'trough' in between. These model waves reflected different images or revealed the colour of the river, according to their orientation. The reflections were then calculated geometrically, based on the viewer's position above the water and the size and placement of each form to be mirrored. Transferred to the final painting, the mechanical exactness of the drafted reflections was blurred by brushwork that gave painterly interest as well as an illusion of movement to the water. The effect, also seen in *John Biglin in a Single Scull* (no. 10), was lively, but far more precise and scientific than *plein air* observation could be expected to produce.[7]

The need for separate drawings for each phase of his preparations and the economical directedness of these drawings, which waste no effort on redundant information or unnecessary prettiness, reveal much about Eakins's compartmentalized and businesslike procedures. His drawings have a hallucinatory beauty that comes from extreme fineness of detail set within a conceptual, non-representational world of line and text, but Eakins aimed to please no one but himself, and

he wasted no effort in making them 'artistic' or in caring for them after they had served their purpose. Their mission was larger and more enduring than the drawing itself, for they served the 'passion for perspective' that Margaret McHenry noted as the motivation for the entire rowing series. Like variations on a theme, each of the rowing pictures solves the basic perspective problem differently: depicting an odd, complex object, 35 feet long and 15 inches wide, so that the character of the boat and the action of the men is clearly described. Changes in personnel, boats, lighting and action are obvious from painting to painting, but the subtler variations in the perspective schema only become clear in the drawings. These show that no two paintings in the series (aside from watercolour replicas) had the same eye level, or the same figure scale, the same angle of recession for the shell, or the same ratio of viewing distance (from the spectator to the painting) to object distance (from the spectator to the figures). These choices have a profound impact on the legibility of the scene, the character of foreshortening, the sense of distance or proximity, and the design of the surface, and all of these decisions had to be made before brush was set to canvas. In these drawings, we discover the bedrock of Eakins's creativity in the imaginative planning that preceded observation or painting.[8]

Academic, conceptual and anti-impressionist as these drawings show Eakins to have been, the last message of these perspectives is one of a locatedness closely allied to the intentions of the most radical realists of his period. The specificity of viewer position, topography, and time of day implied in these drawings gives priority to the contemporary, the transitory, and the subjective experience of the artist. While the manifest labour of planning and execution deny the possibility of a truly spontaneous impression of the events depicted, Eakins's drawings reveal him as a modern as well as an academic.[9]

KAF

1. Donald Walker's book, first published in London under the title *British Manly Exercises*, appeared under Philadelphia imprints by 1837; the 11th edition appeared in 1865. Elizabeth Johns has outlined the history and the meaning of rowing in America as a context for Eakins's work, 1983 (1), pp.19–45. In emphasizing the themes of modernity and expertise in Eakins's work, Johns also notes that no other artist of this period outside the realm of popular printmaking gave attention to rowing. Eakins's rowing paintings have also been well surveyed by Sewell 1982, pp.15–23; see also Schendler 1967, pp.33–41; and Goodrich 1982, vol.I, pp.81–7, 96–100. On *Max Schmitt*, see Spassky 1985, vol.III, pp.588–94.

2. The example of his master, Gérôme, may also have encouraged his interest in rowing themes; see Ackerman 1969, p.240.
3. Goodrich op. cit., vol.I, p.83. Johns documents this race, op. cit., pp.42–3. Eakins habitually spelled the name 'Biglen'.
4. Eakins's record book 2 (at the Pennsylvania Academy of the Fine Arts), records this image as *The Biglens under the Bridge*, and *The Biglens Practicing*, p.14.
5. The manuscript of Eakins's unpublished text is at the Philadelphia Museum of Art; see Siegl 1978, p.109. Drafts for this text and the ink illustrations for the projected publication are in Charles Bregler's Thomas Eakins Collection at the Pennsylvania Academy of the Fine Arts; see Foster forthcoming 1994, nos. 92–144.
6. See Siegl's excellent analysis of these two drawings 1976 and 1978, cited in the literature below. From these drawings, he reconstructed the plan that Eakins must have used. Drawings recently discovered in Charles Bregler's collection include a plan of a four-oared shell, probably similar to a boat plan Eakins must have used to complete *The Pair-Oared Shell*; see Foster op. cit., no. 149.
7. See Siegl 1976, pp.391–3.
8. McHenry was the first to focus on Eakins's enthusiasm for perspective, 1946, p.23. The larger meaning of drawing to Eakins is analysed by Michael Fried 1987; Eakins's use of drawing and his manipulation of perspective techniques, particularly in the rowing paintings, is discussed at greater length in Foster op. cit., chapter 2, 'Drawing', and chapter 3, 'The Rowing Pictures'.
9. Goodrich compared Eakins's work to that of the Impressionists, op. cit., vol.I, p.97; earlier, Schendler remarked that 'time and light' were the principal themes of *The Pair-Oared Shell*, op. cit., p.35.

Provenance: Mrs Thomas Eakins; given to Charles Bregler in 1930; purchased from him, 1944.

Exhibitions: Philadelphia, Museum of Art, 1944, no. 16; Philadelphia, Museum of Art, 1976, no. 336b; Philadelphia, Museum of Art, 1982 (1), no. 16.

Literature: Goodrich 1933, no. 51, p.164; Canaday 1964, pp.88–105, ill. p.93; Schendler 1967, p.35; Dibner 1967; Hendricks 1974, p.71, ill. checklist no. 238, p.339; Siegl 1976, pp.391–3, ill. p.392; Siegl 1978, no. 10, p.56, ill. p.55; Johns 1979, ill. p.131; Goodrich 1982, vol.I, p.99, ill. pl. 38; Sewell 1982, pp.17–21, ill. p.20; Johns 1983 (1), p.21, ill. fig.18; Homer 1992, p.137, ill. pl.126.

10

John Biglin in a Single Scull
1873–4
Oil on canvas, 61.9 × 40.6 cm (24$\frac{5}{16}$ × 16)
Signed and dated on verso in black:
Eakins 1874

Yale University Art Gallery, Whitney
Collections of Sporting Art. Given in memory
of Henry Payne Whitney, BA 1894, and
Payne Whitney, BA 1898, by Francis P.
Garvan, BA 1897, MA (Hon.) 1922 (1932.263)

John Biglin was the most frequent model in Eakins's series of sculling pictures, appearing five times rowing stroke with his brother Barney at the bow oar (as in *The Pair-Oared Shell*; fig.9a), and five times in a single scull. Perhaps he was a friend and an exceptionally patient model; certainly, being exactly Eakins's age and a professional rowing champion, he represented the artist's alter ego as an athlete.[1] The oil study, no.10, was made in preparation for a watercolour (fig.10a) that Eakins showed in New York at the American Watercolour Society's annual exhibition early in 1874, before sending it off to Paris as a gift to his master, J.-L. Gérôme. No other oil composition using Biglin in this pose survives, suggesting that this canvas – first referred to as a 'sketch' in Eakins's record book, and then amended to read 'study' – was always intended as a preparatory piece for a watercolour.[2] This unusual procedure demonstrates Eakins's pre-meditated approach, which sought maximum control of his subject prior to beginning a final image, and it also may reflect his newness to the watercolour medium, which he had not used since his student days. Probably inspired by an unusually exuberant display at the

Watercolor Society in the spring of 1873, Eakins no doubt took extra care with his first submissions to their next show the following January. Already a methodical worker, his cautious preparations allowed him greater confidence when he turned to the less tractable watercolour medium.[3]

In this new venture, Eakins also must have gained assurance from working on a subject that he had already undertaken several times. All of his watercolours exhibited that year were based on rowing or sailing compositions first done in oil. The Biglin subject had been commenced the previous spring in a related watercolour (likewise sent to Gérôme, and now lost), that showed the oarsman in mid-stroke. Gérôme's critique of this pose, which he found too static, led to this revised image, with Biglin at the top of his stroke.[4] In tandem with the oil study, Eakins also prepared a perspective drawing at the same scale, mapping the position of the shell and reflections on and from the water (Museum of Fine Arts, Boston), in the fashion of the drawings for *The Pair-Oared Shell* (see no.9). Specialized, like these drawings, the oil deals with different concerns: the perspective drawing analyses contour, detail

and the geometrical schematization of space, while the oil tackles colour, light, three-dimensional form and the tactile presence of the surface. The drawing is airy, conceptual, abstract, non-visual; the oil, surely studied outdoors and from life, is weighty and sensual, 'like a colored relief'.[5]

In reducing the large, dense oil and its companion perspective by half to produce the watercolour, Eakins created an effect of great precision and delicacy, turning his cautious method to advantage at a time when fine finish was popular among watercolour artists and patrons. He also transformed his image by opening out the space around Biglin, who is seen against the New Jersey shoreline of the Delaware River, and by exploiting the luminosity of watercolour, with its transparent pigments and reflective white paper. Glittering with light and exquisitely detailed, his pictures of scullers and their 'beautifully ugly muscles' won praise from New York critics, and Eakins went on to establish a reputation as a watercolourist that, by 1878, exceeded his celebrity in New York as an oil painter.[6]

The success of this debut may have inspired him to send the second Biglin watercolour to Gérôme as evidence of his progress, and to prepare a replica for himself (Metropolitan Museum of Art). Before sending off the original watercolour along with his Salon entries in the spring of 1874, he also may have re-worked the oil study, which is dated that year and shows signs of finish that are rare in Eakins's preparatory work. Powerfully modelled and uncharacteristically signed, dated and completed to the edges of the stretcher – unlike most of his sketches and studies – the image also shows signs of new paint layered over the sky, perhaps to subdue a blueness judged later as too harsh.[7] The addition of the bow of another shell at the left – a detail not included in this spot in either watercolour, but which adds a sense of space and narrative – also suggests Eakins's consideration of this piece as a composition in its own right, even though it was never exhibited or sold in his lifetime. As a working study developed into a strong and satisfying independent painting, it is unique in Eakins's *œuvre*.

KAF

Fig.10a
John Biglin in a Single Scull
1873
Watercolour, 42.9 × 60.8 (16$\frac{7}{8}$ × 23$\frac{15}{16}$)
Collection of Mr and Mrs Paul Mellon,
Upperville, Virginia

1. On Biglin, see Goodrich 1982, vol.I, pp.83–7; and Johns 1983 (1), p.43; she comments on the metaphorical potency of the image of the lone oarsman, noting that Eakins was 'a single sculler all his life'.

2. The entry in Eakins's record book 2 (Pennsylvania Academy of the Fine Arts) reads: 'Sketch of [deleted]/Study of a man rowing (John Biglen for water/color)', p.59. This entry may be by Susan Eakins.

3. See Hoopes 1971, especially p.22 on the Biglin subject. Eakins's response to the watercolour movement in America in this decade is analysed in Foster 1982, pp.193–262.

4. On the two gifts to Gérôme and the related correspondence, see Goodrich op. cit., vol.I, pp.113–18.

5. Sewell 1982, pp.18–19. On the perspective drawing, see Stebbins Jr. 1976, pp.190–1.

6. *New York Daily Tribune*, 14 February 1874, p.7. The technical development of this image from the perspective and the oil study, the creation of the replica watercolour, and the course of Eakins's reputation in the 1870s as a watercolourist are further analysed in Foster forthcoming 1994, Chapter 2, 'Watercolor'.

7. Other landscapes from the late 1870s and early 1880s, such as *Mending the Net* and *The Fairman Rogers Four-in-Hand* (no. 19), show this same layering of a grey tint over an initially blue sky, suggesting that the reconsideration of his bright skies may have come later.

Provenance: Mrs Thomas Eakins; consigned to Babcock Galleries, N.Y.; purchased by Col. Henry Penn Burke, of Philadelphia, *c*.1928; purchased through Macbeth Galleries by Francis P. Garvan, *c*.1932; given by Garvan to Yale University, 1932.

Exhibitions: Philadelphia, Pennsylvania Academy of the Fine Arts, 1917, no. 97; Philadelphia, Department of Fine Arts, Sesqui-Centennial International Exposition, 1926, probably no. 353; New York, Museum of Modern Art, 1930, pl.92; New York, Museum of Modern Art, 1939, no. 31, ill.; New York, World's Fair, 1940, no. 308, ill. p.213; Boston, Museum of Fine Arts, 1944, no. 27, pl.V; Milwaukee, Art Institute, 1947, no. 26; Washington, DC, National Gallery of Art, 1961, no. 7, ill. p.41; New York, Whitney Museum of American Art, 1970, no. 13, ill. p.9 and cover; Oakland, California, Oakland Museum, 1971; Philadelphia, Museum of Art, 1982 (1), no. 19; Paris, Louvre, 1984, no cat. no., not ill.

Literature: Eakins's record book 2, Pennsylvania Academy of the Fine Arts, p.59; Burroughs 1924, p.329, size given as 24 × 20 inches; Marceau 1930, no. 24, p.19; Mather Jr. 1930, p.24; Watson 1930, ill. p.631; Bruening 1932, ill. p.261; Goodrich 1933, no. 59, p.165; Pach 1936, ill. p.13; Sizer 1938, pp.50–1, ill. frontis; Faison Jr. 1958, ill. p.37; Green 1966, ill. p.407; Schendler 1967, p.243, pl.121; Goodrich 1970, no. 13, ill. p.9; Hoopes 1971, p.22, ill. p.24; Ritchie and Neilson 1972, ill. no. 66, n.p.; Hendricks 1974, p.74, ill. checklist no. 13; Goodrich 1982, vol.I, p.280, ill. vol.I, p.103; Sewell 1982, pp.16–19, ill. p.22; Stebbins and Gorokhoff 1982, no. 466, ill. p.47; Cabe, in Shestack ed. 1983, p.66, ill. p.67; Johns 1984, pp.73–9.

11
Sailboats (Hikers) Racing
on the Delaware
1874
Oil on canvas, 60.9 × 91.5 (24 × 36)
Signed at r. on side of boat: *Eakins/74*

Philadelphia Museum of Art. Gift of Mrs
Thomas Eakins and Miss Mary Adeline
Williams (29.184.28)

In a lecture to his students at the Philadelphia
Academy, Eakins once said:

I know of no prettier problem in perspective than
to draw a yacht sailing ... A boat is the hardest
thing I know to put into perspective. It is so much
like the human figure, there is something alive
about it. It requires a heap of thinking and
calculating to build a boat.[1]

As the most spirited of the handful of sailing
paintings that Eakins did in 1874, no. 11 exhibits both Eakins's enthusiasm for the sport of
sailboat racing and his fascination with the
pictorial problems involved in depicting boats
in motion.

By 1874, Eakins was a devoted recreational
sailor, so enthusiastic about the sport that he
purchased a boat of his own. He enjoyed sailing on the Delaware with his friend William
Sartain on a nearly weekly basis.[2] The 'hiker',
however, unlike Eakins's boat, was a racing
boat, with a tall mast, a long boom, and a dis-
proportionately large sail which made for
speed, but also an unfortunate tendency to capsize.[3] The race depicted in *Sailboats Racing* is

possibly a regatta held on 31 August 1874, the
year of the painting. That summer many races
were held on the Delaware for sailboats of this
kind, but given the large number of vessels on
the water in the painting, it is likely that
Eakins's intention was to describe the late
August event.[4]

As with his sculling paintings (see no. 9), the
artist was particularly careful in planning the
composition of his sailing pictures. In *Sailboats
Racing*, he chose a basically geometric pattern
with the triangular mainsail of the central
vessel as the dominant motif which is repeated
over and over throughout the picture. Each sail
of each boat is essentially bisected by the horizon line, giving the work coherent balance
and a sense of order. In a photograph taken
around this time (fig.11a), Eakins found that a
group of sailboats close together translates
rather flatly to a two-dimensional surface, with
their hoisted sails becoming simple, broad
patches of white. In his painting, however, he
made great efforts to amend this problem by
experimenting with progressions of scale and

colour to suggest spatial depth. The sailboats, especially those to the right of the primary racer, reduce in size evenly, almost with arithmetic precision, and the eye is led into the distance beyond the race. Eakins also chose colour carefully in this central passage – bright red is used for the skipper's shirt in the boat in the foreground, for the crew's uniforms in the next boat to the right, and for the hull of the hiker itself beyond. Through such tightly controlled usage of perspective and colour, Eakins suggests a hierarchy which operates within each racing unit: the captain makes decisions which dictate how the crew in turn control the boat.

As the race passes from left to right before us, Eakins has employed several devices to inject the scene with the dynamics of a closely-fought race. The crew members of the vessel in the foreground lean far out over the water in an effort to fight the wind and waves which will otherwise capsize the vessel. The extreme foreshortening of their bodies parallels visually the foreshortened hiker to the far left, which seems almost to fall over as it realigns itself towards the foreground. A racer just ahead of the central boat is boldly cropped by the right edge of the painting, caught an instant too late by Eakins's eye, and shadows on the water to the left of the central boat let us know that another racer is right on the tail of our boat, no. 25. Eakins engages us as spectators by offering us the excitement and tension of the race.

It is possible that Eakins knew the men in the central hiker, but we as viewers cannot see their faces, so they remain to the viewer individual but anonymous. The interesting dichotomy of portraiture and genre painting is one which Eakins addressed in other works such as *Max Schmitt in a Single Scull* (fig.2), but in no. 11 he has left identities much more ambiguous. The agents exist as teams, not as individualized sportsmen, and they are nameless except for the numbers printed on their sails which designate their identities solely within the context of the race. So, too, does Eakins leave unclear whether the boats in the far background, beyond the spectator ship, are involved in the race or if they simply contain recreational sailors like himself. These uncertainties work together to present a full scene of the sailing life on the Delaware, both specific and generalized at the same time, and suggestive of moments and activities beyond the captured moment of the regatta.

Sailboats (Hikers) Racing on the Delaware was one of four paintings that Eakins sent to his former teacher Jean-Léon Gérôme for submission to the 1875 Salon exhibition in Paris. However, trouble with transportation of the paintings resulted in them arriving too late for submission, and the painting was finally shown in Goupil's gallery instead.[5] In 1881, Eakins attempted to sell the work at a price of $800, which would have made it one of his highest priced paintings; however, he eventually reduced the price to $600 when the work failed to sell. Still, it is clear that this, one of the few paintings by Eakins which successfully presents a scene of action, was one of his favourites.

WPH

1. Quoted by Goodrich 1982, vol.I, p.183.
2. Hendricks 1974, p.84.
3. Goodrich op. cit., p.89.
4. Hendricks op. cit., p.84.
5. It is unclear whether Gérôme sent the painting to the Goupil's branch in England or if it was shown in the Paris branch. Goodrich notes that it remained in Paris, whereas Sewell 1982 states that it, along with the other paintings that Eakins sent, was sent to London by Gérôme '...perhaps assuming that they would find a better market in England'.

Provenance: Given by the artist's widow, Susan Macdowell Eakins, and Mary Adeline Williams, 1929.

Exhibitions: Paris, Goupil's, 1875, no cat. no.; London, Goupil's, 1875, no cat. no.; Philadelphia, Pennsylvania Academy of the Fine Arts, 1883, no. 115; New York, American Art Association, 1884, no. 41; New York, American Fine Arts Society Galleries, 1892, no. 112; New York, Metropolitan Museum of Art, 1917, no. 6; Philadelphia, Pennsylvania Academy of the Fine Arts, 1917, no. 100; Cleveland, Museum of Art, 1928, no cat. no.; Philadelphia, Pennsylvania Museum of Art, 1930, no. 37; Cleveland, Museum of Art, 1937, no. 54; New York, Kleeman Galleries, 1939, no. 16; Philadelphia, John Wanamaker's department store, 1940, no cat. no.; Philadelphia, Museum of Art, 1944, no. 22; London, Tate Gallery, 1946, no. 69; Brooklyn, Brooklyn Museum, 1948, no. 43; Philadelphia, Museum of Art, 1953, no. 21; Philadelphia, Pennsylvania Academy of the Fine Arts, 1955, no. 91; New York, American Academy of Arts and Letters, 1958, no. 13; Toronto, Art Gallery of Toronto, 1961, no. 19; Washington, DC, National Gallery of Art, 1961, no. 16; New York, National Art Museum of Sport, 1968, no cat. no.; Bloomington, Indiana University Art Museum, 1970, no cat. no.; New York, Whitney Museum of American Art, 1970, no. 15; Philadelphia, Museum of Art, 1982 (1), no. 22.

Literature: McKinney 1942, ill. p.66; Porter 1959, ill. pl.15; Schendler 1967, p.49, ill. pl.19; Rennie 1968, pp.12–22, ill. p.18; Wilmerding 1968, pp.226–7, ill. pl.151; Valsecchi 1971, pp.43–4, 341, ill. pl.279; Hendricks 1974, pp.84, 340, ill. no. 240; Siegl 1978, pp.52–8, ill. pl.12; Goodrich 1982, vol.I, pp.89, 97, 118–19, ill. pls. 31–2; Homer 1992, pp.63–4, ill. pl.54.

Fig.11a
Sailboats
*c.*1874
Photograph, 7.9 × 8 ($3\frac{1}{8}$ × $3\frac{3}{16}$)
Philadelphia Museum of Art. Gift of Seymour Adelman

12
Professor Benjamin Howard Rand
1874
Oil on canvas, 152.4 × 121.9 (60 × 48)
Signed and dated c.l.: *Eakins 74*

Jefferson Medical College of Thomas
Jefferson University, Philadelphia
(1877 + e.P.01)

Benjamin Howard Rand, MD (1827–1883), Professor of Chemistry at Jefferson Medical College in Philadelphia, sits behind a profusely cluttered desk in Eakins's large-scale, full-length portrait of 1874. Significantly, Dr Rand was the first person to sit to the artist outside Eakins's circle of family and close friends, and no. 12 was the first in a long series of portraits of physicians and scientists (see also nos. 13, 25, 31, 32 and 36).

The two had been acquainted since Eakins's student days at Philadelphia's Central High School where Rand had held the Chair of Chemistry, a post he later filled at the Franklin Institute and at the Philadelphia Medical College. Rand became Professor of Chemistry at Jefferson Medical College in 1864. That same year, Eakins joined medical students there to study anatomy, which involved dissection, surgical lectures, and attendance at surgical clinics.

Rand was Dean of the medical school from 1869 to 1873 and held the chemistry chair until 1877. An 1848 graduate of Jefferson, he contributed numerous articles to medical journals and wrote and edited several texts on chemistry. He was a member of the American Medical Association and the American Philosophical Society, a fellow of the College of Physicians of Philadelphia, and Secretary of the Academy of Natural Sciences.

Contemporary accounts note that he was kind and obliging to his students, who valued his emphasis on applied rather than theoretical chemistry in the practice of medicine. His career was tragically halted after he accidentally inhaled a poisonous gas during a medico-legal investigation; the ensuing lung ailment compelled him to retire at the age of fifty in 1877. He remained almost housebound for several years until his death in 1883, when Jefferson's Alumni Association noted that the organization had '...sustained a loss of one of its sincere friends and most active and faithful members'.

Eakins asked Rand to sit for his portrait in 1874, when the artist was enrolled in a second anatomy course at Jefferson Medical College to supplement his already extensive artistic training in depicting the human figure. Aged thirty and optimistic about his future as a portrait painter, Eakins was confident enough to portray the distinguished physician boldly, unconventionally, and with kindly humour.

A traditional composition would have placed the scholar in front of or next to his desk in the foreground, but Eakins situated Dr Rand in the middle ground, on the far side of an expansive partner's desk. The murky interior of his home study is largely unde-

scribed architecturally, and the prevailing dark tones are punctuated by light entering the room on a raking angle from the right.

The reticent, sober-faced scholar is so engrossed in private thoughts that he ignores the viewer. One hand points to a passage in an open book. His other hand is placed awkwardly on the arched back of a dark grey cat, which insouciantly rests a front paw on the book. One cannot determine whether the bespectacled professor's downward gaze is focused on the book or on the cat, which has probably just interrupted Dr Rand's reading. At first glance, it is difficult to detect the presence of this congenial house pet; but eventually its upright tail, proprietary stance, red collar, and direct outward stare engage one's attention.

The physician's self-effacing posture and locale prompt most viewers to scrutinize the desk top first. Its surface is crowded with a gleaming array of objects, ranging from the scientific and academic to the personal and domestic. Brightly highlighted brass instruments on the left include a compound microscope and a beam balance. Behind is a wooden rack with test tubes, and to the right of this group, a red, conical, graduated cylinder with a spatula. Reading materials and quills are strewn about left and centre. On the far right is a bright pink rose, and a sheet of crinkled, cool-white tissue paper hangs over the edge of the desk. Blurred forms behind appear to be a perpetual calendar and some fruit. In the right foreground is a brilliant pink, tasselled, afghan or shawl draped over the back of a chair. Below the desk is a red-figured oriental rug, and on the left a fur rug in a pyramidal heap, and an open desk drawer.

The physician's attire and some of the nearby objects suggest non-academic, social pursuits. He has removed his necktie, and his highlighted white shirt is wrinkled. Do the white waistcoat and the flower suggest a recent return from some special evening occasion, and do the shawl and the flower suggest the unseen presence of a woman? Eakins does not provide the answers, but it is known that Dr Rand remarried in 1869 after having been a widower for fifteen years.

Rand must have been satisfied with his portrayal, for he wanted the painting to hang at Jefferson. In a letter of 21 April 1877, Rand offered to place his portrait 'at the disposal of the Board of Trustees'. Board minutes of 1 May 1877 state that he sent another letter saying, '... as soon as it was decided where his portrait was to be hung he would send it'. An 1881 report of the Board of Trustees mentions that the portrait was hung in the reception room of the Jefferson Medical College Hospital. By 1915 it was hanging in the west lecture room of the Medical College Building, in the same room as Eakins's *The Gross Clinic* (fig.4; see also no. 13).

Several scholars have conjectured about Eakins's choice of the estimable Dr Rand as his first public portrait subject. Ellwood Parry pointed out that in 1874 Eakins would have been aware that Jefferson's Alumni Association was beginning its tradition of commissioning portraits.[1] Starting in the early 1870s, Jefferson had begun to commission and collect portraits of illustrious professors at the behest of Samuel D. Gross, MD, the eminent Professor of Surgery.

William Gerdts developed this line of thought, noting Eakins's probable admiration for Rand and that 'he wanted to create a notable portrait that would advertise his talents'.[2] Elizabeth Johns contributed information about a more personal connection between Eakins and Rand, their mutual interest and participation in the popular sport of rowing and rowing clubs.[3]

Another personal connection between artist and sitter is the profession of their fathers — both were writing masters. In *The Writing Master* (1882; Metropolitan Museum of Art), Eakins depicted his father, Benjamin (1818–1899), bending over an official document he is inscribing. Benjamin Eakins taught writing at several local private schools, at one of them for fifty-one years.[4] Benjamin Howard Rand the elder (1792–1862), also an educator, taught penmanship for more than twenty-five years and published four popular books on the subject.[5]

A contemporary Jefferson Medical College ledger states that both writing masters were employed to 'fill in' student diplomas, Rand from 1843 to 1845, and Eakins from 1846 to 1878.[6] It is not known whether the two writing masters knew each other personally, but it is likely that their sons knew that their fathers shared the same profession.

Further, Thomas Eakins surely would have heard about Jefferson Medical College and its curriculum from his father, and that might have encouraged him to study anatomy there. It might also have emboldened him to request a portrait from Dr Rand, who as Dean of the college must have been aware of Benjamin Eakins's role in inscribing the diplomas.

The artist lost an enthusiastic supporter early in his career when Rand became incapacitated and died shortly thereafter. Had he lived longer, the Dean might have been influential in helping to secure more portrait commissions of physicians for Eakins.

Successive generations of Thomas Jefferson University students, professors and staff have admired Eakins's insightful portrayal of Dr Benjamin H. Rand. They respond affectionately to the wry humour of the cat and the controlled clutter of disparate objects on the desk. They identify with the preoccupied and reticent professor as a familiar type, so appropriately depicted in a private moment at home.
JSB

1. Parry 1969, pp.373–4.
2. Gerdts 1981, pp.60–2.
3. Johns 1983 (1), pp.23–4. Later, in footnote 20, p.54, Johns states that Rand retired from the faculty in 1873, so perhaps the portrait was painted as a 'retirement tribute'. In fact, his retirement as in 1877, not 1873.
4. See Goodrich 1982, vol.I, pp.2–3.
5. *Appleton's Cyclopaedia of American Biography*, New York, 1888, p.168.
6. The present author is researching Benjamin Eakins's career and studying official documents of the type he is 'filling in' to ascertain whether he is inscribing a Jefferson Medical College diploma in his portrait.

Provenance: Given by Professor Benjamin Howard Rand, 1878.

Exhibitions: Philadelphia, Art Exhibition at the Centennial Exposition, 1876; Philadelphia, College of Physicians of Philadelphia, 1887, no. 83; New York, Metropolitan Museum of Art, 1917, no. 5, ill; Philadelphia, Pennsylvania Academy of the Fine Arts, 1917, no. 121, ill; Philadelphia, Pennsylvania Academy of the Fine Arts, 1955, no. 77; Toronto, Art Gallery of Toronto, 1961, no. 18; Philadelphia, Museum of Art, 1965, no. 67, ill. p.75; Philadelphia, Museum of Art, Summer Loans, 1969; New York, Whitney Museum of American Art, 1970, no. 18; Birmingham, Alabama, Museum of Art, 1981, ill. p.61; Collegeville, Pennsylvania, Fetterolf House at Ursinus College, 1986, no. 18, ill. p.1.

Literature: McHenry 1946, p.31; Schendler 1967, pp.27, 33, ill. fig.10, p.32; Gerdts 1981, pp.60–2, ill. p.61; Goodrich 1982, vol.I, pp.73, 75, ill., pl.20, p.72, fig.21, p.73; Johns 1983 (1), pp.23–4, 53–4, ill. fig.35; Berkowitz 1990, p.787, ill. cover; Homer 1992, p.56, ill., pl.47, p.58.

13
Sketch for The Gross Clinic
1875
Oil on canvas, 66 × 55.9 (26 × 22)
Signed l.r.: *E.*; inscribed l.r. by Mrs Eakins:
T.E. 75.

Philadelphia Museum of Art. Gift of Mrs
Thomas Eakins and Miss Mary Adeline
Williams (29.184.31)

In this catalogue, the sketch for *The Gross Clinic* stands as proxy for the completed painting (fig.4) that was not available for loan to the exhibition. The oil sketch, however, deals with many of the fundamental issues of composition, colour, and tone addressed in the final, large version of *The Gross Clinic*. The sketch, of course, is smaller, measuring 26 by 22 inches, but in its own way is monumental in treatment.

The Gross Clinic may be seen both as a symbol of Philadelphia medicine, in which one of its great heroes, the surgeon Dr Samuel D. Gross, was celebrated; and also as a summary of all that Eakins stood for at the time that he executed the painting. His most ambitious early work, undertaken as an independent project when he was only thirty-one, it represents Gross in his clinic at Jefferson Medical College, Philadelphia. He pauses in the midst of lecturing on an operation he performs: the removal of a piece of dead bone from the thigh of a young man suffering from osteomyelitis. He is assisted by several other doctors and witnessed by an adult woman, on the left, presumably the patient's mother. Eakins singled out Gross by placing him so that a shaft of light falls onto the great dome of his forehead. This carefully selected raking light strikes him at an angle that beautifully reveals the innate intelligence and character of the face; shadows block out non-essentials. It is one of the most telling portraits in the history of American art.

Through Gross's skill in operating and his authoritative writings, he was an important force in that nineteenth-century movement which strove to elevate surgery to a high and respected professional level. From the beginnings of medicine, the surgeon had been vastly inferior to the physician, the former being associated with painful amputations that were seen as no more than operations requiring manual or mechanical skills; and the latter (the physician) being of higher social standing, involved with the treatment of internal ailments and dignified by the presence of intellectual theories.

By Gross's time, the role of the surgeon had gained a measure of recognition and approval, thanks in part to his own efforts. Eakins acknowledges this achievement in the painting, but according to Elizabeth Johns,[1] *The Gross Clinic* was also Eakins's response to Philadelphia's, and more broadly the nation's, pride in itself and its achievements on the eve of the Centennial of Independence celebrated by a major exposition held in the city in 1876. Certainly Gross was a citizen of wide renown, one in whom the country could take great pride. And the surgical theme, it follows, would have been congenial to Eakins, given his interest in medicine and anatomy and his belief in the scientist as a hero.

With the coming of the Centennial Exposition, Eakins's native country would have its first concerted opportunity to compare its accomplishments favourably with exhibits from all over the civilized world. The Centennial promised to showcase virtually every form of human activity, including the fine arts. As a result, Eakins planned *The Gross Clinic* not only as a tribute to the noted surgeon, but also, as reported by his friend David Wilson Jordan, as 'the finest thing he could possibly do for so great an event'.

To document his subject, Eakins took photographs of Gross, and presumably the other doctors as well (now lost), and in his studio made a penetrating oil study of Gross's head and shoulders. In the finished work, not only are the doctors in the operating theatre specific individuals – from left to right, Dr Charles S. Briggs, Dr William Joseph Hearn, Dr James M. Barton and Dr Daniel M. Appel – but also the recorder and spectators, including Eakins himself, seen on the right, are each identifiable portraits. Oil studies for many of these were made, but only one has survived: that of Robert C.V. Meyers, seated in the back row. Most of this visual information, in turn, was organized broadly within no. 13. Eakins may have made the sketch from the actual operation taking place before him, or from memory, painting quickly with summary strokes, including work with the palette knife.

The overall impression is one of hurried sketchiness, yet secure decision-making in the placement of Gross and his assistants. They are shown working in a dark interior, much gloomier than that of the completed painting. Indeed, this sketch could be viewed as a series of highlights in a murky blackish interior that is not particularly legible. Dr Gross's head looms out of the darkness to the left of centre, and strong accents of white are found in the anaesthetic cloth, thigh of the patient, and sheet covering the operating table. Lesser indications of light appear on the heads of the assisting doctors. The mother of the patient, on the other hand, is not fully articulated, and the recorder is not present in this sketch. There is no indication, either, of the surgical instruments that appear at the left in the final painting.

Here, Eakins presents his human subjects as simplified massive forms, without any attention to detail, using confident strokes to capture the essential features of the composition. Though rough in execution, the work holds together as a formal unity and illustrates Eakins's practised command of tonal painting. It reflects, especially, the tradition of the seventeenth-century masters Rembrandt, Ribera, and Velázquez, whose work he greatly admired and which he here recast so effectively in nineteenth-century terms.

The Gross Clinic was an heroic effort for Eakins, a major work that might well have been followed by others of the same kind if he had enjoyed encouragement from his contemporaries. As it was, most critics, reflecting the fashionable taste for prettified academic art, condemned it. The painting was thought to be brutal and vulgar, particularly because of the prominent blood on the doctor's hands. So this work, now regarded as a masterpiece of American art, received very little acclaim at the time it was painted. When Eakins submitted it to the art jury of the Centennial Exposition it was rejected and instead of hanging in the art building had to be shown in the nearby US Army Post Hospital Exhibit, among medical displays. It was purchased two years later by the alumni association of Jefferson Medical College for the paltry sum of $200. It remains one of their treasured possessions today, quietly enshrined in a tastefully appointed Eakins Gallery.

WIH

1. Johns 1983 (1), pp.55–6.

Provenance: Given by the artist's widow, Susan Macdowell Eakins, and Mary Adeline Williams, 1929.

Exhibitions: Philadelphia, Pennsylvania Academy of the Fine Arts, 1917, no. 9; Philadelphia, Pennsylvania Museum of Art, 1930, no. 38; Philadelphia, Museum of Art, 1944, no. 27; Pittsburgh, Carnegie Institute, 1945, no. 77; New York, American Academy of Arts and Letters, 1958, no. 19; Westmorland County, Museum of Art, 1959, no. 37; Washington, DC, National Gallery of Art, 1961, no. 20; Philadelphia, Museum of Art, 1965, no. 60; Philadelphia, Museum of Art, 1982 (1), no. 34.

Literature: Goodrich 1933, p.168; Fosburgh 1958, pp.24–7, 50–1; Porter 1959, p.28; Parry 1967, pp.2–12; Novak 1969, p.199; Hendricks 1969, pp.57–64; Parry 1969, pp.373–91; Siegl 1969–1970, p.49; Hendricks 1974, p.90, ill. pl.17; Siegl 1978, p.64, ill. p.64; Homer 1992, p.75.

Fig.13a
The Gross Clinic (detail of fig.4)
1875
Oil on canvas, 243.8 × 198 (96 × 78)
Jefferson Medical College of Thomas Jefferson University, Philadelphia

14
Baby at Play
1876
Oil on canvas, 81.9 × 122.8 ($32\frac{1}{4}$ × $48\frac{3}{8}$)
Inscribed l.c.: *Thomas Eakins/76*

National Gallery of Art, Washington,
John Hay Whitney Collection (1982.76.5)

The subject of this remarkable canvas is Eakins's niece, Ella Crowell, born to his sister Frances Eakins and her husband William Crowell in December 1873. Lloyd Goodrich writes:

When she was about two and a half her uncle painted her sitting on the brick pavement of the backyard, playing with blocks and a toy horse and wagon. The painting is far from the usual baby picture – no prettifying, no rosy flesh. The child's face, looking down, is shadowed, almost somber. The picture is equally far from what an impressionist would have made of a child playing in sunlight. The figure is sunlit, but its warm tones against the red brick and green foliage create a color harmony that is deep and powerful, not brilliant... The last quality one would expect in a portrait of a two-year-old girl is monumentality, but this is the quality it has.[1]

Goodrich's remarks (with one exception) are accurate but more can be said. In my book *Realism, Writing, Disfiguration: On Thomas Eakins and Stephen Crane* I argue that Eakins's art was structured by an implicit opposition between two fundamentally different modes of representation: the first, which I call 'graphic' because of its connection with writing and drawing, is oriented to the horizontal plane of inscription; the second, or 'pictorial', is oriented to the vertical plane of the surface of the canvas. Both terms of the opposition are historically and culturally specific. In my account it is crucial that Eakins as a student in Philadelphia's Central High School was trained according to a pedagogy that regarded writing and drawing as two aspects of a single discipline and that imagined the operations of that discipline to be confined to, or at least primally situated in, the horizontal plane. (The key text was Rembrandt Peale's *Graphics*, which went through numerous editions starting in 1834.) The association between oil painting and verticality may seem inevitable, but Eakins's lifelong commitment to the rigorous perspective construction of space was such that he habitually worked on a canvas that was held *absolutely* vertical, not merely approximately so, a practice that if not unique was at any rate far from universal. Something of the complex mutual entanglement of the two modes of representation in his work is suggested by the fact that the study of perspective was part of his early 'graphic' training, which is to say that it was precisely his reliance on a representational practice keyed initially to the horizontal plane of writing/drawing that required that the plane of the painting be defined as vertical (and thus be made to stand in a relation of considerable tension with the representation as such).

Two further observations are directly perti-

nent to *Baby at Play*. First, a marker of Eakins's profound involvement with writing/drawing is the prominence in his paintings of 'graphic' signs and objects of various sorts: letters, numerals, musical notes, graffiti, maps, diagrams, equations, stencils, posters, signatures, and the like. In *Baby at Play* there are the child's wooden blocks, every face of which bears a carefully delineated capital letter – except for one block face, towards the right, that improbably bears *three* letters, 'XVI', which I take as signifying the last three numbers of the painting's date in Roman numerals. (Once alerted to the possibility that letters on the blocks might be meaningful, it is likely to occur to the viewer that the capital 'C' just to the left of the 'XVI' might stand for 'Crowell' and that the upside down 'T' on a face of one of the two blocks near the bottom centre of the canvas could signify 'Thomas' – in any case, it's typical of 'graphic' seeing that it tries to *read* Eakins's paintings in one way or another. In his mature portraits, it attributes to the often lined faces of his sitters effects of what invariably has been called *character*.) Second, on a number of occasions, including *Baby at Play*, Eakins signed a painting by placing his characteristic signature in script *in the horizontal plane*. (The signature together with the abbreviated date '76' may be found in a pair of bricks visually abutting on Ella Crowell's left foot.) But whenever he did so he was also at pains to distinguish between the signature's particular orientation *within* that plane and the dominant orientation of the material ground itself – in *Baby at Play*, between the rightward slant of the signature and the dominant leftward bias of the brickwork floor. I take this to be a further expression of the opposition between the two modes of representation discussed above: that is, not only is there in Eakins's work a certain tension between the representation as such and the vertical plane of the picture, there is also a tension between the representation and the horizontal plane of writing/drawing, which cannot simply be identified with the depicted ground or floor. Put slightly differently, the representation as such belongs exclusively to neither mode but rather is the site of their unending struggle.

All this is to insist on the essentially conflictual nature of Eakins's art; in these and other respects his paintings are internally riven and seek to elicit from the viewer an impossible because divided aesthetic stance. Hence my one disagreement with Goodrich, who finds in *Baby at Play* 'a color harmony that is deep and powerful, not brilliant'. Against this view I suggest that *Baby at Play* is not colouristically harmonious at all; rather, the contrast

between its strong greens and vivid reds is so intense as to forestall the very possibility of colouristic integration. Indeed it is as if the viewer is simultaneously thrust back from the surface of the canvas by the explosive force of the contrast (or perhaps simply by the incandescent reds) *and* drawn into the painted scene by the persuasiveness of the perspective construction, by the lettering on the blocks and the signature on the ground, by the dramatic foreshortening of the black-costumed doll lying brokenly on the brick pavement towards the right, and, not least important, by the sense of something like mental effort or, say, inwardness on the part of Ella Crowell herself. In short, *Baby at Play* is not only a magnificent and original image of a small child; it is also a work that is structured through and through by oppositions and tensions that are virtually allegorized in *The Gross Clinic*, Eakins's masterpiece of the previous year and a painting with which *Baby at Play* has much in common.[2]

MF

1. Goodrich 1982, vol.I, p.79.
2. On *The Gross Clinic* from this point of view, see my *Realism, Writing, Disfiguration*, pp.2–89, *passim*. Jules Prown also connects *Baby at Play* with *The Gross Clinic*, 1985, pp.121–7.

Provenance: Mrs William J. Crowell, Avondale, Pennsylvania: Dr James W. Crowell, Claremont, California; (M. Knoedler & Co., New York); Mr and Mrs John Hay Whitney, New York; given, 1982.

Exhibitions: San Francisco, M. H. de Young Memorial Museum, 1935, no. 100; Baltimore, Museum of Art, 1936, no. 1; New York, M. Knoedler & Co., 1944, no. 12; Wilmington, Delaware, Society of Fine Arts, 1944, no. 12; Des Moines Arts Center, 1948, no. 34; London, Tate Gallery, 1961, no. 26; Washington, National Gallery of Art, 1961, no. 22; Philadelphia, Museum of Art, 1982 (1), no. 7; Washington, National Gallery of Art, 1983, no. 69; Chicago, Terra Museum of American Art, 1987, no cat. no.

Literature: Goodrich 1933, p.169; Schendler 1967, p.70, ill. p.71; Hendricks 1974, p.111, ill. pl.20; Goodrich 1982, vol.I, p.79, ill.24; Sewell 1982, p.10, ill. p.11; Prown 1985, pp.121–7, ill. p.125; Parry 1986, pp.21–41, ill.1; Fried 1987, pp.22, 77, ill. p.26; Wilmerding 1988, p.130, ill. p.131; Homer 1992, pp.91, 93, ill. p.92.

15

Elizabeth at the Piano

1875

Oil on canvas, 183 × 122.4 (72⅛ × 48³⁄₁₆)

Signed l.l.: *Eakins/75*

Addison Gallery of American Art,
Phillips Academy, Andover, Massachusetts.
Gift of anonymous lender (G 87)

One of Eakins's favourite works, *Elizabeth at the Piano* is the culmination of a four-part sequence of paintings illustrating various female family members at the piano.[1] While each piece in the cycle is individually significant, Eakins's final performance surpasses its predecessors as a demonstration of the spiritual and physical union requisite to music making. Yet, aside from a commentary on musicianship, *Elizabeth* also reflects the artist's keen admiration for the European masters and fond appreciation of the Eakins family circle. In spite of its nearly life-size scale, this painting of Eakins's young sister-in-law,[2] Elizabeth Crowell (1858–1929), is an intimate, family picture, rather than a grand exhibition portrait. Nonetheless, with its consummate play of light and darkness, clarity and opacity, *Elizabeth* emerges as one of Eakins's most skilled and sensitive early works.

A profile view of Elizabeth as she plays the piano, Eakins has arranged an uncomplicated, seemingly ordinary, composition that is invigorated and dramatized by the opposition of sombre shadows and bright highlights. Perched on a carved wooden bench with an upholstered seat, Elizabeth leans slightly towards the piano with her forearms extended and her fingers poised on the keyboard as if to observe a musical rest, but ready to play again. Although the front of the piano is visible, revealing the black and white keys and sheet music resting on a carved leaf, the instrument is truncated, dramatically reducing its length and mass. As a result, the pianist and the piano are balanced, if not merged: one is not subsumed or dominated by the other. As its title implies, this painting is at once a portrait of a family member and a vignette about music making.

This sort of duality permeates *Elizabeth*. While the painting's subtle composition suggests restraint and sobriety, Eakins infuses this arrangement with drama and life, using the light and shadows he observed in the paintings of Rembrandt, Velázquez, and of one of his teachers, León Bonnat. The overall effect of Eakins's restricted palette of slatelike hues ranging from black to blue to grey, is dark and obscure. Only the most subtle tonal differences

distinguish the sitter's black dress from the piano's ebony body and the shadowy blue-grey wall that serves as a vague backdrop for the two. Even the oriental rug underneath, colourfully patterned in blues, golds, and reds, is still mellow and unimposing. The sombre atmosphere that Eakins paints not only reflects the typically subdued palette of low-lit Victorian interiors, but more importantly sets the stage for a virtuosic demonstration of light's behaviour and effect as it bounces off one surface and on to another.

Yet, the painting's gloomy tenor is alleviated as an indefinite light source beyond the painting's frame illuminates the right side of the picture from behind Elizabeth. As in several of Eakins's works, this mysterious light brings forth the painting's pivotal characters, objects, and actions, while subordinating less important features – a technique he would have generally observed in Rembrandt's painting (see, for example, *Titus Reading* [fig.15a]). Light falls upon the back of Elizabeth's head, revealing a small scarlet flower pinned in her hair (a touch of red being a curious and consistent hallmark of Eakins's paintings) and caressing her jawline with a certain tenderness and affection. Next, travelling diagonally along the trajectory from Elizabeth's shadowy eyes to her right hand, light strikes the piano keys, accentuating the warm, ivory surface. At the same time, Eakins demonstrates his anatomical expertise as he directs this light to Elizabeth's carefully modelled hands and fingers resting delicately upon the keys, while also suggesting the musculature and manual dexterity of a skilled pianist. The third component of Eakins's tripartite play of light is the sheet music, which is brightly lit, emerging as the painting's most salient feature. Although Elizabeth does not look at the sheet music (perhaps she knows the piece by heart or plays a different composition by memory), an interesting symbiosis is evoked as Elizabeth's head casts a dark shadow on to the printed page while in return, the reflection of the white sheet highlights her face, ever so slightly, to reveal an expression of serenity, confidence and concentration.

It is precisely this mood that pervades so many of Eakins's interior scenes of 'feminine activities' (see, for example, no. 7). The artist paints women involved in informal, indoor activities, 'simple actions', writes Michael Fried, 'that assume a dignity by virtue of having been represented as manifestly and intensely *absorptive*'.[3] Ensconced in the gas-lit shadows of a Victorian parlour, Elizabeth meditates upon the musical tones she produces, paying no apparent attention to the

Fig.15a
Rembrandt van Rijn, *Titus Reading*
c.1657
Oil on canvas, 24 × 30 (9½ × 11¾)
Kunsthistorisches Museum, Vienna

printed notes before her. The player's fingers seem delicate and controlled, her movement slow and tender, yielding what can be imagined as a soft, murmuring passage of music. By painting the keyboard as a brilliant bar of light interrupted only by the shadow of the pianist's hands, Eakins isolates a musical rest in the composition, a transient moment between notes. The artist gives particular attention to this rhythmic silence during which the player pauses briefly to ruminate the resonance of the notes just played and to anticipate the sounds of the next measure. Having well established an atmosphere of rapt concentration, Eakins compels the viewer to follow suit: to thoughtfully linger on his lush painting technique just as Elizabeth lingers on the notes she plays. The eye is immediately drawn to precisely rendered items, such as the flower in Elizabeth's hair, the almost legible sheet music, and the detail around her collar and cuff, but is distracted by the textural variations that emerge from areas of heavy *impasto*. The work of both the artist's brush and knife results in a curious combination of meticulous features that invite close investigation as well as loose, sketchy, and even clumsy, forms (such as the left thumb that passes under the right hand) that register correctly only when viewed from afar.

Yet, if Eakins's alluring techniques are an invitation into his painting, his subject, Elizabeth, is not interested in receiving guests. The parlour's dark, shadowy interior can be read as an analogue to the pianist's psychological interior as she focuses on her activity and allows all else to become obscure so as not to interfere with her concentration. Alone and wholly absorbed in her music making, Elizabeth turns inward, intent upon her playing, but apparently unconcerned with her performance. Eakins's probe of the complex alliance of spirit and technique intrinsic to music making reveals an unmistakable, visible (and nearly audible) harmony.

A family portrait, an homage to the masters he so admired, and a successful inquiry into the creative nature of music, *Elizabeth at the Piano* was finally a provocative inspiration for Eakins's continued dedication to the theme of music and musicianship.

JME

1. This sequence, including *Frances Eakins* (*c*.1870; fig.15b), *Home Scene* (*c*.1870–1871; no. 7); *At the Piano* (*c*.1871; fig.1) and lastly *Elizabeth at the Piano*, (1875; no. 15), is discussed in Johns 1983 (1).
2. Elizabeth King Crowell was the sister of William Crowell, who married Thomas Eakins's older sister Frances in 1872. Peterson 1971, pp.12–14, indicates that Elizabeth Crowell was a 'skillful pianist' who studied with Rudolf Louis Henig (who also posed for Eakins) at the Philadelphia Academy of Music. After graduating in 1879, she continued her music career as a piano teacher in California, where she lived with her husband Townsend Harvey Sharpless until her death.
3. Fried 1987, p.42.

Provenance: Thomas Eakins, 1875; Mrs Susan Eakins, 1916; William MacBeth, Inc. through Mr C.W. Cramer, 1927; Thomas Cochran, 1928; Addison Gallery of American Art, Gift of Stephen C. Clark, 1928.

Exhibitions: New York, Metropolitan Museum of Art, 1917, no. 8; Philadelphia, Pennsylvania Academy of the Fine Arts, 1918, no. 118; New York, Museum of Modern Art, 1943, no. 82; New York, M. Knoedler & Co., 1944, no. 10; Detroit, Institute of Arts, 1944, no cat. no.; Boston, Symphony Hall, 1946, no cat. no.; New York, American Academy of Arts and Letters, 1958, no. 8; Philadelphia, Museum of Art, 1982 (1); Williamstown, Williams College Museum of Art, 1983, no. 31; Clinton, New York, Fred L. Emerson Gallery, 1984, no. 14; Andover, Massachusetts, Addison Gallery of American Art, 1990, no cat. no.

Literature: Goodrich 1933, p.167, no. 87; Porter 1959, ill. no. 18; Schendler 1967, p.27, ill. p.31, no. 9; Sewell 1982, p.9, ill. p.13, no. 11; Johns 1983 (1), pp.120–1, ill. no. 8; Fried 1987, pp.42, 45, 53–4, 77, ill. fig.5.

Fig.15b
Frances Eakins
c.1870
Oil on canvas, 61 × 50.8 (24 × 20)
Nelson-Atkins Museum of Art, Kansas City, Missouri. Nelson Fund

16

**Will Schuster and Blackman
Going Shooting**

1876

Oil on canvas, 56.2 × 76.8 (22⅛ × 30¼)

Signed and dated l.r.: *Eakins 76*

Yale University Art Gallery. Bequest of
Stephen Carlton Clark, BA 1903 (1961.18.21)

Will Schuster and Blackman Going Shooting is
one of a series of rail hunting pictures dating
from about 1873, when Eakins abandoned the
sport after contracting malaria on a rail hunting trip, to 1876. The rail, no larger than a
small chicken, was the prize of leisure hunters
from Philadelphia prospecting in marshes on
the outskirts of the city or, in Eakins's case,
further south along the Cohansey Creek in
New Jersey, where the artist's father owned a
boathouse. Normally elusive, the bird loses
much of its reed cover during high tides. Easily
detected and frightened into a slow flight, it is
as easily shot.[1]

The painting enlarges a passage from *Pushing for Rail* (fig.16a), done two years earlier.
When Eakins had finished *Pushing for Rail*,
he sent the work to Gérôme in Paris for his
former master's critique, which proved a vital
influence on the composition of *Will Schuster
and Blackman*. 'The execution is very good',
Gérôme deemed the frieze-like, dispersed

scene. 'Perhaps a little equal all over, a fault
which it is necessary to avoid for it is only with
the aid of certain sacrifices that one succeeds in
giving interest to the principal parts of a picture ... try to draw from it all the interest possible, either by the dramatic side, or by the
plastic side'.[2]

Eakins reacted in *Will Schuster and
Blackman* with a tauter, more dramatic, thoroughly realistic presentation, the theme of
which is the moment of the kill. Eakins had
described to Gérôme how, using a long pole to
propel and to steer the boat, 'the pusher gets up
on the deck and the hunter takes the position
in the middle of the boat ... when a bird starts
to rise ... [the pusher] cries 'Mark', and being
on the pusher's deck, stiffens up and tries to
stop the boat or at least hold it firmer'.[3] He
added that 'the inertia of the boat makes considerable pressure against the thigh, pressure
which he resists with his weight'.[4]

It is this instant that Eakins depicts in *Will*

Schuster and Blackman. From the glints of light on the wet pole and the denser growth on the picture's left, we can deduce that the boat has come from deep water and heads towards the reeds where the birds hide. From his elevated position, the pusher has spotted an ascending bird, which we do not see and possibly only he sees. He calls his warning and steadies the boat. Punctuating the moment is the red dot that comprises the hunter's finger on the trigger. The scene is a frozen instant, the spell of which the blast of his gun will shatter, an instant when both men are in a perfect equipoise of opportunity and dependence. Eakins's fascination with the tension and precision of co-ordinated energy between men also informs his sailing scene, *Starting Out After Rail*, and his sculling paintings. It relates fundamentally to the artist's interests in movement, anatomy, and scientific achievement, so important in his art, and this quality situates the rail hunting scenes comfortably within his *œuvre*.

Eakins departs from the conventions of American landscape of the generation preceding his own by placing a moment of human action at the centre of the picture. His treatment of landscape is remarkable in other respects[5], differing as it does from the work of the 'luminists' who dominated landscape painting until the 1870s.[6] *Will Schuster and Blackman* suggests some luminist conventions in its expression of natural elements in strong, long lines that lock the scene in place and in time and create a sense of quiet absorption.[7] The work, though, lacks luminism's vistas, sharp details, and steady spatial recession. There is no poetic mood in *Will Schuster and Blackman*, and, rather than timelessness, we discern that time has stopped for only a moment. His landscape soft and surprisingly notational, the atmosphere richly humid, Eakins draws from Barbizon painterliness. His figures, though, are distinctly detailed and retain a strong formal structure. The artist thus emerges as an intermediary between traditional American landscape art and a French style he would have known from his stay in Paris in the 1860s.

Eakins invests his black subjects with individuality, dignity, and responsibility, eschewing in most but not all cases the demeaning stereotypes marking their portrayal during the century.[8] Eakins painted the artist Henry Tanner's portrait (no. 39), but blacks otherwise appear only in a handful of his small body of genre scenes. Despite his occasional bohemianism, in many respects Eakins was a man of his epoch, and in these genre paintings of blacks there is no question of actual equality. The first indication of Eakins's views is the

title of *Will Schuster and Blackman*, which names one figure but identifies only the other's race, though both are depicted with the attentiveness of a portrait. The choice of title is interesting but not necessarily decisive since the provenance of titles often does not descend directly from the artist. More significant is the presentation of the two figures. In *Will Schuster and Blackman*, a white man and a black man are paired in a partnership involving mental and physical co-ordination. One is white, affluent, and sportily urban. The other is black and countrified, a hired hand. Yet in navigating the boat, spotting the birds, steadying the boat for the kill, and recalling where birds fell for later retrieval, the pusher does most of the work, and certainly all the hard physical work. Reserved to the red-shirted hunter is the central role of killer, the role demanding what Eakins would have perceived as the greatest skill. It is a dichotomy of superiority and inferiority Eakins explored earlier in *The Artist and His Father Hunting Reed-birds* (Virginia Museum, Richmond), where the lanky young man assumed the pusher's role. Eakins's consignment of blacks to a status such as this, only a decade after the Civil War's end, reveals the country's desire for a speedy return to 'normality', leaving economic and social integration even of northern blacks largely unachieved. (See also no. 39 for a further discussion of the portrayal of blacks in Eakins's work.)
BTA

1. Bryant 1977, p.29.
2. Quoted in Goodrich 1982, vol.I, p.116.
3. Goodrich op.cit., p.320.
4. Ibid.
5. Roughly 30 per cent of Eakins's lifetime work features some landscape component. Of the works painted before Eakins's forced retirement from the Pennsylvania Academy of the Fine Arts, when he began to concentrate almost exclusively on portraiture, nearly half include landscape. See Foster 1990, p.69.
6. The most extensive and comprehensive recent scholarship on the luminist movement is Wilmerding 1989. Eakins's place in the movement is discussed on pp.148–50 and pp.287–8.
7. Novak 1969, pp.191–6.
8. McElroy 1990 describes the depictions of blacks in American art.

Provenance: Bequest of Stephen Carlton Clark, BA 1903.

Exhibitions: New York, Forum Gallery, 1967, no. 19; New York, Whitney Museum of American Art, 1974, no. 114; Washington, DC, Corcoran Museum of Art, 1990, no cat no.

Literature: Schendler 1967, pp.70–3; Parry and Chamberlin-Hellman 1973, pp.20–46; Goodrich 1982, vol.I, pp.116–20; Fried 1987, pp.70–3, McElroy 1990, p.85.

Fig.16a
Pushing for Rail
1874
Oil on canvas, 33 × 76.4 (13 × 30$\frac{1}{16}$)
The Metropolitan Museum of Art,
Arthur H. Hearn Fund, 1916

17
William Rush Carving His Allegorical
Figure of the Schuylkill River
1876–1877
Oil on canvas (mounted on Masonite),
51.1 × 66.4 (20⅛ × 26⅛)
Signed l.r. on piece of wood: *EAKINS. 77.*

Philadelphia Museum of Art.
Gift of Mrs Thomas Eakins and
Miss Mary Adeline Williams (29.184.27)

William Rush (1756–1833), an ornamental wood carver famous in the late eighteenth century for figureheads and other decorative work for ships, and a leader in the artistic and civic life of Philadelphia, is shown in his workshop, carving the personification of the Schuylkill River that he made in 1809. Eakins described this figure, a fountain intended to stand in front of the neoclassical pumphouse designed by Benjamin Henry Latrobe for the city's first waterworks, in a statement he wrote to accompany his painting when it was exhibited:

The Statue is an allegorical representation of the Schuylkill River. The woman holds aloft a bittern, a bird loving and much frequenting the quiet dark wooded river of those days. A withe of willow encircles her head, and willow binds her waist, and the wavelets of the wind-sheltered stream are shown in the delicate thin drapery. . . . The idle and unobserving have called this statue Leda and the Swan and it is now generally so miscalled.[1]

Two other sculptures Rush made for public sites can be seen in the dim background of the shop: a full-length, life-size figure of George Washington carved in 1814, and a seated woman with her arm extended over a waterwheel, an allegorical representation of the second city waterworks, made in 1825. Eakins consulted Rush's own sketchbook for the carved scrolls on the workshop floor and drawings of other scrolls on the right wall; the notation, 'finish scrolls/for S. Girard/Augt. 13' refers to Stephen Girard, Philadelphia's wealthiest merchant shipper, who was Rush's most important client.

William Rush Carving His Allegorical Figure of the Schuylkill River is entirely different in subject and scale from *The Gross Clinic* (fig.4) painted a year or two earlier, yet it is as ambitious and as elaborately prepared in its own way as the larger picture. While it lacked the shock value of Dr Gross's bloody hands, this comparatively small, extensively researched, depiction of an artist in his studio, a subject popular in Europe at the time, may well have been inspired by the same impulse to astound the public with a masterpiece. Eakins's painting of a female nude – and Rush's model was the only nude woman he ever portrayed in a finished work – even one accompanied by a chaperone and veiled by history, was virtually unprecedented and potentially sensational in American painting at the time.

The intimate scale and historical subject of the *William Rush* recall the work of Eakins's teacher at the Ecole des Beaux-Arts, Jean-Léon Gérôme, who specialized in exquisitely finished genre scenes taken from history, and from contemporary life in North Africa and the Near East, many with female nudes at the centre of the composition (fig.17a).[2] A few years earlier, Eakins had solicited Gérôme's opinions about some of his rowing and sailing subjects (see nos. 10, 11 and 16), and modified them at his teacher's suggestion. In this, however, the most directly comparable to Gérôme's of all of his work, Eakins appears to have been inviting comparison with his teacher deliberately; acknowledging his indebtedness, yet defining his independence by adapting Gérôme's subject and style in a way that was personal and remarkably original.

Gérôme's paintings of famous artists such as *Bramante Showing Raphael the Sistine Ceiling* or *Rembrandt Etching* (both paintings now unlocated) among others, may have suggested the Rush theme to Eakins. Instead of depicting European Old Masters, as did Gérôme and his European contemporaries and European-trained Americans who painted such subjects slightly later, Eakins characteristically chose an historical event that was almost as much a part of his immediate experience as his earlier paintings of family and friends. Two versions of the *Water Nymph and Bittern*, the wooden original and a bronze cast of it made in 1872, stood in the park on the banks of the Schuylkill, not far from the Eakins's family house on Mount Vernon Street, and additional examples of the sculptor's works were easily studied at the Pennsylvania Academy of the Fine Arts and other sites around the city.

Eakins and his contemporaries were beginning to reject the marble neoclassical sculpture produced by the previous generation, and he must have admired Rush's vigorous, idiosyn-

Fig.17a
Jean-Léon Gérôme,
Queen Rodope Observed by Gyges
1859
Oil on canvas, 67.3 × 99 (26.5 × 39)
Museo de Arte de Ponce, The Luis A. Ferré Foundation, Inc., Ponce, Puerto Rico

cratic style and have developed an idea of the sculptor as a dedicated, unpretentious workman.[3] Susan Macdowell Eakins later recalled that her husband admired the 'intelligent and refined work' of Rush, whose 'attitude in art he greatly admired'.[4]

Eakins used Gérôme's painstaking academic method to construct his painting; the numerous preparatory materials that survive constitute the most complete documentation of all of his works. He interviewed people who remembered Rush, photographed, sketched, and made wax models of his sculpture, studied costume from paintings and fashion plates of the time, and assembled the final painting from oil studies and perspective drawings.[5]

However, Eakins's concept of time differs significantly from the unified narrative moment that Gérôme depicts. By including sculpture dating from 1815 and 1825, ship scrolls of the kind that Rush began making in the 1780s, and a Philadelphia Chippendale chair from 1760–1770, besides the *Water Nymph and Bittern* of 1809, he encompassed a wider period of time, presenting a summary of Rush's entire career that amounts to a tribute to the old sculptor.[6] As opposed to Gérôme's continuously modulated light and detail, Eakins's use of strong chiaroscuro – based upon a light effect that he observed in an actual woodcarver's shop on the Delaware riverfront – and of selective focus to vary the sharpness of detail and strength of colour in different areas, similarly disrupts the unity of the painted scene, weighting the relative importance of different areas to the narrative. In this approach to history, Eakins is in keeping with the nostalgic and evocative representations

of the American past characteristic of the Colonial Revival style that had its beginnings around the time of the Centennial.

The central events of Eakins's painting, however, are deliberate fabrications. It is extremely improbable that a young woman, especially the daughter of 'an esteemed merchant' as Eakins tells us, would have posed nude for an artist in the United States in 1809, and Rush is shown incongruously carving his draped figure from the nude model. At this time Eakins was beginning to teach at the newly reopened Pennsylvania Academy, and his emphasis on study of the nude in life classes was already controversial. In *William Rush* he is using the impeccable reputation of the distinguished sculptor, an elected member of City Council for twenty-five years, and one of the two artists who were founding members of the Pennsylvania Academy in 1805, as a respectable local precedent in his argument. A sentence from a review by Earl Shinn, Eakins's friend and fellow student in Gérôme's classes, confirms this view:

The painter of the fountain seemed to have a lesson to deliver – the moral, namely, that good sculpture, even decorative sculpture, can only be produced by the most uncompromising, unconventional study and analysis from life, and to be pleased that he could prove his meaning by an American instance of the rococo age of 1820.[7]

Beyond the tribute to Rush, and justification of his own educational beliefs, Eakins's painting serves as a specific definition of his own aesthetic. The presence of the chaperone recalls his plea in a letter of early 1877 to the Academy board of trustees to hire better models. Instead of the 'degrading' practice of

Fig.17b
William Rush Carving His Allegorical Figure of the Schuylkill River
1876
Oil on canvas, 51.3 × 61 ($20\frac{3}{16}$ × 24)
Yale University Art Gallery;
The James W. and Mary C. Fosburgh Collection

Fig.17c
William Rush and His Model
1907–1908
Oil on canvas, 89.5 × 120 ($35\frac{1}{4}$ × $47\frac{1}{4}$)
Honolulu Academy of Arts, Honolulu, Hawaii

hiring prostitutes who were 'coarse, flabby, ill formed & unfit in every way for the requirements of the school', Eakins suggested that the advertisement state that 'Applicants should be of respectability and may on all occasions be accompanied by their mothers or other female relatives'. He argued that such a course 'will insure in these times a great number of applicants among whom will be found beautiful ones with forms fit to be studied'.[8]

The model dominates the painting, and Eakins has lighted her to compel study of the figure. Compared to the sleek, idealized nudes in Gérôme's paintings, the woman Eakins portrays is imperfectly proportioned and quite individual. An early study (fig.17b) and other preparatory sketches show Eakins rearranging the model from a huddled, stocky figure, to the rhythmic balance and long silhouette of the figure in the finished painting, finding beauty in the unidealized form. Eakins's friend William Clark summed up this concept of beauty in his review of the painting:

The substantial fact is that the drawing of the figure in this picture – using the word drawing in its broadest sense to indicate all that goes to the rendering of forms by means of pigments on a flat surface – is exquisitely refined and exquisitely truthful, and it is so admitted by all who do not permit their judgement to be clouded by prejudices and theories about what art might, could, would, and should be were it something else than, in its essence, an interpretation of nature, and of an order of ideas that must find expression through the agency of the facts of nature if they are to find any adequate expression'.[9]

Eakins first showed *William Rush Carving His Allegorical Figure of the Schuylkill River* in spring 1878. At the first annual exhibition of the newly founded Society of American Artists in New York, whose members were for the most part artists recently returned from training in Europe, it proved to be controversial, and, in general, was unfavourably received by the critics. Although Eakins's talent was recognized, the painting was faulted for lack of colour and the ungraceful treatment of the nude figure, among other defects. The critic for the *Times* was disturbed by 'the presence in the foreground of the clothes of the young woman, cast carelessly over the chair. This gives a shock, which makes one think about nudity – and at once the picture becomes improper'.[10] Only Eakins's friends William Clark and Earl Shinn, who had defended *The Gross Clinic*, gave the painting unqualifiedly favourable reviews.

As with *The Gross Clinic*, Eakins may have intended the painting to be provocative, but may also have underestimated its power to offend his audience. *William Rush* never found a buyer, whereas *Seventy Years Ago* (The Art Museum, Princeton University), a large water-colour of the chaperone alone, one of more than a dozen 'old-fashioned' subjects – water-colours and small oils showing women in late-eighteenth/early nineteenth century costume knitting or spinning amidst colonial furniture – appealed to current taste for Colonial Revival subjects and sold almost immediately.

In 1908, Eakins returned to the William Rush subject, making studies and two large paintings. One (Brooklyn Museum of Art [fig.14]) is a loose reinterpretation of the earlier painting. In the second, Eakins's memories of Rush and Gérôme (who had died in 1904) seem to merge (fig.17c). Gérôme had done a series of humorous, rather arch self-portraits as a dapper, white-haired sculptor paying close attention to his nubile model in the late 1880s and 1890s. Instead of Gérôme's lithe form however, Eakins has given his sculptor his own bulky silhouette from the side, dressed in the same work clothes, the rumpled waistcoat and shirt in which he portrayed Rush in the later canvases. Only the carved ornamental scroll in the foreground recalls his painting of William Rush thirty years earlier.

DS

1. Quoted in Goodrich 1982, vol.I, p.146.
2. Under the title *King Candules*, this painting was first published in conjunction with Eakins's work by Sellin 1976, p.60. Eakins's indebtedness to Gérôme is discussed by Ackerman 1969, pp.235–47, and Weinberg 1984, pp.35–47.
3. A variety of reasons for Eakins's interest in Rush are presented in Johns 1983 (1), pp.83–90.
4. Susan Macdowell Eakins, letter of 15 September 1917, to William Sartain (Sartain Collection, Historical Society of Pennsylvania), quoted in Johns op. cit., p.99.
5. Eakins's elaborate preparatory studies are reviewed by Foster in forthcoming 1994.
6. The idea of the painting as a tribute to Rush is developed by Johns op. cit., pp.88–9, 98–9.
7. [Earl Shinn], 'Fine Arts: The Lessons of a Late Exhibition', *The Nation*, vol.26 (11 April 1878), p.251, quoted in Sellin 1976, p.60.
8. Eakins, letter to the Committee on Instruction, Pennsylvania Academy of the Fine Arts, January 1877, quoted in Goodrich 1982, vol.I, p.170.
9. William Clark, Philadelphia *Evening Telegraph*, 13 March 1878, Sellin 1976, p.61.
10. *New York Times*, 28 March 1878, quoted in Siegl 1978, p.72.

Provenance: Given by the artist's widow, Susan Macdowell Eakins, and Mary Adeline Williams, 1929.

Exhibitions: Boston, Art Club, 1878, no. 170; Brooklyn, Art Association, 1878, no. 313; New York, Kurtz Gallery, 1878, no. 8; Philadelphia, Pennsylvania Academy of the Fine Arts, 1881, no. 242; Chicago, Inter-State Industrial Exposition, 1882, no. 501; Toronto, Ontario Society of Artists, 1885, no cat. no.; Philadelphia, Earle's Galleries, 1896, no cat. no.; New York, Metropolitan Museum of Art, 1917, no. 11; Philadelphia, Pennsylvania Academy of the Fine Arts, 1917, no. 85; New York, Whitney Studio Club, 1921, no. 44; Philadelphia, Department of Fine Arts, 1926, no. 366; New York, Museum of Modern Art, 1930, no. 97; Philadelphia, Pennsylvania Museum of Art, 1930, no. 61; Chicago, Art Institute, 1934, no. 395; Paris, Musée du Jeu de Paume, 1938, no. 53; Philadelphia, Museum of Art, 1940, no. 25; New York, M. Knoedler & Co., 1944, no. 14; Philadelphia, Museum of Art, 1944, no. 34; London, Tate Gallery, 1946, no. 74; Frankfurt, American Federation of the Arts and United States Information Agency, 1953, no. 44; New York, American Academy of Arts and Letters, 1958, no. 45; Washington, DC, National Gallery of Art, 1961, no. 27; Washington, DC, Corcoran Gallery of Art, 1969, no. 1; New York, Whitney Museum of American Art, 1970, no. 27; Philadelphia, Museum of Art 1976, no. 350; Philadelphia, Museum of Art, 1982, no. 41; Philadelphia, Pennsylvania Academy of the Fine Arts, 1991, no cat. no.

Literature: Mather, Morey and Henderson 1927, p.57, ill. p.57; LaFollette 1929, ill. f. p.154; Goodrich 1933, no. 109, ill. p.17; Smith 1956, pp.28–33, 61–3, ill. p.33; Larkin 1960, ill. pl.12; Schendler 1967, p.79, ill. pl.34; Hendricks 1968, pp.382–404, ill. fig.1; Garrett *et al.*, 1970, p.253, ill. pl.190; Parry and Chamberlin-Hellman 1973, pp.20–45, ill. p.26; Gerdts 1974, ill. pp.120–1; Hendricks 1974, pp.111–15, 341, ill. pls.24–5; Sellin 1976, ill. p.55; Siegl 1978, pp.70–2, ill. pl.28; Sewell 1982, pp.46–57, ill. p.46; Goodrich 1982, vol.I, pp.145–57, ill. pl. 64; Johns 1983 (1), pp.82–114, ill. pl.7; Homer 1992, pp.93–7, ill. pl.84.

18
The Spinner (A Sketch)
*c.*1878
Oil on canvas, 76.7 × 63.9 ($30\frac{3}{16} \times 25\frac{3}{16}$)
Inscribed along bottom edge:
[S] TUD [Y FOR P] ICTURE [OF]
SPINNING E [AKINS]

Worcester Art Museum, Worcester,
Massachusetts (1929.123)

During the 1870s, even while he was painting scenes of modern life – outdoor sports or his own home and family – Eakins undertook several subjects of poetic, historical, and even illustrative interest.[1] Some of his ideas, such as for paintings of Christopher Columbus in prison, or the Confederate general Robert E. Lee at his surrender, progressed no farther than a preliminary oil study. But as *William Rush Carving His Allegorical Figure of the Schuylkill River* (no. 17) attests, Eakins could develop imaginative and historical themes with the same determination he displayed in his rowing pictures or the *The Gross Clinic* (fig.4; see also no. 13)

The Spinner (A Sketch) testifies further to the importance that Eakins attached to 'fanciful' subjects, which, except for the William Rush series with its clear autobiographical overtones, have long been accorded only slight attention by scholars eager to define Eakins as the virile painter of contemporary life and heroic portraits. Eakins completed at least five images of spinners; he kept a spinning wheel in his studio, and the early works of many of his first students at the Pennsylvania Academy portray seamstresses and spinners and old-fashioned subjects.[2] It was no passing fancy.

The Spinner shows a young woman dressed in an Empire-style gown, seated at a spinning wheel, pumping its treadle with her foot and drawing the thread between her fingers. Painted on a canvas of standard portrait size, the study reveals by its workmanship an emphasis on physical labour driven by mental concentration. Lit strongly from the left, the woman's right arm and the right side of her face and neck are developed almost to the point of finish. Other details, while more sketchily rendered, are still fully descriptive and leave no question as to the solidity of the woman's body, or the intensity with which she focuses on her work. Her head lowered and her eyes indistinct, she almost appears to be praying.

Eakins squared this canvas for transfer, and used this study in reduced format for a painting called *The Courtship* (fig.18a). Neither study nor final work is dated, but since *The Courtship* was sold in 1878 to Dr Horatio C. Wood (see no. 25), it is likely that both were painted in 1877 or 1878, either while Eakins was working on his William Rush picture, or very soon after he finished it. For the figure of the spinner, Eakins relied on Anna W. Williams, the model who posed for the nude figure of Louisa Van Uxem in his Rush painting (no. 17).[3] Like the chaperone in the Rush painting, who is seated in a Chippendale chair and knitting intently, this spinner concentrates on handiwork that recalls another era, general in its feminine nature, specific in its references to the American colonial past.[4]

Eakins had painted a very explicit essay on this topic in 1876, which he called *In Grandmother's Time* (fig.18b). The figure's old-fashioned costume no less than the work's nostalgic title suggest that Eakins had taken a special interest in the American past and colonial custom. This personal concern coincides with a more general interest in national history then growing among the American public, which manifested itself in significant ways at the Philadelphia Centennial of 1876. This major international exposition commemorated one hundred years of American nationhood with a proud display of the country's accomplishments in science, technology, manufacturing, and the fine arts; Eakins himself was represented by six works, including *The Gross Clinic* (fig.4) and *Elizabeth at the Piano*, (no. 15).

Fig.18a
The Courtship
*c.*1878
Oil on canvas, 50.8 × 61 (20 × 24)
The Fine Arts Museums of San Francisco,
Museum purchase by exchange. Gift of Mrs
Herbert Fleishhacker, M. H. de Young,
John McLaughlin, J. S. Morgan and Sons,
and Miss Keith Wakeman

Fig.18b
In Grandmother's Time
1876
Oil on canvas, 40.6 × 30.5 (16 × 12)
Smith College Museum of Art, Northampton,
Massachusetts

Other displays at the fair attempted to deal with at least certain parts of the American past. One of its most popular attractions was the New England Log House and Modern Kitchen. 'Colonial kitchens' first appeared at the Sanitary Fairs organized by Union women to support the war effort during the 1860s, but the professed inspiration for the 1876 kitchen was an exhibit of Hungarian and Tyrolean peasant life that had appeared at the Vienna Exposition of 1873.[5] Thus appealing to a burgeoning interest in the American past and especially to the more picturesque and nativist roots of American culture, the New England house and kitchen featured 'a combination of quaint architecture [and] antiquated furniture', attended by women dressed in 'epochal costumes', who introduced visitors to New England life as they imagined it had been lived in the seventeenth and eighteenth centuries.[6] Among these attendants was a woman working at a spinning wheel – a woman who readily invited associations with Priscilla Mullins, the Plymouth Bay Colony Puritan whose marriage to John Alden was celebrated in Henry Wadsworth Longfellow's 'The Courtship of Miles Standish'. Early in the poem, Alden interrupts Priscilla's spinning to deliver, Cyrano-like, a marriage proposal on behalf of his captain Miles Standish. In canto VIII, 'The Spinning-Wheel', Alden watches Priscilla at her wheel 'as if the thread she was spinning was that of his life and fortune'; he is helping her wind a skein of yarn when the news of Standish's death arrives, freeing them to marry. Visitors to the 1876 exposition could readily spin similar conflations of romance and history when they realized that Alden's actual writing desk was exhibited not far from the spinning wheel in the colonial kitchen.

Eakins probably drew on such associations himself. He had professed in 1867 a belief that Longfellow created 'the most beautiful poetry – far better than any Englishman of today, even Tennyson', and around 1874 he attempted a composition inspired by Longfellow's poem 'Hiawatha'.[7] He eventually gave up work on that painting, finding it 'too poetic'; perhaps for that reason his composition of *The Courtship* shows no obvious references to a specific literary source, even while it invites comparison to Longfellow's poetry. While the older sitter and more detailed setting of *In Grandmother's Time* evoke a specific moment in the colonial past, *The Courtship* works on a more suggestive level. A compositional study (Private Collection) reveals that Eakins at one point envisaged a more complex background of fireplace and ornamented mantel for *The Courtship*. But eventually the artist decided on

an undeveloped background similar to that of *The Spinner*, thus reducing any narrative solely to the relationship between two figures.

The subject of courtship was timely for Eakins, given his own long courtship with Kathrin Crowell (see no. 8). Some scholars have suggested that the lack of interaction between the figures in *The Courtship* reflects Eakins's lukewarm interest in his fiancée, who was not his artistic or intellectual equal.[8] *The Spinner* belies this reading. Depicting a woman with strong arms and almost reverent concentration, this sketch suggests that Eakins, like the suitor who occupies his final composition, and like John Alden who pondered over Priscilla Mullins, Eakins was attentive to, even enthralled by, his beloved's body and the mundane process of her work. And Eakins continued to explore this process. Nearly twenty paintings, watercolours, and sculptural reliefs executed between 1876 and 1882 testify to the power Eakins invested in the image of a single woman in an interior, sewing, knitting, or especially, spinning. As a time-honoured symbol of both woman's work and feminine nature, the spinning wheel provided a theme within which Eakins could reflect on female roles and feminine potential.[9] By casting his spinning women in the guise of colonial dames, Eakins not only catered to the prevailing taste for old-fashioned subjects, but also seems to have pulled a veil across what may have been intensely personal considerations.

Eakins's last essay on the spinning theme, a sculptural relief intended as a chimneypiece ornament for a Philadelphia home, was undertaken in 1882. Before Eakins finished the commission in 1883, his favourite sister Margaret (see no. 6), who had posed in 1881 for two watercolours of spinning, *Spinning (Homespun)* (fig.7) and *Spinning* (Private Collection), died. The next project for which Eakins made extended studies and related paintings was the elegiac Arcadian series.[10] He never returned to the subject of spinning.

SM

1. See Parry and Chamberlin-Hellman 1973, pp.20–45.
2. See Goodrich 1933, nos.106, 119, 144, 146, and 504. Goodrich gave only a paragraph of mention to Eakins's spinning subjects in this monograph, although he corrected the balance somewhat in his 1982 revision. Other scholars, including Schendler, Hendricks, Johns, and Homer, have followed his early lead, however, apparently finding little 'heroism of modern life' in the subject of spinning. A spinning wheel appears in the photograph of Eakins's studio reproduced in Hendricks 1974, p.206; for the work of Eakins's students, see Casteras 1973, especially nos. 3 and 6; also Danly 1991, p.84.
3. 'Nannie' Williams, an instructor in the Philadelphia House of Refuge, was the friend of one of Eakins's sisters. She became a popular model and her profile appears on several United States coins minted between 1876 and 1882, including the 'Liberty' silver dollar. Williams returned to Eakins's studio at least long enough to pose for some of his photographs of the early 1880s, including one which shows *The Spinner* in the background. See Goodrich 1982, vol.I, pp.148ff. Her photo appears in Hendricks 1972, p.55.
4. For the 1877 watercolour *Seventy Years Ago* (The Art Museum, Princeton University), Eakins again turned to Mrs King, who had posed for the chaperone in the Rush painting. Revising her costume and setting somewhat, he again showed this older woman knitting, but now seated next to a spinning wheel.
5. Roth 1985, pp.174–5.
6. *Frank Leslie's Illustrated Magazine*, quoted in Sewell 1982, p.59; see also Roth op.cit., pp.175–81.
7. Goodrich 1982, vol.I, p.113; also Parry and Chamberlin-Hellman op.cit., pp.20–3.
8. See, for example, Homer 1992, pp.98–9. This reading seems biased in favour of the sturdy and talented Susan Macdowell, who attracted Eakins's attentions after Kathrin Crowell's death and who married the artist in 1884.
9. For the association between women and spinning wheels, one need only recall the Grimm Brothers' retelling of *Dornröschen*, the fairy tale of a princess who pricked her finger on a spindle. For the theme in visual art, see Schlapeit-Beck 1987, pp.20–31. Eakins's spinning subjects are described generally in Sewell op. cit., pp.58–62; see also Goodrich 1933, nos.106, 114–17, 119–23, 131–2, 140–1, 144–7, and 504–5.
10. See Simpson 1987, pp.71–95.

Provenance: Mrs Thomas Eakins; purchased from Clarence W. Cranmer (agent for Mrs Eakins), Philadelphia, 1929.

Exhibitions: New York, National Academy of Design, 1916, no. 96 (as *The Spinner* and assumed to be no. 18); Chicago, Art Institute, 1916, no. 91 (as *The Spinner* and assumed to be no. 18); New York, Metropolitan Museum of Art, 1917, no. 22; Washington, DC, National Gallery of Art, 1961, no. 29; Worcester, Art Museum, 1976, no. 34.

Literature: G. W. E. [George W. Eggers] 1930, p.88, ill. p.89; Goodrich 1933, p.172, no. 121; Hendricks 1974, ill. p.329, no. 142; Goodrich 1982, vol.I, ill. p.160.

19
A May Morning in the Park
(The Fairman Rogers Four-in-Hand)
1879–1880
Oil on canvas, 60.3 × 91.4 (23¾ × 36)
Signed at l., on bridge masonry: *Eakins./79*

Philadelphia Museum of Art.
Given by William Alexander Dick (30.105.1)

A May Morning in the Park (also known as
The Fairman Rogers Four-in-Hand) was commissioned in 1879 by Fairman Rogers, a Philadelphia civil engineer and coaching
enthusiast. Independently wealthy, Rogers
had devoted himself to various civic and cultural causes, including service to the Pennsylvania Academy of the Fine Arts, where he was
a member of the board and chairman of the
Committee on Instruction. He was Eakins's
ally and friend, backing the artist's teaching
innovations and curricular reforms at the
Academy.

It is natural that Rogers should have
ordered this work from Eakins — an accurate
portrayal of himself driving his friends in his

own coach – for the artist possessed a thorough knowledge of equine anatomy and motion. The two men shared a scientific outlook upon the world and undoubtedly thought the correct representation of this moving subject was a worthy goal.

Rogers owned an impressive private coach (or park drag) built in London by Barker & Co. and a team of four horses to draw it. In such a coach, Rogers would take his friends for pleasure drives or attend meets with fellow coachmen. The scene portrayed by Eakins is a drive through Philadelphia's Fairmount Park – the stone bridge and verdant landscape visible behind the coach-and-four is still there today – and it shows Rogers holding a whip, flanked by his wife, and, on the bench behind them, Mr and Mrs Franklin A. Dick (Mrs Rogers's sister) and Mr and Mrs George Gilpin (George Gilpin was Mrs Rogers's brother). At the rear are seated two African-American grooms.

Starting in the late spring of 1879 and possibly working through May 1880, Eakins made oil sketches for various parts of the painting – heads of the riders, the landscape, and the coach-and-four. Rogers invited him to come to his summer home at Newport, Rhode Island, in order to make further studies. During the first of his visits, Eakins had the coach driven past him again and again on Shore Drive to study its movement. From this effort came an oil sketch (fig.19a) that captures the placement of the horses' legs with startling accuracy, as no other artist had ever presented them before.

Six or seven years before Eakins began to plan this picture, the English-born photographer Eadweard Muybridge was working in Palo Alto, California, for ex-governor Leland Stanford, who is said to have made a bet that, at one point in the trotting gait, a horse had all four feet off the ground at once. To settle the matter, Stanford hired Muybridge to take instantaneous photographs of his horse 'Occident'; these proved him correct. Stanford became so interested in Muybridge's method that he employed him to carry out large-scale photographic investigations at his horse farm between 1877 and 1879. Muybridge lined up batteries of twelve or twenty-four cameras and fired them off in a rapid succession as the horse ran down the track. With this method, Muybridge produced the first successful serial photographs of a rapidly moving horse in June 1878.

In that year, some of these images were published in widely-read American and European periodicals and immediately attracted the attention of horsemen, artists, and scientists. Rogers and Eakins were among those who took notice. Eakins, who must have been frustrated by trying to decode the mystery of the movement of the horses' legs, undoubtedly welcomed Muybridge's ingenious solution. In an article published in *The Art Interchange* on 9 July 1879, Rogers stated that 'shortly after the appearance of the [Muybridge] photographs, Mr Thomas Eakins ... took them up for examination'.[1] Close scrutiny of Eakins's paintings (the finished work and the Newport study) and the sculptural studies he made for them reveals his knowledge of Muybridge's sequential photographs. A high degree of correspondence will be found if one compares Eakins's four sculptures of Rogers's team which undoubtedly served as 'models' from which he painted (fig.19b); and Muybridge's photographs of the horse in the trotting gait (fig.19c).

A May Morning in the Park exists in time present. But recently discovered drawings[2] by Eakins in the Charles Bregler collection, now in the Pennsylvania Academy of the Fine Arts, show that Eakins had thought of giving the painting an historical dimension. One of the drawings testifies that Eakins had the idea of introducing a rider on a horse at the left, moving toward the four-in-hand, and a man walking with a knapsack at the right. In the middle distance there is a Conestoga wagon (horse-drawn canvas-covered wagon), and further behind is a sketchy indication of a hilly landscape. Another drawing presents the subject much as it appears in the final work but includes small marginal sketches of a horse and rider, a man with a pole, two men in a

Fig.19a
Sketch for 'A May Morning in the Park'
1879
Oil on wood, 26.7 × 37.5 (10½ × 14¾)
Philadelphia Museum of Art.
Gift of Mrs Thomas Eakins and
Miss Mary Adeline Williams

skiff, and a sailboat, together with rough sketches of locomotives (these engines, old and new, were the subject of additional drawings by Eakins). In all likelihood, discussions between Rogers and Eakins had led to the artist's effort to place coaching in historical perspective. But the experiment failed, no doubt because references to past eras, except in a few nostalgic figure pieces, were so alien to Eakins's artistic temperament. As it turned out, Eakins satisfied himself (and presumably Rogers) by returning to a single moment in the present.

Aside from its technical-photographic 'thesis', *A May Morning in the Park* remains a satisfying work of art. It functions not only as a problem-solving painting but also as a group portrait, a faithful record of Fairman Rogers and his friends enjoying a challenging equestrian activity. It is, too, a social document of that avocation, enjoyed then as now by a select few. The prescribed rituals of coaching, outlined in Rogers's own definitive manual on that subject, published in 1899, survive relatively unchanged, and Rogers remains a model and hero to enthusiasts of the sport today.[3]
WIH

1. Rogers 1879, p.2.
2. Two of the principal drawings under discussion are reproduced in Homer 1992, pp.110, 113.
3. I am indebted to Donald J. Rosato, MD, who shared his extensive knowledge of coaching with me and thus enriched this essay.

Provenance: Commissioned by Fairman Rogers and given to the Museum by his grandson, William Alexander Dick, 1930.

Exhibitions: Philadelphia, Pennsylvania Academy of the Fine Arts, 1880, no. 349; New York, National Academy of Design, 1881, no. 645; New York, Metropolitan Museum of Art, 1917, no. 16; Philadelphia, Pennsylvania Academy of the Fine Arts, 1917, no. 61; Philadelphia, Pennsylvania Museum of Art, 1930, no. 71; Philadelphia, Museum of Art, 1944, no. 38; Washington, DC, National Gallery of Art, 1961, no. 37; New York, Whitney Museum of American Art, 1970, no. 31; Philadelphia, Museum of Art, 1982 (1), no. 61; Philadelphia, Pennsylvania Academy of the Fine Arts, 1991, no cat. no.

Literature: Strahan 1880, p.6, ill. p.7; Marceau 1931, pp.20–5, ill. p.20; Goodrich 1933, pp.65–6, ill. pl.20; Homer and Talbot 1963, pp.194–216, ill. p.200; Hendricks 1965, pp.48–64, ill. p.48; Schendler 1967, pp.73–4, ill. pl.30; Hendricks 1974, pp.115, 118–20, 342, ill. pls.26–7; Siegl 1978. p.81, ill. pl.35; Goodrich 1982, vol.I, pp.264–8, ill. pls. 132–3; Johns 1983 (1), pp.47n, 164n; Homer 1992, pp.108–13, ill. pl.99.

Fig.19b
Trotting Horses: Models for 'A May Morning in the Park'
1879 (cast 1946)
Bronze, marble base, each 26 (10$\frac{1}{4}$) high
Mr and Mrs Paul Mellon, Upperville, Virginia

Fig.19c
Eadweard Muybridge,
Photograph of 'Edgington' Trotting
c.1878
Photograph
Free Library of Philadelphia

20

The Poleman in the Ma'sh

*c.*1881

Brown wash heightened with white over
graphite, and black chalk on paper,
27.9 × 14.9 (11 × 5⅞)
Inscribed at top in black chalk: *On block*
3½ × 4½/The Poleman/In the Ma'sh; on verso
in letterpress: *This picture is presented*
to/A. W. Drake [name inscribed in pen and
brown ink]/*by THE CENTURY*
CO.,.........18./ It has been engraved, published,
and/copyrighted by THE CENTURY
CO.,/NEW YORK, and must not be repro/
duced or published without consent; also
inscribed on verso in black chalk: *by Thomas*
Eakin [sic], and stamped: *JSH* [in ligature].

National Gallery of Art, Washington, Julius
S. Held Collection, Avalon Fund (1984.3.9)

During the years 1878–1881 Eakins produced
several illustrations for popular American
magazines. This was the only occasion during
his career when he worked as an illustrator,
and the results were not generally among his
most memorable achievements. This small
drawing is, however, an exception, for one
would be hard pressed to find another work of
such small scale in all of late nineteenth-
century American art that achieves as much
presence and monumentality.

The Poleman in the Ma'sh was one of a pair
of drawings commissioned from Eakins to
accompany an article entitled 'A Day in the
Ma'sh', which appeared in *Scribner's Monthly*
magazine in July 1881.[1] The second, published
with the caption 'Rail Shooting' (fig.20a),
reproduced the central portion of his 1876
painting *Will Schuster and Blackman Going*

Shooting (no. 16). *The Poleman*, published as
'A Pusher', was derived from a figure in the
painting *Pushing for Rail* of 1874 (fig. 16a). 'A
Day in the Ma'sh' described the landscape and
inhabitants of 'The Neck', a marshy area south
of Philadelphia bordered by the Delaware
River. According to the author, Maurice F.
Egan, The Neck was not often frequented by
'fashionable Philadelphians', being 'celebrated
for its cabbages, its pigs, its dogs, its dikes, its
reed-birds, its inhabitants, and, above all, for
its smells'.[2]

The 'Ma'sh', so-called following local pro-
nunciation of the word 'marsh', was an
expanse of low-lying land along the Delaware
punctuated with dikes, banks, and vast stands
of tall reeds. Most of the inhabitants of the
firmer areas of The Neck lived on small truck
farms (farms producing vegetables for
market), while many in the Ma'sh made their
home on picturesque canal boats known as
'Rudder Granges'.[3] There was also a group of
small boat houses where Philadelphia sportsmen kept skiffs and hunting boats. In the fall,
when the reeds turned golden and rails and
reed-birds congregated in great numbers, the
Ma'sh would be dotted with boats and hunters
and the air would be filled with the sounds of
gunshots.

Eakins knew the Ma'sh well, and he also
knew the intricacies of hunting its elusive
fowl. During the 1870s he executed a series of
paintings, including *The Artist and His Father*
Hunting Reed-birds (*c.*1874, Virginia
Museum, Richmond), *Starting Out After Rail*
(1874, Museum of Fine Arts, Boston), *Pushing*
for Rail (fig.16a), and *Will Schuster and*
Blackman Going Shooting (no. 16) that
detailed various episodes of rail hunting. The
quarry, the clapper rail, was a hen-like bird
best hunted at high tide, when the flooded
marsh offered fewer hiding places and a flat-
bottomed skiff could be poled over and among
the reeds.[4] Eakins himself provided a detailed
description of the hunt in an 1874 letter to
Gérôme about *Pushing for Rail* (see also
no. 16):

The first [painting] represents a delightful hunt in
my country, a hunt arranged so that one arrives at
the edge of the marsh two or three hours before
the height of the tide. As soon as the water is high
enough for the boat to be floated on the marsh,
the men get up and begin the hunt. The pusher
gets up on the deck and the hunter takes a
position in the middle of the boat... The pusher
pushes the boat among the reeds. The hunter kills
the birds which take wing... The pusher always
cries out on seeing birds, for... it is he who sees
first because of the more elevated position of the
deck... When a bird is killed, the hunter fires his
gun if he is going to discharge his second barrel

and then the pusher, having well in mind the place where the bird fell, goes there and picks up the dead birds by means of his net. Sometimes in going to see the dead bird, he sees a number of birds take wing and there will finally be a dozen dead birds shot down before the pusher can reclaim one...It is principally in recalling well the exact locations...after just one turn of the head that the good pushers distinguish themselves.[5]

Clearly then, the role of the pusher, or poleman, was to Eakins of central importance in the sport. In his oil *Pushing for Rail* he took pains to show the pushers in the three positions that typified their role in the hunt: at the left the pusher stands relaxed with his pole upright while the gunner reloads; in the middle the pusher leans heavily against the pole to propel the boat forward while the gunner waits with his gun ready; and at the right the pusher struggles to steady the boat so the gunner can get off a shot at the rail rising at the far left.[6] The difficulties of the task were obvious. Manipulating a pole some twelve to fifteen feet long required considerable strength, guiding the boat required expert skill, spotting the birds required sharp eyesight, and finding the fallen prey required a keen memory. Eakins surely appreciated these qualities. Not only had he hunted rail himself, he had also served as a pusher, and that is how he chose to depict himself in *The Artist and His Father Hunting Reed-birds*.

This poleman was, then, precisely the sort of man that Eakins admired and deemed worthy of depiction in his art. Although we do not know his name, the incisiveness of Eakins's portrayal makes it clear he was an actual individual, not a generalized type.[7] By isolating the figure and omitting the details of the hunt, Eakins forces us to encounter this man directly as another human being. He stands confidently before our eyes as the very embodiment of relaxed energy and grace, a nineteenth-century equivalent of the antique *Doryphoros* (spear bearer). The comparison is not far-fetched, for Eakins greatly admired ancient sculpture, even though he had no patience for the endless copying from casts that was the routine in academic instruction.[8] As he told his students: 'The Greeks did not study the antique...[they] modeled from life, undoubtedly. And nature is just as varied and just as beautiful in our day as she was in the time of Phidias'.[9] Pointing to a cast in the Pennsylvania Academy collection he observed: 'You doubt if any such men as that Myron statue in the hall exist now, even if they ever existed? Well, they must have existed once or Myron would never have made that, you may be sure. And they do

now'.[10] Such men most certainly did exist for Eakins, and they were for him the very mainstay of his art. And whether he found them teaching in hospital operating rooms, rowing on the Schuylkill River, or poling a simple flat-bottomed boat across the waters of a marsh, Eakins time and time again in his art paid moving homage to their dignity, their strength, and their intelligence.

FK

1. For a discussion of this article and of Eakins's work as an illustrator generally, see Parry and Chamberlin-Hellman 1973. The other illustrations were supplied by Joseph Pennell and Harry R. Poore. A. W. Drake, whose name appears on the verso of this drawing, was the art editor of *Scribner's*; it was presumably he who made the notations at the top of the sheet, the erasure of the top of the pole, and the folds. His purpose was to fit the image into a window of text in the article and maximize the use of the page. Eakins's drawing – or, more precisely, the portion of it below the erasure – was transferred photographically to a wood block using a process that allowed the image to appear without reversal.
2. Egan 1881, p.343. Although now greatly changed by the spread of industry and pollution (both of which had already begun to affect The Neck in Eakins's day) and criss-crossed with interstate highways, the area is still predominantly marshy.
3. Ibid., p.350.
4. See the descriptions of the sport in ibid., p.352 and in Goodrich 1982, vol. I, p.90.
5. Quoted in McHenry 1946, p.39.
6. Parry and Chamberlin-Hellman op.cit., p.40, have noted this narrative progression, which Spassky 1985, p.597, considers a means of unifying the three distinct pairs of figures pictorially.
7. Parry and Chamberlin-Hellman op. cit., p.42. This same man also appears as the unnamed 'Blackman' in *Will Schuster and Blackman Going Shooting* (no. 16) and in *Rail Shooting from a Punt* (fig.20a). Although it has been observed with good

reason that this failure to identify the man except in terms of his race 'provides pointed perspective' on the prejudices of the day (McElroy 1990, p.85), Eakins did name several other black men who appear in works of this same time (see Goodrich 1982, vol.I, p.94).
8. Goodrich op. cit., vol.I, p.173.
9. Quoted in Brownell 1879, p.742.
10. Ibid. Although Eakins further observed that 'our business is to do something exclusively for ourselves, not to copy Phidias', he did on several occasions pose figures in his works in ways that strongly recall antique sculptures. Perhaps the most obvious instance of this is the pediment-like arrangement of the figures in *The Swimming Hole* (c.1883–1885, Amon Carter Museum, Fort Worth, Texas; fig.8).

Provenance: Commissioned by *Scribner's Monthly*, c.1881; Alexander W. Drake, New York; Berry-Hill Galleries, New York; purchased by Julius S. Held, 9 June 1966; National Gallery of Art, 1984.

Exhibitions: New York, State University Art Gallery, 1970; no. 5, Hartford, Connecticut, Wadsworth Atheneum, 1973, no. 65; Williamstown, Massachusetts, Clark Art Institute, 1979, no. 51: Washington, Corcoran Gallery of Art, 1990, no cat. no.

Literature: Egan 1881, p.348 (reproductive engraving); Goodrich 1933, p.174; McHenry 1946, p.38; Parry and Chamberlin-Hellman 1973, pp.42–4, ill. fig.29, p.44; Robinson 1973, pp.144–5, no. 65, ill. p.145; Hendricks 1974, p.147; Parry 1974, pp.150–2, ill. fig. 104, p.149; Giles, Milroy and Owens 1979, no. 51, pp.63–4, ill. fig.51; Spassky *et al.* 1985, vol.II, pp.595, 597, ill. p.596; McElroy 1990, p.86, ill.

Fig.20a
Rail Shooting from a Punt
Wash drawing, 22.5 × 31 ($8\frac{7}{8} \times 12\frac{3}{16}$)
Yale University Art Gallery,
The Mabel Brady Garvan Collection

21
The Pathetic Song

1881
Oil on canvas, 114.3 × 82.6 (45 × 32½)
Signed and dated l.l.: *Eakins, 1881*

The Corcoran Gallery of Art, Washington,
DC, Museum Purchase, Gallery Fund (19.26)

Fig.21a
*Margaret Harrison posing for
'The Pathetic Song'*
1881
Bromide print from dry plate negative,
10.2 × 12.7 (4 × 5)
The Pennsylvania Academy of the Fine Arts,
Philadelphia. Charles Bregler's Thomas Eakins
Collection. Purchased with the partial support
of the Pew Memorial Trust

The Pathetic Song was Eakins's last and most ambitious interior genre scene. Following a period during the mid-1870s in which he painted women performing household tasks of the colonial era and wearing period attire (see no. 18), Eakins returned to images of contemporary life.

Early in his career Eakins expressed a deep love of music and regard for its performers. His own household was the scene of many musical gatherings, and provided the background for his early portraits of his sisters (see no. 7). He subscribed to the common belief of the era that the ability to sing or play an instrument was an admirable skill. Singing conveyed pure emotion and women, by the purity and virtuousness of their nature, were thought to possess the most ideal singing instrument.[1] *The Pathetic Song* is the first time in Eakins's *oeuvre* that a woman demonstrating her skill is presented as the hero of the painting. Due to the sheer physical nature of singing, the subject is in many ways the female complement to the theme of rowing which Eakins explored (see no. 10). Through his depiction he convincingly translates an auditory experience into a visual one.

Set in a Victorian parlour, the scene of many recitals during the latter part of the nineteenth century, Eakins focuses on the vitality of the young woman, Margaret Alexina Harrison who was a student of his. Unlike other painters of this period whose depictions of women tended towards idealism, Eakins never glamorized his subjects. Instead, they expressed an inner strength and a strong sense of their own individuality. Holding the sheet music at waist level, and looking up, Margaret reveals her mastery of the composition and her total identification with the emotional content of the song. The tendons in her neck visibly show the physical demands of singing. In the shadowed background to the right Susan Macdowell, Eakins's student and future wife, plays the piano while she listens intently to the singer, sensitive to her artistic interpretations. To the left is C.F. Stolte, a cellist and long-standing member of the Philadelphia Orchestra, who is fully immersed in his task. The crisp, clear, and solid handling of Margaret Harrison's elaborate lavender dress contrasts with the soft and refined modelling of her face and hands. Each crinkled fold and scalloped detail of her sleeve is precisely rendered while the features of her face and hands are less rigidly, but nonetheless strongly, defined.

Compared to this salient relief of the singer, the two accompanists in the background are relatively insubstantial, their essence captured but their details suppressed. The subdued quality of the touches of colour which can be seen in the carved picture frame, the oriental rug, and the blue-green floriated vase on the mantelpiece reinforce the sombre moment. The pyramidal grouping of the figures, with their advancing and receding profiles, implies an unmoving and trancelike state. The entire image is unified by the broad brushstrokes, the mottled green wallpaper, and by the sense of communal concentration and effort that is being portrayed. Eakins's depiction is powerful yet there is also an undercurrent of deep, restrained feeling. This painting and *The Artist's Wife and His Setter Dog* (no. 22) show a profound exploration of consciousness in Eakins's work that attained its height of expression in the portraits of the early 1890s.

Eakins's belief that music was a vehicle through which anyone could find spiritual peace and form communal bonds was again explored by him in 1887 in his series of the cowboy singing. In *Home Ranch* (fig.46a), like *The Pathetic Song*, the cowboy is in an interior setting. He sits in the ranch kitchen, instead of a parlour, while a companion seated at a nearby table listens to his impassioned songs of loneliness.

While it has been thought that the recital shown here took place at 1729 Mount Vernon Street,[2] a series of ten photographs, taken sometime between late 1880 and early 1881, reveal that the recital did not necessarily take place, and that Eakins in fact reconstructed the scene in his studio. The photographs provide fascinating information about Eakins's working process, and illuminate Eakins's conception for *The Pathetic Song*.

The photographs are studies of Margaret Harrison, clothed in the extravagant dress that she wears in the painting, in identical or nearly identical poses to that of the finished oil. In addition, among these photographs are full-length, three-quarter-length, and head-and-shoulders poses that seem to show that Eakins not only took the photographs with the intent of using them as studies for paintings, but also intended them to be portraits in their own right. It is quite possible that this was his first foray into the realm of portrait photography, a theme he would pursue and fully develop during the 1880s and 1890s.[3]

Of the full-length studies it appears that they were taken during two separate sittings. In all of them, Margaret stands, music in hand, to the left side of the desk which serves as a piano. In one set Eakins's cluttered and disarrayed studio is clearly visible, while in the other he apparently had cleared the space of extraneous objects. In the right hand corner of the photographs of the second group, the

actual oil painting *The Pathetic Song* is visible (fig.21a), and serves as a document to Eakins's painting methods. The nearly completed figure of Margaret has already been placed on the canvas, and is set against a mottled background which appears to mimic the wallpaper of Eakins's studio. The figures of Stolte and Susan were conceived separately and added as subsidiary elements at a later time. A perspective drawing of the painting further supports this view, as it mathematically calculates Margaret's positioning on the canvas, and sets the form of the piano in a geometric space, but excludes the other two figures.

The photographs also answer the question of the source of the late afternoon light that flows from the left of the canvas, illuminating Margaret's right side. It is actually Eakins's studio window, its light manipulated in the oil painting to fall on the primary figure. By physically separating the singer from the rest of the group and casting her in a luminous light, Eakins places her in a spiritual realm, and suggests the isolation of the solo performer.

The photographic images were taken during the painting process, which suggests that Eakins used them primarily as memoranda after the model had left. In addition, since there is practically no variance between the photographic studies, it appears that these were not taken as explorations to determine the eventual pose of the singer. Eakins knew exactly what he wanted before he began painting. In one of the photographs, Eakins cropped off Margaret's lower legs and the top of the head, intending the photograph as a study for the ill-fitting bodice and skirt of the richly textured dress. It is evident from Margaret's relaxed downward tilt of her head and closed mouth in the photograph that she was aware of Eakins's intentions. Another photograph is arresting because of Margaret's direct yet sensuous gaze. Such involved and deliberate studies help to explain Eakins's profound mastery in portraying both character and inanimate details with *trompe l'œil* accuracy.

The painting was first exhibited as *Singing a Pathetic Song* at the fourth Annual Exhibition of the Society of American Artists on 23 October 1881.[4] The 'pathetic' song was a particular type, expressing a poignant tale of loss or regret, that had gained in popularity during the 1860s and 1870s. Eakins had been commissioned by the director of the Pennsylvania Academy of the Fine Arts at the time, Edward Horner Coates, to paint *The Swimming Hole*. Upon seeing the completed work, however, Coates was so taken aback by its flagrant

nudity that he bought *The Pathetic Song* instead. A watercolour version of the larger oil was done in 1881, and was given to Margaret for her assistance in modelling.[5]

BSB

1. See Johns 1983 (1), p.126.
2. Goodrich 1982, vol.II, p.83.
3. It has not yet been definitely ascertained which photographs are studies and which portraits; some may have been used as both.
4. Johns op. cit., p.134.
5. *The Metropolitan Museum of Art Bulletin*, vol.40, spring 1980.

Provenance: Edward Horner Coates from the artist, 1885; Gallery Fund Purchase, 1919.

Exhibitions: New York, Society of American Artists, 1881, no. 21; Washington, DC National Gallery of Art, 1961, no. 40; New York, Brooklyn Museum, 1967, no. 82; New York, Metropolitan Museum of Art, 1970, no. 156; New York, Whitney Museum of American Art, 1970, no. 37; New York, Whitney Museum of American Art, 1974, no. 109; Washington, DC, Corcoran Gallery of Art, 1981, no. 21.

Literature: Hendricks 1974, pp.169–170, ill. pl.30; Schendler 1967, pp.86–7, ill. p.85.; Johns 1983 (1), pp.133–6, ill. f.93.; Goodrich 1982, vol.I, pp.201–6, ill. p.204.; Homer 1992, pp.117–120, ill. p.119.

22
The Artist's Wife and His Setter Dog
Oil on canvas, 76.2 × 58.4 (30 × 23)
Unsigned and undated

The Metropolitan Museum of Art, New York.
Fletcher Fund, 1923 (23.139)

Susan Eakins (1851–1938), born Susan Hannah Macdowell, married the artist, who was seven years her senior, on 19 January 1884.[1] Her father, a well-known Philadelphia engraver, had encouraged her interest in art and her studies at the Pennsylvania Academy, where she worked from 1876 to 1879 with Christian Schussele and from 1876 to 1883 with Eakins. Between 1876 and 1882 she showed paintings in six of the Academy's annual exhibitions and won prizes in two of them. Although Eakins deemed her one of his most promising pupils, she gave up her career after their marriage, dedicating herself to assisting his work. During her widowhood she sought to enhance his reputation by arranging loan exhibitions, encouraging biographers, and placing his paintings (including this one) in major collections.

Eakins probably began this portrait shortly after their marriage, re-using a canvas on which, X-rays reveal, he had made and abandoned a study of a woman's head. The result is unusual in scale for Eakins, who much more often painted portraits at life size. The artist's wife, a slender woman of thirty-three when work on the portrait began, is shown seated in three-quarter view to the left, her body slumped and her head slightly inclined. She wears an old-fashioned high-waisted dress of light-blue silk with deep lace cuffs. On her extended right foot is a fuzzy bright scarlet stocking and a soft black slipper. Her direct gaze at the viewer is uncompromising. Glaring light from the overhead studio skylight casts her gaunt features into relief and mercilessly reveals her sunken chest, careless topknot, and the rings under her red-rimmed eyes. She seems melancholic, neurasthenic.

Mrs Eakins sits in a chair in the mid-eighteenth-century Philadelphia Queen Anne style. She holds in her lap an open book of Japanese art, probably by Hiroshige, resting on its edge her large, ruddy left hand, palm up, enervated, a metaphor for her entire body. Dozing at her feet lies Harry, the dark red setter dog that Eakins had inherited from his sister Margaret in 1882. The locale is Eakins's studio at 1330 Chestnut Street, where he and his bride lived until July 1886. On the wall to the right of a red-flecked ochre drapery hangs Eakins's 1883 plaster relief *Arcadia*, an homage to the Parthenon frieze.[2] Unidentified paintings hang on the back wall over a brown secretary desk; one is a study of a woman knitting or crocheting similar to the figure of the chaperone in Eakins's *William Rush Carving His Allegorical Figure of the Schuylkill River* (no. 17).

The portrait echoes popular late nineteenth-century formulas for images of women: the lady at leisure, the aesthetic female. But it is also by far one of Eakins's most personal images, containing autobiographical elements and reflecting key aspects of his work and career. For example, *The Artist's Wife and His Setter Dog* recalls Eakins's training, taking up the theme of the artist's studio that attracted his Beaux-Arts teacher, Jean-Léon Gérôme.[3] Eakins had explored the theme in the Rush series, of which we are reminded by the painting of the woman on the back wall and by Susan Eakins's old-fashioned dress. The dress also recalls Eakins's use of old costumes in other post-Centennial paintings and sculptures (see no. 18). The *Arcadia* relief, too, refers to Eakins's earlier work, bespeaks his competence as a sculptor, and documents his appreciation of ancient Greece as the wellspring of art.[4] The breadth of Eakins's interests is announced by the Japanese book which, eastern and contemporary, balances the western, quasi-antique relief. The dialogue between western and eastern is reiterated by the juxtaposition of the Queen Anne chair – which also locates the studio in Philadelphia – with the ruby-red oriental carpet.

The Artist's Wife and His Setter Dog is the culmination of a series of images by Eakins of female models with animals.[5] The portrait also owes a considerable debt to a painting of 1878 by Susan Eakins that depicts her father, William H. Macdowell, in the family parlour with a dog at his feet.[6] Shown at the Pennsylvania Academy annual exhibition in 1879 and reproduced in an article on the art schools of Philadelphia in the same year, it was certainly known to Eakins.[7] By reiterating it, Eakins seems to suggest that, having taken a wife, he will adopt her art too. That Mrs Eakins wears the costume of a studio model rather than ordinary dress similarly diminishes her independent identity as an artist. The pattern of her complaisance – signalled as well by her passive pose – was being established; much later, in 1899, the former artist told her diary: 'I try on rich stuffs to tempt Tom to paint'.[8]

That Eakins's ego subsumed his wife's is also implied by the technical evolution of the portrait. A photogravure of it reproduced in October 1886 in *The Book of American Figure Painters* (Philadelphia: J.B. Lippincott) reveals a younger and healthier woman than appears on the canvas (fig.22a). Before and after publication of the photogravure Eakins reworked the portrait. Autoradiographs reveal that he painted over Mrs Eakins's face and made other changes, tinkering with the portrait perhaps as

late as 1889. It is probably no coincidence that Eakins's alterations to the portrait occurred while he was experiencing a crisis at the Pennsylvania Academy. Taking an image that was emblematic of his work as a teacher – a portrayal of a star pupil who began to study just after he began to teach – he seems to have projected onto it his own difficulties and disappointments. The portrait of *The Artist's Wife and His Setter Dog* is, thus, in great measure a portrait of the artist himself.

HBW

1. Indispensable sources for this essay are Spassky *et al.*, 1985, pp.613–19; Parry 1979, pp.146–53; Cheryl Leibold, 'The Life and Papers of Susan Macdowell Eakins', in Foster and Leibold 1989, pp.259–68.
2. For an account of the extant and recorded plaster and bronze reliefs of arcadia see Rosenzweig 1977, p.111.
3. Even anti-academic French painters such as Gustave Courbert and Camille Corot investigated the theme of the studio interior, and Eakins's compatriot, William Merritt Chase, similarly resistant to Beaux-Arts standards, would make the theme a speciality beginning in the 1880s.
4. While the musical subject of *Arcadia* (which includes a devoted dog gazing up at the music maker) may refer to Susan Eakins's actual accomplishments as a pianist – she had also posed for the pianist in *The Pathetic Song* (no. 21) – that function in the portrait seems secondary.
5. Early examples are *Elizabeth Crowell and Her Dog* (*c*.1871–1872; San Diego Museum of Art); *Kathrin* (no. 8). Apparent studies for *The Artist's Wife and His Setter Dog* are an albumen print of a women in a laced-bodice dress with a setter dog at her feet (*c*.1883; Pennsylvania Academy of the Fine Arts, Philadelphia); and an oil sketch entitled *In the Studio – Girl and Dog* (*c*.1884; Hyde Collection, Glens Falls, New York).
6. Entitled *Portrait of Gentleman and Dog* (1878, Collection of Mary Macdowell Walters, Roanoke, Virginia), illustrated in Casteras 1973, p.9. See also Sellin 1977 for this and other related works by Susan Eakins.
7. The painting was reproduced in a wood engraving by Alice Barber in Brownell 1879, p.745.
8. Susan Macdowell Eakins diary entry, 16 February 1899, quoted in Foster and Leibold op. cit., p.265.

Provenance: William Macdowell; Mrs Thomas
Eakins; bought 1923.

Exhibitions: New York, Society of American
Artists, 1887, no. 53; Chicago, Art Institute, 1889,
no. 112; New York, Society of American Artists,
1892, no. 115; New York, Brooklyn Museum, 1915,
no. 34; New York, Metropolitan Museum of Art,
1939, no. 256; Chicago, Art Institute, 1939, no. 52;
Philadelphia, Museum of Art, 1944, no. 52; New
York, M. Knoedler & Co., 1944, no. 38; Pittsburgh,
Carnegie Institute, 1945, no. 17; Washington, DC,
Corcoran Gallery of Art, 1969, no. 14; New York,
Whitney Museum of American Art, 1970, no. 45;
Philadelphia, Museum of Art, 1982 (1), no. 134.

Literature: T. Eakins's account book 10 September
1886, p.108; Van Rensselaer 1886, ill. pl.[24];
MMA Bulletin, 18 December 1923, ill. p.281;
Goodrich 1933, p.96; McHenry 1946, pp.41, 58–9,
70, 111; Baldinger 1946, p.212, figs.1 and 2,
pp.218, 221, 223–4, 225; Schendler 1967, pp.87, 88,
89, 120, 172, fig.39; Hendricks 1974, pp.128–9,
pl.32, pp.174, 284, 332, p.334; Rosenzweig 1977,
pp.94, 95, 96, 111, 168; Siegl 1978, pp.27, 107, 113,
137, 156–7; Wilmerding 1979, p.108, pl.109,
pp.111, 112; Chamberlin-Hellman 1979, p.137;
Dinnerstein 1979, p.142; Parry 1979, p.146, fig.1,
p.147, fig.2, pp.146–52; Goodrich 1982, vol.I,
pp.224, 226, 330–1, no. 224, vol.II, p.165, 167, 256,
274, 278; Johns 1983 (1), p.130; Spassky 1985,
pp.613–19; Foster and Leibold 1989, p.88; Homer
1992, pp.117, 120, 126–7.

Fig.22a
The Artist's Wife and His Setter Dog
*c.*1884–1886
Photogravure, reproduced in Mariana Griswold
van Rensselaer, *The Book of American Figure
Painters*, 1886

23

Walt Whitman

1887–1888

Oil on canvas, 76.5 × 61.6 ($30\frac{1}{8}$ × $24\frac{1}{4}$)

Signed and incorrectly dated t.r.: *Eakins/1887;*
inscription on verso: *Walt Whitman Painting
from Life by Thomas Eakins 1897/1887*

Pennsylvania Academy of the Fine Arts,
Philadelphia. General Fund (1917.1)

Walt Whitman (1819–1892) began *Leaves of Grass*, his great book of poems, by proclaiming: 'I celebrate myself'. Soon after its publication in 1855, he found himself surrounded by admirers. Like a cult figure, he became a popular subject for many nineteenth-century photographers, painters, and sculptors. Despite the numerous images of the poet that were produced, the portrait by Thomas Eakins was held in special esteem by Whitman: 'I do not see how anyone can doubt but it is a masterly piece of work'.[1] To him, it was 'strong, rugged, even daring'.[2] Although Whitman did have some initial reservations, his appreciation of Eakins became so consummate that he could forcefully assert: 'All that Eakins does has the mark of genius'.[3]

No exact date is known for when Eakins may have first met Whitman, but it seems most likely that the two were introduced by Talcott Williams (1849–1929), an editor at the *Philadelphia Press*. In the fall of 1887 after Eakins's return from the Dakota Territory, Williams brought the painter to Whitman's house at 228 Mickle Street in Camden, New Jersey, only a couple of kilometres across the Delaware River from Philadelphia. Whitman later recalled that 'He came over with Talcott Williams: seemed careless, negligent, indifferent, quiet: you would not say retiring, but amounting to that'.[4] After this initial meeting, Eakins made many visits to the poet's Mickle Street home. By the later 1880s, Whitman's house had become a virtual pilgrimage destination for Philadelphia's intelligentsia. However, it is surprising that the two had not met earlier since Whitman moved to Camden in 1873 and Eakins had been living in nearby Philadelphia.

Until his death in 1892, Whitman maintained a close friendship with Eakins, whom he believed was not just a painter but 'a force'.[5] In spite of their career differences, the two men had much in common.[6] As early as 1883, Eakins painted *The Swimming Hole* (fig.8), a bold, direct representation of nude male bathers that comes very close to the spirit of companionship advocated in Whitman's poetry, yet the canvas predates their meeting by four years.

Less than a month after what was undoubtedly their initial meeting, Eakins returned to the poet's home to begin the portrait. Whitman recalled that he 'turned up again – came alone: carried a black [possible typographical error that should read blank] canvas under his arm: said he had understood I was willing he should paint me... so he set to: painted like a fury'.[7] The commencement of

the portrait sittings may not have been so unexpected and unplanned. An appointment was conceivably made, for Whitman had written in a letter dated 19 November 1887: 'Mr Eakins the portrait painter, of Phila:, is going to have a whack at me next week'.[8] The poet remembered: 'After that he came often – at intervals, for short sketches'.[9] Between late November 1887 and April 1888, there are numerous references in Whitman's papers to Eakins's visits to work on the canvas in Camden: 'He would spend from half an hour to an hour – and he was a man good to have around – possessed of marked peculiarities'.[10] On 15 April 1888 Whitman acknowledged: 'It is about finished'.[11]

Whitman never committed to print any of his views about Eakins's art. His thoughts about the painter and the portrait are only known from private comments, which certainly do reveal enormous respect for the Philadelphia artist. On the other hand, there are no direct comments by Eakins concerning his feelings about Whitman. The most often quoted remark attributed to the painter was recalled by Weda Cook Addicks, who posed for *The Concert Singer* (no. 26); she supposedly remembered Eakins saying 'Whitman never makes a mistake'.[12] His penetrating portrait is perhaps the artist's most genuine tribute to the Camden resident. At the poet's seventy-second birthday party, Eakins reminisced about working on the painting: 'I began in the usual way, but soon found that the ordinary methods wouldn't do – that technique, rules, and traditions would have to be thrown aside; that, before all else, he was to be treated as a *man*'.[13]

His tribute is underscored by an attitudinal frame of reference. In 1889 at his mid-career, Eakins painted *The Agnew Clinic* (see no. 36), a medical group portrait that depicts a mastectomy, which the directors of the Academy felt was 'not cheerful for ladies to look at'. *The Agnew Clinic* was the most significant commissioned work painted by Eakins during the time of his friendship with Whitman. On one level, it is a portrait of a celebrated Philadelphia surgeon and his students. On the other hand, this canvas may be an image of tribute to his friend from Camden. In 'In Paths Untrodden', Whitman proclaimed that he was 'Resolved to sing no songs to-day but those of manly attachment'. In the all-male group of medical students who are viewing the operation in *The Agnew Clinic*, Eakins has arranged a few pairs that seem more than coincidental couplings, and perhaps are visual images to illustrate the homoerotic essence of Whitman's 'need of comrades'.[14]

Eakins depicts the sixty-eight-year-old poet as if he were a 'Dutch toper'.[15] Whitman is seen leaning back, wearing an open-collared shirt with lace trim, a favourite garment made by Mary Davis, his housekeeper.[16] Unlike a *portrait d'apparat*, this is a seemingly simple, straightforward representation of a contented gentleman with little attention to accessories and no interest in the setting. Whitman observed: 'The Eakins portrait gets there – ... in correct style, without feathers – without any fuss of any sort'.[17] In his unpretentious manner, the poet felt the picture was 'like sharp cold cutting true sea brine'.[18]

The paint is freely applied so that the canvas surface is visible at the lower left and upper right corners. Nonetheless, the sketch-like strokes do effectively present the thinness of Whitman's long hair and his ruddy complexion. The lighting directed from the left makes his silvery-white beard seem to glow. His eyes are open, yet they do not appear to focus. Only his left eye looks to the viewer; the right eye crosses to the left. Eakins has captured what may be a nerve palsy resulting from the poet's paralytic stroke in 1873.[19] The smaller oil sketch of Whitman at the Museum of Fine Arts in Boston (fig.23a) appears more imme-

diate. Whitman is depicted napping, and a sense of intimacy is enhanced by the close-up point of view. There is no suggestion of clothes; it is only a study of the poet's head. Whitman asserted that the oil painting 'keeps close to nature – slurs nothing – faces the worst as well as the best'.[20] For the poet, this portrait affirmed the essence of Eakins's artistic sensibility: 'insists on the truth – the utter truth – the damnablest: that the subject is not titivated, not artified, not 'improved' – but given simply as in nature'.[21]

Eakins gave the portrait to Whitman, who recalled: 'As I always understood Eakins, half of the picture is his, half mine'.[22] It remained in the poet's possession and was hung downstairs on the first floor in Whitman's home, where it was seen 'in a peculiar half-light, from the gas in the hall'.[23] In January 1891 the canvas just titled *Portrait of the Poet* was loaned to the Academy's annual exhibition by Whitman, who was listed as its sole owner. The picture then received a very positive notice in the *Philadelphia Press*, and the unidentified writer, who may have been Talcott Williams, proclaimed: 'Mr Eakins' Walt Whitman is by odds and far the best portrait yet made of an heroic figure in our letters'.[24]

After the portrait was completed in 1888, the friendship between Eakins and Whitman remained strong through the last four years of the poet's life. The artist continuously visited at the Mickle Street house and was 'always welcome – always'.[25] On 27 March 1892, the morning after Whitman died, Eakins immediately went to Camden with Samuel Murray and two assistants. For three hours, he supervised the making of a death mask and a cast of the poet's hand. Horace Traubel noted: 'Eakins threw back the shirt from the shoulders – ... They worked & worked'.[26] At the funeral on 30 March, the painter served as one of the honorary pallbearers.

Whitman's death must have been a great loss for Thomas Eakins, who had benefited not only from the friendship but from the poet's appreciation of his artistic capabilities.[27] Whitman had described Eakins: 'He is a man you would like: artistry, all that – but a *man*, too',[28] echoing Eakins's reported view of him. These two heroic figures of American culture were bonded by their mutual admiration of one another.

FBA

Fig.23a
Walt Whitman
*c.*1887
Oil on panel, 13.3 × 13.3 (5¼ × 5¼)
Museum of Fine Arts, Boston.
Helen and Alice Colburn Fund

1. Traubel, vol.6, p.470.
2. Traubel, vol.3, p.526.
3. Quoted from unpublished Traubel diaries in Homer, 'New Light on Thomas Eakins and Walt Whitman in Camden', in Sill and Tarbell, 1992, p.93. See also Traubel, vol.1, p.39, where Whitman mentioned to his close friend, Horace Traubel, as early as 15 April 1888: 'It was not at first a pleasant version to me, but the more I get to realize it the profounder seems its insight'.
4. Traubel, vol.4, p.155.
5. Traubel, vol.1, p.284.
6. See Traubel, vol.4, p.155, in which Whitman acknowledged that like himself Eakins lacked 'social gifts'. Many writers have pointed out their similarities. Blaser 1978, p.113, wrote: 'In Eakins, Whitman found an American artist with a vision akin to his own'. See also Wilmerding 1985, pp.998, 1001; Goodrich 1982, vol.II, p.28; Johns 1983 (1), pp.145–9, 151–3; Homer 1992, pp.8, 217–19; and Matthiessen 1941, pp.604–605. On p.605, Matthiessen does acknowledge that the 'divergences in the scope of their realism mark them unmistakably as belonging to different generations'. That age difference is typical of several relationships in Eakins's life, where he develops a closeness with older men rather than his own peer group. See Fried 1987, pp.38–9.
7. Traubel, vol.4, p.155.
8. Miller 1969, vol.4, p.133. The letter was sent to Leonard M. Brown, a schoolteacher and friend of the artist, Herbert Gilchrist, who had also painted a portrait of Whitman now at the University of Pennsylvania.
9. Traubel, vol.4, p.155.
10. Traubel, vol.6, p.315.
11. Traubel, vol.1, p.39. Although the painting is signed and dated, this does not seem to be the original signature. In the curatorial files at the Pennsylvania Academy of the Fine Arts, a conservation report by Dr J. Schindler dated 7 February 1944 reveals: 'The second '8' is changed – *after* cleaning a '9' under the '8' is clearly visible. The new '8' does not contain any similar medium used in the signature'. Ten years later, in another conservation report, dated 24 December 1954, Theodor Siegl noted: 'Under the name 'Eakins' too [*sic*] traces of a previous signature with the same outlines are apparent. Although it appears quite obvious that the signature and date as it appears now were added several years after the picture was painted, this does not seem sufficient proof that it was done by an other hand'. I am most grateful to both Susan Danly, formerly Curator, and Elyssa Kane, Assistant to the Registrar, at the Pennsylvania Academy for making these files available to me. I found no evidence to substantiate the statement by Johns op. cit., p.144, n.2: 'under the '7' of 1887 is a '9', which apparently had covered an earlier '7'. During this same period, Eakins also painted a small oil sketch of Whitman (fig.23a). This wood panel painting remained in Eakins's possession. When the Museum of Fine Arts at Boston purchased the painting from Eakins's pupil Samuel Murray in 1930, he wrote that it was 'a first sketch and color scheme for this large portrait now owned by Pennsylvania Academy of the Fine Arts'. (Letter dated 18 January 1930 to William Gricom, Jr. in the curatorial file at the MFA,

Boston.) Samuel Murray (1869–1941) was a student of Eakins's when he taught at the Art Students' League of Philadelphia following his resignation from the Academy. Murray became an art teacher and sculptor. He enjoyed a close friendship with Eakins, and the two shared studio space at the same time that Eakins was regularly visiting Whitman in Camden.
12. Quoted in Goodrich op. cit., vol.II, p.31.
13. Ibid., p.38. This male tribute is also reinforced by Wanda Corn, 'Postscript: Walt Whitman and the Visual Arts', in Sill and Tarbell op. cit., p.173: 'Whitman's celebrants were in the vast majority, men, not women. Eakins went to visit Whitman with his male associates, we remember, not with his wife, who was an artist, or his female students'. In a letter dated 11 September 1886 to Edward H. Coates, a member of the Pennsylvania Academy board who requested the artist's resignation, Eakins asserted: 'I do not believe that great painting or sculpture or surgery will ever be done by women'. (Quoted in Foster and Leibold 1989, p.157).
14. The prominent inclusion of a nurse is also perhaps an allusion to Whitman who cared for wounded Civil War soldiers in Washington and recalled in Traubel, vol.1 (1905), p.434, that it was the 'most nearly real work' of his life.
15. Miller op. cit., vol.4, p.157.
16. Folsom 1986–1987, p.57. Although she made many shirts for him, there are numerous photographs in which he wears this same shirt with its lace trim. Homer 1992, p.212, refers to the garment as 'the poet's trademark'.
17. Traubel, vol.1, p.153.
18. Miller op. cit., vol.4, p.160.
19. See Trent 1948, p.113–21. I am grateful to Douglas Winterich, Curator, Walt Whitman House, State Historic Site, New Jersey Division of Parks and Forestry, for bringing this article to my attention and providing me with a reprint. On p.4 of the reprint, Trent notes that Whitman did not wear eyeglasses and seems to have enjoyed 'good vision until late in life'.
20. Traubel, vol.2, p.295.
21. Traubel, vol.6, p.416.
22. Traubel, vol.7, p.413. Whitman promised his portion of ownership to Dr Richard Bucke. In 1917 the Pennsylvania Academy purchased the portrait directly from Henry Colin Pope, Dr Bucke's son-in-law. Eakins may have regarded this arrangement in a very casual manner, or Bucke possibly bought Eakins's portion. Whitman, in Traubel, vol.7, p.414, stated: 'in paying Eakins, his part, too, he may in the end own the picture outright . . . you can now witness my wish in this matter'.
23. Traubel, vol.5, p.413.
24. Quoted in Traubel, vol.7, p.444. Traubel notes that Whitman was 'pleased' by the remark and felt that the portrait 'deserves all they say about it'.
25. Traubel, vol.1, p.367.
26. Homer op. cit., p.95.
27. Schendler 1967, p.133: 'For the better part of six years following the death of Whitman, Eakins appears to have painted only fitfully'. This observation may best reflect the deep personal loss that the painter felt.
28. Traubel, vol.7, p.413.

Provenance: Given by artist to Walt Whitman; by descent to Dr Richard Maurice Bucke, London, Ontario, Canada, 1892; by descent to Jessie Clare Bucke Pope and Harry Colin Pope, Moose Jaw, Saskatchewan, Canada, 1902; Purchased by present owner from H.C. Pope, 1917.

Exhibitions: Philadelphia, Pennsylvania Academy of the Fine Arts, 1891, no. 89; New York, Metropolitan Museum of Art, 1917, no. 2; Philadelphia, Museum of Art, 1937; London, Tate Gallery, 1946, no. 72; New York, American Academy of Arts and Letters, 1954, no. 125; Madrid, National Library, 1955, no. 34; Pittsburgh, Carnegie Institute, 1957, no. 68; New York, American Academy of Arts and Letters, 1958, no. 16; Washington, DC, National Gallery of Art, 1961, no. 52; Trenton, New Jersey State Museum, 1965; New York, Whitney Museum of American Art, 1970, no. 47; Philadelphia, Museum of Art, 1982 (2).

Literature: Traubel, vol.1 (1905 [rpt. 1961]), pp.39, 41, 42, 72, 131, 153–6, 192, 199, 266, 284, 367, 387, 390, 434, ill. p.145; Traubel, vol.2 (1907 [rpt. 1961]), pp.107, 156, 289, 290, 295, 353, 409; Traubel, vol.3 (1912 [rpt. 1961]), p.526; Goodrich 1933, pp.121–4, 179, ill. pl.32 (G220); Matthiessen 1941, pp.604–10, ill. p.606; Traubel, vol.4 (1953), pp.104, 135, 136, 155–6, 227; Traubel, vol.5 (1964), pp.413–14, 499; Schendler 1967, pp.96–100, 102–4, ill. pl.41; Miller, 1969, vol.4, pp.132, 134, 135, 143, 147, 154, 157, 160, 163; Miller 1969, vol.5, pp.52, 155, 200, 208, 209; Hendricks 1974, pp.179–182, 192, ill. p.181; Rule 1974, pp.7–57, ill. p.20; Goodrich 1982, vol.II, pp.16, 28–38, 53, 167, 275, ill. p.32; Sewell 1982, p.106, no.115, ill. p.108; Traubel, vol.6 (1982), pp.174, 232, 301, 315, 416, 470; Johns 1983 (1), pp.144–9, 163, 169, ill. pl.13; Wilmerding 1985, pp.996–1003, ill. p.1002; Homer, 'New Light on Thomas Eakins and Walt Whitman in Camden', in Sill and Tarbell 1992, pp.85–98, ill. p.86; Traubel, vol.7 (1992), pp.413–14, 444; Homer 1992, pp.7, 8, 73, 116, 210–19, ill. pl.200, p.211.

24
Douglass Morgan Hall
*c.*1889
Oil on canvas, 60.9 × 50.8 (24 × 20)
Unsigned

Philadelphia Museum of Art.
Gift of Mrs William E. Studdiford
(75.90.1)

Thomas Eakins, shunned by many as an annihilator of vanity, was surprisingly deft in conveying the romance of youth. Viewed as both a prominent painter and teacher, his love for teaching and his camaraderie with his students is reflected in many of his portraits of them. One of the most sensitive, and least considered, is his portrait of Douglass Morgan Hall, painted when the subject was about twenty-two years old.

The son of a prominent Philadelphia opthalmologist, Douglass Morgan Hall first enrolled in the Pennsylvania Academy of the Fine Arts in 1885 at the age of eighteen and studied drawing from casts of antique sculpture, the school's most elementary class. He continued at the Academy in the spring of 1886, the time when Eakins was deposed as its director, and after the summer vacation returned for the fall semester. He was not among the fifty-five students petitioning the Academy's trustees to reinstate Eakins in March 1886, though he eventually joined Eakins in 1887 as one of his students at the Art Students' League, established by Eakins at the request of his students after he left the Academy. Hall remained at the League until 1890.[1]

Douglass Hall's surviving sketchbooks, housed in the Philadelphia Museum of Art, date from 1884 to a final drawing done in 1891. They show some talent, emphasizing landscapes, seascapes, and birds, modest, perhaps, but since Hall was advanced enough for Eakins's portraiture class, his work must not have been regarded as strictly amateur. The museum's collection also includes a small self-portrait dated 1884 and quite similar to Eakins's portrait.

Dwelling on the young man's attractive face and casual bearing evokes a certain pathos when one learns of his death in 1912, at the age of forty-four,[2] evidently in the Pennsylvania Hospital for the Insane,[3] where he is said to have suffered from syphilis.[4] Never married, never having pursued a career, apparently a remittance man, he seems to have utterly disappointed the expectations his bourgeois, Victorian upbringing must have imposed upon him. 'I remember the portrait, as I remember Douglass', Mrs Eakins sympathetically wrote to his sister in 1931, 'most dear memories'. The young man 'was a great favorite with the pupils of the Art Students' League, as well as with my husband'.[5]

The warmth of Mrs Eakins's letter notwithstanding, the portrait of Douglass Morgan Hall joins the lengthy list of Eakins works once consigned to closets, attics, furnaces, or dumps by unhappy owners. The subject's sister owned the portrait until the 1950s, keeping it face down against a closet wall. While recognizing its importance as an Eakins work and properly caring for it, she was however also offended by its lack of ornamented finish and by Eakins's casual presentation, which suggested to her that her brother was working-class.

If the subject's presentation is informal and suggests manual work, it is because Eakins, as part of his classes in portraiture, often invited students to his studio to observe him painting and, occasionally, to pose themselves to learn the subject's point of view. Eakins gave the finished portraits to his students as gifts. About thirty different pupils appear either in portraits or in group works, with several portrayed more than once. Many of Eakins's masterpieces in this period, such as *The Swimming Hole* (fig.8), *The Bohemian* (fig.9), *The Crucifixion* (fig.45), and the portrait of Amelia Van Buren (no.27), depict students for whom modelling was an intrinsic part of their instruction as fledgling artists.

A series of wistful, affectionate portraits of his male students emerged from this practice, of which the portrait of Douglass Morgan Hall is a prime example. The picture best suggests the physical and emotional incongruity of a teenager lurching into manhood. Hall's arm drapes casually, perhaps cavalierly, over the side of the chair, stretching his open-collared shirt across his chest and hinting it is too tight for his developing body. His face is broad and full yet angular, its colour ruddy but his stubborn mouth topped by an uneven, sparse moustache. Tousled sandy hair and intelligent but bloodshot eyes complete the conflation of boy and man, a dialogue between uncertainty and brashness.

Yet it is not a judgement harshly rendered. It only invites a misreading of the portrait to view Eakins's representation as a presentiment of Hall's subsequent troubles. Whatever weakness or self-indulgence Eakins discerns in Douglass Morgan Hall is blended with a sensuality that ultimately is as sympathetic as it is absorbing. The subject, too, is as much the unworldly, beguiling qualities of youth generally as the young Douglass Morgan Hall particularly. Eakins's *Francis Ziegler*, the dandified *Art Student* and *Samuel Murray*, all portraits of Eakins's students of the late 1880s, explore the amalgam of young men's maturity and immaturity in very similar ways.[6] In provocative contrast, Eakins's portraits of his women students, such as Amelia Van Buren and Letitia Bacon, are far less tender.

The portrait's austere, direct composition, thinly painted canvas, and dominance of greys, browns, and whites have more in common with Eakins's late portrait style than most of his works from the period. After 1900, Eakins produced head-and-shoulders portraits in great quantities, mostly for friends, using the same spartan formula as in the portrait of Douglass Morgan Hall. Hall is not of the intellectual calibre of the British worthies painted by George Frederic Watts, but the work's dreamy restraint and the introspection of its subject recalls the portraiture of Watts, who was still very active in the 1880s.

BTA

1. Attendance records are found in Chamberlin-Hellman 1981, appendix.
2. It was reported in Goodrich 1933, p.180 and 1961, p.85 that he died at the age of twenty-seven, but his correct date of death from his obituary in the Philadelphia newspapers is 9 March 1912.
3. C. Bregler interview with L. Goodrich, Goodrich Archives, Philadelphia Museum of Art.
4. Siegl 1978, p.121.
5. Letter from Susan Eakins to Mrs William E. Studdiford, Jr., Philadelphia Museum of Art, archives.
6. For a discussion of the romantic qualities of the Murray portrait, see Schendler 1967, p.111.

Provenance: Given to the subject by the artist; by descent to Mrs William E. Studdiford, given by her, 1975.

Exhibitions: Washington, DC, National Gallery of Art, 1961, no.53; Philadelphia, Museum of Art, 1982 (1), no.113.

Literature: Goodrich 1933, ill. pl.233; Siegl 1978, pp.121–2, ill. pl.72; Goodrich 1982, vol.I, ill. pl.146.

25
Dr Horatio C. Wood

*c.*1890

Oil on canvas, 162.6 × 127 (63½ × 50)

Signed l.r.: *Eakins*

The Detroit Institute of Arts. City of Detroit
Purchase (30.296)

In 1917, nearly thirty years after he sat for his
portrait by Eakins, Dr Horatio C. Wood
(1841–1920) and the artist's widow became
engaged in an ownership dispute over the
painting. In the fiery exchange of letters,
Susan Macdowell Eakins replied to Wood's
ingenuous remarks upon the portrait's worth-
lessness, giving a bristling defence of the
painting:

This portrait of you ... is a good likeness,
representing you in your younger days, not
smiling with a bunch of flowers in your hand, but
after the manner of Mr. Eakins' portraits, engaged
at your noble work, as in the case of the portraits
of Dr. Henry Beates, Dr. Forbes, Dr. Gross,
Dr. Agnew, Professor Roland [*sic*] and others all
serious and showing them interested in their
lifework. Mr. Eakins, too, ever worked to honor
the Medical Profession....[1]

Thus Susan Eakins ranked the portrait of
Wood among Eakins's great portraits of professional men, people who had elicited the artist's
admiration and kindred feeling. Unlike most
of the medical professionals whom the artist
portrayed, Eakins and Wood appear to have
had a close friendship; at the end of his life
Wood still recalled Eakins as his 'warm personal friend'.[2] Following the blow of his forced
resignation from the Pennsylvania Academy
in 1886, Eakins was in need of a therapeutic
change of scenery. It was most likely to have
been Dr Wood who suggested that Eakins take
a recuperative trip to the B.T. Ranch in the
Dakota Territory, which Wood partly owned.[3]
Wood, a Philadelphia specialist in nervous
diseases, recognized the hazardous effects of a
careworn existence in modern urban society;
like many contemporary physicans, he advocated the 'camp cure' – a complete immersion
in nature – as a treatment for nervous exhaustion and overwork.[4] In 1887 Eakins was working alongside the ranch hands by day and
camping out by night, and he wrote ebullient
letters home from the B.T. Ranch that attest to
the success of this therapy.

Although it is not known when Eakins and
Wood became acquainted, their friendship was
well-established before Eakins's troubles in
1886, possibly even in their youth, when Wood
spent years studying penmanship with Benja-

min Eakins.[5] Wood's background suggests
many similarities with Eakins's that must have
encouraged the two mens' empathy for each
other. Born in 1841, three years Eakins's
senior, Wood too came from a modest middle-
class Quaker family in Philadelphia. Like
Eakins, Wood developed a resilient mind and
body in early childhood: as the smallest boy in
boarding school, Wood learned to endure
'punishment without flinching', a toughness
which he claimed prepared him well for
adulthood.[6] Wood also possessed the empirical
temperament, so admired by Eakins, that
marked him as a modern man of science and
reason. He first entered the field of science as a
botanist, illustrating his own books and
articles; the hundreds of meticulous drawings
Wood made from the microscope exhibit a
manual dexterity and accuracy that must have
been fostered by his studies with Eakins's
father.

In 1862 Wood graduated with a medical
degree from the University of Pennsylvania,
which opened his career as a medical botanist.
He assumed the chair in Botany there in 1866,
where he became a highly regarded teacher,
and began his associations with some of the
other doctors and academicians whom Eakins
admired, such as Dr D. Hayes Agnew (see
no. 36), S. Weir Mitchell and Eadweard Muybridge.[7] Thereafter, he became increasingly
interested in the nascent field of 'mental medicine', which was soon to earn permanent
recognition as 'psychiatry' under the lead-

Fig.25a
Dr John H. Brinton
1876
Oil on canvas, 199 × 145 (78⅜ × 57⅛)
Medical Museum of the Armed Forces Institute of
Pathology; on loan to the National Gallery of Art

Fig.25b
Professor William D. Marks
1886
Oil on canvas, 194 × 137.5 (76⅜ × 54⅛)
Washington University Gallery of Art, St Louis,
University Purchase, Yeatman Fund, 1936

ership of Sigmund Freud. Bringing his extensive knowledge of botany to bear on his study of medicine, Wood became a pioneer in American pharmacology, experimenting with the therapeutic potential of botanicals such as marijuana, henbane and belladonna. In addition to being a vocal proponent of experimentation on animals, Wood experimented upon himself and his wife, displaying a personal commitment to his work which parallels that of Eakins.[8] Though his laboratory was known to be engaged in important research, a 'school' failed to gather around him.[9]

Wood's independence, intelligence, and outdoormanship struck a responsive chord with Eakins and made him an obvious choice as a portrait subject. At Eakins's request, Wood sat for a full-length portrait at some time following the artist's dismissal from the Academy, probably during Eakins's period of fresh productivity following his return from the Dakota Territory in 1887.[10] The portrait, depicting Wood seated at his desk, recalls Eakins's earlier portraits *Professor Benjamin Howard Rand* (no.12) and *Dr John H. Brinton* (fig.25a). Wood's pose relates even more closely to the roughly contemporary portrait *Professor William D. Marks* (fig.25b), in which Marks is seated casually in three-quarter view behind his desk. As in these earlier portraits, Eakins created an environment for Wood suggestive of intellectual life, using the accoutrements of books, pens, papers, a wastebasket and cluttered desk to identify Wood as a thinker and a writer.

In the Wood portrait, however, there is a pervasive sense of optimism which sets this work apart from Eakins's other portraits of professional men. Using a warm palette and bright, indirect light, Eakins renders Wood and his environment without the enveloping shadows that characteristically suggest his sitters as remote and brooding individuals. At the time of the portrait sitting, Wood had recently completed a popular health primer, *Brainwork and Overwork*, in which he prescribed the mastery of the individual will over the emotions and anxieties that plagued modern Americans, especially' brain-workers'. Dressed in a smoking jacket and thoughtfully pressing a pen to his cheek in animated bemusement, Wood is offered as the proof of his own tenets, a contented man who calmly pursues his work for its intellectual rewards, which in turn feed the mind's vigour. It is a characterization in keeping with Samuel Murray's memory of Dr Wood as 'a great man, childlike, simple, [and] humorous'.[11]

The disposition of the portrait upon its completion is somewhat confused, for after Eakins's death the painting was still in the artist's studio, which suggests that it was not favourably received. Furthermore, the 1917 incident between Wood and Susan Eakins prompted several comments from the doctor which give another complexion to his regard for Eakins. Wood sparked the feud with Susan Eakins when he requested that she allow him to donate the portrait, still in her possession, to the College of Physicians at the University of Pennsylvania. Out of the exchange of increasingly hostile letters, a struggle ensued over the ownership of the work − although Wood did not remember paying for the portrait he believed that it was tacitly understood at the time that he should have it.[12] Citing the recollections of his sons, who had also known Eakins, Wood ventured that he had originally brought the portrait home but it was 'received with so much disfavor that Mr Eakins, hearing the criticism, asked me to bring it back to him, and he would try if he could make it more of a likeness'.[13] Wood's conclusion was that he never retrieved the portrait, though it was still owed to him for the time he spent indulging Eakins's desire to paint him − time which was worth more to him as a doctor than Eakins's time as a painter.[14] While Wood admired the artist's abilities as a painter of genre, he flatly declared that Eakins was 'never strong in portraiture', and implied that he sat only begrudgingly for the portrait.[15] These comments, whether sincere or hastily made in anger, prompted Susan Eakins's trenchant response:

Mr. Eakins [also] painted ... portraits of your sons James and George ... I can only regret that they were accepted and carried from the house, had they been left here unappreciated and forgotten as in the case of your portrait, they would now be my property, to add, as I explained to you was my greatest hope, to a collection of Mr. Eakins' works ... I know well the regard Mr. Eakins held for you and your work. He comprehended the principles of foundation and construction in Art and Music and in the Sciences, without which all work is weak and purposeless.[16]

Wood's portrait therefore remained in Susan Eakins's possession until 1930 when it was purchased by the Detroit Institute of Arts.

LVD

1. Letter from Susan Macdowell Eakins to Horatio C. Wood, 2 April 1917, Pennsylvania Academy of the Fine Arts, archives.
2. Letter from H.C. Wood to S.M. Eakins, 3 April 1917, Pennsylvania Academy of the Fine Arts, archives.
3. Foster and Leibold 1989, p.92. The authors also mention the possibility that the trip was suggested by Wood's son James, one of Eakins's students.
4. Wood 1880, p.107.
5. Letter from H.C. Wood to S.M. Eakins, 7 April 1917, Pennsylvania Academy of the Fine Arts, archives.
6. Roth 1939, p.39.
7. McHenry 1936, p.81. In the course of his photographic series on the human body in motion. Muybridge received permission from Wood to photograph the doctor's patients with abnormal gaits.
8. Roth op. cit., p.42.
9. Sonnedecker 1976, p.496. Dr John Abel, Wood's student, was ultimately recognized as 'The Father of American Pharmacology'.
10. Goodrich 1982, vol.II, p.166. Although Wood's portrait is undated, in 1886 Eakins recorded payments in his journal for $50 and $100, for 'Dr Wood's portrait'. However, writing to Susan Eakins in 1917. Wood did not recall having paid for the portrait. The similarities between the Wood portrait and the seated portrait of Professor William D. Marks, signed and dated 1886 (fig.25b), seem to support the claim that the Wood portrait was painted around the same time.
11. McHenry op. cit., p.81. It is worth mentioning that Murray also remembered Wood as a nervous, perhaps compulsive, person. Thus it may have been that the doctor suffered from the same temperament which he attempted to treat in others.
12. Letter from H.C. Wood to S.M. Eakins, 3 April 1917, Pennsylvania Academy of the Fine Arts, archives. See also n. 10 above.
13. Letter from H.C. Wood to S.M. Eakins, 7 April 1917, Pennsylvania Academy of the Fine Arts, archives.
14. Letter from H.C. Wood to S.M. Eakins, 7 April 1917, Pennsylvania Academy of the Fine Arts, archives.
15. Letter from H.C. Wood to S.M. Eakins, 7 April 1917, Pennsylvania Academy of the Fine Arts, archives. Wood was indeed a patron of Eakins's genre works; in 1878 he purchased *The Courtship* (1878; fig.18a), and later bought a watercolour version of *Mending the Net* (1881). Susan Eakins offered to exchange Wood's portrait for the two works in Wood's collection, but he refused to part with them.
16. Letter from H.C. Wood to S.M. Eakins, 4 April 1917, Pennsylvania Academy of the Fine Arts, archives.

Provenance: Purchased from Susan Macdowell Eakins (Clyde H. Burroughs, agent) by the Detroit Institute of Arts, 1930.

Exhibitions: New York, Metropolitan Museum of Art, 1917, no. 25; New York, Whitney Museum of American Art, 1933, no. 239; Philadelphia, Museum of Art, 1965, no. 52.

Literature: *DIA Bulletin*, vol.XII, no. 2, November 1930, p.21; Marceau 1930, no. 114, p.23; Porter 1959, pl.41; Schendler 1967, pp.9, 116, 118, no.49; *DIA Handbook* 1971, p.147; Hendricks 1974, fig.162; 'Family Art Game', 26 April 1981, p.19; Johns 1983 (1), fig.110, pp.78, 136, 160, 161.

26

The Concert Singer

c.1890–1892
Oil on canvas, 190.8 × 137.8 ($75\frac{1}{8}$ × $54\frac{1}{4}$)
Signed t.r.: *Eakins/92*

Philadelphia Museum of Art.
Gift of Mrs Thomas Eakins and
Miss Mary Adeline Williams (29.184.19)

Fig.26a
Sketch for 'The Concert Singer'
c.1890
Oil on canvas, 35.6 × 27 ($13\frac{3}{4}$ × $10\frac{3}{8}$)
Philadelphia Museum of Art. Gift of Mrs Thomas
Eakins and Miss Mary Adeline Williams

Of all of Eakins's musical portraits, *The Concert Singer* best captures his fascination with musical performance. The model, the Philadelphia contralto Weda Cook,[1] is shown in the midst of singing; her mouth open, neck extended, head tilted slightly upwards and to the right, and eyes gazing out above the crowd, she is fully absorbed in and subsumed by her effort. The fine detail and modelling of Cook's mouth and throat emphasize to the viewer a technical mastery of the voice that together with the isolation of the performer and centrality of the rose taffeta dress as colour and substance create a musical portrait of personal achievement and deep emotional experience.

Apart from the figure of Cook herself the composition is remarkably barren, including only what Eakins must have considered the minimum props necessary to provide the narrative context – a formal public performance. Isolated on stage in her radiant gown, Weda Cook is framed and recessed into the canvas by the hand and baton of the conductor, the single palm frond and the bouquet of roses lying at her feet as if just thrown from the audience. Even the stage she stands on is only faintly indicated, as the floor seamlessly merges into an undefined and wall-less background. Reinforcing her recession into the space of the canvas is the broad, flat, chestnut frame Eakins made for the picture. Onto it he carved the notes from the opening bars of the aria 'O Rest in the Lord' from Mendelssohn's 'Elijah', an addition which Eakins considered 'ornamental unobtrusive and to musicians I think emphasized the expression of the face and pose of the figure'.[2]

Although never able to sell this painting,[3] Eakins thought highly of it. He exhibited the painting several times during his lifetime and reportedly had it hung above his mantelpiece in the downstairs front hall of his home.[4] In 1914, twenty-two years after completing the portrait, Eakins wrote to Cook in response to her request for the painting that he could not part with it as 'it must be largely exhibited yet'.[5]

In the same letter Eakins wrote of the painting, 'I have many memories of it, some happy, some sad', surely referring to both his long friendship with Weda Cook and the brief hiatus when Cook, after hearing scandalous stories about Eakins's character, stopped posing for the picture.[6] Eakins then hung the empty dress over the slippers in order to complete the painting. Just as this episode is frequently cited as the reason for the awkwardness of Cook's right foot and the resulting pose,[7] Eakins's inclusion of the roses in the lower right similarly has been explained by anecdote – the consequence of Eakins's associate, the sculptor William R. O'Donovan, bringing fresh roses to each sitting because he had fallen in love with Weda Cook.[8] Yet, it is perhaps not so much these stories surrounding the painting of *The Concert Singer* that explain the slightly awkward stance and the presence of the roses, but rather Eakins's own uncertainties and unresolved questions about the final form of the painting.[9] The presence of the roses and palm frond serve in the composition to balance the hand of the conductor and further recess Cook into space, but it is the dress itself, with its brilliant pinks and shimmering effect of light that remains the dominant element of the portrait.[10]

Eakins's desire to emphasize the materiality of Weda Cook's dress as pictorial surface while deeply recessing Cook herself into the canvas and creating a sense of space around her, resulted in an ambiguity of pose and viewpoint. While the roses, lower dress and shoes are apparently seen from a high viewpoint, Eakins, at the same time, reveals the bottom of the shoes and underside of the dress as if the viewer's eye were at floor level, and able to look up at Cook's lavish dress and extended neck. Light comes clearly from the right side of the picture and casts a strong shadow to the left. Yet, inexplicably, the small flowers on the bodice of the dress catch light from the left side of the canvas, casting small shadows just above Cook's hand immediately to the right of the flowers and, further over, creating the peculiar scalloped shadows on her waist inside her left arm.

The Concert Singer is rightly regarded as one of Eakins's greatest works. Yet for all of Eakins's brilliance in depicting both the achievement of the performer and the intensity of the performance, his ambiguous and even conflicting treatment of pose, perspective and light remain curiously unresolved. These types of problems probably provided some of the impetus for Eakins to reduce gradually the number of elements in his paintings. Thus *The Concert Singer* stands at a vital turning-point towards the introspective and sparse portraits like *The Thinker* (no. 38) that are the hallmark of the artist's later years.

PP

1. Weda Cook (1867–1937) came from Camden, New Jersey, near Philadelphia. She sang regularly in Philadelphia starting in 1887, including at the 3rd anniversary celebration in 1889 of Eakins's Art Students' League (see no. 24). She was a friend of the poet Walt Whitman (see no. 23) and it is likely that Eakins first met her during one of his frequent visits to Whitman in 1887–1888 (Siegl 1978, p.126). In 1884 Cook married Stanley Addicks, a pianist and organist, whose portrait bust Eakins painted in 1895 along with another of Weda Cook and her sister Maud Cook (no. 29).
2. Typewritten letter to Professor Henry A. Rowland, 4 October 1897, Addison Gallery of American Art, Andover, Massachusetts, quoted by Siegl 1978, p.128. Eakins also carved the frames of *Professor Henry A. Rowland* (no. 31), *The Agnew Clinic* (fig.36a), *Frank Hamilton Cushing* (fig.30a) and *Salutat* (fig.34a). The latter two frames are now lost. For a discussion of the late nineteenth-century popularity of Mendelssohn's 'Elijah' and its message of spiritual reassurance, see Johns 1983 (1), pp.139–43.
3. *The Concert Singer* is listed in 1893 and 1895 catalogues for sale for $1000, placing it among Eakins's highest priced works before 1900 (Goodrich 1982, vol.II, p.166). In 1914 Eakins raised the price to $5000 as a result of the successful sale of the study of Dr D. Hayes Agnew (no. 36) for $4000 in 1914 (ibid., p.270), yet after his death it was appraised at merely $150 (Goodrich 1982, vol.II, p.278).
4. Hendricks 1974, p.194.
5. Handwritten note quoted in Goodrich 1982, vol.II, p.260, and reproduced in Haughom 1975, p.1184. *The Concert Singer* was exhibited twice in the next two years, 1914 and 1915.
6. Haughom op. cit. reports (p.1184) that the account of Eakins's behaviour was probably told by Eakins's niece Ella Crowell. Cook later determined the stories to be false and renewed her friendship with Eakins. Other mixed memories Eakins may have attached to the painting might have related to the Art Students' League, where Eakins possibly first conceived of the painting while watching Cook sing. The League was disbanded in 1892 for lack of money.
7. See for example Goodrich 1982, vol.II, p.84.
8. Ibid.
9. It was not unusual for Eakins to have trouble with the stance of his full-length figures; see for example *Professor William Smith Forbes*, 1905 (Medical College of Thomas Jefferson University, Philadelphia) and *John McClure Hamilton*, 1895 (Wadsworth Athenaeum, Hartford, Connecticut). Michael Fried goes further, stating that the partially obscured palm frond and severed arm of the conductor 'strongly suggest that at least in this instance a lack of certainty about the status of the limits of the canvas is being given expression within the painting itself'. (Fried 1987, p.38).
10. In the initial oil sketch Eakins made for the painting (fig.26a), he displays as his central concerns the close physiological observation of Cook's throat and neck, her deep recession into space, and the emotionally overwhelming colour and play of light of her dress. Left unresolved are the more precise questions of pose – particularly the feet – perspective and formal arrangement. Weda Cook's right foot and the train of her dress are only sketchily indicated, and apart from Cook herself, only the hand and baton of the conductor are represented by a few quick strokes. The palm frond and roses do not appear at all. The circular form taken by the dress's train in the sketch reappears in the finished painting, but pushed to the foreground and transformed into the bouquet of roses with their pink petals folding like the crumpled fabric of the dress.

Provenance: Given by the artist's widow, Susan Macdowell Eakins, and Mary Adeline Williams, 1929.

Exhibitions: Chicago, 1893, no. 74 (under the title *The Singer*); Philadelphia, Art Club of Philadelphia, 1894, no. 12; New York, National Academy of Design, 1895, no. 432; Washington, DC, Corcoran Gallery of Art, 1914, no. 42; San Francisco, 1915, no. 2960; New York, Metropolitan Museum of Art, 1917, no. 30; Philadelphia, Pennsylvania Academy of the Fine Arts, 1917, no. 107; Philadelphia, Department of Fine Arts, 1926, no. 356; New York, Museum of Modern Art, 1930, no. 105; Philadelphia, Pennsylvania Museum of Art, 1930, no. 161; Paris, Musée du Jeu de Paume, 1938, no. 55; New York, M. Knoedler & Co., 1944, no. 49; Philadelphia, Museum of Art, 1944, no.69; Philadelphia, Museum of Art, 1953, no. 32; Washington, DC, Corcoran Gallery of Art, 1957, no. 31; Washington, DC, National Gallery of Art, 1961, no. 64; New York, Whitney Museum of American Art, 1966, no. 82; New York, Whitney Museum of American Art, 1970, no. 57; Philadelphia, Museum of Art, 1982 (1), no. 101.

Literature: Goodrich 1933, pp.122, 144–5, no. 266, ill. pl.43; Craven 1959, pp.458–9, ill. pl.111; McKinney 1942, ill. p.73; McHenry 1946, pp.99, 109, 121–2; Porter 1959, p.20, ill. pl.44; Schendler 1967, pp.130–2, ill. pl.58; McCaughey 1970, p.57, ill. p.57; Hendricks 1974, no.288, pp.191–4, pl.38, 39; Haughom 1975, pp.1182–4, ill. p.1183; Siegl 1978, no.78, pp.126–9; Goodrich 1982, vol.II, pp.79, 84–6, 260, ill. fig.182, 183; Sewell 1982, no.101, p.93; Johns 1983 (1), pp.116, 138–43, pl.10, fig.97; Fried 1987, pp.35–8, fig.30; Homer 1992, p.223, pl.172.

27
Amelia Van Buren
*c.*1891[1]
Oil on canvas, 114.3 × 81.2 (45 × 32)
Unsigned and undated

The Phillips Collection, Washington, DC
(0632)

Miss Amelia Van Buren, a student of Eakins's
at the Pennsylvania Academy between 1884
and 1885, was a close personal friend of the
artist, as well as one of his favourite pupils.
Even after her departure from Philadelphia to
pursue a career in Detroit, she maintained contact with Eakins, and on occasion returned to
Pennsylvania to stay with him and his wife. It
was during one of these visits that she sat for
her portrait, one of Eakins's most poignant and
psychologically resonant works.

For Eakins, portraiture was the dominant
means of artistic expression, especially in his
later years when his works became deep psychological probings. Much of the introspective
quality of these works has to do with his
declining stature in the established art community in Philadelphia, marked definitively
by his dismissal from the Pennsylvania
Academy of the Fine Arts in 1886. Criticism of
Eakins centred around his teaching methods,
more specifically, his insistence on the importance of working from nude models in order to
study the human figure, which became the
source of much unwanted public controversy
and scandal for the Academy.

A related story concerning Van Buren was
used against Eakins by political adversaries,
such as Frank Stephens, in an effort to discredit
the artist. During her studies with Eakins in
his studio, Van Buren often partook of life
classes with nude models; this in itself was considered questionable behaviour for a respectable young woman of the period, but on one
occasion in particular, Eakins took Van Buren
aside and 'exposed himself' to the young
student, ostensibly to clarify a question of anatomy. It has been noted by some commentators
that Eakins regarded the incident as strictly
professional and mutually unembarrassing,
and that in fact, 'Minnie', as she was called,
continued to study with Eakins, and remained
a close supporter of the artist through the
1890s.[2] However, by the time that criticism of
Eakins was strongest, in 1886, Van Buren had
already left for Detroit, and thus was not close
at hand to defend and exonerate her teacher.

Painted years after, the portrait of Miss Van
Buren reflects the state of disillusionment
which is characteristic of Eakins in the years

following his professional ostracism. Utilizing an essentially pyramidal composition, Eakins leads the eye to examine specific details which contain his message. At the apex, Miss Van Buren's eyes look into the light source of the picture – studio windows which, indeed, one can see reflected in her eyes. Her gaze is inward, however, and spiritually reflective, directed not to material objects and light, but rather infused by deep personal contemplation. Her countenance displays a weariness which borders on despair and is suggestive of a wealth of experience beyond her years, highlighted dramatically by the urgent streaks of white in her tied-back hair.

Miss Van Buren's wrist and hand assert the strength of her left arm as, bathed in the brightest of the light, they emerge from a frilly cuff. The hand, bowed slightly at the wrist, is fleshy and full, smooth and pink. It is very much alive and powerful. The open fist is suggestive of an unspoken potential for great vitality, something beyond the general sense of lassitude apparent here. Together, the forearm, wrist, and hand, through Eakins's sculptural rendering, acquire an almost architectural quality; the three together form a visual buttress which supports in full the weight of her head and upper body, and creates a compositional balance. Solidity, strength, and permanence are expressed through this passage, the anchor of the portrait. By contrast, her opposite side, consisting of her right forearm and a small folding fan which is near-closed, a fallen support. Foreshortened and cast in shadow, her right hand and wrist appear as lifeless as the ones on the left side appear alive. Tendons show through the sallow flesh of this wrist, and her fingers and thumb lie together limply, resting within the folds of her frock. Eakins, here, offers us the verso – fragility, weakness, and, perhaps, death.

Beyond the triangular locus of the image, Eakins includes one other element to underscore the dark tone of the work. The large, looming chair pushes aggressively into the frame and seems to envelop Miss Van Buren. This powerful prop was used to differing effects in a number of Eakins's portraits, and here Eakins manipulated it considerably, giving it a silently ominous character. As evidenced by a photographic portrait by Eakins of Van Buren taken roughly at the time of her enrolment at the Academy, the chair used by Eakins in his studio was, in fact, much smaller relative to Van Buren, and much less threatening. Here, however, with its worn velvet upholstery, rhythmical woodworking, and dark umber palette which appears to fuse with Eakins's ambiguous background, the chair is a veritable presence, an undeniable manifestation of foreboding and of imminent darkness. The artist manipulated the reflection of light off the two knobs at the either end of the arms of the chair in such a way that they repeat the dichotomy of Van Buren's body – the knob of the left arm is polished and bright, whereas the knob of the right arm is painted in sketchy strokes so as to give it a flat dullness. Her body seems suspended, by the chair, in a joyless, two-dimensional limbo, and Van Buren is left with nothing but her own thoughts.

Given this reading of the portrait, Eakins's expressive content is clear – the painting stands for a universal vulnerability and temporality of the human body and spirit. Amelia Van Buren stares, as one sympathetic viewer says, '... with an intelligence and a quiet sort of knowing if not a cynicism'.[3] Indeed, deep understanding is relayed through her reflective expression, and it is of a pessimistic nature. The direction of her gaze, to her right, away from her side of strength and into the light, the metaphoric beyond, speaks of a deep awareness, one only achieved in an advanced state of maturity, which Eakins reinforces in his representation of Van Buren through manipulated formal means. The overall tone of the work is not necessarily nihilistic, but can be read instead as one of resigned acceptance of unhappy realities. In depicting Van Buren in such a powerful psychological posture, as a woman invested with such meaningful knowledge, Eakins's respect for and belief in his sitter are clearly revealed, and to an extent that is perhaps atypical of a teacher depicting his student. It is not presumptuous, therefore, to surmise that Eakins felt an almost intrinsic connection with this particular student, many years his junior. The work can be read as a form of self-portraiture, as well as a portrait of a specific sitter, but regardless of how it is interpreted, *Amelia Van Buren* must be considered one of Eakins's most successful, and certainly most riveting, compositions.

WPH

1. In 1933, Goodrich dated this work to 1891, but then changed the date to 1890 in his revised book of 1982. Most scholars accept 1891 as the date of the work, although Johns believes the earlier date to be more accurate because it was based on information relayed by people close to Eakins himself.
2. Foster and Leibold 1989, p.78.
3. Schendler 1967, p.124.

Provenance: Possible gift of the artist to Amelia Van Buren, Detroit, by 1893; Phillips Memorial Gallery purchase from Van Buren, North Carolina, 1927.

Exhibitions: Chicago, 1893, no.383 (as *Portrait of a Lady*); New York, Museum of Modern Art, 1930, no.102; Los Angeles, Museum Exposition Park, 1930, no.23; New York, Metropolitan Museum of Art, 1932, no cat. no.; Philadelphia, Museum of Art, 1937; New York, Museum of Modern Art, 1939, no.33; Pittsburgh, Carnegie Institute, 1945, no.90; London, Tate Gallery, 1946, no.71; Philadelphia, Pennsylvania Academy of the Fine Arts, 1955, no.89; New York, The Brooklyn Museum, 1957, no.62; Washington, DC, National Gallery of Art, 1961, no.58; New York, Whitney Museum of American Art, 1970, no.56; Chadds Ford, Brandywine River Museum, 1980, no.1; Philadelphia, Pennsylvania Academy of the Fine Arts, 1991.

Literature: Goodrich 1933, p.184, ill. pl.41; Novak 1969, p.207, ill. p.207; Schendler 1967, pp.124, 130, ill. pl.54; Hendricks 1972, pp.124, 130, ill. pl.54; Erwin 1976, pp.109–110, ill. pp.109–110; Goodrich 1982, vol.I, pp.61, 70, 72, 163, ill. pl.176; vol.II, pp.245, 258–9; Johns 1983 (1), p.164; Lubin 1985, p.48; Foster and Leibold 1989, pp.158, 383; Homer 1992, pp.167, 176, 230–1, ill. pl.217.

28
William H. Macdowell
*c.*1890
Oil on canvas mounted on wood panel,
38.5 × 33.1 (15¼ × 13⅛)
Unsigned
Bregler label on reverse: *Painted by Thomas Eakins/study of his father-in-law/William H. Macdowell/1890*

Hirshhorn Museum and Sculpture Garden, Smithsonian Institution.
Gift of Joseph H. Hirshhorn, 1966
(HMSG 1966.1503)

Always one to choose portrait subjects who met his own standards of disciplined achievement and personal integrity, Eakins typically drew out of his sitters' countenances thoughtfulness, caution, and vulnerability. His portraits suggest intellectual and emotional lives that survived, and that sometimes were shaped by, harsh circumstances. In this regard, his own life was a model. The portraits of William H. Macdowell and Maud Cook, ostensibly quite different from each other – one a quickly brushed profile and the other a carefully finished head-and-shoulders – show the threads that held Eakins and his sitters in this community of shared experience. They tell the story of endurance that Eakins found in almost every human life that he admired, both male and female.

At the same time, these portraits demonstrate Eakins's pictorial explorations of different inner lives in men and women. His desire to paint Philadelphians who were prominent in public life was thwarted by the loss fifteen years into his career of his own public position at the Pennsylvania Academy. He subsequently withdrew protectively into a private stance of resistance (sometimes resistance even to decorum), nurtured by close friends and family. He had always enjoyed the friendship of men, especially those older and younger than he; with his father he had a strong, sustaining relationship, and with his many male students at the Pennsylvania Academy and later at the Art Students' League of Philadelphia, virtually all of them considerably younger than he, almost constant companionship. For his portrait subjects during the middle and late years of his career he depended more and more on such friends and on close family members, although he continued to seek out people to pose for him (sometimes friends of friends) who did things well. Men he admired for their intellectual achievements, and, his many portraits suggest, for the virtually impenetrable front with which they faced the world. Women, on the other hand, he felt free to depict as melancholy and diminished rather than self-confident, and in many of the portraits Eakins implied his female sitters' psychosexual longings. His assumptions and liberties were, of course, completely consistent with the social construction of gender roles in the late Victorian, middle-class society in which he lived. The ironical consequence of the freedom he took in his depiction of women is that his female portraits have a power that is lacking in all but a few of the male portraits.

In William H. Macdowell (*c.*1816–1906), the father of his wife Susan, Eakins could hardly have found a more compatible subject. Macdowell was a resilient, independent-thinking male, a family intimate, and an accomplished engraver and photographer. According to family tradition, Macdowell's lively and broad intellectual stances extended to the raising of his children. Peggy Macdowell Walters, the sitter's niece, wrote that Macdowell 'was a fascinating gentleman and he and Mr [John] Wanamaker [the Philadelphia department store entrepreneur who selected his merchandise from around the world] had many things in common. He wanted his daughters – Aunt Susie [who would become Eakins's wife] and Aunt Lyzie (Elizabeth Macdowell Kenton), to paint and he sent his sons out west to learn about this country and some of his daughters to Europe to study and to learn about foreign countries.'[1] Macdowell, like Eakins, was not one to be too attentive to notions of sexual decorum. The patriarch and his sons, along with Eakins, Susan (before she married Eakins), and other family members, took excursions to the shore of New Jersey in

the early 1880s where they made nude photographs of each other in poses inspired by fantasies of antiquity. Many of these photographs are now in the Pennsylvania Academy of the Fine Arts.[2] In Macdowell, then, Eakins enjoyed an unusually sympathetic older counterpart.

In admiration and camaraderie, he painted at least six portraits of Macdowell and made a number of photographs of him as well. Perhaps the photograph most revealing of the attractiveness for Eakins of Macdowell's personality is an undated image in the Metropolitan Museum, *William H. Macdowell in a Window* (fig.28a). The close-up shows the easy familiarity of the photographer with his subject at the same time that it emphasizes a private intensity in the older man. Macdowell's starched white shirt is at odds with the unbuttoned cuff and windblown hair. The wrinkles on the face and prominent veins in the hands are hallmarks of the ageing process that Eakins valued in his painted portraiture; they are signs of a life that had been lived, implying that it has been lived at cost.

In its efficiency and directness no. 28 cap-

tures a man who did not mince words. The profile format is unusual in the artist's *œuvre*. It shows how efficiently he could exploit the expressive possibilities of even such a small format. Using dramatic light to model Macdowell's face, he placed the strong profile against a dark background. His painting method for flesh here is typical for his entire career: he brushed a dark brown form onto the ground, following it with ruddy and succeedingly lighter tones; he let the unmodified brown underpainting serve as the hollow of the cheek – a literal as well as visual depth. To emphasize the depression of the face at that point, Eakins pulled flesh tones up to it, as he also did at the temple. With a dark, slightly disordered eyebrow he conveyed Macdowell's rugged intensity. Then, for lively counterpoint, he laid on a brilliant white collar, bright forehead, and unruly wisps of hair. These few strokes – all of them quite visible – add punch to the quick yet gentle intelligence conveyed in the photograph. Eakins apparently completed the painting at one sitting, as noted much later by his student Charles Bregler, who claimed that the image was 'the result of one painting'.[3]

Fig.28a
William H. Macdowell in a Window
Silver print, 14.6 × 17.2 (5¾ × 6¾)
The Metropolitan Museum of Art,
David A. McAlpin Fund, 1943

Fig.28b
William H. Macdowell
1904
Oil on canvas, 61 × 50.8 (24 × 20)
Memorial Art Gallery of the University of
Rochester, Marion Stratton Gould Fund, 1941

That Eakins considered the work a study, or at least a highly personal interpretation of his father-in-law, is suggested by the fact that he neither signed nor dated it.

A startling contrast to the study of Macdowell, the large, finished profile portrait that Eakins made of William Merritt Chase (no. 35), tells us much about the artist's sensitivity to each sitter's consciously-modelled public self. Restless fluidity, even effrontery, was fundamental to Macdowell, but anathema to Chase. Thus in Eakins's portrait of Chase, also a profile, he modified the brown underpaint almost completely with light flesh tones, subduing and in many areas altogether disguising his brush strokes. Eakins placed his fastidious fellow artist in a large space that suggests the artist's cultivated presence and gave him such accoutrements as the *boutonnière* to convey his mannered delicacy.

As in the Chase and the Macdowell, the qualities that Eakins conveyed in his male sitters always involved assent to their self-presentation. When Eakins painted women, he turned to very different components of the human psyche. What seems to have intrigued him about women was their vulnerability, their emotional tenderness, and their roles as onlookers, as those who wait rather than as those who do. Thus even though many of his women subjects were accomplished musicians or artists, he portrayed them in these more troubled aspects of their social identity. Whether he did so because he liked to think of women in those terms himself, or because he regretted their societal strait-jackets, or because such a conceptualization made more interesting pictures, we do not know. His success in evoking these qualities, however, meant that his female sitters, like Amelia Van Buren (no. 27), Edith Mahon (no. 44), and Susan Eakins (nos. 22 and 37), virtually never appear in charge of their own lives. Almost without exception in his entire body of work, in fact, women seem to be emotionally exposed by the artist, although with compassion rather than cruelty.

His portrait of Maud Cook in her young womanhood is a dramatic example of this practice. We do not know of the special talents of Cook beyond her participation in a very musical Camden family.[4] The sister of his earlier subject Weda Cook, a contralto whose full-length portrait *The Concert Singer* (no. 26) he had painted in 1892, Maud Cook was apparently one of the 'friends of a friend' who formed much of Eakins's constituency after 1886. According to Elizabeth Cramer, whose husband was the grandson of Maud Cook, the sitter was in her twenties at the time of the

portrait, and Eakins carved the frame before presenting her the work.[5] Eakins's image is subtly invasive. Cook tilts her head away from the viewer (and the painter) towards the light source, her eyes focused outside of the picture. Her body position is unstable, and although she may be seen as resisting the role in which her gender cast her, she is also clearly acted upon. The artist has presented her in a very private moment; we suspect that we are even to infer that she has just had an intense experience. With her dress, composed of a variety of pink fabrics tactilely rendered and modestly covering her bosom, Eakins heightened traditional notions of decorous femininity. He undercut this propriety, however, by the sensuality he gave to her face. This is notable in the dimple in her left cheek, her long upper lip, and the irregularity, even disorder, of her hairline at the parting in her middle forehead. As opposed to the physical brusqueness of the Macdowell portrait and the studied public persona of Chase, Eakins would seem to have painted Maud Cook to signify the repressed longings of the body, the urgings of sexuality — feelings known by both genders but depictable only in the 'second sex'. How much more intriguing, and at the same time more disturbing because of its implications about the relations between male artist and female sitter, such a work is than most of Eakins's male portraits. We wonder how Cook saw the picture at the time. In retrospect years later, she seems to have been pleased with the language of sensuality with which Eakins characterized the picture. Lloyd Goodrich tells us that Cook wrote to him in 1930, 'my hair is done low in the neck and tied with a ribbon. ... Mr Eakins never gave [the painting] a name but said to himself it was like a "big rose bud" '.[6] Just how a young woman during the heyday of Victorian flower symbolism would have interpreted this description if not in the association of the rose with virginity, and of the bud with sexual promise, is hard to imagine. Perhaps she understood it all too well, and forgave Eakins for what to many would have been outright impertinence. She, too, may have thought of herself as longing for romance; she did not marry for another eleven years.

A reading of *Maud Cook* as embodying Eakins's association of female identity with sensual desire and repression leads to the

painting's link with the most stunning of such images, *Edith Mahon*, dating from a decade later (no. 44). The face of Mrs Mahon seems to yield up the trials of unhappy experience, a sequel to the hopeful projections of Maud Cook. That very year Eakins painted his last portrait of his father-in-law (fig.28b), whose averted glance and closed jacket may allude to the life of the intellect and the emotions, but on the matter of sexuality seem absolutely silent.

EJ

1. Peggy Macdowell Walters's testimony is in her letter of 4 May 1876 to Abraham Lerner, the Director of the Hirshhorn Museum, copy in the object files at the Hirshhorn Museum. 'Aunt Lyzie' was briefly the wife of the subject of *The Thinker* (no. 38).
2. I discuss these images in my essay 'Nudity and Fantasy in the Photography of Thomas Eakins' in *Eakins and the Photograph*, forthcoming 1994 from the Smithsonian Institution Press.
3. Bregler's letter to Lloyd Goodrich in 1943 is cited in his correspondence in May 1976 to Phyllis Rosenzweig, located in the Hirshhorn Archives. The Macdowell portrait is mounted on a wood panel, possibly having been done so by Bregler, for when the painting was catalogued for the Hirshhorn collection, the conservation report noted that it was badly cracked, held together only by its mounting.
4. Local newspaper and journal articles about the family in the 1890s may be found in the Camden County Historical Society, Camden, New Jersey.
5. Letter from Elizabeth Cramer to Helen Cooper, Yale University Art Gallery, 28 April 1982.
6. Goodrich 1982, vol.II, p.69.

Provenance (no. 28): Given by Susan Eakins to Charles Bregler, Philadelphia; Joseph Katz, Baltimore; M. Knoedler & Co., New York, 1961; Joseph H. Hirshhorn, New York, 1966.

Provenance (no. 29): Maud Cook to Babcock Galleries; Stephen C. Clark; Yale University Art Gallery, 1961, by bequest.

Exhibitions (no. 28): New York, M. Knoedler & Co., 1944, no. 47; Pittsburgh, Carnegie Institute, 1945, no. 65; Washington, DC, Hirshhorn Museum and Sculpture Garden, 1977, no. 66.

Exhibitions (no. 29): New York, Whitney Museum of American Art, 1970, no. 50; Philadelphia, Museum of Art, 1982 (1), no. 131.

Literature (no. 28): Rosenzweig 1977, pp.130–1.

29
Maud Cook
1895
Oil on canvas, 60.9 × 50.8 (24 × 20)
Inscribed on verso: *To his friend/Maude Cook/Thomas Eakins/1895*

Yale University Art Gallery. Bequest of Stephen Carlton Clark, BA 1903 (1961.18.18)

30

Mrs Frank Hamilton Cushing

1895

Oil on canvas, 66.5 × 55.9 (26$\frac{3}{16}$ × 22)

Inscribed l.r. by Mrs Thomas Eakins: *T.E.*

Philadelphia Museum of Art. Gift of Mrs
Thomas Eakins and Miss Mary Adeline
Williams (29.184.4)

Emily Magill Cushing (1860–1920), the wife of the brilliant and controversial ethnologist Frank Hamilton Cushing, was one of the many women who sat to Eakins for portraits in the 1890s. Eakins, who met Frank Hamilton Cushing through a mutual friend in 1894, was naturally attracted by the ethnologist's independence and uncompromising dedication to the study of North American Indians.[1] In 1895 Eakins invited the Cushings to be his guests while he executed a portrait of Cushing.[2] Whether or not they actually stayed at the Eakins's home that autumn is not certain, but during their visit to Philadelphia the artist painted his ambitious portrait *Frank Hamilton Cushing* (fig.30a), as well as this smaller portrait of his wife.

Overshadowed by the magnificent full-length painting of her husband, solemnly attired in Indian dress, the modest portrait of Mrs Cushing has rarely been discussed in the Eakins literature over the years, yet this portrait remains a provocative and perceptive work in Eakins's *œuvre*. The intelligent, sensitive rendering of Mrs Cushing's head and the prominent treatment of her solid arms contrasts with the delicacy of her dress, and invites speculation on the character of this woman whom Samuel Murray once described as both 'cantakerous' and a 'baby doll'.[3]

Contemporary accounts of Emily Cushing suggest that she possessed a duality that may have been the basis of Eakins's interest in her as a portrait subject. A banker's daughter from a middle-class background, Emily Tennison Magill was raised in the cosmopolitan environment of Washington, DC. When she married Frank Hamilton Cushing in July 1882, the ethnologist was enjoying a degree of national celebrity as he accompanied a party of Zuni leaders on a tour of eastern cities. It seems natural that the charismatic Cushing, popular within the circles of the social and political élite, would have appealed to Emily Magill, who reportedly had a fondness for fashion and good society. It is perhaps more remarkable that following their marriage the couple returned to the Zuni pueblo in New Mexico, where Emily Cushing joined her husband in a life which plainly lacked even basic middle-class comforts.[4] While she insisted on maintaining some European/American customs, such as the practice of knocking before entering a private space,[5] reports of her distaste for life at Zuni are probably exaggerated, for she soon became profoundly involved in her husband's arduous work.[6]

It is this contrast between social refinement and physical power that is so striking in Eakins's depiction of Mrs Cushing. As in his contemporaneous portrait of Weda Cook (1895; Cleveland Museum of Art), Eakins chose to set Emily Cushing in a three-quarter view, rendering her head almost in profile. Her chin tips pensively toward her right shoulder as she gazes intently beyond the frame; raking light illuminates her face, neck, and bare arms. Eakins had used the gesture of clasped hands before, in *The Concert Singer* (no. 26), but in his portrait of Mrs Cushing the strength implied by the circular link of the arms is enhanced by their luminous differentiation from the dark folds of her dress. Unlike the complex costumes found in so many of Eakins's female portraits. Mrs Cushing's dress is rendered simply and used as a subtle foil for the corporeality of the sitter. Wearing a fashionable square-necked dress with short puffed sleeves and beaded waistband, Emily Cushing's powerful arms are curiously at odds with the feminine play of black chiffon about them. That Eakins chose to depict Mrs Cushing in half-length on the small canvas, rather than as a head-and-shoulders view as he typically did on canvases of this size, suggests that the sitter's arms and body were of great importance in the artist's conception of the portrait. The physical power in Mrs Cushing's portrait is most evident when compared with that of her husband. While obviously not pendant portraits, there is clearly a thematic relationship between the two paintings. Eakins was apparently pleased with both works and showed them in his 1896 exhibition.[7] In the portrait of Frank Hamilton Cushing, the sitter's physical frailty is painfully central to this characterization of Cushing as a man who risked his health in pursuit of his beliefs. In response to this vision of the ethnologist, Eakins portrayed Mrs Cushing as the patient source of strength behind this emaciated genius; she is also his connection to the white society that Cushing could never completely relinquish. While *Frank Hamilton Cushing* describes Cushing's relationship to spiritual and professional realms, Eakins's portrait of Mrs Cushing is intuitive of her role within her marriage. After her husband's premature death in 1900, Emily Cushing devoted herself to the task of organizing the morass of information that Cushing had gathered over the years; she was largely responsible for the publication of *Zuni Folk Tales*, now a classic text, which is one of Cushing's major contributions to the field.[8]

LVD

1. Cushing had been studying the Zuni people in New Mexico since 1879; his radically interactive approach to ethnology and anthropology was both hailed and criticized by his colleagues in the east. Immersing himself in Zuni culture. Cushing eventually shed his status as a white outsider and was adopted as a member of the Zuni nation.
2. Hendricks 1974, p.228.
3. McHenry 1946, p.112.
4. Ibid. Apparently gathered from her conversation with Samuel Murray, McHenry reported that Emily Cushing had been unable to 'stand the dirt and curiosity of the Indians when Cushing took her down to New Mexico to live'.
5. Notes on Mrs Cushing, 18 May 1977, Pennsylvania Museum of Art, archives.
6. For example, Emily Cushing and her sister accompanied Cushing as curators on the Hemenway expedition in Arizona, charged with the care and classification of specimens. A *Washington Post* article, 3 February 1896, described Mrs Cushing, who was at that time engaged in the restoration of antique Indian pottery from shards, as a 'persevering little woman'.
7. The portraits of the Cushings may have been hung side by side; the reviewer for the *Daily Evening Telegraph* commented upon the two works together, calling the portrait of Frank Hamilton Cushing 'the most conspicuous' work in the show, while simply describing the portrait of Mrs Cushing as 'unfinished'. *Daily Evening Telegraph* (Philadelphia), 16 May 1896, quoted, Siegl 1978, p.140.
8. Letter from Dr Jesse D. Green to the Philadelphia Museum of Art, 20 April 1977.

Provenance: Given by the artist's widow, Susan Macdowell Eakins, and Mary Adeline Williams, 1929.

Exhibitions: Philadelphia, Earles Galleries, 1896, no cat. no.; New York, Museum of Modern Art, 1930, no.101; Philadelphia, Pennsylvania Museum of Art, 1930, no.101; San Francisco, M.H. de Young Memorial Museum, 1935, no cat. no.; Harrisburg, Harrisburg Art Association, 1940, no cat. no.; Philadelphia, Museum of Art, 1944, no. 75; Pittsburgh, Carnegie Institute, 1945, no. 111; New York, American Academy of Arts and Letters, 1958, no. 25.

Literature: Goodrich 1933, no. 275; Burroughs 1923 (2), ill. p.311; *Philadelphia Museum of Art Bulletin*, vol.XXV, no. 133, March 1930, p.23, no. 110; Schendler 1967, p.144, no. 65, ill. p.146; Siegl 1978, pp.140–1, no.90, ill. pl.90; Truettner 1985, pp.48–72, ill. p.52; Homer 1992, pp.191–2, ill. pl.178.

Fig.30a
Frank Hamilton Cushing
1895
Oil on canvas, 228.6 × 152.4 (90 × 60)
Thomas Gilcrease Institute of American History and Art, Tulsa, Oklahoma

31
Professor Henry A. Rowland
1897
Oil on canvas, 203.8 × 137.2 (80¼ × 54)
Inscribed l.l.: *Prof Henry A. Rowland/
Thomas Eakins 1897*

Addison Gallery of American Art, Phillips
Academy, Andover, Massachusetts.
Gift of Stephen C. Clark (G264)

It is almost too tempting to read Thomas
Eakins's remarkable portrait of Professor
Henry A. Rowland – surrounded as it is by a
chestnut frame onto which the artist has
carved circles, lines, mathematical equations
and crudely drawn diagrams – as an affirma-
tion of the correspondence between painting
and science. Eakins's career is filled with
instances of his commitment to a 'scientific'
form of painting: perspective drawings that
map and measure the placement of his figures;
anatomical details that add an air of correct-
ness to his portraits (note the blood vessels
lacing Rowland's right hand); and portraits of
subjects chosen for their medical, scientific or
professional accomplishments.

The portrait of Henry Rowland falls within
the latter category. Rowland (1848–1901) was
one of the leading physicists of his day. A graduate, like Eakins, of Philadelphia's Central
High School, Rowland had been invited at the
age of twenty-seven to join the founding
faculty of Johns Hopkins University. His
career spanned the central controversies of late
nineteenth-century physics: the speed of light,
the mechanical equivalent of heat, the unit of
electrical resistance and of its magnetic analogue permeability, the ratio of the electrosta-
tic force to the electromagnetic force. Rowland
sought answers by clarifying the terms of each
problem. He worked to find the constants – an
absolute mathematical measure – that defined
the forces involved. He succeeded where others
had failed by building better instruments.[1]

When demonstrating his work on solar
spectrums before the Physical Society in
London in 1881, Rowland proclaimed that his
machines could accomplish in one hour what
others required three years to do. Rowland's
remark prompted Sir James Dewar, who had
succeeded Faraday at the Royal Institution, to
respond, 'I struggle with a very mixed feeling
of elation and depression: elation for the wonderful gain to science, and depression for
myself; for I have been at work three years in
mapping the ultra-violet'.[2]

Eakins composed his picture of Rowland as
a *portrait d'apparat*, a form of painting popular

at the time that identifies the subject with his
profession. Rowland sits contemplatively in an
interior space suggestive of a laboratory.
Behind him stands his famous ruling machine,
a revolutionary device that allowed for
measurements of the spectrum up to 1/20,000
of an inch. During six days of non-stop ruling,
the machine cut three miles of grooves on a
five-inch grating, an advance so great upon
previous methods of calibration that 'the study
of spectroscopy as an exact science dated from
his inventions'.[3] In the background, to the
viewer's right, Rowland's assistant and skilled
machinist, Theodore Schneider, works on a
lathe.

Eakins, who felt that Rowland 'ought to be
painted', solicited Rowland's approval for the
project in 1897. He left Philadelphia that
summer to join Rowland for one month at
Rowland's summer home at Seal Harbor,
Maine. The picture wasn't completed until the
end of the year, after Eakins had travelled
from Philadelphia to Baltimore to observe
Rowland's ruling machine first-hand. Eakins
was impressed with what he saw. He made a
perspective drawing of the machine that har-
kens back to his first exercises in mechanical
drawing at Central High School (no. 1). Eakins
informed Rowland that sketching the machine
allowed him to get 'an understanding of it. The
directness and simplicity of that engine has
affected me and I shall be a better mechanic
and a better artist'.[4]

The frame surrounding the canvas is one of
five eccentric, individually carved frames
known to have been made by Eakins.[5] In a
letter to Rowland, Eakins proposed displaying
'some of the Fraunhofer [spectrum] lines
which you were the first man to see'. He asked
for a 'simple & artistic way ... of suggesting the
electric unit that I heard of your measuring so
accurately'. At Rowland's suggestion, Eakins
abandoned the idea of Fraunhofer lines and
turned instead to designs supplied by Rowland
himself. Eakins was pleased with the results.
When the painting was exhibited at the
National Academy of Design in 1904, he wrote
to his friend Frank W. Stokes in New York,
'Have you been to the Academy? I am wonder-
ing where they have hidden my Rowland
whose frame they hate but I like'. In another
letter, he described the frame as 'ornamented
with lines of the spectrum and with coeffi-
cients and mathematical formulae relating to
light and electricity, all original with Professor
Rowland and selected by himself'.[6]

The frame must be understood as an integ-
ral part of the painting. As a disembodied
space, filled with partial notations, fragmented
equations, and schematic drawings, the frame

32

Sketch for Professor Henry A. Rowland

1897

Oil on canvas, 30.5 × 22.9 (12 × 9)

Inscribed on verso: *Sketch for portrait of Professor Roland [sic] painted by Thomas Eakins. Presented to Charles Bregler, 1934, by Mrs Thomas Eakins*; inscribed on recto: *Original sketch for Portrait of Professor Roland [sic] by Thomas Eakins, 1891*

[The inscriptions were both probably done by Mrs Thomas Eakins. The date of 1891 is in error, and should read 1897]

Addison Gallery of American Art, Phillips Academy, Andover, Massachusetts (G265[1940.17])

carries with it the burden of thinking in the painting. It represents what we might term Eakins's 'pragmatic' option within the overall realism of his art. If we understand pragmatism, a philosophical movement concurrent with Eakins's work, as a way of insisting that thinking makes a difference in the world, that mental work is real labour, then the Rowland portrait, like so much of Eakins's *œuvre*, straddles the terms of pragmatic discourse. It is concerned to legitimate thinking as an element essential to worldly endeavour.

Pragmatists like William James and Charles S. Pierce sought to define what James called the 'cash value of ideas'. They insisted that thinking was an activity that could be measured by its practical effects. Eakins's portrait of Rowland, in parallel fashion, understands thinking, like science, as a form of symbolic intervention within the material realm. The painting insists, as part of its programme, that labour in the world requires mental vigilance. It disallows any notion of work that does not also include an account of mind.

We see Eakins develop this dialectic of thought and action in two ways: (1) through the emphasis he places upon Rowland's head and hands, and (2) by the counterpoint he establishes between Rowland and Schneider. In no. 32, an oil sketch of Rowland painted by Eakins upon his arrival in Maine, Eakins defined Rowland's figure as a broken diagonal of light extending from Rowland's forehead, through his shirt (the jacket is unbuttoned), and concluding in Rowland's strongly highlighted right hand. Though Eakins retained this posture in the final portrait, he did away with the axis of light that knits head, body and hands together. Eakins instead costumed Rowland with a tie and waistcoat absent in the oil sketch. As a result, the final portrait de-emphasizes Rowland's torso, which shares the brown tones of the background, while highlighting instead Rowland's head and hands. Eakins wrote to Rowland about this effort to 'simplify' the painting's composition: 'The most prominent thing in the picture will be the head, whereas before it was the whole figure'.[7]

The canvas defines Rowland as a thinker whose contemplative efforts are tethered to the real world. The downward slant of Rowland's right hand, together with the palpable sense of weight attached to the metal grating in the left, function figuratively to anchor Rowland's thoughts. So too with the grating machine, which abuts Rowland's body as if it were another arm, a mechanical extension of his body.

A century earlier, the American portraitist John Singleton Copley painted the silversmith Paul Revere in his work clothes in a fashion that we may understand today as a precursor to the *portrait d'apparat* (fig.31a). Revere, like Rowland, is defined through the counterpoint of head and hand, both highlighted and rounded. Copley's goal in the painting was to interfuse artisanal production with an aura of thought. His portrait achieves a delicate balance between the desire to ennoble art as more than manual dexterity (a form of thinking as well as making) and the need to reassure his viewers that the artist labours, like others, to the practical benefit of mankind. The link between head and hand, for Copley, was thus fraught with ideological significance. On the one hand, it pushed the notion of crafts towards the status of a fine art, while on the other, it disavowed any link between art and aristocracy that might have worried Copley's commercially minded clientele.[8] The highlighting of the head worked to the former end, while the prominence of the hand performed the labour of reassurance.

For Eakins, the status of painting as a fine art is no longer in question. The issue a century later is not the noble nature of painting but the prerogatives of the newly emergent professional and managerial classes of Eakins's day. The scientific graffiti of the frame, when coupled with the emphasis on Rowland's head, reminds the viewer that knowledge has less to do with intuition than it does with education and expertise. Only experts can truly understand, let alone manage, the complex machinery of society. Rowland's hand, in turn, reassures us of the instrumental thrust of all reason: that thought is not without social benefits. It is the task of professional society to oversee the material operations of the world, supervising those laws that govern both men and machines.

Rowland thus embodies what Burton Bledstein has termed the 'culture of professionalism'. He occupies a distinct space linked to 'specialized training, uncommon knowledge, administrative ability, and a professional code of ethics and . . . a distinctive way of life'.[9]

Schneider, in turn, functions less as Rowland's double than as a second set of hands. He performs the tasks that Rowland assigns him, translating the former's thoughts into achieved results. His single-minded dedication to the lathe, which he works, slightly off-focus, in the background, distinguishes him from Rowland, whose abstracted gaze, leisured mode of thought and freed hands all signify not only his scientific but his *class* differences from Schneider. We might, with some exaggeration, see

Schneider and the frame surrounding the canvas as alternate versions of Rowland, each split off from Rowland while embodying those contradictory tendencies that he holds together in his person. Schneider from this perspective represents the *body* in its manual functions, while the frame presents us with a reified version of *thought*.[10]

The portrait as a whole (canvas and frame) thus recapitulates the larger social divisions of Rowland's late nineteenth-century world. It condenses onto its two male figures the separate roles of intellectual and manual labour that undergird a bureaucratic culture. It both abstracts thought from the workaday world at the same time as it redeploys thinking in instrumental fashion to govern that world. Seen from this vantage, Eakins's portrait legitimates professional culture through its notion of *expertise* (head and frame) even as it marks off the class boundaries between a professional élite and those who serve it.

Fig.31a
John Singleton Copley, *Paul Revere*
*c.*1768–1770
Oil on canvas, 88.9 × 72.3 (35 × 28½)
Museum of Fine Arts, Boston. Gift of Joseph W., William B., and Edward H. R. Revere

And yet more is at stake in the painting than professional legitimation. Note Rowland's two hands (see detail, opposite). Their apparent symmetry, each resting comfortably on either of Rowland's thighs, belies the larger oddity that defines their relation to the viewer. While Rowland's right hand faces downward, his left hand faces up, a variation that would be unremarkable were it not for the fact that the left hand almost entirely disappears. The true partner to Rowland's extended right hand is not his left hand but the diffraction grating which he holds in it. Rowland's left hand has been rather conspicuously covered over by a brightly coloured piece of metal, which parallels in both its length and its angle to the picture plane Rowland's right hand. What remains of the hand are the rounded nubs of the fingertips and the inner length of Rowland's thumb. Instead of two hands in parallel position, we see one hand – shadowed, lined, and painted with intense feeling – and its partner, a mechanical object, the only source of large chromatic variation within the canvas.

If the grating reminds the viewer of Rowland's ties to the history of spectroscopy, it also reminds the viewer, through its rich colour, of Eakins's concerns with representation. Like the blood two decades earlier on the scalpel of Dr Samuel Gross in *The Gross Clinic* (fig.31b), the grating in the Rowland portrait is a flat metallic surface held in the hand and showered with colour. It alludes not only to science, but as Michael Fried has demonstrated in *The Gross Clinic*, to the painter's brush and palette.[11] As a startling splash of colour within an otherwise subdued canvas, the grating functions as a synecdoche for the painting as whole.

I am suggesting, in other words, that the details of Rowland's hands are not incidental to the picture, nor a matter of simple convention or 'good' composition, but that, on the contrary, they are essential to the very way that meaning is constructed in Eakins's canvas. They alert us to Eakins's concern with the processes of representation, the manner in which a painting about science very quickly becomes a painting about painting. They help us understand why the Rowland portrait is less a portrait of Rowland's world than Eakins's, less a *portrait d'apparat* than a portrait of the artist. Eakins places science in the service of his own concerns: the reconciliation of mind and body through professionalized modes of behaviour, the transformation of thought into a form of 'expertise', the dual role of expertise as both agency within the world and as a marker of class difference, and the articulation of painting as a mode of professional activity. What began as a *portrait d'apparat*, a confirmation of the links between painting and science, concludes as a utopian fantasy, a study in how representation may be put to the service of class definition and individual agency.

BJW

1. Moore 1982, pp.150–61.
2. Ibid., p.160.
3. Ibid., pp.150–60, and Goodrich 1982, vol.II, p.137.
4. Letter from Thomas Eakins to Henry Rowland, 28 August 1897, Pennsylvania Academy of the Fine Arts, archives.
5. The other four canvases with frames carved by Eakins are *The Concert Singer* (no. 26), mentioned by Eakins in a letter of 4 October 1897, to Rowland, *The Agnew Clinic* (fig.36a), *Frank Hamilton Cushing* (fig.30a) and *Salutat* (fig.34a). The latter two frames have subsequently been lost.
6. Quoted in Goodrich op. cit., vol.II, p.140. For an explanation of the scientific meaning of each image in the frame, see Moore op. cit., p.150.
7. Letter from Thomas Eakins to Henry Rowland, 3 September 1897, Pennsylvania Academy of the Fine Arts, archives.
8. For a discussion of the role of art in colonial American culture, see Ellis 1979, pp.22–38.
9. Bledstein 1976, p.57.
10. For a parallel reading of Schneider's role in the painting, see Clark 1991, pp.5–28.
11. Fried 1987, *passim*.

Provenance (no. 31): Bought direct from Mrs Thomas Eakins about 1929 by Stephen C. Clark; presented to Addison Gallery of American Art by Mr Clark, 1931.

Provenance (no. 32): Consigned by Babcock Galleries to the MacBeth Gallery, 1940; sold to Addison Gallery, 1940.

Exhibitions (no. 31): Philadelphia, Pennsylvania Academy of the Fine Arts, 1917, no. 136; New York, Whitney Museum of American Art, 1933, no cat. no.; Venice, 19th Biennale, 1934; Cambridge, Massachusetts, Fogg Art Museum, 1949, no cat. no.; Washington, DC, National Gallery of Art, 1961, no. 61; New York, Whitney Museum of American Art, 1966, no cat. no.; New York, Whitney Museum of American Art, 1970, no. 63; Philadelphia, Museum of Art, 1982 (1), no. 110.

Exhibitions (no. 32): Hamilton College, E.W. Root Art Center, 1960, no cat.no.; Washington, DC, National Gallery of Art, 1961, no cat no.; Philadelphia, Museum of Art, 1982 (1), no. 111.

Literature (no. 31): Goodrich 1933, no. 264, ill. pl.42; Porter 1959, ill. no. 43; Schendler 1967, pp.104, 105, 121, 289, ill.122, no.51; Sewell 1982, pp.103, 104, 105, ill. pl.110; Johns 1983 (1), p.159; Fried 1987; Clark 1991, pp.5–28.

Literature (no. 32): Goodrich 1933, no. 265; Sewell 1982, p.103, no.111.

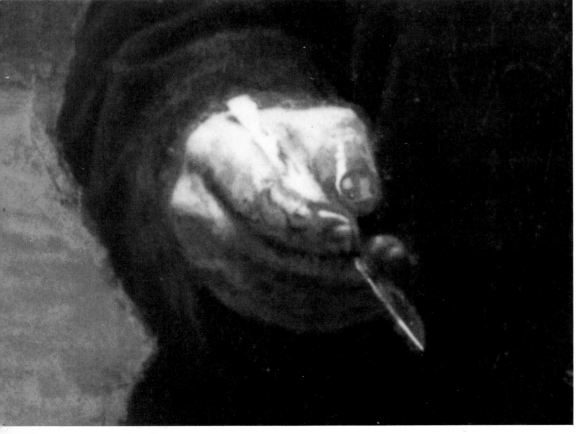

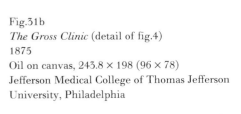

Fig.31b
The Gross Clinic (detail of fig.4)
1875
Oil on canvas, 243.8 × 198 (96 × 78)
Jefferson Medical College of Thomas Jefferson University, Philadelphia

33
Billy Smith
1898
Oil on canvas, 53.3 × 43.2 (21 × 17)
Signed and dated l.r.: *Billy Smith,*
from his friend, Thomas Eakins, 1898

The Roland P. Murdock Collection,
Wichita Art Museum, Wichita, Kansas

Thomas Eakins's portrait of Billy Smith is one
of four oil studies done for the larger canvas
Between Rounds (no. 34) of 1899. In common
with most of Eakins's studies, it stands as a
finished painting, and provides insight into the
character of both the sitter and the artist.

In 1897 or 1898 Samuel Murray, Eakins's
friend from the Art Students' League, began
taking Eakins several times a week to prize-
fights at the old Philadelphia Sports Arena. By
the time Eakins began painting the boxing
series, in 1898, the game had become the leading passion for sports fans in Philadelphia, and
the city boasted one of the liveliest fight scenes
in the country. Prize-fighting, however, was
not yet a spectator sport for high society or for
women. In addition, it did not fit in with the
genteel impressionism of Sargent and Whistler that was currently popular in America, and
therefore would have been considered an
unlikely subject for serious painting. Eakins,
however, was never concerned with what was
appropriate or fashionable, and his choice of
subject was always rooted in contemporary
realities. In addition, he was an avid sportsman
and boxing thus had a natural appeal to him.
Eakins was among the first Americans to paint
this genre scene, anticipating the urban realism of George Bellows and the Ash Can School
by ten years.

Through his association with Murray, and
two Philadelphia sportswriters, Clarence Cranmer and Henry Schlicter, Eakins was introduced to several Philadelphia prize-fighters.
Among them was Billy Smith, with whom he
developed a lifelong friendship. Smith was not
a celebrity, but he was a professional, and
made a living at it for ten years, fighting over
300 rounds.[1] He was a small man, weighing
less than 120 pounds, and fought in the
featherweight division under the name of
'Turkey Point' Billy Smith.[2] Eakins was
impressed by Smith's workmanlike professionalism, and it was for this reason that he chose to
depict him for the painting *Between Rounds*.
As most of his portraits were non-
commissioned, and his sitters were usually
friends or relatives, Eakins often gave his sitters the completed works. Eakins gave this
study to Smith, signing the canvas, 'Billy
Smith, from his friend Thomas Eakins, 1898'.
After Smith retired, he became an evangelist
with the Salvation Army, and he was a great
comfort to Eakins in the artist's later years
when he was sick, paying regular visits to give
Eakins soothing massages, for which Murray
and Susan Eakins were very grateful.[3]

In *Between Rounds*, Eakins chose to depict
Smith seated in his corner, resting between the
first and second rounds, indicated by the

number two over the entrance door. Smith is contemplating possibly both the confrontation that is about to take place as well as the round that has just passed. The view is from below ringside, which accounts for the somewhat awkward foreshortening of the arm, but enables us to glimpse Smith's moment of introspection. In the study, Eakins, directed by his own emotional response to the sitter, captures with powerful insight the essence of the fighter. While recording the physical reality of the athlete, Eakins describes the essential element and vigour of life. Smith's expression is surly and intense as he looks off towards his opponent in the opposite corner, his jaw drawn taut from his clenched teeth. The converging diagonals of his arms and the ropes not only serve to underscore the direction of his gaze, but also frame his chiselled features which convey a youthful determination.

Although Eakins's primary interest here was in portraiture, the study allowed Eakins to indulge himself in his knowledge of anatomy, which was explored in the full-length figure sketch (fig. 33a). Smith's body is too lean to be heroic, but while his form is not graceful, every muscle in his jaw, neck, shoulders, and arm is meticulously crafted. The pumped striations of Smith's powerful forearm convey his strength and inherent abilities. The attention paid to anatomical accuracy also serves to emphasize the mind, reminding us of the rigorous mental conditioning that must accompany the athlete's physical training.

In 1940, after Smith had sold the portrait of himself to Walker Galleries in New York, he was asked for information regarding the picture. In response, Smith, in a highly perceptive manner, described his encounter with Eakins and made the following observations:

It was 1898, when Mr Eakins came to a Boxing Club, to get a modle [sic] for his first [fight] picture, titled, *Between Rounds*. He choose [sic] Me. I posed first for the picture you just sold. Then for the Between Rounds, and next for the one titled Salutat. Mr Eakins, to me was a Gentleman and an Artist and a Realist of Realists. In his work he would not add or subtract. I recall, while painting the portrait you just sold, I noticed a dark smear across my upper lip, I asked Mr Eakins what it was, He said it was my mustache, I wanted it of [sic], He said it was there and there it stayed. You can see that He was a Realist.[4]

The moustache was in fact the result of Smith's intentional neglect to shave, a common practice among boxers, as an unshaven face better absorbed the impact of a punch.

When one compares the portrait study of Billy Smith to the finished painting of *Between Rounds*, it is striking that virtually no change

in the renderings of the figure took place between the sketch and the finished painting. Charles Bregler, one of Eakins's students, commented on the artist's ability to conceive fully the basic idea for a painting in the sketch, which showed that Eakins knew exactly what he wished and intended to do from the start.[5]

Billy Smith was painted during the period in which Eakins was turning almost exclusively to portraiture. Smith was a simple man, and Eakins discovered in him the qualities of perseverance and diligence, qualities that characterized Eakins himself. The study of Billy Smith is a celebration of humanity and a reminder of the heroism within all men.[6]

BSB

1. Goodrich 1982, vol.II, p.144.
2. Smith used the name, which is derived from an area in south Philadelphia, because at the time he began his boxing career the Englishman Billy Smith was currently a champion.
3. Hendricks 1974, p.241.
4. Billy Smith to Maynard Walker Galleries, New York, 15 August 1940, the Archives of American Art. Quoted in Hendricks op. cit., p.236.
5. Bregler 1931.
6. Johns 1983 (1).

Provenance: From Mr William Smith through the Walker Galleries, New York, 1940.

Exhibitions: Philadelphia, Pennsylvania Academy of the Fine Arts, 1917, no cat. no.; Tulsa, Oklahoma, The Phillbrook Art Center, 1969, no cat. no.

Literature: Watson 1940, ill. p.696; Tomko 1972, pp.57–8; Hendricks 1974, p.236; Goodrich 1982, vol.II, ill. pl.215; Rhodes 1990, p.64, ill. pl.27.

Fig.33a
Sketch of Billy Smith
c.1898
Oil on canvas, 50.8 × 40.6 (20 × 16)
Philadelphia Museum of Art. Gift of Mrs Thomas Eakins and Miss Mary Adeline Williams

34
Between Rounds
1899
Oil on canvas, 127.3 × 101.3 ($50\frac{1}{8}$ × $39\frac{7}{8}$)
Signed l.r. *Eakins.99.*

Philadelphia Museum of Art. Gift of Mrs
Thomas Eakins and Miss Mary Adeline
Williams (29.184.16)

In 1898 Eakins began his prize-fighting series.
Introduced to the Philadelphia fight scene
through his friend Samuel Murray, Eakins was
able to explore the male form in a way that he
had not done since his sculling pictures of the
early 1870s.

The series, which includes *Taking the Count*
(fig.10) and *Salutat* (fig.34a) of 1898, culmi-
nates in the forceful and complex composition
of *Between Rounds*. The work encompasses
several themes that underlie many of Eakins's
works, including voyeurism, heroism, and
suspended time, simultaneously revealing
Eakins's power as a full-scale genre painter and
portraitist.

The boxing series allowed Eakins system-
atically to reinterpret the nude through a complex range of poses, and was, in part, developed
out of his photographic studies of the 1880s, in
particular the 'Naked Series' (1883).[1] In these
serial nude images, Eakins captured the
human form performing a sequence of movements; this allowed him to study the nude
frontally, from the side, and from the back (see
no. 51). The influence of photography manifested itself in his compelling work *The Swimming Hole* (fig.8), begun in 1883, and then
again in the boxing series. The human figure
was manipulated into the greatest variety of
poses, by which Eakins captured the action and
suspended it in time.

The three works, *Taking the Count, Salutat,*
and *Between Rounds* in effect form a triptych
celebrating human endurance and achievement through the images respectively of
defeat, victory, and the contemplation of
battle. This epic sense of life does not derive
from a brutal representation of the sport, but
instead emerges through a measured timelessness marking the various stages of human
perseverance.

Between Rounds depicts a match at the Philadelphia Arena that took place on 22 April
1898, in which Billy Smith (see no. 33) was
beaten by another fighter.[2] Smith sits in his
corner, between rounds, his concentration
intense and focused on his opponent as he
waits for the timekeeper's signal. Ellwood
McCloskey, a retired fighter known as 'The

Fig.34a
Salutat
1898
Oil on canvas, 127.3 × 101.6 ($50\frac{1}{8}$ × 40)
Addison Gallery of American Art,
Phillips Academy, Andover, Massachusetts

Old War Horse', leans over and advises Smith.[3] Eakins places the arena in the mid-distance, illuminating Smith's body by the strong overhead light, and isolating him against the wall of spectators.

Eakins's working process involved the preparation of many preliminary studies. For the boxing series, Eakins paid several boxers to come and pose for him in his studio, which he converted, for a time, into a workout gym. In addition to two compositional studies, individual sketches were made of the timekeeper, Clarence Cranmer, and Billy Smith (no.33). These studies were than combined, resulting in the fully developed composition of *Between Rounds*. Thus, although *Between Rounds* represents an actual event, it was essentially recreated, figure by figure, in Eakins's studio.

Eakins's attention to detail and his directed search for character are not confined to the face, hands, and figure of Smith or his attendants. Eakins extends this to the surrounding inanimate setting as well. The still-life of the brass bucket on the floor with its sponge and accompanying cut lemon is rendered with precise, linear accuracy exemplary of Eakins's technical mastery. *Between Rounds* is thus unlike many of Eakins's paintings, which are studies of single figures, notable for their realization of the central object rather than for their design as a whole. The work combines painterly and linear styles, and emotional and physical realities, which result in a complex and powerful composition.

One of the underlying themes of the boxing series is the paradoxical relationship between ephemeral and suspended time. In *Between Rounds* there is an atmospheric stillness derived from the smoky haze which permeates the arena. The flowing lines of Smith's lean legs, which extend out to the body of the attendant fanning Smith, and of the attendant's outstretched arms, which visually connect with those of Smith, create a circular pocket of arrested movement. Time asserts itself as our eye moves from the boxer, to the spectators, to the timekeeper, and to the two attendants. In the foreground the timekeeper diligently watches the time on his stopwatch, his right hand poised to ring the bell. The ritual is fixed in a moment of timelessness which passes under the timekeeper's hand.

The image of the hand played a significant role in Eakins's works. Often compositionally linked to the head of the sitter, either through placement or light, the hand represented the physical manifestation of the mind's will. In *Between Rounds* the timekeeper's power lies in his poised hand, and recalls Eakins's earlier portraits of his sisters playing the piano (see no.15). The representation of this physical manifestation of intellectual training and rational thought reached its fullest development in *The Gross Clinic* (fig.4) and *The Agnew Clinic* (fig.36a), where the physicians lecture to a room filled with students, their hands firmly holding the tools with which they carry out their work.

Other parallels between the boxing and clinic paintings exist. As with the clinic pictures, the setting of *Between Rounds* is that of an arena with the spectators surrounding the action. We become voyeurs, witnessing the scene as if from behind a curtain that has been pulled aside. The theme of public display and judgement have sources early in Eakins's career. These images are, in part, adaptations of the gladiatorial scenes painted by Eakins's teacher Jean-Léon Gérôme. *Between Rounds* and *Salutat*, in particular, are successful reinterpretations of academic subject matter. Gérôme's images of the gladiator in the Colosseum are translated by Eakins into a distinctly American and contemporary context as depictions of the prize-fighter in the sports arena.[4]

Between Rounds was included in the Pennsylvania Academy's annual exhibition of 1900, and received disparaging comments from critics. One wrote, 'you all know ... he can do better'. Eakins offered the painting for $1,600, but when Harrison Morris, Director of the Academy at the time, asked Eakins if he would go down in price, Eakins refused, and the painting remained in his possession until his death in 1916.[5]

In *Between Rounds* balance and order are supplemented by stability and permanence. As in *Max Schmitt in a Single Scull* (fig.2), in *Between Rounds*, Eakins chooses to portray the moment in which there is a lapse in action, and the athlete's rationalization process takes precedence over the physical aspect of the sport. Although Eakins's paintings of athletes and sporting events are celebrations of masculinity and explore the beauty of the human form, there is an essential connection made between the corporal and the cerebral. It is this emphasis on the contemplative and the internal that imbues *Between Rounds* with a monumental sense of dignity and reverence.

BSB

1. See Parry 1980, p.2.
2. Hendricks 1974, p.238.
3. Goodrich 1982, vol.II, p.149, and Ellwood McCloskey in a brochure in the Charles Bregler collection at the Pennsylvania Academy of the Fine Arts.
4. Weinberg 1984, p.39.
5. Hendricks op. cit., p.239.

Provenance: Given by the artist's widow, Susan Macdowell Eakins, and Miss Mary Adeline Williams, 1929.

Exhibitions: Philadelphia, Pennsylvania Academy of the Fine Arts, 1900, no.154; New York, Metropolitan Museum of Art, 1917, no.45; Philadelphia, Pennsylvania Academy of the Fine Arts, 1917, no.92; New York, Whitney Studio Club, 1921, no.46; New York, Museum of Modern Art, 1930, no.106; Los Angeles, Los Angeles Museum, 1932, no.752; Chicago, Art Institute, 1934, no.390; New York, Whitney Museum of American Art, 1935, no.31; Philadelphia, Museum of Art, 1940, no.20; Boston, Museum of Fine Arts, 1944, no.37; Philadelphia, Museum of Art, 1944, no.83; London, Tate Gallery, 1946, no.68; New York, American Academy of Arts and Letters, 1958, no.56; Washington, DC, National Gallery of Art, 1961, no.72; New York, Whitney Museum of American Art, 1970, no.20; Philadelphia, Museum of Art, 1982 (1), no.32.

Literature: Porter 1959, ill. pl.60; Schendler 1967, p.154–5, ill. p.157; Hendricks 1974, pp.236–9, ill. pl.41; Siegl 1978, p.149, ill. pl.97; Smith 1979, pp.403–8, 410, 412, ill.f.p.; Goodrich 1982, vol.II, pp.144–9; Weinberg 1984, p.39; Homer 1992, pp.237–9.

35
William Merritt Chase
*c.*1899
Oil on canvas, 60.5 × 50.8 ($23\frac{7}{8}$ × 20)
Inscribed on verso: *To my friend,*
William M. Chase, Thomas Eakins

Hirshhorn Museum and Sculpture Garden,
Smithsonian Institution. Gift of Joseph H.
Hirshhorn, 1966 (HMSG 1966.1486)

In 1896, ten years after forcing Eakins's resignation, the Pennsylvania Academy of the Fine Arts appointed as instructor the highly acclaimed American painter William Merritt Chase (1849–1916). During the years following Chase's appointment to the Academy, Eakins and Chase agreed to paint each other's portraits, of which only Eakins's portrait of Chase still exists. (Chase's portrait of Eakins is unknown and generally believed to have been destroyed by Mrs Eakins.)[1] While it is clear that the two painters knew each other both before and after Chase came to the Pennsylvania Academy, the extent of their friendship and professional relationship remains unclear. It is in fact hard to imagine the recalcitrant, unsociable, and somewhat embittered Eakins as a close friend of the urbane and successful Chase.

Born in the small town of Williamsburg, Indiana, Chase studied painting at the National Academy of Design in New York and then at the Royal Academy in Munich[2] before returning to New York in 1878, where he almost immediately became a leading figure in the rapidly evolving New York art community. Partly to counter his small-town origins, Chase strove to create for himself a sophisticated and cosmopolitan image of 'genteel bohemianism'. He was unfailingly smart in appearance and his famed Tenth Street studio in New York (fig.35a) quickly became a well-known meeting place for the city's cultural élite and elegant society.[3] A former student of Chase described him in this way:

His neatness in personal apparel is one of his chief characteristics ... He never appears before his classes that he is not perfectly groomed and looking as though he had just stepped from a band-box. He always wears a fresh carnation in the buttonhole of his coat, which offsets the wide black string attached to his nose glasses and making a characteristic color note.[4]

Eakins, on the other hand, intensely focused on his own work and his own world, was little interested in and, not surprisingly, even less appreciated by, high society. After visiting his studio (fig.35b) in 1881 one art critic described Eakins as:

not even a man of tolerably good appearance or breeding. His home and surroundings and family were decidedly of the *lower* middle-class, I shall say, and he himself a big ungainly young man, very untidy to say the least, in his dress ... His studio was a garret room without one single object upon which the eye might rest with pleasure – the sole ornaments some skeletons and some models of the frame and muscles which looked, of course, like the contents of a butchers shop![5]

Eakins himself was aware of this difference and is reported to have once commented, 'Chase's studio is an atelier; this is a workshop'.[6]

Whereas Eakins found it difficult to get along with the Board of the Pennsylvania Academy, the Philadelphia Sketch Club, the Drexel Institute, some of his family relations, and many of his sitters, Chase was not only immensely popular, but also a shrewd and successful bureaucrat. He was a leading figure in the Society of American Artists (SAA), serving as president for eleven years (1880 and 1885–1895), belonged to numerous art organizations, and served frequently on exhibition juries and committees.

Personal and penetrating, Eakins's paintings seem to be informed by a very different aim from Chase's portraits of cultivated society and bourgeois life, with their characteristic glossy surfaces and technical bravura. Frank

Fig.35a
Rockwood, *William M. Chase in his studio*
Photograph, reproduced in *The Commercial Advertiser New York*, 10 February 1900

Fig.35b
Unknown photographer (Susan Macdowell Eakins?), *Samuel Murray, Thomas Eakins, William R. O'Donovan and Harry in the Chestnut Street studio*
*c.*1891–1892
Charles Bregler Archival Collection, Hirshhorn Museum and Sculpture Garden, Smithsonian Institution

Jewett Mather, for example, considered Chase's painting 'as consummate from point of view of sheen and surface as it was deficient in inner gravity'.[7] Eakins himself was also reported to have reservations about Chase's merits as an artist and teacher.[8] Conversely, Eakins's student and long-time friend Samuel Murray (not always a reliable source) maintained that Chase sometimes dissuaded patrons from commissioning portraits from Eakins, and in lectures to his students criticized Eakins as a man 'hide-bound by modeling'.[9]

But Chase in fact used his influence several times to help Eakins. In 1879, when the Pennsylvania Academy hosted a Philadelphia showing of the annual Society of American Artists exhibition, Chase, as a representative of the SAA, came to Eakins's aid by protesting about the Pennsylvania Academy's hanging of Eakins's *The Gross Clinic* outside the main exhibition. While the eventual compromise did not result in the restitution of *The Gross Clinic*, it is likely that Eakins appreciated the SAA's protests on his behalf.[10] The next year, Chase's first as president, the SAA elected Eakins as a member. Chase is also likely to have been responsible for Eakins's presence in the 1883 Munich exhibition and for ensuring that three of his pictures were included in Durand-Ruel's important 1891 Paris exhibition of contemporary American art.[11] Even more directly, Chase served on the award committee and jury at the World's Columbian Exposition in 1893 where Eakins won a bronze medal for *Mending the Net* (1893, Philadelphia Museum of Art).[12]

Chase, indeed, had qualities for which Eakins probably would have had the greatest respect. Like Eakins, Chase was a serious teacher who believed in teaching from life, not casts; and whilst Chase led many expensive summer teaching tours to Europe, he is said to have also taught free classes in Philadelphia using space provided by the public school system.[13] He strongly advocated developing an American school of art, and wanted to see American art students and institutions achieve a level of skill and professionalism which would rival the Europeans.[14]

Certainly Eakins and Chase were, or at least tried on several occaions, to be on good terms or even friends with each other. Samuel Murray (seemingly contradicting his previous tale) also recalled that Eakins and Chase once spent an afternoon together firing pistols in the basement of Eakins's studio, after turning it into a shooting gallery by setting up an iron sheet to stop the bullets.[15] In addition to his portrait, with its dedication on the verso of the canvas, Eakins is known to have also given Chase his

oil of *Arcadia* (1883, Metropolitan Museum of Art) and the oil painting *Sailing* (c. 1875, Philadelphia Museum of Art); he inscribed the latter on the lower right of the canvas 'To his friend William M. Chase/Eakins'.[16] Apart from the portrait Chase reportedly made of Eakins and exchanged with him, there is no evidence that Chase ever reciprocated Eakins's other gifts by giving Eakins any works of his own.[17]

The glimmer of light reflecting off Chase's glasses, plus the slight flash of gold from the clip on the ribbon and the clasp at the shirt collar, seem to allude to the superficiality that has often been noted in Chase's paintings, but the predominant tone is not one of mockery. Hinting at the flash and bravura which became the focus of John Singer Sargent's 1902 portrait of Chase (fig.35c), these subtle suggestions in Eakins's painting remain secondary to the cool monumentality of Chase's bust. With light falling liberally across Chase's forehead and his perhaps overly-broad shoulders and chest, Eakins pays his respects to a successful colleague, secure in his position and nobly serene.

PP

Fig.35c
John Singer Sargent, *William Merritt Chase*
1902
Oil on canvas, 158.8 × 105.1 (62½ × 41⅜)
The Metropolitan Museum of Art.
Gift of the Pupils of William Merritt Chase, 1905

1. Goodrich 1982, vol.II, pp.220–2.
2. First under Alexander von Wagner and later under Karl von Piloty.
3. See Cikovsky 1976, pp.2–14; Bryant 1991, pp.64–74, 241–2. Chase moved out of the Tenth Street studio in 1895, selling all of its contents at auction the following year. While not as remarkable as his New York studio, Chase's Philadelphia studio, which he moved several times, was reportedly still quite ornate.
4. Quoted in Pisano 1983, p.87.
5. According to an 1881 unpublished report submitted to the *American Art Review* by Mariana Griswald Van Rennselaer. Quoted in Goodrich op. cit., vol.I, p.197.
6. Goodrich op. cit., vol.II, p.8. Eakins was probably referring to Chase's Tenth Street studio in New York.
7. Quoted in Mather, Morey and Henderson 1927, p.118.
8. Goodrich op. cit., vol.II. p.222.
9. Quoted in Hendricks 1974, pp.240–1, from the Henry McBride Paper, Archives of American Art.
10. For a fuller account of the incident see Bryant op. cit., p.60; and Goodrich op. cit., vol.I, pp.137–8.
11. Roof 1917, p.57; Siegl 1978, p.35.
12. Siegl op. cit., p.35, cites a letter in the Philadelphia Museum of Art, archives, from Lloyd Goodrich to Henri Marceau, 18 November 1930, claiming Chase served as the one-man jury.
13. Ibid.
14. Much earlier Chase had turned down the offer of a teaching position at the Royal Academy in Munich, preferring to return to New York and participate in the development of American art.
15. Goodrich op. cit., vol.II, p.220.
16. Ibid.
17. Siegl op. cit., p.35.

Provenance: William Merritt Chase, c.1899; Leroy Ireland, Philadelphia, 1917; John F. Braun, Merion, Pennsylvania, 1917–1933?; Macbeth Gallery, New York, 1935; Canajoharie Art Gallery, Canajoharie, New York, 1937?; Robert G. McIntyre, New York; Hirschl & Adler Galleries, New York, 1957–1959; sold to Joseph H. Hirshhorn, New York, 1966.

Exhibitions: Pittsburgh, Carnegie Institute, 1899–1900, no.77; Philadelphia, Pennsylvania Academy of the Fine Arts, 1900, no.433; New York, American Fine Arts Society, 1903, no.140; New York, Metropolitan Museum of Art, 1917, no.55; Philadelphia, Pennsylvania Academy of the Fine Arts, 1917, no.75; Baltimore, Museum of Art, 1937, no.29; Washington, DC, National Gallery of Art, 1961, no.78; New York, Whitney Museum of American Art, 1970, no.75; Washington, DC, Hirshhorn Museum and Sculpture Garden, 1977, no.93.

Literature: Ziegler, 11 November 1917; Burroughs 1924, p.332; Goodrich 1933, no.330; Schendler 1967, pp.174–5, pl.85; Hendricks 1974, pp.241–2, ill. fig.262; Rosenzweig 1977, no.93, pp.170–1; Goodrich 1982, vol.II, pp.220–2.

36
Dr D. Hayes Agnew

c. 1889

Oil on canvas, 124.5 × 80 (49 × 31½)
Signed and inscribed b.l.: *STUDY FOR
THE/AGNEW POR-/TRAIT EAKINS*

Yale University Art Gallery. Bequest of
Stephen Carlton Clark, BA 1903 (1961.18.16)

In the early spring of 1889 a group of students
from the University of Pennsylvania
approached Thomas Eakins, expressing hope
that the artist would accept $750.00 to paint a
portrait of their professor, D. Hayes Agnew,
the eminent surgeon who was retiring from
the University that May. Eakins welcomed
their offer. Susan Macdowell Eakins later
recalled that the students 'asked only for the
head' of their professor, but Eakins, 'delighted
to paint Dr. Agnew, immediately offered to
paint them, for the same sum, a clinic picture,
with not only Dr. Agnew and his assistant
physicians, but also portraits of the class'.[1]

This opportunity marked Eakins's first significant commission since his professional
trauma and personal breakdown of 1886. It
returned the artist to the realm of surgical and
anatomical research with which he had so
many connections, and gave him a chance to
review and reprise the effort he had made with
the 1875 portrait of Agnew's colleague, Samuel
D. Gross (fig.4). The final work, completed in
the record time of only three months, proved to
be the largest that Eakins ever painted
(fig.36a). Yet for all the grandeur of the clinic
setting and the importance of the assistants
and students who surround him, the figure of
Dr Agnew remains set apart. Leaning against
the low railing that separates him from his
students, disengaged from the operation in
which he had been participating, Agnew
stands alone. His singular presence in the final
painting maintains the effect that Eakins
created in no.36, a nearly life-size portrait
study of Dr Agnew.

A rapidly executed composition sketch for
The Agnew Clinic (Private Collection) reveals
that Eakins always planned to isolate the surgeon to the left of his canvas. In the much
larger, more carefully worked portrait study
shown here, Eakins developed this isolated
figure into a dignified and imposing presence.[2]
Agnew apparently sat many times for Eakins,
returning often to the artist's third-floor studio
despite his busy schedule and claims of 'I can
give you only one hour'.[3] The study shows evidence of extended labour, and varying degrees
of finish indicate areas of special concentration.

Deft, summary strokes of paint create the folds
of the surgeon's gown, while patches of colour
define his face, hair, and features. However,
Eakins modelled the surgeon's hands and finished the outline of a drawstring cuff atten-
tively, thus calling attention to the
foreshortened right arm and the three-
dimensional illusion of the right hand projecting into space.

Even in this portrait study, without the
larger setting of the surgical clinic, Eakins
describes a subject actively engaged in his life's
work. The white gown instantly denotes a
practising surgeon, but it also indicates
Agnew's acceptance of the principles of antisepsis (which had not yet advanced to include
surgical masks or gloves), and testifies to the
flexibility of this white-haired doctor willing
to embrace the newest implications of a
theory.[4] Agnew's left hand holds a scalpel, the
primary instrument of his profession (and a
reminder to those who knew him that he was
ambidextrous), while the right hand, extended
with its palm turned upwards, indicates his
teaching role. No blood appears on Agnew's
hands or gown in this studio portrait. Eakins
later acceded to Agnew's request to remove the
blood that had been painted into the final
work. This breach of descriptive truth seems
alien to Eakins's principles, but it also suggests
that the artist was as interested in creating an
image of the modern surgeon as he was in
presenting the realities of that profession.[5]

In this light, Agnew's isolation may imply
more than a momentary pause in the surgical
proceedings. Eakins emphasizes the instruct-
ing half of Agnew's profession: the left hand
shows no evidence of blood, and the scalpel it
holds is idle. With the strong gesture of
Agnew's right hand into the viewer's space,
Eakins appeals to the medical students who
commissioned the portrait. Bernard Uhle's
portrait of a self-contained Agnew provides an
instructive comparison (fig.36b). Painted in
the same year as *The Agnew Clinic*, it was commissioned by Agnew's colleagues in the medical profession.[6] Its formidable likeness suggests
a man of determination and intellectual
strength, but unspecific achievement. Uhle's
portrait strives to transcend the sitter's professional role. Eakins, however, presents an
Agnew of the moment, who steps back from
active performance and gestures to his audience – an appropriate pose for a retiring professor beloved by his students.

David Hayes Agnew (1818–1892) was a
prominent surgeon in Philadelphia, whom
many Americans would have recognized as the
surgeon called in to attend President James A.
Garfield, who was mortally wounded by an

assassin in 1881. Agnew graduated from the University of Pennsylvania in 1838. He worked with his father, a rural doctor, and later in an iron-foundry business, before returning to Philadelphia in 1848 to teach practical anatomy and operative surgery at the Philadelphia School of Anatomy.[7] Agnew became director of the School in 1852, and served in that position for ten years. During his tenure the school grew in size and importance, and Agnew, who by this time was also affiliated with several hospitals, established himself as a practical, rather than theoretical, surgeon. Agnew contracted to serve the United States Army as a surgeon during the Civil War years, and in 1863 was invited to demonstrate anatomy at his Alma Mater. The University of Pennsylvania appointed him to the senior chair of surgery in 1871. Within the medical profession, Agnew was respected as an eminent surgeon of encyclopaedic knowledge, and praised especially for the clarity and thoroughness of his diagnoses, operations, and writings. Agnew was a superb generalist, whose comprehensive outlook would soon be overtaken by the move towards greater research and specialization, even then being practised by his colleagues at Johns Hopkins University in Baltimore, Maryland. But to his students at the University of Pennsylvania, Agnew was 'the most experienced surgeon, the clearest writer and teacher, the most venerated and beloved man'.[8]

Eakins was probably drawn to the anatomist in Agnew, as well as to the practical, experiential basis of his profession, which in so many ways paralleled his own. Eakins studied anatomy at the Jefferson Medical College from 1864 to 1865, but he certainly would have known of Agnew's work at the nearby School of Anatomy. When Eakins became a demonstrator of anatomy at the Pennsylvania Academy of the Fine Arts, he came under the supervision of Dr William W. Keen, Agnew's successor at the School.[9] Both Eakins and Agnew studied the human body as the foundation of their craft; both considered teaching a central part of their profession. These connections seem expressly acknowledged in the final clinic painting.[10]

Fig.36a
The Agnew Clinic
1899
Oil on canvas, 214.3 × 300 (84⅜ × 118⅛)
The University of Pennsylvania Collection of Art, Philadelphia

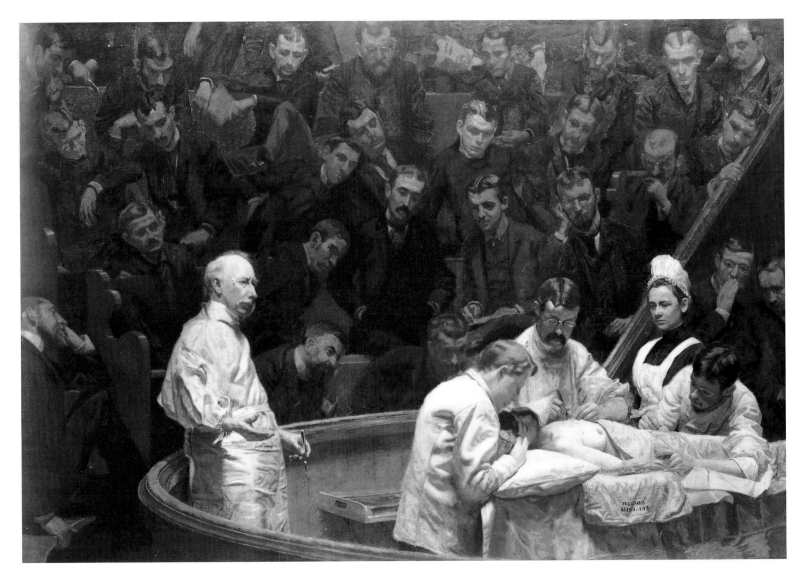

Eakins's study of Agnew remained for many years in the artist's studio, until Eakins decided in 1913 to send it to an exhibition in New York. When the painting appeared the next year at the Pennsylvania Academy, it was hailed as 'the sensation of the annual exhibition', bearing 'the inestimable qualities of a masterpiece'.[11] A bidding war ensued among museums eager to purchase the work; the victor was Albert Barnes. Renowned in 1914 for his collecting activity, and remembered today as an eccentric museum director and educator, Barnes earned his considerable fortune by developing two medicinal compounds.[12] This medical career (from which he immediately retired) began at the University of Pennsylvania in the fall of 1889; Barnes entered the School of Medicine only a few months after Agnew had left it. Perhaps his decision to purchase the Eakins portrait, one of only a few works by an American artist that Barnes ever bought, was swayed by sentiment as much as by admiration for any qualities inherent in the work itself.

Barnes was certainly influenced in his decision by his high school friend William Glackens. An artist who advised Barnes on his collecting, Glackens had taken night classes at the Pennsylvania Academy. Although he had worked under Thomas Anshutz, he recognized the importance of Eakins's work as a precedent to Anshutz's art as well as his own. By encouraging Barnes to purchase the work which caused such a sensation in Philadelphia, Glackens sought to rehabilitate the reputation of an important American artist. Glackens's friend and colleague Robert Henri later wrote to Barnes, congratulating him on his acquisition:

I am happy that you have [the Agnew portrait] and that it has found place in a collection in which there are so many of the best works by men who like Eakins have seen the way before them and have dared to follow it ... I think your purchase of his work is more significant than the purchase of a hundred old masters.[13]

SM

1. Susan Macdowell Eakins to Dr Horatio C. Wood, 4 April 1917; Pennsylvania Academy of the Fine Arts, archives, Charles Bregler collection. See also Goodrich 1982, vol.II, pp.38–46.
2. Slight differences between the figure of Agnew as he appears in the portrait and the clinic painting (such as the collar and folds of the surgical gown, or the position of the left hand against the rail) suggest a less than direct transfer from study to finished work. The study does not appear to be gridded for transfer, but at least one small cross-hair mark is visible to the left of Agnew's chin, implying that Eakins measured and aligned certain reference points to help him move from one format to another. The sketchy quality of many passages, as well as evidence of reworking around the head and railing, indicate that this painting was indeed Eakins's preliminary study from life, and not a work made after *The Agnew Clinic* was completed.
3. Like all his students, Agnew climbed the stairs to Eakins's studio, but apparently unlike those students, maintained himself with great serenity. Eakins also made frequent visits to the University of Pennsylvania to observe Agnew. See McHenry 1946, pp.143–4.
4. See Smith 1987, p.165. Joseph Lister's work in antisepsis, based on Louis Pasteur's germ theory, was published in the 1860s, but gained acceptance very slowly. An 1886 photograph of Agnew performing an operation (which seems to have served Eakins as a partial model for *The Agnew Clinic*) shows a canister of the carbolic acid which Lister advocated spraying around the surgical area. But in the photograph Agnew still wears street clothes, much as Dr Gross had appeared in Eakins's portrait of 1875.
5. See Adams 1892, p.333. Agnew's appeal to propriety was apparently not completely successful, since Eakins was still called a 'butcher' for painting a surgeon at work; see Goodrich op. cit., vol.II, p.46. As Adams pointed out, 'a surgical operation is rarely pleasant to a layman, and consequently such a subject must be more or less repulsive to the general public'.
6. Adams op. cit., p.314. The committee that commissioned Uhle's portrait in 1888 included Drs S. Weir Mitchell and Samuel W. Gross (the son of Samuel D. Gross), both of whom knew Eakins and his work very well. For whatever reason, these men decided to choose another artist for their commemorative portrait.
7. Adams op. cit., provides full, if somewhat effusive, biographical information on Agnew. Adams, himself a doctor, was married to Agnew's niece.
8. This phrase is inscribed in Latin on the frame around *The Agnew Clinic*, which Eakins designed and carved. For changes in the surgical profession, see Smith op. cit., pp.164–9; also Long 1987, pp.185–98.
9. For Keen's relation to the School of Anatomy, see Adams op. cit., pp.93–4. Keen closed the School in 1875, shortly before he began lecturing on 'Artistic Anatomy' at the Pennsylvania Academy. In this course designed for artists, Keen lectured on anatomical principles using skeletons, manikins, diagrams, and the live model; after each lecture, his demonstrators, such as Eakins, would direct the students in dissection. See Goodrich 1982, vol.I, pp.177–9.

10. See Smith op. cit., pp.171–7. Especially on account of Eakins's decision to portray Agnew performing a mastectomy (a procedure for which Agnew was not especially renowned and which he did not particularly advocate), *The Agnew Clinic* raises several provocative issues of content and interpretation that do not appear in the portrait study. For a somewhat different reading of the value systems and gender issues encoded in *The Agnew Clinic*, see Lubin 1985, pp.27–82.
11. *The Philadelphia Inquirer*, 22 February 1914; See also Goodrich op. cit., vol.II, pp.267–8.
12. See Greenfield 1987.
13. This letter appears in full in Rosenzweig 1977, p.222.

Provenance: Purchased from the artist by Albert C. Barnes, 1914; Barnes Foundation, Merion, Pennsylvania, 1914–1944; purchased by Stephen C. Clark [1944?]; by bequest to Yale University Art Gallery, New Haven, Connecticut, 1961.

Exhibitions: New York, National Academy of Design, 1913, no. 29; Philadelphia, Pennsylvania Academy of the Fine Arts, 1914, no. 329; New York, Museum of Modern Art, 1955, no cat. no.; New Haven, Yale University Art Gallery, 1960, no. 37; Birmingham, Alabama, Museum of Art, 1981, no cat. no.

Literature: Barnes 1923, ill. p.26; Barnes 1925, pp.300–1, 503; Goodrich 1933, pp.138–9, 181, no. 237; McHenry 1946, p.69; Schendler 1967, pp.106, 161, 293, ill. p.108; Hendricks 1974, pp.184–5, 317, ill. p.185; Rosenzweig 1977, p.222; Goodrich 1982, vol.II, pp.45, 267–8, ill. p.274; Homer 1992, p.232, ill. p.232.

Fig.36b
Bernard Uhle, *Dr D. Hayes Agnew*
1889
Oil on canvas, 130.8 × 95.3 (51½ × 37½)
The College of Physicians of Philadelphia

37
Susan Macdowell Eakins
c. 1900
Oil on canvas, 51 × 40.8 (20⅛ × 16⅛)
Unsigned and undated

Hirshhorn Museum and Sculpture Garden,
Smithsonian Institution. Gift of Joseph H.
Hirshhorn, 1966 (HMSG1966.1522)

Following his one-man exhibition of May 1896, in which he had gathered many of his portraits and genre scenes from previous years, Eakins hinted that he was contemplating a change in his approach to portraiture. Rather than bringing sitters into his studio to pose, he was considering the notion of painting portraits more personally associated with his clients by depicting them in their own clothes and environment:

I think it an excellent idea. The home surroundings have the effect of giving a natural look to the picture... The discomfort attending a hasty dress, a trip up three flights of stairs to an artist's studio who waits in vain for his subject are all avoided. It is somewhat of an innovation, but I am sure it will become popular and be a great saving of time, both to the sitter and the artist.[1]

The results of this 'innovation' include some of Eakins's grandest paintings – the portrait of Mrs Frishmuth surrounded by her instrument collection (fig.12) and the series of portraits of the clerics at Overbrook seminary (see nos. 47 and 49) – but also a series of more modest works representing his own surroundings. At this moment of rethinking his approach to this genre, he turned to portraits of family members, specific in scope and spare of accoutrement, which recall in size and mood the portraits he painted of his sister Margaret (see no. 6 and fig.6a) upon his return from Paris. Whilst the early works exhibit Eakins's experimentation with the diverse influences of his education, his head-and-shoulders portraits painted at the turn of the century, including no. 37, refined those experiments and confirmed the statement he made to his father shortly before leaving Paris: 'I will never have to give up painting, for even now I could paint heads good enough to make a living anywhere in America'.[2]

The focus of his portrait of Susan is her direct, piercing gaze at the viewer, and by extension, at the artist himself. In the early 1870s Eakins was already exploring the versatility of the frontal view in the portrait of Margaret and even in *The Champion Single Sculls* (fig.2) in which Max Schmitt arrests his activity and peers over his shoulder to return the viewer's glance. Yet apart from these early examples, such direct frontality is unusual in Eakins's *œuvre*, and appears to have been reserved for those he knew – and who knew him – the most intimately.

Both no. 37 and his earlier portrait of Susan (no. 22) show her gazing directly out, as does the late portrait of Susan's father (fig.28b) and Eakins's last self-portrait (no. 41). In these later works Eakins returned to the tasks he had set for himself in the studios of Paris. Although he had turned away from the style of Gérôme, the French artist's powers of expression provided Eakins with the ideal of a portraitist, as he stated in a letter to his sister Frances in 1869: '[who] can paint men like my dear master, the living thinking acting men, whose faces tell their lifelong story?'[3]

In the series of portraits Eakins painted of his family from 1899 to 1904, the 'lifelong story' told in the faces of his sitters is, perhaps, his own. This is nowhere more poignantly evident than in no. 37, the portrait of Susan painted shortly after one of the great tragedies to strike the Eakins family: the suicide of Frances's daughter, Ella Crowell, who had spent the previous years in the Eakins household under the tutelage of her uncle. Her death and the allegations of sexual misconduct that surrounded it brought about the severance of ties between Eakins and his sister, who had supported him during his fight with the Pennsylvania Academy, and to whom he had confided the dreams of his career. If the impact of the break was softened at all it was due to Susan, who once again vehemently defended her husband and condemned her sister-in-law's failed loyalty, calling the charges against Eakins 'detestable and outrageous', and insisting that the Crowells, who then lived on a farm in Avondale, Pennsylvania, be barred from the Eakins home in Philadelphia.[4]

In light of this incident, the frontal portraits focusing only on the heads – and therefore the thoughts and emotions – of the family members who stood by Eakins suggest an impetus more personal than a continued exploration of traditional portrait types. The rupturing of his long-steadfast familial support structure led him not only to nostalgia for the simpler days and experiments of his career, but also to a bold statement of his integrity as an artist, an academician, and as a man. The family members and friends he painted at this time, including Addie Williams (no. 43), Susan, Susan's father, and himself – all in clothes suggesting an urban respectability – appear as witnesses for the defence in a case brought by an unfaithful accuser, Frances Eakins, who would remain conspicuously unpictured – banished – for the rest of Eakins's life. The portrait of Susan, exhibiting Eakins's achievement even as it attests to the deepest sorrows of his career, represents the artist's most stalwart advocate within any forum in which he might have been tried and found wanting. In the weary yet unwavering eyes of Susan Eakins, the artist was exonerated.

DJS

1. Quoted in Hendricks 1974, p.233.
2. Letter to Benjamin Eakins, 24 June 1869, Pennsylvania Academy of the Fine Arts, archives.
3. Letter to Frances Eakins, 1 April 1869, The Archives of American Art, Washington, DC.
4. Letter to Frances Eakins Crowell from Susan Macdowell Eakins, 18 October 1896, Pennsylvania Academy of the Fine Arts, archives.

Provenance: Collection of Mrs Thomas Eakins; given to Charles Bregler, Philadelphia; purchased by Joseph Katz, Baltimore, 1944; to M. Knoedler & Co., New York, 1961; purchased by Joseph H. Hirshhorn, New York, 1966; given by him, 1966.

Exhibitions: Philadelphia, Museum of Art, 1944, no. 89; New York, M. Knoedler & Co., 1944, no. 59; Pittsburgh, Carnegie Institute, 1945, no. 5; Philadelphia, Pennsylvania Academy of the Fine Arts, 1955, no. 81; New York, Whitney Museum of American Art, 1970, no. 72; Washington, DC, Hirshhorn Museum and Sculpture Garden, 1975, no cat. no.

Literature: Rosenzweig 1977, pp.168–9, ill. pl.169; Goodrich 1982, vol.II, ill. p.170; Homer 1992, pp.179–82, ill. p.180.

38
The Thinker: Portrait of Louis N. Kenton
1900
Oil on canvas, 208.3 × 106.7 (82 × 42)
Signed and dated l.r.: *Eakins 1900*; inscribed
on stretcher, probably by Susan Macdowell
Eakins: *'Thinker' T. Eakins*

Metropolitan Museum of Art.
John Stewart Kennedy Fund, 1917 (17.172)

One of Eakins's most memorable portraits –
uncommissioned like the greatest of them –
the painting depicts the artist's brother-in-law
Louis N. Kenton (1865–1947).[1] In 1899
Kenton married Elizabeth Macdowell (1858–
1953), the sister of Eakins's wife Susan, but the
marriage lasted only for a short time. Eakins
showed the picture widely after its completion
in 1900 as *Portrait of Mr Louis N. Kenton*. In
the artist's 1917 memorial exhibition the
painting appeared as *The Thinker*, a title
derived from an inscription on the stretcher,
probably in Mrs Eakins's hand and probably
invented in response to the popularity of
Rodin's image of 1879–1889. Mrs Kenton, who
lent the painting to the memorial exhibition,
sold it to the Metropolitan Museum of Art
after the show closed. Little is known of
Kenton, although his pose suggests a scholarly,
introspective man. The metamorphosis of the
painting's title from the specific to the generic
may have originated with the Eakins family's
estrangement from Kenton; but the new title
seems entirely consistent with the universal
image that Eakins created.

On a white ground on a canvas almost seven
feet high Eakins painted a thin wash of grayed
yellow-ochre to suggest a flat wall rising from
a pale floor of similar hue and slightly darker
tone. A pair of lines parallel to the wall-floor
division denotes a baseboard. Silhouetted at
life size against this unadorned bright backdrop stands a plain-looking man in his mid-
thirties, turned three-quarters to the right. His
flat-footed stance is matter-of-fact, even
ungainly. He wears a rumpled black suit with
long coat and waistcoat. His hands are thrust
deeply into the pockets of his baggy trousers. A
shirt with a starched high collar, a patterned
dark-red necktie, and a gold watch-chain
across his waistcoat complete his austere,
entirely ordinary costume. His gaze is downward, his eyes averted and obscured from the
viewer by a pince-nez; he is absorbed in
thought, indifferent to our gaze. Bright light
from the upper left illuminates the right side
of Kenton's face and body and casts shadows to
his left. These shadows begin to create the illu-

sion of a spatial box in the lower portion of the
flat backdrop. Kenton's cuffless trousers end at
the tops of his laced shoes which are planted
firmly on the floor; it is on the specificity and
weight of these shoes that the illusion of three-
dimensional space finally depends.

One of a late series of portraits of men
shown standing, at life size, *The Thinker*
reveals the durable residue of Eakins's admiration of the works of Velázquez in its restraint,
its flattened space, and its restricted palette.
Yet, while most of his contemporaries found in
the Spanish master's works inspiration for free
and facile rendering of extremely flat and simplified forms, Eakins maintained a commitment to precise accounts of anatomy and
costume, of volume and detail. Close examination of the canvas reveals the artist's long process of adjusting and perfecting, his laboured
reworking in pursuit of correct contours. The
care with which he described Kenton's shirt
collar, watch-chain, and shoes is typical of
Eakins. Unlike Sargent, Whistler, Chase, and
Manet, for example, who also learned a great
deal from study of Velázquez, Eakins tempered
his admiration for Spanish virtuosity with a
durable allegiance to French academic specificity.

Eakins's high esteem for and pride in the
portrait of Louis N. Kenton were reciprocated
by critics who welcomed its directness, its individuality, its avoidance of flattery. These
writers began to appreciate Eakins's style as an
antidote to the grace and preciosity of much
late nineteenth-century American painting.
They enlisted his works as paradigms of a
rugged, masculine, national and therefore
'usable' strain in American art as they cam-
paigned against cosmopolitanism, aesthet-
icism, and the genteel tradition. Typically,
Charles H. Caffin remarked of *The Thinker* in
his 1907 survey of American painting:

It is a picture that in its matter-of-factness and in
its disregard of the elegancies of line, and of the
persuasiveness of colour and tone, might be
charged with ugliness, but as the record of a
human individual is extraordinarily arresting and
satisfactory… here is an instance where a picture
may be superior to a mere work of art; that there
is in Eakins a capacity broader and deeper than
that of simply being an artist. He has the qualities
of manhood and mentality that are not too
conspicuous in American painting.[2]

Simple and vigorous, *The Thinker: Portrait
of Louis N. Kenton* is a probing, intensely realized image of an individual as well as an archetypical portrayal of modern man in the first
year of the new century. (The year is promi-
nently proclaimed, along with the artist's signature, at the lower right corner of the canvas.)

Although Kenton was twenty-one years
younger than Eakins, he seems less invigorated
by his relative youth and by new prospects
than burdened by isolation – the condition
from which Eakins himself suffered – and by
the search for inner strength. Although it is a
convincing response to Kenton's individual
existence, *The Thinker* embodies a more profound generic meaning that is the key to its
unique and durable power and appeal.
HBW

1. Indispensable sources for this essay are Spassky
et al., 1985, vol.II, pp.622–6; Goodrich 1982, vol.II,
pp.179–82. Goodrich, p.182, notes that the
portrait, exhibited at least thirteen times between
1900 and 1916, was one of Eakins's most
frequently shown works. It was exhibited four
times as owned by Mrs Kenton, twice as owned
by Kenton himself, and four times without an
owner's name.
2. Caffin 1907, p.232.

Provenance: Elizabeth Macdowell Kenton; bought,
1917.

Exhibitions: Pittsburgh, Carnegie Institute, 1899,
no. 70; Philadelphia, Pennsylvania Academy of the
Fine Arts, 1901, no. 11; Buffalo, 1901, no. 310; New
York, National Academy of Design, 1902, no. 309;
Worcester Art Museum, 1902, no. 363; Boston,
Copley Hall, 1902, p. 9; Saint Louis, 1904, no. 220;
Detroit, Museum of Art, 1906, no cat. no.;
Washington, DC, Corcoran Gallery of Art, 1907,
no. 150; New York, Metropolitan Museum of Art,
1917, no. 48; Philadelphia, Pennsylvania Academy
of the Fine Arts, 1917, no. 68; New York,
Metropolitan Museum of Art, 1939, no. 263;
Philadelphia, Museum of Art, 1944, no. 90;
Washington, DC, National Gallery of Art, 1961,
no. 77; New York, Whitney Museum of American
Art, 1970, no. 76; Boston, Museum of Fine Arts,
1983, no. 102.

Literature: *International Studio*, no. 14, 1901,
p.xxxii; no. 15, 1902, p.lxi; Caffin 1907, p.232; *New
York Sun*, 11 November 1917, p.12, no. 8; *MMA
Bulletin*, no. 13, p.25; *MMA Bulletin*, no. 18, 1923,
p.282; Mumford 1931, pp.213–14; Goodrich 1933,
pp.137, 139, 190–1, no. 331; McKinney 1942,
ill. p.43; McHenry 1946, p.70; Schendler 1967,
ill. p.191, 192, 194; Hendricks 1974, p.246, fig.264,
pp.280, 282, 283, 334; Sellin 1977, pp. 29–30;
Rosenzweig 1977, p.226, no. 129, n. 2; Siegl 1978,
p.30, fig.8; Wilmerding 1979, p.110; Goodrich
1982, vol.II, pp.179–182, 205, 256, pl.231, fig.232;
Spassky 1985, pp.622–6; Homer 1992, pp.221, 251.

39
Henry O. Tanner
c. 1902
Oil on canvas, 60.2 × 51.4 ($24\frac{1}{16}$ × $20\frac{1}{4}$)
Signed l.r.: *Eakins.*

The Hyde Collection, Glens Falls, New York
(1971.16)

'The question [of race] does not stand alone, but is a part . . . a by no means small part, in the working out of America's destiny'. H. G. Wells, 1906.[1]

Eakins's portrait of Henry O. Tanner portrays the Parisian-based, African-American artist Henry Ossawa Tanner (1859–1937) during a return visit to the United States in 1902. Leaning back in his chair and turned to his right, Tanner is presented in three-quarter pose. The right side of his head stands in strong relief against the painting's dark brown background, while the shadowed side of his face emerges from darkness, blending delicately into highlights along his cheek and brow. His head is accentuated by a dense shock of black hair, exposing a large high forehead, and by a thick brown moustache and goatee. Tanner wears a dark jacket and waistcoat, starched high collar, patterned tie, and a pair of wire-rimmed spectacles.

During the 1870s and 1880s Tanner studied sporadically under Eakins at the Pennsylvania Academy of the Fine Arts, but by 1902, when this painting was completed, Tanner was already a mature artist. Not only did Tanner receive prizes for his paintings in the United States, but he was highly respected in his adoptive home of Europe, accepting honours at the Salons of 1896 and 1897, and at the Universal Exposition of 1900.[2] By the turn of the century Tanner was arguably a more successful artist than his former teacher.

Given the racial climate of late nineteenth-century America, Tanner's decision to reside in Europe is not surprising. In the last quarter of the century many of the social and political gains achieved by blacks during the Civil War and Reconstruction were reversed by government legislation and indifference. This period saw the Compromise of 1877, which halted the Federal government's protection of black rights in the former Confederacy, the overthrow of Reconstruction governments, disenfranchisement campaigns, race riots and an upsurge in lynchings. As Tanner's father, a Bishop in the African Methodist Episcopal Church, wrote at the end of the century, 'In no country in Christendom, except the United States of America, would the color of a man be deemed a subject worthy of consideration. In all other lands it is . . . moral or intellectual status that is discussed'. The elder Tanner concluded that, in America 'color is everything'.[3]

Eakins painted Tanner in an era when Americans concerned with the issue of racial equality were polarized by the competing philosophies of two black leaders, Booker T. Washington and W.E.B. Du Bois. Washington, the more conservative and widely embraced leader, thought that racial equality would come about slowly through individual economic advancement, while Du Bois, the progressive, wanted sweeping changes on the political front. Washington tried to teach blacks practical skills, self-help, and the dignity of labour, confident that blacks who gained economic power would eventually be accepted by whites as equal citizens. Du Bois, conversely, not willing to rely on the munificence of whites, advocated advanced education for the brightest 'Talented Tenth' of black America, in the hope that they would become their people's intellectual leaders.

It was in this highly charged context that Eakins and Tanner depicted blacks. Tanner's black genre scenes and portraits are painted in a quasi-realist style adapted from Eakins, though his fame rests primarily on idealized religious scenes. Tanner's work *The Banjo Lesson* (1893; fig.39a) owes much in its subject matter and presentation to Eakins's painting of *The Dance Lesson* (1878; fig.39b).[4] Both canvases illustrate private moments in the lives of black families. United by art and lost within their creative worlds, the figures in each work focus on a small boy's performance. In both paintings knowledge is patiently being imparted to children, perhaps metaphorically suggesting that black progress will come only with the growth of the next generation.

The paintings appear to offer conservative images, advocating hard work and patience, of the kind that Washington would applaud. But, Tanner's conservative subject matter must be balanced against the progressive context of the work's production. The painting was, after all, produced by a black artist. The practical education Washington promoted for blacks was certainly not to be found at the Pennsylvania Academy of the Fine Arts. Progressives like Du Bois, however, understood how artistic training might encourage black advancement. Not only did he single out Tanner as having contributed significantly to American art,[5] but he wrote, that for the black artist 'who will work, and dig, and starve, there is a chance to do here incalculable good for the Negro race … there is the chance to gain listeners who will know no color line'.[6]

For slightly different reasons Washington, too, was aware that Tanner's achievement could help to encourage equality. While opposing art education for blacks, he felt satisfaction in finding that Tanner was already well received by white audiences. Washington called Tanner an example of the fact 'that any man, regardless of color, will be recognised and rewarded just in proportion as he learns to do something well'. But unable to fully appreciate what Tanner represented, Washington concluded that for blacks success would come from menial jobs, as they learned 'to do a common thing in an uncommon manner'.[7]

Fig.39a
Henry Ossawa Tanner, *The Banjo Lesson*
1893
Oil on canvas, 124.5 × 90.2 (49 × 35½)
Hampton University Museum, Virginia

Fig.39b
Negro Boy Dancing (The Dance Lesson)
1878
Watercolour, 46 × 57.5 (18⅛ × 22⅝)
The Metropolitan Museum of Art, Fletcher Fund, 1925

Besides the portrait of Tanner, Eakins painted blacks merely to illustrate types or as extras in larger genre scenes. Appearing in only ten of his canvases, his representations of blacks rarely display the psychological depth for which Eakins's portraits are known.[8] Formalistically, it makes more sense, in fact, to connect *Henry O. Tanner* not with Eakins's depictions of blacks, but with his head-and-shoulders portraits of his students, or his full-length images of scientific, literary and religious leaders.

Tanner's floodlit form emerges from the darkness of the background. His high forehead, glasses and pensive expression do much to further the impression that Tanner is an intellectual. Tanner's contemplative presentation links him to another of Eakins's late portraits, *The Thinker* (1900; no. 38). With their pensive expressions and wire-rimmed spectacles, both men are clearly lost in thought; staring down and away from the viewer each sitter ignores our gaze. In *The Thinker*, however, the glasses, as emblems of internalized intelligence and thought, obscure the eyes, blocking any access we might have to the figure's world. Tanner's glasses, conversely, function as true lenses for both sitter and viewer alike. Just as the glasses allow Tanner to focus on surrounding objects so they align our sight, permitting us to focus on the eyes which they frame. Although Tanner does not meet our gaze, he seems connected to our world.

The portrait of Henry O. Tanner does not embody a single, obvious ideological stance, but rather gives voice to a variety of beliefs, circulating in America at the turn of the century. This multiplicity of meaning allowed both conservative and progressive groups to find in Eakins's work tenets to applaud. Washington would surely have admired the dignity and respect accorded the figure, appreciative that an artist of Eakins's stature had sought to honour a black colleague, while Du Bois might well have relished the sitter's open, intellectual air, recognizing him as a member of his 'Talented Tenth'.

MAB

1. Wells 1906, p.1317.
2. Tanner's awards up to 1902 are as follows: honourable mention at the Paris Salon of 1896, a third-class medal at the Salon of 1897, the Lippincott Prize in Philadelphia in 1900, a silver medal at the Paris Universal Exposition of 1900, and a silver medal in Buffalo, New York, at the Pan-American Exposition. (Information drawn from the chronology compiled by Kathleen James and Sylvia Young in Mosby and Sewell 1991, pp.39–43.)
3. Tanner 1895, pp.14, 40.
4. Long known as *Negro Boy Dancing*, the work was originally titled by Eakins, *The Dance Lesson*. In Annette Blaugrund, *Paris 1889: American Artists at the Universal Exposition* (Philadelphia: Pennsylvania Academy of the Fine Arts, 1989), no.147.
5. W.E.B. Du Bois, 'The Negro in America', in McDannald 1941, pp.20, 52, quoted in Aptheker 1982, p.189.
6. Du Bois 1898, pp.2–3.
7. Washington 1963, p.202.
8. Eakins's paintings in which blacks appear are: *A Negress* (c. 1867; San Francisco, California Palace of the Legion of Honor), *Pushing for Rail* (1874; fig.16a), *Whistling for Plover* (1874; The Brooklyn Museum), *Will Schuster and Blackman Going Shooting* (1876; no. 16), *The Dance Lesson* (1878; fig.39b), *Shad Fishing at Gloucester on the Delaware River* (1881; Philadelphia Museum of Art), *Drawing the Seine* (1882; Philadelphia Museum of Art), *The Red Shawl* (c. 1890; Philadelphia Museum of Art), *Henry O. Tanner* (no. 39), and *William Rush Carving His Allegorical Figure of the Schuylkill River* (1908; fig.14).

Provenance: Mrs Thomas Eakins; Babcock Galleries, New York?; purchased by Mr and Mrs Louis Hyde between 1933 and 1939.

Exhibitions: San Francisco, 1915, no. 2965; Philadelphia, Pennsylvania Academy of the Fine Arts, 1917, no. 37; Detroit, Art Institute, 1937, no. 17; Washington, DC, Howard University, 1942, no cat. no.; Philadelphia, Art Alliance, 1945, no. 19; Bowdoin, Maine, Bowdoin College Museum of Art, 1964, no. 56; Washington, DC, Smithsonian Institution, 1969, no. 81; Glen Falls, The Hyde Collection, 1972, no. 1; San Jose, California, Museum of Art, 1975, no cat. no.; New York, Metropolitan Museum of Art, 1976, no cat. no.; New York, Whitney Museum of American Art, 1977, no. 33; Philadelphia, Museum of Art, 1982 (1), no. 32; Boston, Museum of Fine Arts, 1986, no cat. no.

Literature: Burrough 1923 (2), p.203–23, ill. fig.6; Goodrich 1933, p.192, ill. no. 345; Kaplan 1966, p.120; Schendler 1967, p.290, ill. fig.137; Mathews 1969, p.30; Hendricks 1974, p.332, ill. pl.167; Parry 1974, p.163, ill. fig.116; Johns 1983 (1), p.149, ill. fig.102.

40
Self-portrait
c. 1902
Oil on canvas mounted on fibre board,
50.8 × 40.9 (20 × 16⅛)
Unsigned and undated

Hirshhorn Museum and Sculpture Garden,
Smithsonian Institution.
Gift of Joseph H. Hirshhorn, 1966
(HMSG 1966.1494)

It is a measure of the degree of Eakins's rejection by his fellow artists that he was not invited to become a member of the National Academy of Design until 1902. Founded in 1826, the National Academy, like the Royal Academy in England on which it was modelled, elected Associates or full Academicians; these were the most prestigious honours available to artists in the United States. Election to the Academy always depended to some extent upon personal connections, but Eakins, a young, European-trained artist who exhibited his work aggressively in the late 1870s and early 1880s, might reasonably have expected to be admitted to the Academy in the mid-1880s, as were many of his less talented contemporaries. Most of Eakins's work was too controversial for wide popularity, however; both established artists and his French-trained contemporaries judged his subjects unsuitable for art and his technique too rigorous.

Eakins's forced resignation from the Pennsylvania Academy in 1886 and the consequent reduction of his efforts to exhibit coincided with a general consensus against his work. The reception of *The Agnew Clinic* was especially painful to Eakins: the Pennsylvania Academy rejected the painting, after inviting Eakins to show it there in 1891; similarly, The Society of American Artists, which had elected Eakins as a member in 1892, and where the artist had shown his most adventurous works, *William Rush Carving His Allegorical Figure of the Schuylkill River* and *The Gross Clinic* in 1878 and 1879, also refused to exhibit it. In 1892 Eakins resigned from the Society of American Artists, his only professional affiliation, and although he was well represented at the World's Columbian Exposition in 1893 with a group of thirteen works, there was some justification, especially during the late 1880s and early 1890s, for his famous statement of 1894 that 'My honors are misunderstanding, persecution, and neglect, enhanced because unsought'.[1]

The revival of Eakins's reputation in the later 1890s was due to two factors: reassessment and qualified admiration of him from peers who had by then achieved security in their own careers; and discovery by a new generation of artists and critics such as Robert Henri and Sadakichi Hartmann. Eakins was made an Associate-elect of the National Academy by unanimous vote on 12 March 1902, and fulfilled the Academy's requirement for Associate membership in remarkably short time, producing his self-portrait in less than two months. This 'diploma picture' was accepted and Eakins was made an Associate on 5 May. With alacrity unprecedented at the

Academy, he was elected a full Academician at the annual meeting on 14 May 1902, and remains the only person in the history of the institution to be elected an Associate and an Academician in the same year.

Apart from including himself as a participant in some of the early sporting scenes, and as an observer in the Gross and Agnew clinics, Eakins had not painted any self-portraits hitherto, and other than showing a side view of himself in one of the late William Rush paintings around 1908 (see fig.17c), he did not make any others after nos. 40 and 41. Charles Bregler and Mary Adeline Williams recalled that both were related to the National Academy election.[2]

At this time Eakins was at the height of his powers as a portraitist, and given the attention that he devoted to subtle adjustments of costume and pose, and to rendering emotional states in his other portraits of this period, the problem of how to present himself to his colleagues and to history must have been especially engrossing. Although there were no painted self-portraits as such, Eakins had been photographed often by professional portrait photographers, and by Susan Eakins, as well as by students, friends and family members. The photographs show Eakins assuming a wide variety of personae, ranging from conventionally formal to outrageously bohemian, and he may have referred to some of them, or even had portrait photographs made specifically as studies for his painting.[3] Charles Bregler interprets Eakins's sketchily-painted garment in the Hirshhorn painting as an old grey sweater,[4] possibly the high-necked, ribbed sweater that Eakins wore in a photograph previously dated 1895 (Pennsylvania Academy of the Fine Arts). His short-cropped hair and beard in the painting also can be seen in this photograph.

For no. 40 Eakins chose a canvas of the small, 20 × 16 inches, size that he had used only for the portrait of Susan Macdowell Eakins a year or so earlier (no. 37), and would use only once again, for the portrait of Edith Mahon in 1904 (no. 44). Compression of the figure in this small format intensifies the effect of physical presence, especially when the sitter looks directly out at the viewer, and Eakins exploited this quality in the Hirshhorn picture by painting a confrontational, full-face view. Bregler recalled that this painting was made in one sitting and never touched again,[5] and although certain passages such as the left eye are well defined, the randomness of the brushwork overall suggests that Eakins did not intend this to be the finished work, but rather an exercise in anatomical note-taking, and an experiment with the emotional tone he wanted to convey. The resulting image is austere and rather intimidating, and perhaps Eakins considered it too hostile and limited in its emotional content. Certainly the portrait in the National Academy suggests a more complex, vulnerable personality.

For the National Academy painting, Eakins adopted a canvas measuring 30×25 inches, larger than his usual 24×20 inches format. Instead of wearing a sweater, he portrayed himself in the conventional garb of dark grey suit and buttoned waistcoat, white shirt and dark tie worn by most of his male sitters. Such formality of dress is offset by his dishevelled hair and unevenly trimmed moustache which covers the left side of his upper lip; the latter detail seems to have interested him, as he also included it in the Hirshhorn sketch. The tension between costume and grooming implies a rebellious spirit constrained by social convention; this reading is supported more specifically through the rendering of anatomy and expression.

The larger format and half-length pose create a greater space around the figure and slightly diminish the sense of physical immediacy, so the viewer is freer to observe, and contact between sitter and viewer depends upon Eakins's direct glance out of the canvas. Direct eye contact between sitter and viewer is a device that Eakins used very seldom, and then only in portrayals of people he knew well. Emphasis on the liquid reflection from the eye in strong light, which enhances the emotionally-charged nature of the glance, is a device that Eakins used even more rarely, to full effect only in portraits of Susan Eakins (nos. 22 and 37), Edith Mahon (no. 44) and William H. Macdowell (fig. 28b).

In many ways, Eakins's self-portrait has fewer affinities with his portraits of men, in which some degree of psychological distance is always maintained, than with some of his portraits of women painted about this time, such as *Addie* (no. 43), *Mrs Susan Eakins* or *Mrs Edith Mahon*. These portrayals of women are disconcertingly intimate and sympathetic, and suggest the existence of profound emotional life through the artist's apparently relentless study of lighting and physical detail. Eakins similarly shows himself as a vulnerable being, capable of deep emotion. In the light of what we know of the history of his career up to this point, it is possible to interpret Eakins's expression as accusatory and sad – and perhaps he intended this quality to be apparent to his fellow members of the National Academy – but the painting's success lies more in its ambiguity of feeling and emotional range.

Eakins provided the Academy with a beautiful example of his technique as well as an image of compelling psychological power. For this work, that inescapably would be compared to those produced by his peers, Eakins seems to have aimed at a demonstration of virtuosity in his own terms. In common with the portraits of Susan Eakins, Edith Mahon, Leslie Miller and Macdowell, painted around this time, the self-portrait is especially notable as an example of Eakins's method of direct painting in which all the idiosyncrasies of individual bone structure, flesh and skin are defined by small, exactly placed, shaped strokes of rather liquid paint which remain distinct on closer examination, but resolve into an illusion of solid form in light. Beautiful technique is not usually considered an important component of Eakins's art, but the thinly painted, even surface of the self-portrait is an unmatched demonstration of his absolute control of the medium.

Election to the National Academy of Design, and the other signs of recognition that began to come to Eakins in the first decade of the twentieth century did not entirely reconcile him to past neglect, and he did not necessarily receive every honour with gratitude. When the Pennsylvania Academy of the Fine Arts presented him with the Temple Gold Medal in 1904, the sixty-year-old artist arrived at the ceremony on his bicycle, and received the medal with the words, 'I think you've got a heap of impudence to give me a medal'.[6] He then pedalled directly to the United States Mint and exchanged it for cash.

DS

1. Quoted in Goodrich 1982, vol.II, p.160.
2. Bregler information in letter from Charles Bregler to Lloyd Goodrich, 22 March 1943, quoted in Rosenzweig 1977, p.180, note 1. Williams information noted by Lloyd Goodrich in notebook entry on the self-portrait, catalogue no. 358, in The Lloyd Goodrich and Edith Havens Goodrich, Whitney Museum of American Art, Record of Works by Thomas Eakins, Philadelphia Museum of Art.
3. Leibold 1991, p.8.
4. Letter from Charles Bregler to Lloyd Goodrich, 22 March 1943, quoted in Rosenzweig op. cit., p.180, note 1.
5. Letter from Charles Bregler to Lloyd Goodrich, 22 March 1943, quoted in Rosenzweig op. cit., p.180, note 1.
6. Quoted in Goodrich op. cit., vol.II, p.201.

Provenance (no. 40): Charles Bregler, Philadelphia; Joseph Katz, Baltimore; M. Knoedler & Co., New York, 1961; Joseph H. Hirshhorn, 1966.

Provenance (no. 41): Given by the artist, 1902.

Exhibitions (no. 40): New York, M. Knoedler & Co., 1944, no. 97; Philadelphia, Museum of Art, 1944, no. 97; Washington, DC, Hirshhorn Museum and Sculpture Garden, 1977, no. 98.

Exhibitions (no. 41): New York, National Academy of Design, *Eighty-Third Annual Exhibition*, 1908, no. 236 [as *Portrait of a Man*]; Philadelphia, Pennsylvania Academy of the Fine Arts, 1917, no. 84; New York, Museum of Modern Art, 1930, no. 110; Baltimore, Museum of Art, 1936, no. 22; Detroit, Art Institute, 1937, no. 24a; New York, The Century Association, 1951, no. 2; New York, National Academy of Design, 1951, no. 47; Philadelphia, Pennsylvania Academy of the Fine Arts, 1955, no. 95; Wilmington, Society of the Fine Arts, 1956, no. 13; New York, American Academy of Arts and Letters, 1958, no. 9; Washington, DC, National Gallery of Art, 1961, no. 83; Washington, DC, National Portrait Gallery, 1968, no cat. no.; New York, Whitney Museum of American Art, 1970, no. 84; Philadelphia, Museum of Art, 1982 (1), no. 126.

Literature (no. 40): Hendricks 1974, no. 107, p.325, ill. p.325; Rosenzweig 1977, no. 98, p.179, ill. p.179.

Literature (no. 41): Goodrich 1933, no. 358, ill. frontis.; Goldwater 1945, pp.106–7, ill. p.107; Smith 1956, pp.28–33, 61–3, ill. p.29; Porter 1959, ill. pl.66; Canaday 1964, pp.88–105, ill. p.89; Flexner 1966, ill. p.150; Frankenstein 1966, pp.76–87, ill. p.82; McLanathan 1968, ill. p.345; Schendler 1967, p.178, ill. pl.84; Rennie 1968, pp.12–22, ill. p.22; Hendricks 1974, p.335, ill. pl.1; Goodrich 1982, vol.II, p.201, ill. vol.I, frontis.; Johns 1983 (1), ill. fig.124.

41
Self-portrait
1902
Oil on canvas, 76.2 × 63.5 (30 × 25)
Unsigned and undated

National Academy of Design, New York
(398–P)

42
Alice Kurtz
1903
Oil on canvas, 60 × 49.9 ($23\frac{9}{16}$ × $19\frac{6}{8}$)
Signed l.r.: *Eakins*

Fogg Art Museum, Harvard University Art
Museums. Gift in part – Mrs John
Whiteman (Alice Kurtz, the sitter);
purchase in part – funds contributed by
Friends of John Coolidge, Director of
the Fogg Art Museum, 1948–1968 (1969.1)

Eakins's portraits before 1900 typically feature an individual costumed or surrounded by the accoutrements of his or her life's work. In these large-scale, full-length works, the subject's character is calculatedly revealed through his or her surroundings and not simply through physical appearance. Around 1900, however, while continuing to work within this style, Eakins also adopted a new format, by scaling down his portraits (almost all of them measure approximately 60 × 49 centimetres), and painting his sitters from the shoulders up without any extraneous details or background props. In these late works, pared down to the face and torso, the artist was able to concentrate on the revelation of the inner lives of his subjects.[1] Painted in 1903, no. 42 exemplifies this late phase of Eakins's portrait *œuvre*, and at the same time illustrates the fundamental principles of realism to which the artist adhered throughout his career.

Presented in a vague, darkened space, the young woman, Alice Kurtz, is comfortably and casually posed. She leans back slightly, apparently seated, with her head gracefully turned to her right, and her arms open. Glancing aside, her eyes reflect the non-specific light source that illuminates the right side of her face while producing shadows on the left. In contrast to the murky background behind her, Kurtz's face is alive and aglow with a range of pink and golden tones. Her neck and arms, however, are comparatively pallid and strikingly incongruous. Having spent the summer playing tennis in a high necked, long-sleeved blouse, the young woman's face was apparently sunburned (while her neck and arms remained pale) when she posed for the artist, who painted her precisely as he saw her.[2] Committed to realism, Eakins did not correct the unevenness of his subject's complexion, but instead accentuated it to indicate an aspect of Alice Kurtz's personality.

With her shiny, blotched skin, heavy eyelids, and thick lips, Alice Kurtz is not portrayed as an idealized beauty. Nonetheless, she is radiant, exuding a sense of warmth, physical vitality and psychological depth that undoubtedly moved Eakins. Drawing on his keen interest in athletic activities, Eakins painted Kurtz as a robust, modern woman with a strong physical presence rather than as an archetypical fair and delicate Victorian model. Her hair is not meticulously styled, but loosely arranged with a few stray wisps. Her face is scrubbed and she wears no jewellery. This absence of adornment emphasizes the bareness of Kurtz's neck and chest, revealing the musculature of a sturdy, vigorous individual. Years after the portrait was painted, Alice Kurtz recalled

Eakins once telling her during a sitting, 'Your back is more like a boy's than a girl's'. He then asked to paint her in the nude. Her mother, a close friend of Eakins, gave permission but was not enthusiastic, so Alice Kurtz decided against it.[5] Still, Eakins paid close attention to the young woman's athletic physique, giving prominence to her clavicle and neck tendons as she gently twists her head.

If these features give Kurtz a somewhat masculine aspect, they are countered by the exceedingly feminine dress that she wears; off-white with an intricately embroidered lace flounce encircling the shoulders, the garment concords Victorian notions of fashion and femininity. Nonetheless, the portrait does not embody the more conventional femininity that is evident in earlier portraits such as *Maud Cook* (no. 29) and *Lucy Lewis* (fig. 42a). The tension that Eakins so skilfully evokes in the sitter's taut anatomical structure marks a latent opposition between masculine and feminine: here is a sporty young woman who has enjoyed the physical challenge of outdoor athletic activity and is now confined within a subdued Victorian interior. Her wistful gaze, directed beyond the boundary of the picture's frame, suggests a longing to be elsewhere, and from this apparent lack of engagement it might be conjectured that she is contemplating her position as young woman in relation to the separate masculine and feminine spheres defined by society, and lamenting their ostensible mutual exclusivity. In Eakins's representation, however, these supposed spheres are not so clearly polarized: having observed the depth and inner life of his subject, Eakins paints Alice Kurtz as the personification of the combined feminine and masculine traits that in fact constitute most individuals. The artist offers a pictorial equivalent to Walt Whitman's celebration of an all-embracing pan-sexuality:

The bodies of men and women engirth me,
and I engirth/them,/They will not let me off nor
I them till I go with them and/respond to them
and love them/ . . . The expression of the body of
man or woman balks account,/The male is
perfect and that of a female is perfect.[4]

Whitman's indiscriminate admiration for the lives, souls, and bodies of both genders is echoed in the fusion of masculine and feminine which informs Eakins's work (see also no. 23).

Indeed, when Eakins presented the portrait to Kurtz, her parents believed it was unattractive, that she looked 'like a bag of bones, like an anatomical sketch. They thought it was hideous, that [she] looked like a boy, with a beard coming'.[5] Like many who viewed Eakins's por-

traits, they were undoubtedly shocked by the unconventional, if not unflattering image of their daughter. Yet, they perhaps did not realize that Eakins located beauty in the evidence of Alice Kurtz's physical vigour, creating a portrait of a real woman, rather than a fictional ideal.

JME

1. John Wilmerding addresses the evolution of Eakins's portraits in the chapter entitled 'Thomas Eakins's Late Portraits', in Wilmerding 1991.
2. Schendler 1967, pp.294–5.
3. Ibid.
4. Whitman 1855, Crowley, ed., 1986, p.116.
5. Schendler op. cit., p.295.

Provenance: Miss Alice B. Kurtz (Mrs John B. Whiteman), 1903; Fogg Art Museum (purchase from Mrs Whiteman), 1969.

Exhibitions: Cambridge, Massachusetts, Fogg Art Museum, 1977, no cat. no.

Literature: Goodrich 1933, p.139, ill. p.379; Unsigned, *Arts in Virginia*, vol.9, no. 1, fall 1961, p.35; Schendler 1967, p.294, figs.143, 265; *Fogg Art Museum Newsletter*, vol.6, no. 3, January 1969; *Fogg Art Museum Acquisitions Report*, 1969–70, ill. p.79; Boulton *et al.*, 1972, no.113; Hendricks 1974, pp.363, 365, ill p.329, no.138; Wilmerding 1978, p.124, ill. fig.3; Goodrich 1982, vol.II, p.91, ill. p.93; Mortimer 1985, p.186, ill no. 212; Homer 1992, p.225.

Fig.42a
Lucy Lewis
*c.*1896
Oil on canvas, 55.9 × 68.9 (22 × 27⅛)
Private Collection

43

Addie

1900

Oil on canvas, 61.3 × 46 (24⅛ × 18⅛)

Unsigned and undated

Philadelphia Museum of Art. Gift of Mrs
Thomas Eakins and Miss Mary Adeline
Williams (29.184.10)

Thomas Eakins's eighty-one-year-old father, Benjamin, died on the next-to-last day of the nineteenth century. The artist, together with his wife Susan, had already lived for some years with Benjamin in the family home at 1729 Mount Vernon Street and was now bequeathed the residence. To make use of Benjamin's empty room, the couple asked a family friend, Mary Adeline Williams (1853–1941), to come to live with them. Addie, as she was known, was forty-six at the time. Many years earlier she had been invited to join the Eakins household after the death of Tom's sister Margaret (see no. 6), who was her best friend. Ten years Addie's elder, Eakins was unmarried then and, perhaps for that reason, she declined.

The artist's biographer Lloyd Goodrich says that Addie loved music but was compelled to neglect her interest in the piano in order to earn a living as a seamstress, by sewing shirts at Wanamaker's Store and fashioning corsets for a certain Mme Murney. She moved to Chicago in the early 1890s to live with one of her brothers but after six years returned to Philadelphia. When Tom's father died, the childless Eakinses asked the unattached Addie to live with them on Mount Vernon Street and this time she accepted; she remained in the house after the artist's death in 1916 and even after his widow's death in 1938.[1]

Eakins painted two portraits of Addie. The first, dating from the spring of 1899 – after her return to Philadelphia but before her move to Mount Vernon Street – is an austere head-and-shoulders portrait in three-quarters profile (fig.43a). It shows a woman with tightly bound hair streaked grey at the temple. Her head seems almost nervous and birdlike perched upon her shoulders as she sits upright in an implicitly straightbacked chair.

Everything about this portrait represents 'spinsterhood' as it was conventionally constructed at the turn of the century: the woman portrayed by Eakins is, to use the familiar modifiers, prim, terse, tight, overdressed, schoolmarmish, and puritanical. The chin-high collar, fastidious hairdo, drawn lips, and perpendicularity of posture were all stereotypical signifiers used for characterizing an unmarried woman of middle age or older. Even the apparent sadness in Addie's eyes would have accorded with romantic notions of the desiccated spinster who had once upon a time known love, even passion (a theme that reached its apotheosis a dozen years later in Edith Wharton's novel *Ethan Frome* and the popular stage play derived from it).

In 1900, when Addie moved to Mount Vernon Street, Eakins painted her in a second portrait, no. 43, clearly intended as a pendant to the first. The result, to invoke musical terms that Addie herself might have appreciated, is a romantic fantasia, or unrestricted variation and development on the original theme. Eakins plays upon the earlier painting in virtually every respect, reversing an element here, opening up another there, or in one way or another deconstructing (to use a term Addie surely would not have appreciated) the previous portrait's construction of spinsterhood.

In no. 43, instead of facing from our left (the so-called 'sinister side') to our right (a term with moral and social as well as directional implications), Addie looks from the right to the left. Eakins has moved in on her, filling more of the frame and providing a closer (more intimate) view. Whereas before her posture was rigidly perpendicular, now she is angled, her head lowered to one side in that subtle gesture of yielding or resignation that Eakins came increasingly to prefer in his late portraits.

The dress of the earlier picture, striped in prison-bar black, has been liberated into torrents of reddish-orange, filament-thin brushstrokes culminating in a pair of bows, one of which trails a transparent ribbon that streaks down across the breast like a vaporous comet. The knotted ivory collar at the neck has been exchanged for a ·coral-coloured scarf loosely gathered beneath the chin. The lips, still pursed, are fuller now both above and below, where an impastoed white highlight conveys a sensual liquidity. The brushwork across the face is looser and richer, with a more liberal use of pink to suggest the flow of blood beneath the flesh.

Eakins has posed the model in such a way as to provide more facial surface than before and fuller, more softened angles. The eyes are wider, moister, more filled with light and, by implication, poignant sensibility. The hair no longer seems artifically affixed to the scalp but emerges from it, indicating a wholeness, an organic integrity, a *naturalness* not apparent in the earlier work. This Addie allows her hair to be out of place. The ear, half-covered before, is now nakedly visible, suggesting a sensual receptivity in the sitter that is not to be found in the artist's earlier view of her.

Gordon Hendricks accounts for the dramatic difference between the two portraits by suggesting that Eakins had an affair with Addie once she moved into his house. He supports this speculation by quoting a relative who told him, 'You know, of course, that Uncle Tom made love to Addie Williams'.[2] Goodrich doubts this to have been the case and proposes instead an interpretation based on a comment by Susan Eakins that the earlier painting shows a woman who was 'worried' and living

alone, whereas the subsequent one shows her to be 'relaxed,' for she was then 'a beloved companion in our house'.[3]

Both of these explanations of the dramatic change in Eakins's representation of his friend rely on traditional assumptions about female fulfilment, as though nothing short of the love of a man or the ambience of a family could account for such an apparent transformation. They also assume that the portraits should be taken as realistic reportage of a specific individual's — Addie's — evolving state of mind. Yet, instead of being seen as documenting a libidinal change in Addie, perhaps they should be seen as indicating a perceptual change in the artist, who by the time of the second painting had come to know his sitter better than before. Even here, though, a strictly biographical reading is too limiting. To the extent that he was a systematic student of the visual representation of modern behaviour and personality types, Eakins was very much interested in portraying specific individuals in socially coded roles (*The Art Student, The Veteran, The Writing Master*).[4] The pair of Addie paintings can be seen in this context as individualizations of two related conventions, 'the lonely old maid' and 'the old maid in love'. Or possibly the pair of paintings served allegorically to register for Eakins the two centuries they bridged, one standing for nineteenth-century repression, the other for twentieth-century expression.

In any event, to fixate solely on the biographical dimensions of *Addie* is to reduce an instance of powerful painting and, as it were, cultural theory into a mere supplementary illustration of a particular family romance involving Addie and the Eakinses. A more holistic approach is to see the painting as the manifest result of a variety of factors, biographical (the death of the artist's father, the incorporation of Addie into the family), sociological (widespread assumptions about unmarried women), and art-historical (the artist's concern to work a variation upon a prior theme).

DML

1. Goodrich 1982, vol.II pp.171–4.
2. Hendricks 1974, p.244.
3. Goodrich op. cit., p.174.
4. See Cikovsky, entry for Eakins, *The Art Student*, in Cikovsky, Kelly and Shaw 1989 pp.126–131.

Provenance: Given by the artist's widow, Susan Macdowell Eakins, and Mary Adeline Williams, 1929.

Exhibitions: Philadelphia, Pennsylvania Academy of the Fine Arts, 1917, no. 106; New York, Museum of Modern Art, 1930, no. 107; Philadelphia, Museum of Art, 1944, no. 91; Washington, DC, National Gallery of Art, 1961, no. 80; New York, Whitney Museum of American Art, 1970, no. 77; Philadelphia, Museum of Art, 1982 (1), no. 138.

Literature: Goodrich 1933, ill. pl.54; McHenry 1946, pp.131–4; Schendler 1967, p.177, ill. p.183; Hendricks 1974, pp.244, 346, ill. pl.45; Siegl 1978, p.154, ill. pl.101; Goodrich 1982, vol.II, pp.171–4, ill. pl.227; Johns 1983 (1), p.167, ill. fig.122; Homer 1992, pp.234–5, ill. pl.169.

Fig.43a
Mary Adeline Williams (Addie)
1899
Oil on canvas, 61 × 51 (24 × 20$\frac{1}{16}$)
The Art Institute of Chicago.
Friends of American Art Collection

44
Edith Mahon
1904
Oil on canvas, 50.8 × 40.7 (20 × 16)
Inscribed on verso: *To My Friend Edith
Mahon/Thomas Eakins 1904*

Smith College Museum of Art, Northampton,
Massachusetts. Purchased, Drayton Hillyer
Fund, 1931 (1931.2)

Edith Mahon (?1874–?1924), as portrayed by
Eakins, emerges from the depths of a sombre
background into the narrow space defined by
her beaded evening gown and the heavy carving of a highbacked chair. Eyes moist, brow
contracted, and face ruddy with colour, she
exudes an undefined yet singularly intense
emotion. However stoical or self-restrained she
may appear, she looks as though she is about
to cry.

The sitter was an Englishwoman who
moved to Philadelphia before the turn of the
century and who, according to the artist's
widow, Susan Eakins, died when she was about
fifty. She was a pianist known for her ability to
accompany singers; these included the legen-
dary mezzo-soprano Ernestine Schumann-
Heink, who performed in Philadelphia often
in the early years of the century. Mrs Mahon
once told the composer John Ireland that she
did not like her portrait but had sat for it and
accepted it as a favour to the artist (it is
inscribed on the reverse 'To My Friend Edith
Mahon/Thomas Eakins 1904').

The art dealer Morris Pancoast remembered purchasing the painting from Mrs
Mahon in 1923 or 1924 when she was dispos-
ing of her possessions before she moved back to
England, where months later she died from
cancer. If Susan Eakins was correct in saying
that Mrs Mahon had died at fifty, the sitter
would have been only thirty at the time of the
portrait, although that appears unlikely. The
artist tended to make his sitters look older than
they were, but this would seem to have been an
extreme case. When the painting was purchased from Pancoast by the Smith College
Museum of Art in 1931, Mrs Eakins recollected
having heard from outside sources that Edith
Mahon 'had suffered from great unkindness'.
Perhaps so, although one wonders if on this
occasion an elderly woman's recall of a quarter
of a century earlier was coloured more by the
portrait itself than by actual information concerning the person portrayed.

As an instance of portraiture, *Edith Mahon*
constitutes a departure from the norm in
American art. From the Colonial era onwards
and throughout the nineteenth century, portraits in America tended to emphasize the sitter's public persona rather than describe a
private mood. Portraits aimed to define qualities which remained constant regardless of
the multitudinous moment-to-moment emotional shifts that the subject may normally
have experienced. Such portraiture eschewed
the ephemera of transient mood and as a result
ruled out grins, grimaces, and tears.

Eakins, however, consistently worked towards an art that could capture the essence of a moment in such a way as to make it seem classical, long-lasting, almost timeless. His rowing pictures, for example, catch the oarsmen at the instant between the conclusion of one stroke and the start of another. *The Swimming Hole* (fig.8) shows a diver arched midway between rock and water. The swift motion, though implied, is frozen, as though forever. This snapshot effect, borrowed from the newly developed techniques of stop-motion photography, clearly fascinated Eakins. He sought ways to apply its principles to the painterly depiction of modern life. His portraiture also responded to the new photography. As a result portraits such as no. 44 constituted a defection from the traditional goals of American portraiture in that they sought to particularize a precise mood, however fleeting.

Edith Mahon may thus be viewed not so much as a realist document attesting to a profoundly sad or introspective disposition on the part of the sitter as it is a quasi-photographic record of a passing emotion: stop-motion, or stop-emotion, portraiture is how we might characterize it. In this respect the painter, who revered seventeenth-century art and learned much from what he observed in his student travels to Madrid, Naples, and Rome, was like those artists of the European baroque who sought to transfix lastingly on canvas or in marble the most ephemeral and elusive of moments. For instance, Bernini's sculptural

portrait of the Blessed Ludovica Albertoni in the church of San Francesco a Ripa in Rome depicts a dying woman at the moment that the agony of death gives way to the ecstasy of the hereafter (fig.44a).

The ornamentation of Edith Mahon's evening gown and the carved back of her chair are themselves baroque elements of the painting, twisting the space before and behind the sitter even as her hair and face seem subject to the twistings of an emotion that wrings her in its grip. The ribbon at her breast, animated with bold black curves, forms a lively contrast to Mrs Mahon's solemnly angular face – and yet also seems a metaphor for a dark and tangled emotion rearing up out of her heart or, alternatively, an incubus weighing down that heart.

The expression of intense transient emotion did not of course originate in the art of the Baroque. Since the early Renaissance artists had shown grief and lamentation in religious art, as in virtually any *Entombment* or *Pietà* (fig.44b). When the Virgin Mother or John the Beloved grieve in such works, or a saintly martyr endures an earthly torment, the facial expression is a response to a specific moment rather than to a long-standing characterological trait, even though that moment is deemed to be of such transhistorical importance that the strong emotion displayed seems to reach beyond local incident and transcend time. To the extent that *Edith Mahon* depicts a moment of similar, albeit lesser, emotional gravity, it falls within this artistic tradition, with the dif-

Fig.44a
Gianlorenzo Bernini, *The Blessed Ludovica Albertoni* (detail)
1671–1674
Marble
Church of Francesco a Ripa, Rome

Fig.44b
Dieric Bouts, *The Entombment of Christ*
Flax, 90.2 × 74.3 (35$\frac{1}{2}$ × 29$\frac{1}{4}$)
National Gallery, London

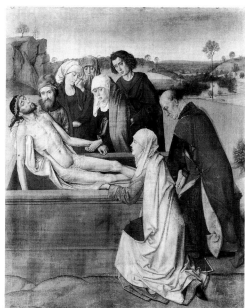

ference being that Edith Mahon's emotion is a private rather than public matter, and secular rather than religious.

Yet the art-historical lineage of the painting surely does not remove it from its own historical moment. It is appropriate to mention here not only still photography but also the recently invented motion picture. In 1903, Edwin S. Porter's *The Great Train Robbery* introduced to narrative filmmaking a technique that came to be known as the close-up. At first, close-ups were used simply for augmenting excitement rather than building characterization – the final shot of *The Great Train Robbery* is a close-up of a bandit firing his gun at the camera. About a decade later, as film director D.W. Griffith began to elicit an underplayed veristic style of acting suitable to the screen instead of the hammy histrionics preferred on the popular stage, the close-up came into its own as a device for showing internalized emotion that could best be revealed by subtle and nuanced gesture or expression (however overplayed these may seem by today's standards). Stars such as Greta Garbo became famous for conveying depths of mood merely by lifting an eyebrow or tilting the head in the radiance of a close-up (fig. 44c).

In the many head-and-shoulders portraits painted late in his career, and in none more so than *Edith Mahon*, Eakins merged the Renaissance tradition of lamentation painting, the immediacy of baroque art, and the principle of stop-motion photography to forge an artistic style unique to American portraiture and one that seems to have anticipated the emotion-saturated close-up of the silent motion picture. Using realist techniques to construct a fictive woman caught on the verge of tears, Eakins seemingly arrests time in a manner that looks both timeless and timely.

DML

Provenance: Given by the artist to Edith Mahon; purchased by Pancoast Galleries of Wellesley, Massachusetts, 1924; purchased by Smith College Museum of Art, 1931.

Exhibitions: Philadelphia, Museum of Art, 1944, no. 74; Washington, DC, National Gallery of Art, 1961, no. 93; Waterville, Maine, Colby College, 1969, no. 20; Philadelphia, Museum of Art, 1982 (1), no. 141; Boston, Museum of Fine Arts, 1983, pp. 330–1. ill. p. 183.

Literature: Goodrich 1933, no. 407, p. 199, ill. pl. 63; Larkin 1949, p. 278, ill.; Schendler 1967, p. 226, ill. p. 113; Hendricks, 1974, pp. 255, 329, ill. pl. 52; Wilmerding 1979, p. 112, ill. p. 111; Goodrich 1982, vol. II, pp. 55, 211, 215, ill. pl. 250; Johns 1983 (1), p. 167, ill. pl. 15; Baigell 1984, pp. 141–2, ill. p. 142.

Fig. 44c
Unknown photographer, *Greta Garbo in 'Anna Christie'*
1930
Bromide print
MGM, courtesy of the Kobal Collection

45
Rear-Admiral George W. Melville
1905
Oil on canvas, 101.6 × 68.5 (40 × 27)
Signed l.r.: *EAKINS*; on verso: *T.E.*

National Gallery of Art, Washington.
Gift (Partial and Promised) of Mr and Mrs H. John Heinz III,
in Honor of the Fiftieth Anniversary of the National
Gallery of Art (1991.33.1)

If it was Eakins's artistic purpose to depict persons of achievement who exemplified the 'heroism of modern life',[1] then few of the men and women who posed for him exemplified it as well as Admiral Melville. Described as 'frank and straightforward[,] ... intolerant always of sham and pretence,... [and] rigidly honest and incorruptible', Melville (1841–1912) possessed virtues very similar to those commonly attributed to Eakins himself.[2] Although Eakins did not know Melville personally before he painted him, perhaps that is why Eakins was attracted to him, and why he sought him out. And perhaps that is why he painted two versions of the subject, the first, now in the Philadelphia Museum of Art, in 1904 (fig.45a), and no.45 a year later.

Melville was approached on Eakins's behalf in the fall of 1903. On 25 September a Dr George C. Stout wrote to Colonel Thomas A. Prince of the US Marine Corps, requesting a letter of recommendation (and describing as well the enterprise of which Melville's portrait was to be a part):

Do you know Melville well enough to give a letter of recommendation to him to a friend of mine who is, I think, the best portrait painter in America, and who wishes to paint the Admiral without cost. He has painted two of our most famous paintings of surgical clinics in Philadelphia, has also painted [Rear-Admiral] Sigsbee and a number of other notables. I shall be very glad to help him get at Melville if I can.[3]

Within a few months Melville had agreed; on 3 January 1904 Eakins wrote to Frank Wilbur Stokes, 'I am about to paint another Admiral late this winter or in early spring'.[4]

On the back of the Philadelphia version, in Roman capital letters much as they might be engraved on the base of a sculptured monument, Eakins listed Melville's vital statistics and principal achievements:

REAR ADMIRAL
GEORGE WALLACE MELVILLE U.S.N.
BORN NEW YORK CITY JANUARY 10 1841
ENTERED U.S. NAVY JULY 29, 1861
1881 CHIEF ENGINEER
1887 ENGINEER IN CHIEF
1898 REAR ADMIRAL
1904 RETIRED
MEMBER OF THE HALL RELIEF
EXPEDITION 1873
CHIEF ENGINEER JEANNETTE
EXPEDITION 1879–82
CHIEF ENGINEER GREELEY RELIEF
EXPEDITION 1883
DEGREES
L.L.D. (PA) D.E. (STEVENS) M.A.
(GEORGETOWN) M.E. (COLUMBIA)

Eakins's inscription, although it reverses the order of their occurrence, gives the principal parts of Melville's career: his heroic participation in several of the important episodes of polar exploration that so occupied the energy and imagination of the nineteenth century, and his crucial contribution, as Chief of the Navy's Bureau of Steam Engineering, to the modern American steam-powered 'New Navy'.[5]

Of all Melville's exploits, the most heroic was the ill-fated *Jeannette* expedition. The *Jeannette*, a bark-rigged steamship captained by Lieutenant George Washington De Long, the expedition's leader, left San Francisco in June 1879 in the first attempt to reach the North Pole by way of the Bering Strait. The expedition was planned on the basis of the untested theory that a thermal current comparable to the Gulf Stream, known as 'the Black Current of Japan', would provide an unimpeded waterway northwards. One year later, his ship firmly in the grip of arctic ice from which it would never be released, De Long wrote in his journal, 'I pronounce a thermometric gateway to the North Pole a delusion and a snare'.[6] For two years the *Jeannette* was held by drifting ice, until June 1881 when she sank, at a position 400 miles north of the Siberian coast to which the ice had carried her. In the greatest ordeal of all, three of the ship's boats attempted to reach the mainland. One sank and the other two were separated. The party commanded by Engineer Melville succeeded in finding a native village and survived. Lieutenant De Long and most of his party, lost in the maze of the Lena Delta, perished. In March 1882, after two attempts, Melville found their remains. In recognition of his efforts, he received the Russian order of St Stanislaus from the Tsar – which he wears in this portrait – and a gold medal from the congress of the United States.[7] Melville told of his experiences in his book *In the Lena Delta*.

About six feet tall, powerfully built, and gruff in manner, Melville was an impressive and somewhat domineering presence. Eakins's first portrait of him (fig.45a) was a conventional three-quarter length three-quarter view in full dress uniform that captured Melville's appearance (compare fig.45b) and his station. His second, no. 45, greatly simplified in dress and pose, with the figure rigidly frontal and filling the picture space like a Byzantine Pantokrator, his head nimbed by a mane of white hair, and his scarred hand an emblem of his trials and fortitude,[8] is an iconic distillation of Melville's character – his great physical strength, his forceful personality, his keen intelligence, and, above all, his indomitable will.

NC Jr.

1. See Johns 1983 (1). Homer 1992 endorses this view of Eakins's enterprise.
2. Cathcart 1912, p.508.
3. Dr George C. Stout to Colonel T.A. Prince, written from 1611 Walnut Street, Philadelphia, 25 September 1903 (Philadelphia Museum of Art). Rear-Admiral Charles D. Sigsbee was Captain of the battleship *Maine* when she was blown up in Havana harbour in 1898 and was Commandant of the League Island Navy Yard in Philadelphia between 1903 and 1904. Eakins painted his head-and-shoulders portrait, now in a private collection, in 1903.
4. Eakins to F.W. Stokes, written from 1729 Mount Vernon Street, Philadelphia, 3 January 1904 (Philadelphia Museum of Art).
5. See Thurston 1903, pp.183–6.
6. Quoted in Guttridge 1988, p.147.
7. Two ships were named after him, a destroyer tender that served in both world wars, and a scientific research vessel launched in 1968. He was so honoured not for his exploits on the *Jeannette* expedition and other events of polar exploration in which he was an important participant, but for warship design and construction in his capacity as Chief Engineer.
8. Frostbitten and calloused by his years of arctic exploration, his left hand also bears the scar of a severe axe wound suffered during the Civil War when the *Wachusett*, on which he was serving, rammed and boarded the Confederate cruiser *Florida*.

Provenance: Mrs Thomas Eakins, Philadelphia; Millicent Rogers; Count Peter Salm; (Lothar Dohna, New York, 1983).

Exhibitions: Pittsburgh, Carnegie Institute, 1905, no. 67; Philadelphia, American Art Society, 1907; Philadelphia, Pennsylvania Academy of the Fine Arts, 1912, no. 201; New York, M. Knoedler & Co., 1944, no. 76; Washington, DC, National Gallery of Art, 1991.

Literature: McHenry 1946, pp.117–19; Hendricks 1974, pp.255–6, ill. p.256; Goodrich 1982, vol.II, pp.208–11, ill. p.209; *Art for the Nation: Gifts in Honor of the Fiftieth Anniversary of the National Gallery of Art*, 1991, p.274, ill. p.275.

Fig.45a
Rear-Admiral George W. Melville
1904
Oil on canvas, 76.8 × 121.9 (30¼ × 48)
Philadelphia Museum of Art. Gift of Mrs Thomas Eakins and Miss Mary Adeline Williams

Fig.45b
Unknown photographer,
Rear-Admiral George W. Melville
Photograph reproduced in *Journal of the American Society of Naval Engineers*, vol.24, May 1912, p.474

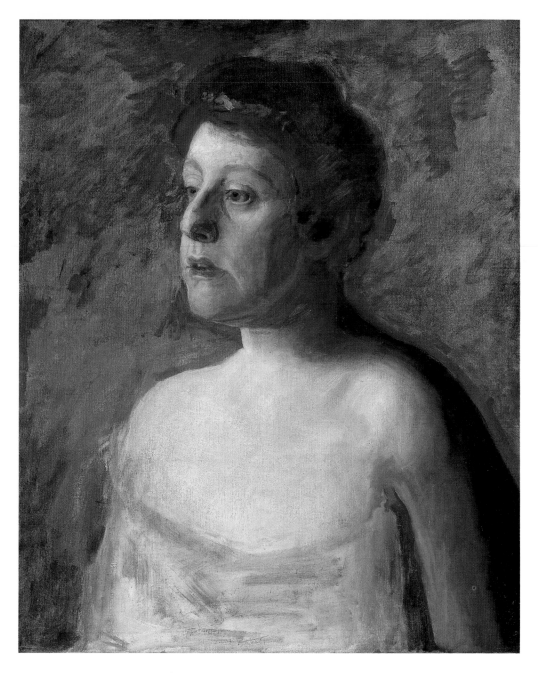

46
A Singer (Mrs W.H. Bowden)
c. 1906
Oil on canvas, 61.9 × 51.7 (24⅜ × 20⅜)
Unsigned and undated

The Art Museum, Princeton University.
Museum purchase, Fowler McCormick Fund
(y1986.85)

Between 1900 and 1910, a period of unprecedented popularity for Eakins, he painted
eighty-five head-and-shoulders portraits of the
same dimensions as *A Singer (Mrs W.H.
Bowden)*. Although he worked with veteran
expertise, some portraits, including no. 46,
apparently remained unfinished. There were
several plausible reasons why deserted projects
existed. Stories by close friends and family and
letters by the artist offer explanations as to why
some projects were abandoned, but it is unclear why this particular painting remained
unfinished.

In instances where portraits were not completed, the sitters often chose not to see a portrait to its final stage. Mrs Elizabeth Duane
Gillespie, for example, refused to return to
Eakins's studio in 1895 because she found his
work attire distasteful.[1] Mrs William Shaw
Ward commissioned a portrait in 1884, but was
unable to remain in Philadelphia long enough
to allow Eakins to finish it. She took the
incomplete painting, and paid the artist half
the agreed price of $400.[2] Although they do not
perhaps have the same aesthetic appeal as the
finished portraits, *A Singer* and the several
other unfinished works are useful tools for
inquiry into the methods of the artist. Stroke
for stroke, the unfinished painting becomes a
telling story, a kind of road map of the artist's
search for the two-dimensional image. Eakins
presumably began each project in earnest with
the intention of completion, and the canvases
left unfinished do not bear his signature.

By the time Eakins began *A Singer*, his technique was not as laboured as in the meticulously worked canvases of his earlier years. His
brush has left notes, abbreviations of placement to be refined at a later time, perhaps the
next sitting, but Mrs Bowden apparently never
made her final visit. He has rendered the sitter's face with care although it is quite possible
that even this, the most completed area of the
canvas, is not the finished product Eakins had
in mind. Many of the head-and-shoulders portraits from this period, such as *Mrs Edith
Mahon* (no. 44), have faces feather-brushed,
leaving a smooth, mirror-like representation.
Little or no under drawings are evident on his
canvases, but Eakins did made notes with his
brush, which gave direction to subsequent sittings. This type of notation can be seen in the
sweeps of paint covering the chest of *A Singer*,
alluding to a strapless garment. This is surely a
painting made from life. The sense of solidity,
even without the final touches, comes through
here as much as in finished works. Eakins's
adjustments to chin, shoulder, and hairline are
preserved for future scrutiny only because the
artist was unable to see the portrait to com-

pletion. This clearly was not a feeble effort cast aside hastily by the artist, and the painting was handled more than once, as evidenced by the layered paint, wet over dry, which is found in several areas of the face.

The exact identity of Mrs W.H. Bowden remains unknown. The unframed canvas was among two hundred paintings consigned to the Babcock Galleries in New York in 1939 by Susan Macdowell Eakins. It was not signed or dated by the artist. Mrs Eakins gave the painting a typological title with a personal identification in parentheses, relying entirely on her memory. This canvas poses many questions. Was Mrs Bowden actually a professional singer or was she one of the many ladies from this time who sang in the parlours of family and friends? Was this work commissioned and subsequently abandoned because the sitter was unhappy with the developing likeness? Did Eakins request Mrs Bowden to model for his representation of a singer as an addition to an existing group of professional types such as *The Oboe Player* (Philadelphia Museum of Art) for which Dr Benjamin Sharp posed in 1904? If the latter was the intent, why would the artist have come so close to completion only to abandon a purely 'descriptive' painting? This seems unlikely when the events surrounding the completion of *The Concert Singer* (no. 26) are taken into account. When Weda Cook, who modelled for *The Concert Singer* early in Eakins's career, refused to continue posing (see no. 26 for a fuller account), Eakins finished the work without his model by hanging her dress over her shoes for reference. Evidently, if a project was important enough, Eakins found a way to effect completion. Further, if Mrs Bowden was a celebrated name in the music world, the enhanced marketability of her portrait would have prompted the artist to finish the painting at least for exhibition if not for sale.

At best, a shadow of Mrs W.H. Bowden's identity exists. The Bowden name is not among those of the first families of Philadelphia. The surname began to appear after the turn of the century in the working-class areas of the city. This leaves the impression that Mrs Bowden was not a notable member of Philadelphia society. Was she a short-term visitor to Philadelphia and, unlike Mrs Ward, not inclined to take the portrait unfinished? In any case, her unfinished portrait survives as a splendid example of work in progress by the artist in his prime. Eakins had not undertaken an open-mouthed, singing image since *Home Ranch* (fig.46a) in 1892. Some of Eakins's most accomplished paintings include individuals singing, but the artist's attempts at representing the figure in song were posed genre compositions rather than portraits as such. Eakins's conception of singing themes reflects the variety found elsewhere in his *œuvre*; the natural parlour amateur, the contrived, costumed cowboy and the trained professional at work. How does *A Singer* fit into this group?

It is interesting to note that the paintings of singers are all titled for the action implied and not for the sitter.[3] Hence, Susan Eakins might have thought it appropriate to continue in this tradition by titling this work typologically as well. The painting was considered less marketable in 1939 because it remained unfinished, but titled as such, the dealer could display this somewhat disguised portrait of Mrs W.H. Bowden in the hope that a collector, without any kinship link to the sitter, would nonetheless recognize an investment in *A Singer*. The neglect of this portrait did not end when Eakins removed it from his easel sometime after the turn of the century, however. It remained unsold by the Babcock Galleries for an additional twenty years, no doubt puzzling those who saw it as much as it continues to intrigue us today.

MRV

1. Goodrich 1982, vol.II, p.75.
2. Ibid., vol.I, p.201.
3. The genre oil paintings of singing are *The Pathetic Song* (no. 21), *The Concert Singer* (no. 26) and *Home Ranch* (fig.46a).

Provenance: Susan Macdowell Eakins; Kleeman and Babcock Galleries, New York, 1957; Leonard and Lisa Baskin, New York, 1959; private collection; Kennedy Galleries, Inc., New York; The Art Museum, Princeton University, New Jersey, 1986.

Exhibitions: Pittsburgh, Carnegie Institute, 1958, no. 66.

Literature: Goodrich 1933, p.202; Schendler 1967, p.235, ill. p.231; Wilmerding 1991, pp.260–1, ill. p.261.

Fig.46a
Home Ranch
1888
Oil on canvas, 60.9 × 50.8 (24 × 20)
Philadelphia Museum of Art. Gift of Mrs Thomas Eakins and Miss Mary Adeline Williams

47
The Right Reverend James F. Loughlin
1902
Oil on canvas, 230 × 115 (90½ × 45¼)
Signed and dated

St Charles Borromeo Seminary,
Overbrook, Pennsylvania

Thomas Eakins was born a member of Philadelphia's Protestant bourgeoisie, and his views on religion appear to have developed from hostility in his youth[1] to a smirking agnosticism on which many of his friends commented later in his life.[2] It is remarkable, then, that among his best works is a series of fourteen portraits of prominent Roman Catholic clerics executed with a single exception between 1900 and 1906. Of these paintings, all but one, the lost portrait of Mother Mary Patricia Waldron, depict priests intimately connected with the St Charles Borromeo Seminary, Philadelphia's and the region's pre-eminent training college for aspiring priests. During Eakins's visits, the seminary's rigorous academic programme included Greek and Latin, philosophy, theology, history, mathematics, elocution and chanting, and seminarians were expected to master these subjects before their ordination could take place.[3] St Charles Seminary is still located in the Italianate complex Eakins would have known, set in extensive grounds in Overbrook, a suburb of the city.

Painted by Eakins in 1902, Monsignor James Loughlin (1851–1911) taught Greek, canon law, and music at St Charles Seminary.[4] He also served for many years as editor of the *American Catholic Encyclopedia* and as associate editor with Monsignor James P. Turner, another Eakins subject (see no. 49), of the *American Catholic Quarterly Review*, a scholarly journal exploring not only strictly doctrinal concerns but also questions of history, philosophy, and ethics. His pastoral vocation included the rectorship of Philadelphia's Church of the Nativity of the Blessed Virgin and Eakins's portrait hung in the parish house there until 1930. With six others from Eakins's Overbrook series, it is now displayed in the Eakins Room, a reception hall at St Charles Seminary. Easily accessible, well maintained, but almost never loaned, the portraits are among the small number of works in Eakins's *œuvre* which can still be viewed in locations relating to the environments for which they were originally painted.

Eakins had first showed an interest in Philadelphia's Roman Catholic hierarchy in 1876, when he asked Archbishop James F. Wood to sit to him. The young, ambitious artist painted this major figure of early Philadelphia Catholicism without payment, possibly with hopes of broadening his client base to include future paid commissions from the Catholic community, which was exploding in size because of immigration and consequently building new schools, churches, and rectories for which decoration was needed. Though the Wood portrait was well received, Eakins's effort to generate

more business from Roman Catholic sources was not successful. Until 1900, his only other painting on a religious subject was the powerful and controversial *Crucifixion* (fig. 45) done in 1880 and deemed irreligious, even sadistic, because of its emphasis on Christ in torment.[5]

It was around 1900 that Eakins was reintroduced to Overbrook through his protégé, Samuel Murray, a Philadelphia sculptor whose sister was a Roman Catholic nun and whose patrons included the St Charles Seminary.[6] Murray and Eakins often cycled to the picturesque and serene seminary on Sundays, remaining for lunch or for an entire day of conversation with the priests and ending with Vespers in the evening. Several members of the faculty became Eakins's close friends, and it was from these friendships, so often the source of Eakins's portraiture, that the paintings arose.

Certainly Eakins felt a strong intellectual kinship with his Overbrook friends, who were neither merely parish priests nor solely religious in their scope of interests, but men of significant achievement as intellectuals and leaders. Among these was Loughlin, described by a contemporary as possessing 'habits of study that were almost suicidal',[7] as well as other professors at St Charles Seminary, two archbishops, and three cardinals. As Roman Catholic clerics, too, Eakins's Overbrook subjects were outsiders, set apart, like the increasingly alienated artist, from the mainstream of Philadelphia society into which Eakins had been born but from which he had, by 1900, endured considerable scorn.

Eakins continued his visits to Overbrook over a period of years, possibly until his death, but almost all the ecclesiastical portraits were painted before 1903 and none after 1906. They range from spartan head-and-shoulders portraits to full-length works such as the portrait of Archbishop Diomede Falconio (no. 48) for which Eakins sought to borrow such conventions of Old Master clerical portraiture as august bearing and elaborate vestments. Some of these works are among the masterpieces of his career, and while it is perhaps incorrect to include the portrait of Monsignor James F. Loughlin in this category, the painting, which has been discussed with disparagement[8] where it has not been ignored altogether, succeeds to a far greater extent than acknowledged. Eakins drew the viewer's attention to the upper portion of Loughlin's face by dramatically highlighting his eyes and forehead. His eyeglasses, which seem to magnify the eyes like microscope lenses, and his wide, broad brow convey the man's 'suicidal habits of study' better than any contemporary obser-

vation. Eakins connected head and hand through the long, strong line of his cloak. This device conveys emphatically the union of Loughlin's inquiring, lively mind with the physical man, the latter suggested in the beautifully painted hand emerging from ample vestments. If the vestments themselves are unfinished, Loughlin's completely painted face and hand would have constituted, in Eakins's view, an intellectually robust conception of his subject. It is not ungenerous to suggest that Loughlin, in this conception, is a plain man, possibly even a homely one. Yet the austerity and introspection Eakins invested in many of his clerical subjects do not generally evoke a sense of sadness, anxiety or loss, as the same qualities do in his portraits of the laity. (Restraint is more readily expected of priests, so Eakins's goal of reaching the contemplative man is more easily and positively achieved.) See also nos. 48 and 49 for a further discussion of Eakins's ecclesiastical portraits.

BTA

1. Eakins's views as a young man on Catholicism are expressed in letters published in Goodrich 1982, vol.I pp.45–6.
2. 'Eakins used to smile superciliously when anyone spoke about future life', a friend wrote, 'it was contrary to the knowledge of science he possessed'. Quoted in Hendricks 1974, p.160. See also Goodrich op. cit., vol.II, p.194; Schendler 1967, p.199; Siegl 1978, p.24; McHenry 1946, p.129.
3. The seminary's history from its establishment in a Philadelphia rectory in 1832 through its relocation to its own facility at Overbrook in 1871 to the modern era is detailed in Connelly [1979]. The seminary's reputation for academic excellence was quickly established and its success is regarded today as an important foundation for the Roman Catholic college movement in the United States. A measure of this success is the visit of Pope John Paul II to Overbrook shortly after his election to the papacy as part of his first American tour.
4. In Goodrich 1933, p.194, Loughlin's date of birth is incorrectly given as 1867. For Loughlin's biography, see Connelly op. cit., p.86.
5. The painting is considered in Milroy 1989, pp.269–84.
6. Connelly op. cit., p.308.
7. Ibid., p.86.
8. Schendler op. cit. described it as insipid and speculates that the lack of finish in the vestments indicates Eakins's lost interest in the work (p.211).

Provenance: Given to the subject by the artist, 1902; displayed in the rectory of the Church of the Nativity of the Blessed Virgin, Philadelphia, transferred to St Charles Borromeo Seminary, Overbrook, 1930.

Literature: Goodrich 1933, p.194; Schendler 1967, p.211.

48
Archbishop Diomede Falconio
1905
Oil on canvas, 183.2 × 137.7 (72⅛ × 54¼)
Inscribed on verso (covered by lining fabric):
HANC EFFIGIEM ILLMI AC REVMI
DIOMEDI FALCONIO
ARCHLARISSENSIS ET DELEGATI
APOSTOLICI IN STATIBUS
FOEDERATIS AMERICAE
SEPTEMTRIONALIS PINXIT THOMAS
EAKINS WASHINGTONII MDCCCCV/
EAKINS

National Gallery of Art, Washington
Gift of Stephen C. Clark (1946.16.1)

Fig.48a
His Eminence Sebastiano Cardinal Martinelli
1902
Oil on canvas, 200 × 152.3 (78⅜ × 60)
The Armand Hammer Collection, The Armand
Hammer Museum of Art and Cultural Center,
Los Angeles

Beginning at about the turn of the century, Eakins painted fourteen portraits of Roman Catholic clergymen, often ambitious full-length ones such as no. 48. Why Eakins, who was avowedly irreligious, elected to paint them has never been clearly established. It is said that he liked the company of these learned and cosmopolitan churchmen, and, despite his irreligiousness, found their accomplishments admirable.

According to Lloyd Goodrich, 'All of Eakins' portraits of the clergy were evidently done at his request, not commissioned'.[1] That is true of most of his ecclesiastical portraits, a number of which were presented to their sitters and are now owned by St Charles Borromeo Seminary in Overbrook, Pennsylvania; many of the portraits were associated with the seminary, which Eakins often visited, and many of them were painted there (see nos. 47 and 49 for a further discussion of Eakins's ecclesiastical portraits). It was Eakins's common practice, especially in his later life, to solicit sitters of all kinds whom he admired and to present them with their portraits (see no. 45). This was not the case, however, with the Falconio portrait: Eakins did not initiate it, nor did he seem to have any special admiration for the sitter.

In a letter to his friend William Sartain, written in March 1905, Eakins wrote that, as soon as he finished some work then in progress, he would 'go down to Washington to paint Falconio the Apostolic Delegate for the Catholic University of America'.[2] His language can only indicate that Falconio's portrait was commissioned by the university, or at very least that he undertook to paint it with the expectation that the university would acquire it. Three years

earlier Eakins had painted a similarly conceived and similarly ambitious portrait of the previous Apostolic Delegate, Sebastiano Cardinal Martinelli (fig.48a), which did belong to the Catholic University.[3]

Eakins's language in a series of letters to his wife written from Washington, where he was at work on Falconio's portrait, indicates a less than perfect regard for his subject.[4] On 8 May 1905, Eakins wrote: 'I had an engagement with the Archbishop at 10.[5] I waited for him to come in from the next room and he waited for me to knock at his door and I did not see him until dinner time. He posed at 1 o'clock for 50 minutes most of that time asleep. You bet I will knock tomorrow at 10 o'clock'. A week later, on 15 May, Eakins wrote: 'I had the good man for 56 minutes today and I fairly flew over my work. He was somewhat critical today before commencing. He told me his time was very valuable and I told him so was mine. He said it was very hot. I told him I felt it. That was all but it had a good effect, and he came in two or three times and noticed how hard I was working up to supper time.' The next day he reported, 'The good man gave me a long sitting to day. An hour and a half. I got the whole head and neck except the eyes. I guess I will finish in 2 or 3 days . . .'. And on the next, in the last letter pertaining to the painting, he wrote: 'When I got done to day's work the old man asked me if I had finished so I told him yes. Then he want to know if I could do more to it, if he gave me more time. I said yes. He said he would not mind sitting twice more and then he had to go away. I will see him tomorrow only . . .'.

Falconio's portrait was never finished; that can be seen in the painting itself, of course, but can as easily be deduced from Eakins's last letter. Henry McBride believed that Falconio 'refused to continue the poses when he saw the sort of effigy that was growing between the painter's brushes'.[6] But from Eakins's facetious references to Falconio as 'the old man' – born in 1842, he was in his early sixties and only two years older than Eakins – and 'the good man', and from his reports of their strained, clipped conversations, this was clearly a project which neither participant relished, and which, indeed, Falconio was evidently more willing to complete than was Eakins. Goodrich thought Falconio's face – the most fully finished part of the painting and, as a photograph shows (fig.48b), an excellent likeness – has an expression of meditation and reverie'[7] yet it is just as possible to read in it an unpleasant self-importance and a sternness bordering on sourness that may well have put Eakins off, as his letters suggest, not to mention a worldly toughness and shrewdness very different from the values Goodrich saw in it.

Eakins left no other major painting as partially finished as this one. McBride admired the painting the more for its lack of finish. Goodrich thought it a virtue, too, and wished 'Eakins more often left well enough alone'.[8] It is not clear how Eakins regarded it. In certain respects he treated it as a finished picture. He never destroyed it, never repainted it, inscribed it elaborately on its back (in Latin), and in 1907, in reply to a letter from Professor John Pickard of the University of Missouri, requesting information about him and a list of his 'most representative paintings' for a course he was preparing on the history of American painting, Eakins included the Falconio portrait with some of his other most important – and fully finished – paintings.[9] But he never exhibited it during his lifetime, and it is shown leaning unframed against the wall in a photograph of Eakins's Mount Vernon Street studio made about 1910.[10]

Angelus Raphael Januarius Falconio (1842–1917) was born in Pescocostanzo in Italy. Upon entering the Franciscan Order at the age of eighteen he received the name Diomede. He left Italy for America in 1865, and became an American citizen in 1871. He was ordained in 1866, and two years later, at twenty-six, became president of St Bonaventure College. He subsequently held many important positions in the Church, becoming Bishop of Lacedonia in 1892, Archbishop of Acerenza and Matera in 1895, the first Apostolic Delegate in Canada and titular Archbishop of Larissa in 1899, and three years later, the third Apostolic Delegate to the United States. He served in that position until 1911, and in that year was created Cardinal.

As Apostolic Delegate in Canada 'he remained a poor Franciscan friar', and 'although gray silken garments had been prepared for him he never wore them'.[11] He seems to have made an exception for Eakins, doing so, perhaps, at the request of Eakins, who often asked people to wear what they themselves ordinarily would not have chosen.

NC Jr

1. Goodrich 1982, vol.II, p.188.
2. Letter to William Sartain, from 1729 Mount Vernon Street, Philadelphia, 13 March 1905 (Sartain Papers, Archives of American Art, Smithsonian Institution, Washington, DC).
3. When it was exhibited the year after it was painted a reviewer commented: 'Mr. Eakins is showing his portrait of Cardinal Martinelli, lent by the Catholic University, for which it was painted' ('Brilliant Display of High-Class Art', *The Philadelphia Inquirer*, 18 January 1903). The university frequently let Eakins exhibit the painting, always indicating its ownership whenever it did so. The Catholic University sold the painting in 1970. It was acquired by Armand Hammer.
4. All are written from the Saint James hotel, Washington, DC (Pennsylvania Academy of the Fine Arts, archives, Charles Bregler Papers). Like Martinelli's portrait before it, Falconio's was painted at the residence of the Apostolic Delegate, perhaps even in the same panelled room.
5. For some reason, despite Eakins's inscription on its back, whenever the painting was exhibited and cited, until it was formally changed by the National Gallery of Art in 1978, Falconio's title was given as Monsignor.
6. 'Thomas Eakins II', *New York Sun*, 11 November 1917, in McBride 1975, pp.138–9.
7. Goodrich op. cit., vol.II, pp.188, 191.
8. Ibid., p.191.
9. Letter from John Pickard to Thomas Eakins, written from Columbia, Missouri, 20 June 1907 (Philadelphia Museum of Art). Eakins's list included *The Gross Clinic, The Agnew Clinic, The Crucifixion, The Concert Singer*, as well as five other ecclesiastical portraits, among them that of Cardinal Martinelli.
10. Goodrich op. cit., vol.II, fig.175, p.269.
11. *Il Cardinale Diomede Falconio, O.F.M.*, L'Aquilia, 1968, p.18.

Provenance: Mrs Thomas Eakins, Philadelphia, to 1922/1923; Reginald Marsh, New York, to 1943; (William Macbeth, New York); Stephen C. Clark, New York, by whom given to the National Gallery of Art, 1946.

Exhibitions: New York, Metropolitan Museum of Art, 1917, no. 51; Philadelphia, Pennsylvania Academy of the Fine Arts, 1917, no. 138; New York, Museum of Modern Art, 1930, no. 113; Pittsburgh, Carnegie Institute, 1945, no. 106; Washington, National Gallery of Art, 1961, no. 91.

Literature: H. McBride, 'Thomas Eakins II', *New York Sun*, 11 November 1917, in McBride 1975, pp.138–9; Goodrich 1933, p.201, ill. pl.66; McKinney 1942, p.15; Schendler 1967, p.208, ill.104; Hendricks 1974, p.255, ill.275; Gerdts 1979, pp.154–5, ill. p.155; Goodrich 1982, pp.188, 191, ill.237; Homer 1992, pp.226–7.

Fig.48b
Unknown photographer, *Monsignor Falconio, the Present Apostolic Delegate to the Church in the United States*
Photograph reproduced in
The Catholic World, vol.76, February 1903, p.568

MGR. FALCONIO,
THE PRESENT APOSTOLIC DELEGATE TO THE CHURCH IN THE UNITED STATES.

49

Sketch for Monsignor James P. Turner
Oil on cardboard, 36.8 × 26.7 ($14\frac{1}{2}$ × $10\frac{1}{2}$)
Unsigned; inscribed l.r. by Susan Macdowell
Eakins: *Sketch/T.E.*

Philadelphia Museum of Art. Gift of Mrs
Thomas Eakins and Miss Mary Adeline
Williams (30.32.15)

When interviewed after his death, Eakins's
family and friends said that he was an agnostic.
But though he may never have professed a
religion, Eakins demonstrated a cautious fascination with the Roman Catholic church and
her clergy throughout his career.[1] While
studying in Paris during the late 1860s, he
attended services at St Sulpice, primarily to
listen to the choir. In 1876, he requested permission to paint a full-length portrait of The
Most Reverend James Wood, recently elevated
to the rank of Archbishop of Philadelphia.
Four years later, Eakins completed his powerful and enigmatic *Crucifixion* (fig.45), a painting he may have hoped to sell to the
Philadelphia archdiocese for the chapel of the
diocesan seminary of St Charles Borromeo at
the new Overbrook campus.[2] By the late 1890s,
probably due to his close friendship with the
sculptor Samuel Murray, who was a Roman
Catholic, Eakins became a regular visitor to the
seminary. According to Murray, the two men
would bicycle to Overbrook on Sunday after-
noons, frequently staying for dinner. Murray
recalled that Eakins sometimes attended
Vespers as well.[3]

At the seminary, the one-time Director of
Schools of the Pennsylvania Academy was
welcomed into a close-knit all-male community of scholars and teachers. But Overbrook
was by no means a cloister. The faculty and the
many parish priests who regularly visited the
seminary – most of them, like Eakins, native
Philadelphians – were influential civic as well
as religious leaders. By 1900, the balance of
power in Philadelphia was shifting inexorably
out of the hands of the traditional Protestant
establishment and into the hands of the
500,000 citizens who professed Roman Catholicism, almost thirty per cent of the city's popu-
lation. Since the violent Anti-Catholic Nativist
riots, which had occurred during the year of
Eakins's birth, the number of Catholic parishes
and schools in Philadelphia had increased
exponentially. And as a resident of the Fairmount district of the city which had grown
correspondingly more Catholic during his own
lifetime, Eakins was surely aware of this.[4]

Just as he had portrayed the leaders of the
artistic, medical and scientific communities, so
too Eakins was attracted to the leaders of the
Catholic community as portrait subjects. Over
the course of a decade, from around 1900 until
1909, Eakins produced at least fourteen portraits of Roman Catholic clerics. Some of these
paintings were commissioned; others Eakins
volunteered to paint, as was his custom: in
many cases, as with the earlier Wood portrait,
the portrait commemorated some specific
event of honour in which the sitter was

involved. Eakins's subjects included such distinguished sitters as Sebastiano Cardinal Martinelli (fig.48a), Apostolic Delegate to the United States from 1898 to 1902, his successor as Apostolic Delegate, Archbishop Diomede Falconio (no.48), and Archbishop William Henry Elder of Cincinnati (fig.46). Other sitters included the founder of Villanova University, the Very Reverend John Fedigan OSA; Bishop Edmond Prendergast, later named Archbishop of Philadelphia, and Bishop Denis Doughtery, Prendergast's successor to the archdiocese, who would be named Cardinal in 1921.[5]

In 1906, Eakins produced a full-length portrait of Monsignor James P. Turner (fig.49a), on the occasion of Turner's appointment as Domestic Prelate and subsequent promotion to Protonotary Apostolic. Eakins already had painted a head-and-shoulders portrait of Turner, indeed this seems to have been the first in the clerical series, and the fact that Turner posed twice may indicate that a particular bond of friendship existed between the two men. It could well have been Turner, in his capacity as Vicar-General of the Archdiocese, who introduced the artist to his other sitters and secured commissions for Eakins. Born in the Southwark district of Philadelphia, James P. Turner (1857–1929) was among the first to be ordained by Archbishop Wood from the St Charles Borromeo Seminary and, despite delicate health, he proved to be an especially talented and devout diocesan priest. After serving at parishes in Colorado, California, and Philadelphia through the 1880s and 1890s, in 1898 Turner was appointed assistant rector at the Cathedral of Sts Peter and Paul. In the October of that year, Turner also became associate editor of the influential *American Catholic Quarterly Review*, of which he was later editor. In 1901, The Most Reverend Patrick John Ryan, Archbishop of Philadelphia, named Turner Chancellor of the diocese and in 1903, Vicar-General. With this promotion, Turner became the archbishop's chief deputy: he assisted Archbishop Ryan in the government of the archdiocese and was delegated to exercise episcopal jurisdiction in spirituals and temporals. Turner resigned both of these offices in 1911 with the death of Archbishop Ryan. From then until his death in 1929, Turner was rector of the Church of the Nativity at Allegheny Avenue and Belgrade Street in the north-east section of Philadelphia.[6]

In keeping with the academic procedure he had learned in the ateliers of Gérôme and Bonnat in Paris, Eakins first developed the portrait of Turner in no. 49, the oil sketch, siting the figure within a format, and roughing out colour relationships and the dominant areas of light and shadow (see nos. 13 and 32). As a Monsignor holding the office of Protonotary Apostolic, Turner was a 'prelate di mantellata', granted the privilege of wearing a distinctive red cassock, with white lace rochet, sleeveless red mantellata and the biretta with red pompom. Turner's vestments provided Eakins with an ideal opportunity to manipulate the colour red on a large scale, exploring the visual tension created by the mix of brightly-lit red glazes as these combine to push the figure of Turner forwards out of the cool brown setting in which he is posed. Having established the basic design of his composition, Eakins then plotted the dimensions of the setting and the exact scale and siting of the figure in a series of detailed perspectival diagrams (now in the collection of the Pennsylvania Academy of the Fine Arts). These calculations were transferred to the canvas, and the painting completed.[7]

Eakins made no changes to the composition of the figure when expanding the portrait from oil sketch to life size to canvas. Turner is shown standing in a darkened interior, holding a Roman Missal. To his right is a low altar rail, decorated with the initial 'M' and beyond this, hanging over his right shoulder, a painting of the Assumption of the Virgin. As Kathleen Foster has pointed out, Turner was the only cleric whom Eakins posed in an ecclesiastical setting, but it is difficult to ascertain whether Eakins intended the space to be read as a specific site. A painting of the Assumption did hang in the sanctuary of the Cathedral, but the placement of the painting in the Eakins portrait does not correspond to that sanctuary area. The space could perhaps be entirely fictitious.[8]

According to legend, Eakins was inspired to paint this portrait of Turner after watching him celebrate a funeral mass; and the painting of the Assumption could be interpreted as a reference to death.[9] But as Foster has noted, Turner is not portrayed in the act of celebrating mass; rather he stands immobile, simply posing. The funeral legend is also contradicted by Turner's vestments which are not those he would have worn for a funeral mass, and by the fact that he wears the biretta, indicating he is standing outside the high altar sanctuary – therefore cannot be celebrating the mass. Indeed, he need not have been engaged in any activity, for simply by posing in the brilliant red vestments of a senior prelate, Turner embodied episcopal authority and spiritual jurisdiction.[10]

EM

Fig.49a
Monsignor James P. Turner
*c.*1906
Oil on canvas, 223.5 × 106.7 (88 × 42)
The Nelson-Atkins Museum of Art, Kansas City, Missouri. Gift of the Enid and Crosby Kemper Foundation

1. David W. Jordan told Lloyd Goodrich he thought Eakins liked priests 'because "they were human and told good stories, because they were intelligent, not too other-worldly like Protestants" '. Quoted in Homer 1992, p.226. Writing home to his mother while crossing the Atlantic to France in 1866, Eakins described a Jesuit fellow-passenger: 'He is the most learned man I ever saw and talks French with me by the hour. He had read all the books with which I am acquainted and knows them. He chats about authors, painters, musicians, colleges, the animals of the south, those of France. He knows anatomy, medicine & all the languages of Europe. He has never tried to convert me although he knows I belong to no church, and the only moral advice he ever gave was to abstain from gaming in Paris which he says ruins many Americans. The most striking thing about him is his modesty'. Thomas Eakins to Caroline Eakins, 1 October 1866 (Charles Bregler's Thomas Eakins Collection, Pennsylvania Academy of the Fine Arts, Philadelphia).

2. For a discussion of this work, see Milroy 1989, pp.269–84.

3. See Turner 1970, pp.195–8; Hendricks 1974, pp.253–5; Goodrich 1982, vol.II, pp.186–98; and Homer 1992, pp.225–8.

4. By 1900, St Charles Borromeo was the third largest diocesan seminary in the United States, a thriving academic and theological centre with an internationally renowned faculty and some 115 students preparing for pastoral work in the diocese. See Connelly [1979]. For a history of Catholics in Philadelphia, see Kurlin 1909, and Connelly 1976. My thanks to Lorena Boylan and Shaun Weldon at the Archdiocese, and Elizabeth Anderson, for their generous assistance.

5. The clerical portraits were first described by Lloyd Goodrich in the catalogue appendix to his 1933 monograph. For the paintings still at Overbrook, see Connelly [1979], pp.303–8. Eakins's debts to Velázquez, as well as his own teacher Léon Bonnat, in these portraits are discussed in Gerdts 1979, pp.154–7.

6. Obituary, *Catholic Standard and Times*, 8 June 1929. Samuel Murray was an honorary pallbearer at Turner's funeral.

7. The drawings are part of Charles Bregler's Thomas Eakins Collection, Pennsylvania Academy of the Fine Arts, Philadelphia. In her forthcoming catalogue of this collection, Kathleen Foster provides a detailed analysis of the drawings and their relation to Eakins's final construction of the Turner portrait. See Foster forthcoming 1994, nos. 215–19.

8. The question of the location of this interior is discussed by Foster op. cit. Dr Foster generously made the pertinent sections of her manuscript available to me, as well as sharing her insights into the Turner portrait, for which I am deeply grateful.

9. This was told to Lloyd Goodrich by one of Turner's relatives who inherited the finished portrait, and who actually named the deceased, one Peter Dooner. The story is repeated by Siegl 1978, no. 111, p.164 and by Goodrich 1982, vol.II, p.192.

10. The inclusion of the altar painting of the Assumption might refer to a theological issue which is likely to have been debated by Turner and Eakins. In the letter of 1869, Eakins's only surviving explicit criticism of Roman Catholicism, the young artist derided in particular the recently promulgated doctrine of the Immaculate Conception (1854): 'Then think of the contemptible catholic religion the three in one & one in "3" 3 = 1 1 = 3 3 × 1 = 1 which they call mystery & if you don't believe it be damned to you & the virgin mother than afterwards married a man look at it, isn't it ridiculous & the virgin grandmother for his grandmother was made so recently by Pope Pius IX dont you remember the solemen conclave & the date in gold letters at the head quarters at Saint Peters. Its beyond all belief'. Thomas Eakins to Frances Eakins, 1 April 1869 (Archives of American Art, Smithsonian Institution, Washington, DC). By 1900, discussion was ongoing about a similar redefinition of the status of the Assumption, that is whether the Virgin Mary simply died in a natural way, with the reunion of her body and soul occurring in heaven shortly thereafter, or whether her body and soul were assumed together into heaven at the end of her earthly life. It was not until 1950 that the generally held belief in the Assumption was promulgated as doctrine.

Provenance: Given by the artist's widow, Susan Macdowell Eakins, and Miss Mary Adeline Williams, 1929.

Exhibitions: Philadelphia, Pennsylvania Museum of Art, 1930, no. 299; Philadelphia, Museum of Art, 1944, no. 111; Overbrook, Pennsylvania, St Charles Borremeo Seminary, 1970, no. 15.

Literature: Siegl 1978, no. 11, p.164.

Thomas Eakins and the Art of Photography

Susan Danly

Photographs, especially those of the human figure, played an important role in the art of Thomas Eakins. He used newly available photographic equipment and techniques to explore picture-making in terms of what appears to be a set of opposing artistic principles: realism and romanticism. Photography, more than any other medium, provided him with a means both to capture spontaneous events that occurred outdoors (fig. 40) and to create consciously artistic images in the studio (no. 50). Although some of these images are related to his paintings, for the most part Eakins's photographs should be seen as independent works of art. His choice of photographic subjects, use of certain effects of cropping and lighting, and experimentation with a variety of printing techniques allowed Eakins to explore portraiture in an aesthetic realm that had its own set of formal principles and social history.

Thomas Eakins took up photography at a time when this relatively new mode of visual representation was in a period of transition. The daguerreotype, the earliest and simplest form of photography, was introduced to the United States in 1839 shortly after the process was publicly unveiled at the French Academy of Sciences in Paris. Over the following three decades, commercial photographers dominated the field producing numerous forms of portrait photographs: daguerreotypes in a variety of sizes, cheap ambrotypes and tintypes, and more costly albumen prints ranging in size from small cartes-de-visite to large imperial prints.[1] While most artists viewed photography merely as a tool – a mechanical means by which to record a likeness or to provide figure studies for paintings – in Philadelphia there was an active group of photographers and publishers who ardently believed that photography also had an aesthetic component that was closely allied with painting.[2] They argued that photographs, whether they were portraits or landscapes, should be artfully composed and printed.

By the 1850s and 1860s, Philadelphia's photographic businesses were centred in the commercial district on Chestnut Street in the neighbourhood where Thomas Eakins attended high school and, later, art classes at the Pennsylvania Academy of the Fine Arts. Each day Eakins would have passed by shop windows filled with advertisements for these commercial studios and the photographic equipment that they sold. And his family, like many middle-class families of the period, ardently collected photographic portraits of relatives and friends which they mounted in leather-bound albums.[3]

The *Philadelphia Photographer*, one of the nation's leading photographic journals, encouraged amateurs to take up this medium as a means of artistic expression. Articles in the journal in the late 1860s and 1870s provided not only technical guidance, but also suggested areas of study most appropriate for the amateur.[4] Among the areas mentioned were art history, perspective, anatomy, and optics – all of which were of particular interest to Thomas Eakins throughout his artistic career. Another important element of amateur photography of the period was the group outing or excursion, organized with the intention of taking outdoor photographs. Such activities were a mainstay of local amateur photographic societies such as the Photographic Society of Philadelphia. The journal regularly reported on their outings and public exhibitions of their photographs.

In the early 1880s, the Pennsylvania Academy of the Fine Arts hosted a series of photographic exhibitions and lantern slide lectures for the Society. At the time, Eakins was director of instruction at the Academy and knew several of the Society's members.[5] Although he exhibited only once with the group, Eakins must have been familiar with their activities and aims.[6] Many of his photographic studies made at the Academy utilize the same processes, particularly cyanotype and platinum, preferred by amateur photographers. Moreover, the types of subjects that Eakins produced – including portraits, landscapes, and figure studies – were the mainstay of the Society's exhibitions at the Pennsylvania Academy.[7]

Eakins, however, kept apart from the kinds of social gatherings around which amateur photographic societies were organized. Although he was held in high regard by many of his students, others, especially women, were often offended by Eakins's brusque manner and defiance of conventional social rules. His personal difficulties with students and the board of the Pennsylvania Academy were further exacerbated by his activities as a photographer. In part, because he insisted on taking nude photographs of his students and participated in the practice himself (no. 51), Eakins eventually incurred the wrath of the board, which forced him to resign from his teaching post in 1886.[8]

The new style in photography which appeared in the 1880s emphasized the aesthetic as opposed to commercial concerns of the medium. Although this style eventually became known as pictorialism, in the period of Eakins's greatest activity as a photographer it had no name or precise definition. It was an

50
Female nude, semi-reclining from rear
*c.*1889
Platinum print, 9.8 × 13.5 ($3\frac{7}{8}$ × $5\frac{5}{16}$)

Charles Bregler's Thomas Eakins Collection.
Purchased with the partial support of the
Pew Memorial Trust (1985.68.2.503)

51
Circle of Thomas Eakins
**Motion study: Thomas Eakins nude,
running to left**
1884 or 1885
Modern print from glass-plate negative,
9.2 × 11.8 ($3\frac{5}{8}$ × $4\frac{5}{8}$)

Charles Bregler's Thomas Eakins Collection.
Purchased with the partial support of the
Pew Memorial Trust (1985.68.2.992)

emerging style that often relied on aspects of commercial work in both its conception and production. The degree of Eakins's photographic invention becomes more evident, however, when his portrait photographs are compared to those produced by a commercial photographer, such as Frederick Gutekunst (fig.39). While some professional portrait photographers used elaborate lighting to create what they called 'Rembrandt effects', for the most part they kept the process simple, using a skylight or single light source from the side to cast part of the face into shade. This helped to emphasize the three-dimensional character of the head and gave some pictorial interest to the portrait. To increase the volume of work and thus maximize profits, these photographers often posed their sitters in standardized frontal or three-quarter views. Frequently they used a brace to hold the sitter's pose during the long period of time needed to expose the negative plate. This often resulted in stiff, formal poses that lacked a sense of naturalness or spontaneity.

The very first photographs that Eakins made illustrate some of these characteristics, but they also introduce innovative elements. In a series of informal portraits of his family and his pets taken in the backyard of his home at 1729 Mount Vernon Street, Eakins imbued his subjects with an unprecedented sense of indi-

viduality and familiarity conveyed by their facial expression and body language. In a portrait of his sister Margaret, Eakins posed the subject casually outdoors on the back steps (fig.40). She sits hunched over with her knees spread apart in what would have then been considered a rather unladylike demeanour. One hand supports her large head, while the fingers of her other are splayed across her skirt. Margaret Eakins does not engage the camera directly, but casts her gaze to one side, lending a contemplative mood to this picture. The expression and pose of the dog lying next to her, with its head and paws hanging over the step, reinforce the glum expression on her face. Even when Eakins photographed Margaret in a more formal situation (no. 52), he made no attempt to flatter her plain features. Instead he shows her slumped in a chair, confronting the camera directly with her large eyes and serious expression.

Eakins's involvement in photography began at a crucial juncture in the technological evolution of the medium, at a time when slower and more complex processes were giving way to smaller, commercially prepared negative plates and simpler, more portable cameras. The invention and commercial distribution of gelatin dry plates allowed amateur photographers to use their cameras on excursions to the countryside and to develop the results at

their leisure once they returned home. The numerous photographs that Eakins took at the nearby New Jersey shore (fig.6b) and at his sister's farm in Avondale, Pennsylvania, just outside Philadelphia (fig.41), attest to his use of the camera in such a way. Eakins relied on elements of nature – an empty expanse of sea and sand or a bower of overhanging branches – to set off the figures.

Eakins's unrelenting pursuit of artistic truth is perhaps best seen in his study of the human nude. In photography, this practice began within the sanctioned setting of the studio, but it soon spread to the outdoors, where it was linked to Eakins's firm belief in the close relationship between nature and the human form. Some of his most provocative images were made on photographic excursions with his students to the beach and the rural environs of Philadelphia. Photographic studies for paintings such as *The Swimming Hole* (fig.8) and the Arcadia subjects, although not strictly portraits, are images whose human subjects are clearly identifiable. Another, even more daring series of nude studies with horses includes views of his wife Susan Macdowell Eakins (no. 53), his students, and even Eakins himself.

Fig.41
Susan Macdowell and the Crowell children in a rowboat at Avondale, Pennsylvania
1883
Gelatin printing-out-paper print, 9.4 × 11.7 ($3\frac{11}{16} \times 4\frac{5}{8}$)
Charles Bregler's Thomas Eakins Collection, Pennsylvania Academy of the Fine Arts, Philadelphia. Purchased with the partial support of the Pew Memorial Trust (1985.68.2.325)

Fig.40
Margaret Eakins and Eakins's setter dog Harry on the doorstep of 1729 Mount Vernon Street
c.1881
Albumen print, 7 × 8.3 ($2\frac{13}{16} \times 3\frac{1}{4}$)
Charles Bregler's Thomas Eakins Collection, Pennsylvania Academy of the Fine Arts, Philadelphia. Purchased with the partial support of the Pew Memorial Trust (1985.68.2.75)

52
Margaret Eakins
*c.*1881
Albumen print, 8.9 × 7.6 (3½ × 3)

Charles Bregler's Thomas Eakins Collection.
Purchased with the partial support of the
Pew Memorial Trust (1985.68.2.74)

53
Susan Macdowell Eakins nude, from rear,
leaning against Eakins's horse Billy
*c.*1890
Platinum print, 9 × 11 ($3\frac{9}{16}$ × $4\frac{5}{16}$)

Charles Bregler's Thomas Eakins Collection.
Purchased with the partial support of the
Pew Memorial Trust (1985.68.2.549)

54
William H. Macdowell
*c.*1884
Platinum print, 21.9 × 17.2 ($8\frac{5}{8}$ × $6\frac{3}{4}$)

Charles Bregler's Thomas Eakins Collection.
Purchased with the partial support of the
Pew Memorial Trust (1985.68.2.820)

55
Circle of Thomas Eakins
Mrs William H. Macdowell
*c.*1890
Platinum print, 23.6 × 19.7 ($9\frac{1}{4}$ × $7\frac{3}{4}$)

Charles Bregler's Thomas Eakins Collection.
Purchased with the partial support of the
Pew Memorial Trust (1985.68.2.800)

Many of the outdoor nudes, among them scenes of Eakins's nephews 'skinny-dipping' (fig.41), seem to have been made without any intention of serving as models for paintings. For Eakins, such images established a close relationship between nudity and nature and they evoked the idealism of the classical past. These photographs also set an important precedent for the pictorialist photographers of the turn of the century. Classical nudes were to become an important component in the work of American pictorialist photographers such as Clarence White, Robert Conklin, and Herbert Hess.[9]

Eakins's incipient pictorialism is most evident in his platinum prints. All of the glass-plate negatives that have survived from Eakins's studio are 4 × 5 inches in size. These negatives were used to produce small contact prints in a variety of photographic media including cyanotype, albumen, collodion, and platinum. In addition, over the course of his ten-year involvement with photography, Eakins selected certain negatives to enlarge and print in platinum. More than any other photographic medium, platinum allowed Eakins to manipulate the character of light and atmospheric effects in his images. Most often he used commercially-produced 'platino-type' papers which were precoated with the platinum salts that produced soft tonal grada-tions ranging from silvery grey to deep black.[10]

On occasion, however, Eakins experimented with hand-coated papers, which he, his wife, or perhaps the professional photographer Frederick von Rapp prepared.[11] In a remark-able pair of platinum portraits of his wife's parents, William and Hannah Macdowell, Eakins captured the subtle nuances of individ-ual character and human experience in their time-worn faces. The portrait of Mr Mac-dowell (no. 54) shows the elderly gentleman wrapped in a shabby overcoat with the brim of his tall, slightly lop-sided hat casting a shadow over his gaunt face and deeply set eyes. His long grizzled hair and shaggy beard further enhance the effect of informality in this view. In another uncropped version of the image (fig.42), it is apparent that Macdowell sat for his portrait in front of a stretched canvas improvised to provide a studio-like backdrop in Eakins's backyard. Behind him, the legs of a second person are visible at the base of his chair. Such realist details add a peculiar sense of the actual photographic moment to the pic-ture. But when Eakins eliminated these inci-dental details in other prints made from the same negative, he consciously sought to create portraits, not just snapshots.

In addition, Eakins's use of hand-coated papers for Macdowell's portrait demonstrates his desire to gain greater control over the tonality and surface quality of his photo-graphic portraits. The evidence of hand-coating appears at the left edge of one print (fig.42), where the marks of the rag-covered rod used to apply the salts to the paper are still visible. In the portrait of Mrs Macdowell (no. 55), the wipe marks extend downwards to the bottom of the image as if they were an extension of the fabric in her dress. Eakins may have deliberately left these signs of the photo-graphic process to underscore the aesthetic pro-cess and hand craft involved in the making of a print. These latent photographic marks, in many ways, are equivalent to the sketchy brushwork that Eakins often used in the backgrounds of his carefully detailed, painted portraits.

An inscription on a variant of Mrs Mac-dowell's portrait in the collection of the Metro-politan Museum of Art suggests that Thomas Eakins may have collaborated with his wife and perhaps his sister-in-law in making photo-graphic portraits of the sitter.[12] We know from Susan Eakins's diaries and from other inscrip-tions[13] that both she and her sister, Elizabeth Kenton, were active photographers during the 1880s and 1890s. Susan even exhibited a por-trait of a child, probably her niece Betty Rey-nolds, at one of the Photographic Salons held at the Pennsylvania Academy in 1898. She also produced both casual snapshots and formal portraits of her husband, several of which sur-vive in the collection of the Pennsylvania Academy. The most sophisticated and artfully printed is a platinum portrait of Eakins made about 1889 (no. 56).

Fig.42
William H. Macdowell
*c.*1884
Platinum print, 29 × 22.4 ($11\frac{7}{16}$ × $8\frac{13}{16}$)
Charles Bregler's Thomas Eakins Collection, Pennsylvania Academy of the Fine Arts, Philadelphia. Purchased with funds donated by the Pennsylvania Academy Women's Committee (1988.10.22)

56
Attributed to Susan Macdowell Eakins
Thomas Eakins sitting, hand to forehead
*c.*1889
Platinum print, 17 × 15.3 ($6\frac{11}{16}$ × 6)

Charles Bregler's Thomas Eakins Collection. Purchased with the partial support of the Pew Memorial Trust (1985.68.2.37)

57
Woman in laced-bodice dress, sitting with
her setter dog at feet
*c.*1883
Albumen print, 9 × 11.4 (3⁹⁄₁₆ × 4½)

Charles Bregler's Thomas Eakins Collection.
Purchased with the partial support of the
Pew Memorial Trust (1985.68.2.265)

58
Weda Cook in classical costume
*c.*1892
Platinum print, 15.9 × 7.9 (6¼ × 3⅛)

Charles Bregler's Thomas Eakins Collection.
Purchased with the partial support of the
Pew Memorial Trust (1985.68.2.245)

Although Eakins made photographic portraits of several individuals who appear in his paintings, these images were not always used as studies for his oils. For example, almost all of the photographs of Walt Whitman that Eakins had tacked to his studio wall (see fig.35b) were made after Eakins had painted his portrait in 1887 (no. 23). The only portrait for which there is a significant body of related photographic studies is *The Pathetic Song* (no. 21). The dress worn by the sitter Margaret Harrison was extremely elaborate in its detail and scholars have suggested that, in this case, Eakins may have felt the need to rely on photographs rather than lengthy sittings, to get it right (see also no. 21 for a discussion of the related photographs).

The documentary nature of the photographs of Margaret Harrison sets them apart from photographic figure studies that relate to other paintings by Eakins. For example, in a photograph of a woman posed in a manner very like that of the figure of Susan Eakins in *The Artist's Wife and His Setter Dog* (no. 22), Eakins has created a related, but independent photographic image (no. 57). Here an unidentified woman is shown seated in a laced-bodice, colonial dress that differs from the loose, empire-style gown that Susan Eakins wears in the painting. Although the compositions are reversed, in both images Eakins's setter dog lies comfortably ensconced on an oriental rug at the feet of the sitter.

A similar relationship exists between a painting of Weda Cook, known as *The Concert Singer* (no. 26), and a series of photographs made at about the same time. In the painting, Weda is shown on stage clad in an evening gown, but in the photographs she is dressed in classical garb.[14] A platinum enlargement of one of the photographs (no. 58) depicts Weda in a pose that is almost the exact reverse of her stance in the painting, with her hands clasped and head tilted to one side. The camera also records the details of what appears to be a rather hastily improvised costume and backdrop, full of wrinkles as if they had just been removed from a box of studio props.

The sense of immediacy created by such details is strangely at odds with the idealizing conception of the overall image. The dreamy mood of this portrait or figure study (it is difficult to make a precise distinction in this case) comes close to that of English photography of the period. Noteworthy photographers, such as Julia Margaret Cameron (fig.43) and Clementina, Viscountess Hawarden, also dressed up female friends and family in historical costume or fancy dress and posed them in such a way as to create an idyllic mood. Like Eakins, these English photographers stressed the artistic conception of their work and eventually made a significant contribution to the development of a pictorialist aesthetic.[15] Cameron's work, in particular, was well known in American photographic circles. She had exhibited at Philadelphia's Centennial Exhibition in 1876 and one of her works appeared on the cover of *Harper's Weekly*, a popular illustrated magazine.[16]

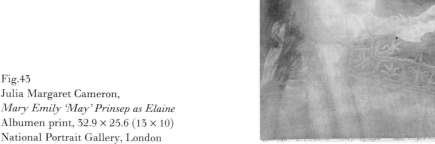

Fig.43
Julia Margaret Cameron,
Mary Emily 'May' Prinsep as Elaine
Albumen print, 32.9 × 25.6 (13 × 10)
National Portrait Gallery, London

59
Amelia Van Buren,
sitting with cat on shoulder
*c.*1891
Platinum print, 8.9 × 10.2 ($3\frac{1}{2}$ × 4)

Charles Bregler's Thomas Eakins Collection.
Purchased with the partial support of the
Pew Memorial Trust (1985.68.2.712)

Amelia Van Buren was another of Eakins's sitters who posed for portraits both in front of the easel (see no. 27) and the camera. Although these portraits share a quiet mood, formally there is even less of a direct relationship between the painted and photographic images. In a small platinum contact print (no. 59), Eakins gave an unusual narrative focus to her portrait. He shows Amelia engrossed in a book, with a cat perched rather precariously on her shoulder. Carefully lit from the side, the cat's soft fur, the wisps of the sitter's hair, and the pages of an open book form the brightest areas of the composition. These highlights are contrasted with the deep shadows that accentuate the luxuriant folds of Amelia's elegant leg-o-mutton sleeves. Even without the aid of colour, Eakins was adept at conveying the texture of a variety of materials in his photographs. The deliberate inclusion of genre elements, such as the cat and book, add further pictorial interest to the image and connect Eakins's photographic work with that of his contemporaries, most notably George Bacon Wood and Robert S. Redfield, members of the Photographic Society of Philadelphia.

The poise and elegant execution of Eakins's most accomplished portraits aptly convey his skill in composition, lighting, and printing of the photographic image. It is the romantic mood of these portraits that distinguishes them from family snapshots and ultimately makes them works of art. As in his painted portraits, Eakins did not have to please a patron or accede to commercial demands of production. His photographs were taken for personal pleasure and to explore his own aesthetic interests. Perhaps because he did not draw very often during these years, photography afforded him the best means by which to achieve the delicate balance between realism and romanticism that lay at the very heart of all of his artistic endeavours.

1. For a discussion of the early years of American photographic history see Welling 1978 and Sandweiss 1991.

2. Marcus Aurelius Root, the noted daguerreotypist, was one of the first Americans to publish a book on the aesthetics of photography, *The Pencil and the Camera, or, the Heliographic Art*, Philadelphia, 1864. Numerous articles on how to compose photographs also appeared in the *Philadelphia Photographer*, for example see the lengthy series 'Art Principles Applicable to Photography', vol.4, 1867, pp.337–8, 371–3 and vol.5, 1868, pp.49–52, 71–3, 117–18, 265–7, 331–2, 367–9, and 438–9.

3. One album containing carte-de-visite portraits produced by commercial photographers is now in the collection of the Pennsylvania Academy of the Fine Arts, which houses an extensive collection of Eakins's photographs. Most were acquired as part of a large cache of drawings, photographs, and manuscripts left in Eakins's home after the death of his wife. Preserved by his student Charles Bregler, this collection is discussed by Foster 1989, pp.1128–37; for a discussion of the manuscripts see also Foster and Leibold 1989.

4. See for example, 'The Education of Photographers', *Philadelphia Photographer*, vol.12, September 1875, pp.281–3.

5. A more detailed discussion of these exhibitions and Eakins's activities as a photographer will appear in the forthcoming catalogue of his photographs in the collection of the Pennsylvania Academy of the Fine Arts edited by Susan Danly and Cheryl Leibold. I would like to thank Ms Leibold for her assistance both on this essay and the more extensive cataloguing project.

6. Eakins lectured on his photographic motion studies in 1885 and showed one of them, entitled *History of a Jump*, in the 1886 exhibition of the Society.

7. For a report on the activities of the group see 'The Annual Exhibition of the Photographic Society of Philadelphia', *Philadelphia Photographer*, vol.20, May 1883, p.147. Further discussions about the Society appear in Panzer 1982, pp.8–11; and Fehr and Homer 1984, pp.5–6.

8. For a discussion of Eakins's use of nude photographs see Foster, ' "Trouble" at the Pennsylvania Academy', in Foster and Leibold 1989, pp.75–9 and Homer 1992, pp.167–174.

9. The work of these photographers is discussed in Bunnell 1992.

10. One such purveyor of platinum papers, John Bradley, was located at 47 North 13th Street in Philadelphia, just a block from the Pennsylvania Academy. An advertisement for his printing paper which appeared in the Academy catalogue for the Photographic Salon of 1901 claimed 'the article is endorsed by all leading Professional and Amateur photographers as being "the paper on which Masterpieces of photography are made" ' (Pennsylvania Academy of the Fine Arts, archives).

11. Susan Eakins noted in a diary entry for 20 April 1899: 'Fred Von Rapp over to print' (Pennsylvania Academy of the Fine Arts, archives).

12. This profile portrait was annotated on the verso by A. Hyatt Mayor, presumably with information he received from Charles Bregler: 'Neg. by Thos. and Susan M. Eakins/Platinum print by Mrs Eakins/Letter from Mrs. Kenton to Charles Bregler/21 Aug. 1944 'That which I took of/mother is splendid'. The glass-plate negative of the image is in the collection of the Pennsylvania Academy.

13. Several photographs in the collection of the Macdowell family, Roanoke, Virginia, and two at the Pennsylvania Academy bear Elizabeth Kenton's signature.

14. The Pennsylvania Academy owns several photographs of Weda Cook in classical garb, some of which are mounted in an album together with other figures in similar attire.

15. For a discussion of the development of the pictorialist aesthetic in England see Seiberling and Bloore 1986; Weaver 1989; and Dodier 1991, pp.196–207.

16. The photograph, *The Parting of Sir Lancelot and Queen Guinevere*, was published in an edition of Alfred, Lord Tennyson's *Idylls of the King*, London, 1875, and reproduced as a wood engraving in *Harper's Weekly*, vol.21, 1 September 1877, p.682. Cameron's work was even compared to the work of old master painters by Vogel 1876, p.287.

The Critical Reception of Thomas Eakins's Work

I: Lifetime

Amy B. Werbel

When reviewing Eakins's entries in the 1875 Paris Salon for *L'Art*, Paul Leroi displayed a mixture of appreciation, mystification and complaint that set the tone for many critics that followed him during the next four decades. He wrote:

... et M. Thomas Eakins, un disciple de M. Gérôme, qui envoie de Philadelphie un bien étrange tableau; c'est loin toutefois d'être sans mérite. *Une Chasse aux États-Unis* (no. 757) est un véritable ouvrage de précision; ... Ce produit exotique vous apprend quelque chose, et son auteur n'est pas à oublier ...[1]

This mixed review of *Pushing for Rail* (fig.16a) expressed sentiments shared by American critics of Eakins's early work, who found the mundane subject matter of his boating and home scenes 'curious' and 'peculiar', while still remarking on the artist's 'marked ability' and 'conspicuous promise'.[2]

While these early writers found it possible both to mildly praise and to criticize Eakins, the exhibition of the artist's unconventional *Gross Clinic* (fig.4) and *William Rush Carving His Allegorical Figure of the Schuylkill River* (no. 17) between 1875 and 1879 established his reputation as a maverick who impressed and horrified audiences simultaneously. William Clark, writing for Philadelphia's *Daily Evening Telegraph* in 1876 stated that 'nothing finer' than the explosive Gross portrait had ever been attempted in the country.[3] At the same time, more conservative artists and critics refused the painting a place at Philadelphia's Centennial Exhibition.[4] Clark was irate when

the painting was relegated to the exhibition's 'United States Hospital Building', writing 'It is rumored that the blood on Dr. Gross's fingers made some of the members of the Committee sick but judging from the quality of the works exhibited by them we fear that it was not the blood alone that made them sick'.[5]

Perhaps hoping for a more favourable response in New York, Eakins tenaciously entered his *Gross Clinic* three years later at the Society of American Artists' second annual exhibition. Most city newspapers reviewed the work extensively, the *Herald* terming it 'decidedly unpleasant and sickeningly real in all its gory details, though a startlingly life-like and strong work'. Others found the painting 'powerful', 'horrible', 'compelling', nausea-provoking, 'revolting' and 'fascinating'. Following on Leroi's mixed reactions, even those critics most vehemently opposed to the painting typically admitted that it held some praiseworthy aspects, particularly admiring the artist's superb technical skills and ability as a portraitist. Clarence Cook, the influential *New-York Daily Tribune* art critic, wrote of the picture that 'The more we study Mr Thomas Eakins' 'Professor Gross', the more our wonder grows that it was ever painted, in the first place, and that it was ever exhibited, in the second. As for the power with which it is painted, the intensity of its expression, and the skill of the drawing, we suppose no one will deny that these qualities exist ...'[6]

A year earlier, at the Society's first exhibition in 1878, exhibition of *William Rush* had engendered a similar response as critics argued about the appropriateness of the subject matter while praising the artist's technical skills. Cook again disparaged Eakins's choice of subject, writing: 'Mr Thomas Eakins has an amusing, but disappointing, and, artistically, not very credible picture ... If belles have such faults as these to hide, we counsel them to hide them'. William Clark, in a typically supportive review, wrote that 'considering it simply as a specimen of workmanship, there is not a picture in the display ... that is at all up to the high standard of Mr Thomas Eakins' *William Rush*'.[7]

By 1880, then, Eakins was a controversial figure in the eyes of American art critics. Clarence Cook had blasted *The Gross Clinic* and *William Rush* while leaving some room for praise.[8] Reviews by Earl Shinn, writing as Edward Strahan in Philadelphia, were similarly ambivalent. At the same time, William Clark had fixed his place as a staunch defender of Eakins's canvases.[9]

Despite this lack of consensus, some of Eakins's works were generally well received.

Fig.44
The Chess Players
1876
Oil on canvas, 29.8 × 42.5 (11¾ × 16¾)
The Metropolitan Museum of Art.
Gift of the artist, 1881

Even Clarence Cook praised Eakins's water-colour efforts in 1878, terming his *Negro Boy Dancing* (fig.39b) the work of a 'scientific draughtsman who ... sees as far into human nature [as Detaille] and can just as well represent that nature in action ... Other charms may be wanting, beauty of color, skill of handling, but here is life, and when an artist has this he has all'.[10] Two years later, the response to the exhibition of Eakins's *The Chess Players* (fig.44) at the newly opened Metropolitan Museum of Art also helped to offset earlier vehemence, as critics uniformly praised the painting.[11]

Eakins's most steadfast supporter, William Clark, was joined by another friendly voice in the 1880s – that of Mariana Griswold van Rensselaer, a New York aesthete who equally admired the artist. Just as Clark's Philadelphia prejudices were likely to have influenced his support for Eakins's work, van Rensselaer's judgement was swayed by her desire for America to produce a 'national' school; this resolve was fuelled by the patriotic sentiments aroused by the country's centennial. She saw Eakins, with his local subject matter and original style, as an embodiment of the ideals such a school would promote. Van Rensselaer was also among the most sensitive and astute admirers of Eakins's painting capabilities. In 1881, she wrote, 'There is no one who is doing more than Mr Eakins to show how our native material, unglossed and unpoeticized, may be made available in artistic work'.[12] Unfortunately for the artist, van Rensselaer's columns in the *American Architect and Building News* were interspersed with those of Leslie Miller, Eakins's later portrait subject (fig.47), who by contrast voiced harsh rebuke.

Critique of Eakins's works in the 1880s grew more sophisticated and specific as the field expanded. Often, reviewers complained that the artist, though a gifted draughtsman, was too much of a scientist, and not enough of a poet. Such criticisms were particularly common in reviews of Eakins's *A May Morning in the Park* (no. 19). A contributor to the *Philadelphia Press* wrote:

As a mechanical experiment it may be a success;
on this point we express no judgment, but as to
the matter of framing the experiment, hanging it
in a picture gallery, and calling it A Spring
Morning in the Park, we have to express judgment
decidedly adverse.[13]

Even van Rensselaer rejected the painting, noting that Eakins's painstaking study of the subject had rendered a painting 'scientifically true, but artistically false'.[14] Still, Eakins continued to garner praise on technical grounds

from even his harshest critics. Summing up the sentiments of many frustrated critics, a *Nation* reviewer wrote of *The Pathetic Song* (no. 21): 'It is a characteristic picture; nothing here is more powerful, more admirable in a dozen ways – or more annoying'.[15]

In 1882, these strains of criticism were focused on Eakins's stark *Crucifixion* scene (fig.45). Rejected by the Society of American Artists, Eakins's *Crucifixion* hung in a New York 'salon de refusés', and was castigated by critics. One reviewer went so far as to title his essay 'Christ Crucified by Eakins'.[16] Another critic wrote: 'To those who from deep sacred feelings invest the person of Christ with ideal characteristics and qualities, the manner in which Mr Eakins has treated the subject can never seem anything else than offensively repulsive'.[17] Van Rensselaer was alone in defending the work. She wrote that 'after seeing a hundred crucifixions from modern hands this one seemed to me not only a quite original but a most impressive and haunted work'.[18]

Despite van Rensselaer's devoted praise, she could not prevent the artist's increasing isolation. Between 1886 and 1903, Eakins sent few paintings to exhibitions, and received little attention from critics for the works that were shown.[19] A *persona non grata* in the art world following his dismissal from the Pennsylvania Academy of the Fine Arts in 1886, many pictures were now rejected, and others were hung so high on the wall that viewers could barely see them.[20] As early as 1887, a reviewer for the *Art Age* noted that Eakins, 'who used to be one of the most prominent of the irreconcilables, is falling into comparative obscurity'.[21]

A decade later, Eakins made a bold attempt to break out of this obscurity. In 1896, the artist mounted a solo exhibition of his portraits at the Earle Galleries in Philadelphia. Rejection loomed yet again, as the exhibition was largely ignored by the city's press. Riter Fitzgerald, whose portrait was included in the show, summed up many of the reasons for Eakins's rejection in his own review of the show for the *Philadelphia Item*:

... he paints his subjects as he finds them. This is
all very well from an 'art for art's sake' standpoint,
but in the progressive work-a-day world of the
present time, the portrait painter, the same as
everyone else, must trim his craft to the trade
winds.[22]

Eakins had indeed consistently sailed against the 'trade winds' of the late nineteenth century, ignoring the nation's taste for bright, impressionist works such as those by Cecilia Beaux, William Merritt Chase, and John Singer Sargent.

Fig.45
The Crucifixion
1880
Oil on canvas, 243.8 × 137.2 (96 × 54)
Philadelphia Museum of Art.
Gift of Mrs Thomas Eakins and
Miss Mary Adeline Williams

Despite Eakins's efforts to revive his reputation with the Earle Galleries exhibition, another eight years passed before he re-emerged in the critical mainstream. In 1904, the artist won the Temple Gold Medal for his portrait of Archbishop William Henry Elder (fig.46). This was the highest honour given by the Pennsylvania Academy of the Fine Arts, in one of the nation's most prestigious yearly exhibitions. Despite the limited attention this honour received outside Philadelphia, between 1904 and the artist's death in 1917, a wider group of critics and artists came to respect Eakins's work.

Following the lead of William Clark and Mariana van Rensselaer, new voices were now heard speaking of Eakins as 'the Dean of American Painting', and the 'foremost living American painter'.[23] The tributes of painters John Singer Sargent, Robert Henri and Edwin Austin Abbey were published, and for the first time in his career, Eakins also faced purchasers anxious to acquire his work. In 1914, the eccentric art collector Alfred Barnes purchased Eakins's study of D. Hayes Agnew (no. 36) in competition with several other bidders, who had flocked to the painting after critics promised that it would 'one day be amongst the most treasured possessions of some great American museum'.[24] Although many years passed before Eakins's work was widely known and collected, this last burst of enthusiastic critical support for the artist set the stage for his posthumous rebirth as America's great 'old master' painter.

1. Leroi 1875, p.276. Another review of Eakins's contributions to the Salon was given by Lagenevais 1875, p.927.
2. These criticisms were noted by Hendricks 1974, p.70. They appear in the *Philadelphia Inquirer* (27 April 1871) and the *Philadelphia Evening Bulletin* (28 April 1871) and were written in response to the exhibition of *Max Schmitt in a Single Scull* and an unlocated portrait of family friend M.H. Messchert at Philadelphia's Union League Club.
3. Clark 1876 (1), p.4.
4. For a thorough account of these events, see Hendricks 1969, pp.57–64.
5. Clark 1876 (2), p.2.
6. Cook 1879. Another critic concurred with Cook's negative assessment, stating that the picture 'ought never to have left the dissecting room . . . The scene is revolting to the last degree, with the repulsiveness of its almost Hogarthian detail' (Unsigned, 'The Society of American Artists', *The Art Interchange*, vol.2, no. 6, 19 March 1879, p.42).
7. Cook 1878 (1), p.5; Clark 1878.
8. Jo Ann Weiss notes that Cook's negative reactions to Eakins's *Gross* and *Rush* were based on his general disapproval of paintings he considered 'silly, alien or disagreeable'. Cook placed both in the latter category. Weiss 1976, p.112.
9. Clark, for example, had taken up defence of Eakins's *William Rush* in 1878, ridiculing the prudish complaints of viewers. Clark 1878.
10. Cook 1878 (2), p.5; Earl Shinn also praised these watercolours in the *Nation*, vol.26, no. 66, 28 February 1878, p.156.
11. See for example Strahan [Earl Shinn] May 1880, p.116. Eakins's exhibition of *At the Piano* at the Society of American Artists' exhibition in 1880 also received favourable reviews.
12. Van Rensselaer 1881, p.311. William Brownell concurred with van Rensselaer in admiring Eakins for his technique and original 'national' style. See Brownell 1880, pp.1–15.
13. Unsigned, 'Art at the Academy. Second Annual Exhibition of the Philadelphia Society of Artists', *Philadelphia Press*, 25 November 1880, p.5.
14. Van Rensselaer 1880, p.303.
15. Unsigned, 'Fifty-Sixth Annual Exhibition of the National Academy of Design – I', *Nation*, vol.32, no. 822, 31 March 1881.
16. Unsigned, 'The Anorexe Exhibition – Suggestive Pictures – Christ Crucified by Eakins', *New York Times*, 4 May 1882, p.5.

17. Unsigned, 'The Fine Arts', *Philadelphia Evening Bulletin*, 13 November 1882, p.8.
18. Van Rensselaer 1882, p.231. For an excellent discussion of van Rensselaer's critique, see Dinnerstein 1979, p.140–5.
19. Goodrich 1982, vol.II, p.161.
20. Reviewers frequently mentioned the bad hanging spots of Eakins's work, including that of his *Professor William D. Marks* at the National Academy of Design in 1891; see Unsigned, 'The Academy's Exhibition', *New York Times*, 6 April 1891. Eakins's paintings were also 'hung above the line' at the Pennsylvania Academy of the Fine Arts as noted in the *Philadelphia Ledger*, 23 December 1895, p.12; For a review of Eakins's exhibition history in these years, see Goodrich 1982, vol.II, pp.199–203.
21. Unsigned, 'Society of American Artists' Exhibition', *Art Age*, vol.5, June 1887, p.68. Eakins received slightly more attention at the Columbian Exposition in Chicago in 1893.
22. Fitzgerald 1896, p.1. Fitzgerald wrote the only critical review of this exhibition. Other city newspapers reported that the exhibition had opened, but little else. See Turner 1979, pp.100–107. This was the only solo exhibition of Eakins's work during his lifetime.
23. The *Philadelphia Inquirer* referred to the artist as 'the Dean of American Painting' (Unsigned, 8 February 1914, p.14); the *Philadelphia Press* in the same month published an article on Eakins, in which it wrote: 'Mr Eakins is considered to be the foremost living American painter'. See 'Eakins Chats on Art of America', *Philadelphia Press*, 22 February 1914, p.8.
24. The artist's tributes were published in Unsigned, 'Noted Picture and Its Maker', *Philadelphia Record Magazine*, 29 March 1914, part 3, p.4; the *Philadelphia Inquirer* praised Eakins's study of Agnew, 8 February 1914, p.14.

The author wishes to thank Darrel Sewell, and other members of the staff of the Department of American Art, Philadelphia Museum of Art, for generously providing access to exhibition reviews located in their extensive Thomas Eakins Archives.

Fig.46
Archbishop William Henry Elder
1903
Oil on canvas, 168 × 114.6 (66⅛ × 45⅛)
Cincinnati Art Museum; Louis Belmont family in memory of William F. Halstrick, Bequest of Farny R. Wurlitzer, Edward Foote Hinkle Collection and Bequest of Friends of Frieda Hauck by exchange

The Critical Reception of Thomas Eakins's Work

II: Posthumous

Jennifer Hardin

'Frank', 'brutal', 'raw', 'uncompromising', 'analytical', 'manly', and 'diabolically realistic': art writers in the early twentieth century used such terms to describe the work of Thomas Eakins. These commentators included Sadakichi Hartmann, Charles Caffin, Bryson and Alan Burroughs, Robert Henri, Frank Jewett Mather, and Lloyd Goodrich, as well as other important art critics, educators, and museum professionals. Their combined efforts helped to establish Thomas Eakins's reputation as one of the pre-eminent figures in the history of American art: by 1930 his name had joined those of Winslow Homer and Albert Pinkham Ryder to constitute the great triumvirate of nineteenth-century American painters.[1] The three painters came to represent what was essentially 'American' in American art, in contradistinction to their compatriots James McNeill Whistler, John Singer Sargent, and William Merritt Chase, who chose to travel extensively and work abroad, and who were generally regarded as embodying a European sensibility.

But compared to Homer, or even Ryder, Thomas Eakins was little known in his own country before 1930. Honours gained by other artists earlier in their careers came late to Eakins. Born in 1848, he won his first gold medal at fifty-three at the Pan-American Exposition in Buffalo, New York, and was not elected to the National Academy of Design until 1902, but at his death in 1916 Eakins's art still remained something of an enigma. Although some recognition came immediately following his death, as is the case with many artists, the contribution made by his early supporters played a significant part in the construction of his subsequent reputation, and Eakins's work could not otherwise have commanded the public attention that it did by 1930.

Many of these promoters were also painters, or were close friends of painters. Their purpose was typically two-fold: to enhance his reputation, and to provide a precedent for their own art or the art that they supported. They saw in Eakins's example an important lesson for American artists in the 1910s and 1920s when European modernism was gaining what some considered too much acceptance. Critics viewed his art as not only possessing essentially 'American' qualities of realism and masculinity, but also depth, humanity, and substance. Thus, his art was often regarded as a crucial antidote to the uninspired imitations of Impressionism, Futurism, Cubism, and Expressionism which were then fashionable. Eakins was a significant precursor to artists like Robert Henri, who eschewed elitist subject matter, and searched below the surface for the beauty inherent in the most mundane subjects. It is no accident that in the 1910s, an era when artists became involved with left-wing politics, Eakins's work came to the forefront. During this period artistic organizations in New York such as John Weichsel's People's Art Guild attempted to reach out to a broader audience, while artists including John Sloan were actively involved in socialism and contributed to left-wing magazines like Robert Minor's *The Masses*.[2] The time seemed right for the emergence of an artist who had sought to paint American subjects in an unsentimentalized manner, and who aspired to portray people as they were, not as they might want themselves to be portrayed.

Eakins was by no means a radical leftist, but throughout his life he was a democrat with a great sense of national pride. He recognized the need for an indigenous 'American' art, and saw that American artists should be trained at home rather than abroad, and should paint their own life and people. It was a stance that appealed to those younger American artists who were trying to find their own way in a maze of cross-cultural influences in the early twentieth century. By 1914 Eakins was himself publicly advocating ideas akin to those of his early twentieth-century promoters. In the pages of the *Philadelphia Press* he endeavoured to re-create his early experiences and to advise a younger generation. He maintained that American artists should stay in their own country, rather than travelling to Europe as he had:

In the days when I studied abroad conditions were entirely different. The facilities in this country were meager. There were even no life classes in our art schools and schools of painting... It would be far better for American art students and painters to study their own country and portray its life and types. To do that they must remain free from any foreign superficialities.[3]

The painter seems to have exaggerated the scarcity of life classes, since they did take place in the United States, and he himself attended them (see nos. 2 and 3), although they were admittedly limited prior to the Civil War. More significant is Eakins's antagonism towards new movements from abroad. In this interview he went on to describe Cubism and Futurism as 'hysterical imaginations of pathological temperament....'[4] His artistic isolationism may have been a reaction to the influx of European modernism in America, so prevalent at the 1913 Armory Show in New York. He also stressed the need for the younger generation to create what he described as 'a distinctly American art'. Not that he promoted stagnation, however; he advised artists to 'add something new but sane, something which arises out of the new realities of life'.[5]

While Eakins's supporters did not overtly state prejudices against European modernism, many stressed his native qualities, and used their writings on his work as a forum for discussing their notion of an 'American' art. Writers emphasized as components of his Americanness – and his place in an American artistic tradition – his realism, his intellect, and his manliness. Sadakichi Hartmann's *History of American Art* of 1902 represented the first of such publications. Hartmann is well known for his critical writings in *Camera Notes* and *Camera Work*. Interestingly, Hartmann had met Walt Whitman in 1884 and used to visit him in his early years in Philadelphia, and by the time he left for Boston in 1887, the year Eakins met Whitman, Hartmann had absorbed much of Whitman's artistic philosophy, which had much in common with Eakins's (see no. 23).[6] In his survey Hartmann compared Eakins with Homer, describing both as 'strong' and 'frank', and maintained that each had 'decided ways of expressing something American'.[7] Using the example of *The Gross Clinic* (fig.4), which he believed viewers would find 'brutal', he proclaimed Eakins's art to be an antidote to works by many contemporaries:

Our American art is so effeminate at present that it would do no harm to have it inoculated with just some of that brutality. Among our mentally barren, from photograph working, and yet so blasé, sweet caramel artists, it is as refreshing as a whiff of the sea, to meet with such a rugged powerful personality. Eakins, like Whitman, sees beauty in everything. He does not always succeed in expressing it, but all his pictures impress one by their dignity and unbridled masculine power.[8]

In his reaction against European-influenced turn-of-the-century art, whether derivative Impressionism or debased academicism, Hartmann linked Eakins to his own mentor Whitman, as did many subsequent writers. While Eakins's artistic forms are not avant-garde like Whitman's free verse, Hartmann still perceived an essential tie between the intentions of their art: both glorified the plain and commemorated the commonplace.

Charles Caffin too coupled Eakins's name with Homer's, underscoring their 'qualities of manhood and mentality that are not too conspicuous in American art'.[9] Caffin's art writings were characterized by a desire to make art more accessible to the average person. In keeping with more progressive components of the New York art world in the 1910s, he wrote *Art for Life's Sake* in 1913. Here Caffin, like the artists of the so-called 'Ashcan School', propounded a more egalitarian notion of art.[10] In *The Story of American Painting* of 1907, Caffin established a tie between Eakins and the great French realist Gustave Courbet. He believed that the Realist movement had affected even the Academy by the 1860s, as exemplified by Gérôme's synthesis of history and genre painting, and by Bonnat's 'exact and analytical study'. Thus, according to Caffin, Eakins, as a pupil of both men, was an inheritor of Courbet.[11]

Despite increasing interest from these writers, few individuals or institutions collected Eakins's paintings before the mid-1920s. Two important acquisitions were made on the recommendation of the artist's peers. In 1914, with the encouragement of painters William Glackens and Robert Henri, Albert Barnes bought the single figure portrait of Dr Agnew (no. 36). The Metropolitan Museum of Art purchased *Pushing for Rail* (fig.16a) just before Eakins's death, an acquisition proposed by the Metropolitan's curator Bryson Burroughs at the suggestion of the painter Julian Alden Weir.[12] Burroughs had known of Eakins's work prior to Weir's suggestion, however, and was himself a painter and art teacher.[13] He saw Eakins as a great, neglected master and organized the 1917 memorial exhibition at the Metropolitan, which marked a turning-point in interest in Eakins. Like Hartmann and Caffin, he emphasized the masculine qualities of Eakins's work, writing in 1916 of its 'manliness and single-minded sincerity'.[14] His thoughts on Eakins were more fully expressed on the occasion of the memorial exhibition. Burroughs believed that in addition to creating 'manly and thoughtful art' full of character, Eakins was the most consistent of American realists. He also alluded to Eakins's international significance by putting him within the historically important Realist movement, 'the main characteristic of the nineteenth century'.[15]

Renown did not immediately follow the memorial exhibition. A reason for this was proposed by the art critic Henry McBride, in a supportive review of the 1917 show, where he noted that Eakins was not represented in major museums. He believed that Eakins's work was too serious for its current audience, whom he felt wanted to be distracted by 'light and trifling' works – paintings that catered to the mood of escapism engendered by America's entry into the First World War. (Significantly, between 1918 and 1922 very few articles on Eakins appeared.) The critic did, however, note that one specific audience appreciated the depth and importance of Eakins's art – the artists.[16]

Robert Henri was a well-known member of this audience. He had studied at the Pennsylvania Academy with Eakins's former student, Thomas Anshutz, had trained in Paris, and had absorbed old masters such as Hals and Rembrandt. He and his followers John Sloan, George Luks, and Everett Shinn, who began their careers by illustrating newspapers, were later dubbed the 'Ashcan School', due to their fondness for depicting the seamier side of city life. Henri rarely painted subjects as unrefined as Sloan, Luks, Shinn and George Bellows, Henri's young pupil, yet, with his dark palette and emphasis on human character, he departed from the bright colours, impressionistic style and complacent bourgeois scenes of much of early twentieth-century art.

Henri advised his pupils at the Art Students' League to study Eakins's works at the memorial exhibition carefully. He emphasized Eakins's attention to 'humanity', and the integrity of his art, which he saw as standing outside the vagaries of fashion. Henri stressed the artist's manliness, as had Hartmann, Caffin, and Burroughs. He cited the portrait of Leslie Miller (fig.47) as an example, describing it as 'a man's feeling for a man'. Henri wished his students to learn from these works: 'I expect them to fill you with courage and hope'.[17]

Only later, in the 1920s, did interest in Eakins truly develop, however. One of the most significant early articles was written by Bryson Burroughs's son Alan.[18] The younger Burroughs's essay appeared in *The Arts* in 1923. Until its demise in 1931, this magazine was an important forum for the reassessment of Eakins's art. It also promoted contemporary American art and solicited articles written by the artists themselves.[19] Burroughs's essay began with a quote from *The New Laokoon*, written by the Harvard professor and literary critic Irving Babbitt in 1910: 'Man is a living paradox in that he holds with enthusiasm and conviction to the half truth and yet becomes perfect only in proportion as he achieves the rounded view'. Burroughs believed Eakins had successfully captured the whole truth about society and its participants. Furthermore, he understood more completely than any previous writer that Eakins had adapted his French academic training and study of old masters such as Velázquez and Rembrandt to depicting American life as one would 'the glories of a great civilization'. Burroughs believed that Eakins searched for truth and character, painting the 'eternal value of no matter how plain a fact'.[20] He concluded by terming Eakins a humanist – although one without formal philosophy – implicitly connecting him to Babbitt's New Humanism.[21] New Humanism was in part a reaction against science and technology, and a reassertion of the importance of the thinking individual. It also criticized what it supposed to be the limited taste of the democratic masses.[22] Burroughs thus cast Eakins as a humanist, an individualist, who had declined to follow popular taste and market trends.

In the mid-1920s critics still continued to speculate as to why Eakins was not being collected. In 1923 the editor of *The Arts*, Forbes Watson, brazenly challenged dealers and curators: 'Why every museum in America has not already an Eakins is inexplicable'.[23] He proposed that Eakins's directness may have in part been responsible, for, like Courbet, 'no sweetness and fluff adorn his work'.[24] Interest in collecting Eakins's works gradually grew during the decade, as evidenced by the number of works in public and private collections loaned to the Museum of Modern Art's exhibition of Homer, Eakins and Ryder in 1930.

According to the writer Van Wyck Brooks, the art historian Frank Jewett Mather, Jr. was the first to link Homer, Eakins and Ryder, and to assert their importance over Whistler and Sargent for American art.[25] While Mather continued the discussion of the 'masculine propensities' of Eakins's work, unlike other writers he de-emphasized the artist's biography.[26] Also, instead of seeing Eakins as a great portraitist, as did Henri, Mather believed that the artist's true strength lay in genre painting, and he referred to both clinic pictures as such:

What is strange is that nobody sufficiently realized the greatness of Thomas Eakins in genre at a moment when masterpiece followed masterpiece – *The Chess Players, Salutat, William Rush*, the rowing pictures. No doubt this neglect rested partly on the error of the times and partly on Eakins' own character. He was never relaxed or sentimental and so failed to catch the crowd, whereas persons of taste had been mistaught that the picture with a story is a vulgarity.[27]

Like Caffin and Hartmann before him, Mather separated Eakins from contemporaries who followed the French Impressionists, and believed the 'massive and truthful Americanism of Eakins' work is one of our best legacies from a generally too cosmopolitan period'.[28] Like Alan Burroughs, he saw Eakins as 'one of our greatest painters among those who essayed the delicate task of saying an American thing in a pictorial language essentially French'.[29]

The event that was most instrumental in thrusting Eakins to the fore was the exhibition devoted to Homer, Ryder and Eakins held at the new Museum of Modern Art in 1930. It was an early attempt by the Museum to focus on less avant-garde art, and was held in the wake of exhibitions presenting European modernism and American contemporary art. The exhibition also followed the 1929 stock market crash that ushered in the Great Depression and with it an increase in critical and public attention to the Regionalists – the painters of the 'American scene'. The exhibition, accompanied by a catalogue written by Bryson Burroughs, Mather, and Lloyd Goodrich, provided the public with the opportunity to view at first hand a wider range of Eakins's works than had been possible in the pages of magazines like *The Arts* and in smaller shows of New York dealers. From this point on, Eakins was seldom referred to as 'neglected'. In addition to the 1930 exhibition and another at the Philadelphia Museum of Art organized to celebrate the bequest of Susan Macdowell Eakins and Mary Adeline Williams in 1930, the gift of a late portrait, *Clara* (c.1900, Musée d'Orsay, Paris), in 1932 to the Louvre from the Philadelphia Museum further enhanced Eakins's posthumous reputation.[30]

Eakins's work was made available to a much wider audience through Lloyd Goodrich's monograph and catalogue of 1933. Prior to its publication, Goodrich had written two major pieces on Eakins for *The Arts*. His first, a review written in 1925, stressed pictorial qualities, such as the strong structural elements of Eakins's work and his ability to distil a sitter's personality.[31] A 1929 article was more ambitious and laid the foundation for his subsequent writings.[32] Although Goodrich acknowledged the influence of Gérôme and Bonnat, he disassociated Eakins from their work, however; Eakins had 'none of Gérôme's cold pseudo-classicism ... and whatever likeness he showed to Bonnat's machine-made art was only to the latter's strong, sober portraits. Eakins' art was far more vital and human than that of these high priests of French officialdom ... his art had a reality theirs lacked'.[33] By distancing Eakins from his French teachers and by stressing his 'visual innocence', Goodrich directed attention to his native qualities. Further, he contended that Eakins's painting was a 'Puritanical art, austere, sombre, bitter', and placed him into a tradition of American realism, which included Copley, Johnson, and Kensett.[34]

The 1929 piece also reveals Goodrich's commitment to early twentieth-century American realism and depictions of American life, which he believed were being slighted by critics: Goodrich argued that Eakins provided an important precedent and inspiration for these artists. Eakins had been unafraid to paint what he saw and felt; contemporary realists should not be dissuaded from doing the same. Goodrich wrote:

His art was a direct reflection of his environment, and for the present generation that environment represents all that is dull and hideous, everything from which they have been trying to escape. We are still too close to Eakins' period; in another twenty-five years, perhaps ... his viewpoint on his times is so thoughtful, so serious, so real, that it repels the average contemporary.[35]

Fig.47
Professor Leslie W. Miller
1901
Oil on canvas, 223.8 × 109.8 (88⅛ × 43¼)
Philadelphia Museum of Art.
Gift of Martha P.L. Seeler

Previous writers had asserted the didactic value of Eakins's example, but Goodrich expressed it more strongly than most:

We need the example of Eakins' art today, perhaps more than ever. Our modern system of 'pure' aesthetics, with its disdain of 'literary' and naturalistic elements, tends to make us conceive of art as a sort of pleasing pastime, an exquisite, high type of enjoyment, rather than as an expression of life and character. We are neglecting the experiential sources of art in favor of *a priori* concepts of beauty, and as a result our painting is in danger of degenerating into pretty pattern-making – a new academism as far removed from reality as the old. We need more of Eakins' spirit – his full-blooded power of extracting art from the elements of his own experience, his courage to paint life in any of its aspects, his firm roots in reality.[36]

Here Goodrich took an anti-modernist position by calling the new abstract movements 'academic'. Although they may have appealed to him earlier – he apparently attended the Armory Show several times – his profound interest in promoting American realism took precedence over any interest in European modernism, as evidenced by his writings on 'American scene' painters such as Edward Hopper and Thomas Hart Benton. Goodrich's friends included many contemporary artists who painted the 'American scene', such as Reginald Marsh, to whom he dedicated the 1933 monograph, and John Stewart Curry. Like other early supporters of Eakins – Caffin, Bryson Burroughs, and Henri – Goodrich had also painted early in his career, taking classes in the 1910s at the Art Students' League alongside Marsh.

Is Eakins, then, merely a painter's painter? In 1929 Goodrich estimated that it would take twenty-five years for Eakins to be fully appreciated by the art establishment and the public. However, it was not until the 1970s that Eakins studies truly exploded. This flood of scholarship occurred at the very time when American art was undergoing a much-deserved change in status. In 1979 *Arts Magazine* devoted an entire issue to Eakins. Several important books followed, whose authors included Goodrich, Elizabeth Johns, David Lubin, Michael Fried, and William Innes Homer. Appreciation for the richness and variety of Eakins's work has increased; these modern commentators have explored a far wider range of interpretations than their counterparts in the early twentieth century, and these readings have enabled us to achieve a rounded view of Eakins's art.

1. See Goodrich 1930, p.6.
2. See Stavitsky 1991, pp.12–19.
3. *Philadelphia Press*, 22 February 1914, p.8.
4. Ibid. Here, Eakins concurred with the critical stance of an artist and art critic from a younger generation, Kenyon Cox. Cox is best remembered for his public murals rendered in a conservative manner and his negative reaction to the Armory Show, which he characterized as 'pure insanity or triumphant charlatanism'. See Cox 1913, p.10.
5. *Philadelphia Press*, 22 February 1914, p.8.
6. Hartmann and Eakins must have been in contact by 1895, when Hartmann dedicated his *Conversations with Whitman* to the painter. See Weaver 1991, p.24. Hartmann, who was also a poet and playwright, lived a life that was even more unconventional than the artist he championed. At Christmas 1893 he was jailed in Boston following the publication of his play, *Christ*, loosely based on Oscar Wilde's *Salomé*, which called for nude scenes and an orgy; see Weaver op. cit., p.3.
7. Hartmann 1902, vol.I, p.193.
8. Ibid., vol.I, p.203.
9. Caffin 1907, p.233.
10. Caffin, however, was more interested in the philosophy behind works by Henri's group than the works themselves. The rhetoric of Henri and Caffin are quite similar. Caffin wrote, 'The supreme art of the New Democracy is to be the art of Human Life; the molding of the individual and collective life into forms, efficient, healthy and happy, that shall embody with ever-increasing realization the Democratic ideal – Life, Liberty, and the Pursuit of Happiness'. Art was no longer to be for an élite segment of the public: 'not for selfish indulgence, but for the widest possible benefit to all' (Caffin 1913, pp.5–6, 10). The book embodies all the important components of Caffin's art theory, which has its roots in John Ruskin's writings. See Lee 1983, pp.23–35.
11. Caffin 1907, p.230. In an earlier book on American art, *American Masters of Painting* of 1901, Caffin did not mention Eakins. He included the work of Inness, La Farge, Whistler, Sargent, and Winslow Homer, and discussed the latter in terms similar to Eakins. Homer's art possessed 'qualities of earnest force', and was 'not traceable to European influences' (p.71). Caffin laid greater stress on Eakins's position in a European context than Hartmann; this may have been the result of his interest in the art of other nations. His *Story of Dutch Painting* appeared in 1911, *The Story of French Painting* in 1915, and *The Story of Spanish Painting* in 1917. Caffin was born in England and educated at Oxford. He was also a painter, and had emigrated to the United States in order to work on the decorations at the 1893 Columbian Exposition in Chicago. He began his career as a critic four years later. See Lee op. cit., pp.7–13.
12. Goodrich 1982, vol.II, pp.267–8, 270–1.
13. Before leaving for Paris in 1890 to study at the Ecole and at the Académie Julian, Burroughs attended the Art Students' League in New York; one of his teachers was Kenyon Cox. He returned in 1895 and taught at the League and at the Cooper Union until accepting a position at the Metropolitan Museum of Art in 1906. See 'Bryson Burroughs Curator and Painter Dies at Sixty-five', *Art News*, 24 November, 1934, pp.8, 11; and William M. Ivins, Jr., intro. in *Bryson Burroughs: Catalogue of a Memorial Exhibition of His Works*, Metropolitan Museum of Art, 1935.
14. 'B.B.' [Bryson Burroughs] 1916, p.132.
15. 'B.B.' [Bryson Burroughs] 1917, p.199.
16. McBride 1917, pp.46–8.
17. Letter to Art Students' League, reproduced in Henri 1923, pp.86–8. The impetus for Henri's letter was actually Bryson Burroughs, who asked if Henri could 'boost the show', because 'Eakins is not very well known generally...'. See Goodrich 1982, vol.II, p.276.
18. Alan Burroughs later worked at Harvard University's Fogg Art Museum and wrote a book on American portraiture. See Burroughs 1936.
19. Hamilton Easter Field began *The Arts* in 1920. Following his death in 1922 the art critic Forbes Watson enlisted the aid of Gertrude Vanderbilt Whitney to help continue the magazine. It ceased publication in 1931 when Whitney put her efforts into the Whitney Museum of American Art. For a history of the journal see Goodrich 1973, pp.79–85. Edward Hopper wrote articles on Charles Burchfield and John Sloan; Thomas Hart Benton discussed his art theory in a five-part essay, 'The Mechanics of Form Organization'. See Goodrich 1973, p.83.
20. This piece was ostensibly a review of a show at Brummer Galleries. Alan Burroughs 1923 (1), p.185.
21. Ibid., p.189.
22. For discussions of Babbitt and New Humanism see Nevin 1984; and Morgan 1989, pp.141–7. Mather was, in fact, a close friend of Babbitt's and taught with him at Williams College.
23. [Watson] 1923, p.225.
24. Ibid. Watson echoed this idea in a brief review of a 1927 exhibition of Eakins at Babcock Gallery. See Watson 1927, p.329.
25. Brooks is inferring this from Mather's stance on each of these artists in Mather's *Estimates in Art: Sixteen Essays on American Painters of the Nineteenth Century* of 1931. See Brooks 1952, p.402. However, it should be noted that Hartmann discussed the three in *American Art* in 1902, although he separated Ryder from Homer and Eakins. Bryson Burroughs also linked them together, but added Inness and Whistler. See 'B.B.' [Bryson Burroughs] 1917, p.177.
26. Mather, Jr. 1930, p.44.
27. Mather *et al.* 1927, p.51.
28. Ibid.
29. Ibid., p.58.
30. This event was discussed by Pach 1933, pp.19–20, 48, 50.
31. The piece was a relatively brief review of a 1925 Eakins exhibition at Brummer Galleries. Goodrich 1925, p.345.
32. Goodrich's monograph and catalogue of 1933 must have drawn on work done on Eakins by both Burroughses. *The Arts* had printed Alan Burroughs's catalogue list of over three hundred Eakins works in its June 1924 number (pp.328–33).
33. Goodrich 1929, p.74.
34. Ibid., pp.76, 83.
35. Ibid., pp.72, 74.
36. Ibid., p.83.

The author wishes to thank Professor John Wilmerding as well as colleagues in the graduate program at Princeton University, Sally Mills, and especially Doug Nickel, now at the Museum of Modern Art, San Francisco for their thoughtful comments on earlier versions of this essay.

Bibliography

ABBOTT, E.A., *The Great Painters*, 1927.

'The Academy's Exhibition', *New York Times*, 6 April 1891.

ACKERMAN, G.M., 'Thomas Eakins and his Parisian Masters, Gérôme and Bonnat', *Gazette des Beaux-Arts*, vol. 73, April 1969.

ADAMS, H., *The Education of Henry Adams*, Sentry (ed.), Boston, 1961.

ADAMS, J.H., *History of the Life of D. Hayes Agnew, M.D., LL.D.*, Philadelphia, 1892.

'American Art Gallery', *Art Journal*, vol. 5, May 1881.

ANDREWS, W. and MCCOY, G., 'The Artist Speaks, Part III: Realists and Mystics', *Art in America*, vol. 53, August-September 1965.

'The Annual Exhibition of the Photographic Society of Philadelphia', *Philadelphia Photographer*, vol. 20, May 1883.

'The Anorexe Exhibition – Suggestive Pictures – Christ Crucified by Eakins', *New York Times*, 4 May 1882.

APTHEKER, Herbert, *Writings by W.E.B. Du Bois in Non-Periodical Literature Edited by Others*, Millwood, 1982.

'Art at the Academy. Second Annual Exhibition of the Philadelphia Society of Artists', *Philadelphia Press*, 25 November 1880.

Art for the Nation: Gifts in Honor of the Fiftieth Anniversary of the National Gallery of Art, exh. cat., National Gallery of Art, Washington, DC, 1991.

Arts and Decoration, vol. 8, November 1917.

Arts in Virginia, vol. 9, no. 1, fall 1961.

BAIGELL, M., *A Concise History of American Painting and Sculpture*, New York, 1984.

BALDINGER, W.S., *Art Quarterly*, vol. 9, summer 1946.

BALDWIN, C., 'Thomas Eakins: *le sculpteur W. Rush ciselant une statue allegorique du fleuve Schuylkill, 1877. Nue pris comme modele*', *Connaissance des Arts*, no. 254, April 1973.

BARNES, A.C., 'Some Remarks on Appreciation', *Arts*, vol. 3, 1923.

BARNES, A.C., *The Art in Painting*, Merion, 1925.

'Belated Tribute to a Troubled Artist', *Photography Bulletin*, no. 89, June 1971.

BENJAMIN, S.G.W., 'The Exhibitions – VII. National Academy of Design, Fifty-Sixth Exhibition', *American Art Review*, vol. 2, part II, 1881.

BERKOVITZ, J.S., 'Professor Benjamin Howard Rand', *Journal of the American Medical Association*, vol. 264, no. 7, 15 August 1990, p.787.

BLASER, Kent, 'Walt Whitman and American Art', *Walt Whitman Review*, vol. 24, no. 3, September 1978.

BLAUGRUND, Annette, *American Artists at the Universal Exposition*, Philadelphia, 1989.

BLEDSTEIN, B.J., *The Culture of Professionalism: The Middle Class and the Development of Higher Education in America*, New York and London, 1976.

BOIME, A., *The Academy and French Painting in the Nineteenth Century*, London, 1971.

BOULTON III, Kenyon C., HUENICIK, Peter, POWELL III, Earl A., RAND, Harry Z., SEXTON, Nanette, *American Art at Harvard*, exh. cat., Fogg Art Museum, Cambridge, Massachusetts, 1972.

BREGLER, Charles, 'Thomas Eakins as a Teacher', *Arts*, October 1931.

'Brilliant Display of High-Class Art', *Philadelphia Inquirer*, 18 January 1903.

BROOKS, Van Wyck, *The Confident Years: 1885–1915*, New York, 1952.

BROWN, M.W., *American Art to 1900: Painting, Sculpture, Architecture*, New York, 1977.

BROWNELL, William C., 'The Art Schools of Philadelphia', *Scribner's Monthly Magazine*, vol. 18, no. 5, September 1879.

BROWNELL, William C., 'The Younger Painters of America, First Paper', *Scribner's Monthly Illustrated Magazine*, vol. 20, May 1880.

BRUENING, M., 'A Gallery of American Painting', *London Studio*, vol. 4, November 1932.

BRYANT JR., K.L., *William Merritt Chase: A Genteel Bohemian*, 1991.

BRYANT, N., 'Wood, Field & Stream: Flushing Out Rail Birds', in *New York Times*, 11 November 1977, p. 29.

BUNNELL, P., 'The Art of Pictorial Photography, 1890–1925', exh. cat., in *Record of the Art Museum*, vol. 51, Princeton, 1992.

BURROUGHS, Alan, 'Thomas Eakins', *Arts*, vol. 3, no. 3, March 1923 (1).

BURROUGHS, Alan, 'Thomas Eakins, the Man', *Arts*, vol. 4, December 1923 (2).

BURROUGHS, Alan, 'Catalogue of Works by Thomas Eakins (1869–1916)', *Arts*, vol. 5, no. 6, June 1924.

BURROUGHS, Alan, *Limners and Likenesses: Three Centuries of American Painting*, Cambridge, Massachusetts, 1936.

'B.B.' [Bryson Burroughs], 'Recent Accessions', *Bulletin of the Metropolitan Museum of Art*, vol. 11, no. 6, June 1916.

'B.B' [Bryson Burroughs], 'Thomas Eakins', *Bulletin of the Metropolitan Museum of Art*, vol. 12, no. 10, October 1917.

BURROUGHS, Bryson, *Bulletin of the Metropolitan Museum of Art*, vol. 13, January 1918.

BURROUGHS, Bryson, *Bulletin of the Metropolitan Museum of Art*, vol. 18, December 1923.

BURROUGHS, Bryson, *Bulletin of the Metropolitan Museum of Art*, vol. 29, September 1934.

BUTLER, J.T., 'The American Way with Art', *The Connoisseur*, vol. 176, no. 709, March 1971.

CAFFIN, Charles H., *American Masters of Painting*, New York, 1901 (1).

CAFFIN, Charles H., *International Studio*, no. 14, October 1901 (2).

CAFFIN, Charles H., *The Story of American Painting*, New York, 1907.

CAFFIN, Charles H., *Art for Life's Sake: An Application of the Principles of Art to the Ideals and Conduct of Individual and Collective Life*, New York, 1913.

CANADAY, J., *Mainstreams of Modern Art*, New York, 1959.

CANADAY, J., 'Familiar Truths in Clear and Beautiful Language', *Horizon*, vol. 6, no. 4, autumn 1964.

CASTERAS, Susan P., *Susan Macdowell Eakins, 1851–1938*, exh. cat., Pennsylvania Academy of the Fine Arts, Philadelphia, 1973.

Catalogue of the Forty-First Annual Exhibition of the Pennsylvania Academy of the Fine Arts, exh. cat., Pennsylvania Academy of the Fine Arts, Philadelphia, 1864.

CATHCART, W.L., 'George Wallace Melville', *Journal of the American Society of Naval Engineers*, 24 May 1912.

CHAMBERLIN-HELLMAN, Maria, *Arts Magazine*, vol. 53, May 1979.

CHAMBERLIN-HELLMAN, Maria, 'Thomas Eakins as a Teacher', unpublished Ph.D. thesis, Columbia University, 1981.

CHILD, T., *Art Amateur*, 17 June 1887.

CIKOVSKY Jr., Nicolai, 'William Merritt Chase's Tenth Street Studio', *Archives of American Art Journal*, vol. 16, no. 2, 1976.

CIKOVSKY Jr., Nicolai, KELLY, Franklin and SHAW, Nancy Rivard, *American Paintings from the Manoogian Collection*, exh. cat., National Gallery of Art, Washington, DC, 1989.

200

CLARK, Kenneth, *The Nude: A Study in Ideal Form*, London and Washington, DC, 1956.

CLARK, W., 'The Fine Arts: Eakins' Portrait of Dr. Gross', Philadelphia *Daily Evening Telegraph*, 28 April 1876 (1).

CLARK, W., 'The Centennial. The Art Department: American Section – Eakins', Philadelphia *Daily Evening Telegraph*, 16 June 1876 (2).

CLARK, W., 'American Art. New Departure – The Exhibition of the Society of American Artists in New York', Philadelphia *Daily Evening Telegraph*, 13 March 1878.

CLARK, William J., 'The Iconography of Gender in Thomas Eakins's Portraiture', *American Studies*, no. 32, fall 1991.

COKE, V., *The Painter and the Photograph, from Delacroix to Warhol*, Albuquerque, 1972.

COOK, Clarence, 'Letter to the Editor, A New Departure. Association of American Artists, First Annual Exhibition', *New-York Daily Tribune*, 9 March 1878 (1).

COOK, Clarence, 'The Water-Color Society Exhibition at the Academy', *New-York Daily Tribune*, 9 February 1878 (2).

COOK, Clarence, 'The Society of American Artists, Second Annual Exhibition', *New-York Daily Tribune*, 22 March 1879.

CONNELLY, J.F. (ed.), *The History of the Archdiocese of Philadelphia*, Philadelphia, 1976.

CONNELLY, J.F., *St. Charles Seminary, Philadelphia*, Philadelphia, [1979].

CORN, W.M., *The Color of Mood*, exh. cat., M.H. de Young Memorial Museum, San Francisco, and California Palace of the Legion of Honor, San Francisco, 1972.

COUTURE, T., *Conversations on Art Methods*, S.E. Steuart (trans.), New York, 1879.

COX, K., 'The Modern Spirit in Art, Some Reflections Inspired by the Recent International Exhibition', *Harper's Weekly*, vol. 57, 15 March 1913.

CRAVEN, T., *A Treasury of Art Masterpieces from the Renaissance to the Present Day*, New York, 1939.

DANLY, Susan, *Telling Tales*, exh. cat., Pennsylvania Academy of the Fine Arts, Philadelphia, 1991.

DAVIDSON, M.B., *et al.*, *The American Heritage History of the Artist's America*, New York, 1973.

DAYER GALLATI, Barbara, *A Celebration of American Ideals: Paintings from the Brooklyn Museum*, 1990.

DE KAY, C., *Art Review*, 1 April 1887.

Detroit Institute of Arts Bulletin, vol. 12, no.2, November 1930.

DIBNER, C.W., '*The Pair-Oared Shell* by Thomas Eakins', unpublished paper, University of Pennsylvania, 1967.

DINNERSTEIN, L., 'Thomas Eakins' *Crucifixion* as perceived by Mariana Griswold van Rensselaer', *Arts Magazine*, vol. 53, no. 9, May 1979.

DODIER, V., 'From the Interior: Photographs by Clementina, Viscountess Hawarden', *Antiques*, vol. 139, January 1991.

DU BOIS, W.E.B., *Two Addresses Delivered by Alumni of Fisk University in Connection with the Anniversary Exercises of Their Alma Mater, June, 1898*, Nashville, Fisk University, 1898.

DU BOIS, W.E.B., 'The Negro in America' in *The Encyclopedia Americana*, A.H. McDannald (ed.), New York, 1941.

'Eakins Chats on Art of America', *Philadelphia Press*, 22 February 1914.

EDMONDS, F., *History of the Central High School of Philadelphia*, Philadelphia, 1902.

'The Education of Photographers', *Philadelphia Photographer*, vol. 12, September 1875.

EGAN, Maurice F., 'A Day in the Ma'sh', *Scribner's Monthly Illustrated Magazine*, vol. 22, 1881.

ELLIS, Joseph J., *After the Revolution: Profiles of Early American Culture*, New York and London, 1979.

ERWIN, Joan Smith, 'Miss Van Buren', in *The Classical Spirit in American Portraiture*, Brown University, 1976.

FAISON Jr., S.L., *A Guide to the Art Museums of New England*, New York, 1958.

'Family Art Game', Detroit Institute of Arts Advertising Supplement, *Detroit Free Press*, 26 April 1981.

FEHR, A. and HOMER, William Innes, 'The Photographic Society of Philadelphia and the Salon Movement' in *Pictorial Photography in Philadelphia: The Pennsylvania Academy's Salons, 1898–1901*, Philadelphia, 1984.

'Fifty-Sixth Annual Exhibition of the National Academy of Design – I', *Nation*, vol. 32, no. 822, 31 March 1881.

'Fifty-Sixth Annual Exhibition of the National Academy of Design – II', *Nation*, vol. 32, 21 April 1881.

'The Fine Arts', *Philadelphia Evening Bulletin*, 13 November 1882, p.8.

FITZGERALD, R., *Philadelphia Item*, 12 May 1896, p.1.

FLEXNER, J.T., *The World of Winslow Homer, 1836–1910*, New York, 1966.

Fogg Art Museum Acquisitions Report, 1969–1970.

Fogg Art Museum Newsletter, vol. 6, no. 3, January 1969.

FOLSOM, E., ' "This Heart's Geography's Map": The Photographs of Walt Whitman', *Walt Whitman Quarterly Review*, vol. 4, nos. 2–3, fall/winter 1986–1987.

FOSBURGH, J.W., 'Music and Meaning: Eakins' Progress', *Art News*, vol. 56, February 1958.

FOSTER, Kathleen A., 'Makers of the American Watercolor Movement, 1860–1890', Ph.D. dissertation, Yale University, 1982.

FOSTER, Kathleen A., 'An Important Eakins Collection', *Antiques*, vol. 130, December 1989.

FOSTER, Kathleen A., 'Realism or Impressionism? The Landscapes of Thomas Eakins', *Studies in the History of Art*, no. 37, 1990.

FOSTER, Kathleen A., *Thomas Eakins Reconsidered*, New Haven, forthcoming 1994 (catalogue of Charles Bregler's Thomas Eakins Collection, Pennsylvania Academy of the Fine Arts).

FOSTER, Kathleen A. and Cheryl Leibold, *Writing about Eakins: The Manuscripts in Charles Bregler's Thomas Eakins Collection*, Philadelphia, 1989.

FRANKENSTEIN, A., 'American Art and American Moods', *Art in America*, vol.54, March 1966.

FRIED, Michael, 'Realism, Writing, and Disfiguration in Thomas Eakins's *Gross Clinic*', *Representations*, no. 9, winter 1985.

FRIED, Michael, *Realism, Writing, Disfiguration: On Thomas Eakins and Stephen Crane*, Chicago, 1987.

GABRIEL, R.H. (ed.), *The American Spirit in Art*, vol. 12 of *The Pageant of America*, 1927.

GARRETT, W.D., NORTON, P.F., GOWANS, A., and BUTLER, J.T., *The Arts in America: The Nineteenth Century*, New York, 1969.

GERDTS, William H., *The Great American Nude: A History in Art*, New York, 1974.

GERDTS, William H., 'Thomas Eakins and the Episcopal Portrait: Archbishop William Henry Elder', *Arts Magazine*, vol. 53, May 1979.

GERDTS, William H., *The Art of Healing: Medicine and Science in American Art*, exh. cat., Birmingham Museum of Art, Alabama, 1981.

GILES, Laura, MILROY, Elizabeth and OWENS, Gwendolyn, *Master Drawings from the Collection of Ingrid and Julius S. Held*, exh. cat., Clark Art Institute, Williamstown, Massachusetts, 1979.

GOLDWATER, R., 'Art and Nature in the Nineteenth Century', *Magazine of Art*, vol. 38, March 1945.

GOODRICH, Lloyd, *Arts*, vol. 8, no. 6, December 1925.

GOODRICH, Lloyd, 'Thomas Eakins, Realist', *Arts*, vol. 16, no. 2, October 1929.

GOODRICH, Lloyd, *Winslow Homer, Albert P. Ryder, Thomas Eakins*, exh. cat., New York, 1930.

GOODRICH, Lloyd, *Thomas Eakins, His Life and Work*, New York, 1933.

GOODRICH, Lloyd, *Thomas Eakins: A Retrospective Exhibition*, National Gallery of Art, Washington, DC, 1961.

GOODRICH, Lloyd, *Thomas Eakins: Retrospective Exhibition*, exh. cat., Whitney Museum of American Art, New York, 1970.

GOODRICH, Lloyd, '*The Arts* Magazine: 1920–31', *American Art Journal*, vol. 5, no. 1, May 1973.

GOODRICH, Lloyd, *Thomas Eakins*, 2 vols., Cambridge, Massachusetts, Washington, DC, and London, 1982.

GOODRICH, Lloyd and MARCEAU, H., *Philadelphia Museum Bulletin*, vol. 39, May 1944.

GREEN, S.M., *American Art: A Historical Survey*, New York, 1966.

GREENBERG, C., *Art Digest*, vol. 28, 1 January 1954.

GREENFIELD, H., *The Devil and Dr. Barnes: Portrait of an American Art Collector*, New York, 1987.

'Greta's Boston Letter: The Art Club's Exhibition', *Art Amateur*, vol. 4, March 1881.

GUTTRIDGE, L.F., *Icebound: The Jeannette Expedition's Quest for the North Pole*, New York, 1988.

'G.W.E.' [George W. Eggers], 'Thomas Eakins', *Bulletin of the Worcester Art Museum*, vol. 20, 1930.

HALE, R.B., *Metropolitan Museum of Art Bulletin*, vol. 12, March 1954.

HAMILTON, J.M. and MORRIS, H.S., *Metropolitan Museum of Art Bulletin*, vol. 12, November 1917.

HARTMANN, Sadakichi, *A History of American Art*, 2 vols, Boston, 1902.

HAUGHOM, S., 'Thomas Eakins's *The Concert Singer*', *Antiques*, vol. 108, December 1975.

HENDRICKS, Gordon, 'A May Morning in the Park', *Philadelphia Museum of Art Bulletin*, vol. 60, spring 1965.

HENDRICKS, Gordon, 'Eakins's William Rush Carving His Allegorical Statue of the Schuylkill', *Art Quarterly*, vol. 3, no. 4, winter 1968.

HENDRICKS, Gordon, 'Thomas Eakins's *Gross Clinic*', *Art Bulletin*, vol. LI, March 1969.

HENDRICKS, Gordon, *The Photographs of Thomas Eakins*, New York, 1972.

HENDRICKS, Gordon, *The Life and Work of Thomas Eakins*, New York, 1974.

HENRI, Robert, *The Art Spirit*, Philadelphia, 1923.

HOMER, William Innes, *Thomas Eakins: His Life and Art*, New York, 1992.

HOMER, William Innes, and TALBOT, J., 'Eakins, Muybridge and the Motion Picture Process', *Art Quarterly*, vol. 26, summer 1963.

Home Scenes: American Genre Paintings from the Brooklyn Museum Collections, New York, 1987.

HOOPES, D.F., *Eakins Watercolors*, New York, 1971.

HOWARD, H.N., *Brush and Pencil*, vol. 9, February 1902.

Il Cardinale Diomede Falconio, O.F.M., L'Aquila, 1968.

Index of Twentieth Century Artists, vol. 1, January 1934.

JACKMAN, R.E., *American Arts*, 1928.

JOHNS, Elizabeth, 'Thomas Eakins: A Case for Reassessment', *Arts Magazine*, vol. 53, May 1979.

JOHNS, Elizabeth, 'Drawing Instruction at Central High School and its Impact on Thomas Eakins', *Winterthur Portfolio*, vol. 15, no.2, summer 1980.

JOHNS, Elizabeth, *Thomas Eakins: The Heroism of Modern Life*, Princeton, 1983 (1).

JOHNS, Elizabeth, 'Thomas Eakins and "Pure Art" Education', *Archives of American Art Journal*, vol. 23, no. 3, 1983 (2).

JOHNS, Elizabeth, 'Body and Soul', *Art and Antiques*, vol. 7, September 1984, pp. 73–9.

JOHNS, Elizabeth, 'Nudity and Fantasy in the Photography of Thomas Eakins' in *Eakins and the Photograph*, forthcoming from Smithsonian Institution Press.

KAPLAN, Sidney, 'The Negro in the Art of Homer and Eakins', *Massachusetts Review*, vol. VII, winter 1966.

KATZ, L., *Arts*, vol. 30, September 1956.

KOEHLER, S.R., 'The Exhibitions – III', *American Art Review*, vol. 2, part 1, 1881.

KURLIN, L.J., *Catholicity in Philadelphia*, Philadelphia, 1909.

LAFOLLETTE, S., *Art in America*, New York, 1929.

LAGENEVAIS, F., 'Le Salon de 1875', *Revue des Deux-Mondes*, vol. 9, 1875.

LARKIN, Oliver W., *Art and Life in America*, New York, 1949, 1960.

LEE, Sarah Underwood, *Charles H. Caffin: A Voice for Modernism 1897–1918*, Ann Arbor, Michigan, 1983.

LEIBOLD, Cheryl, 'The Life and Papers of Susan Macdowell Eakins' in Kathleen A. Foster and Cheryl Leibold, *Writing About Eakins: The Manuscripts in Charles Bregler's Thomas Eakins Collection*, Philadelphia, 1989.

LEIBOLD, Cheryl, 'The Many Faces of Thomas Eakins', *Pennsylvania Heritage*, vol. XVII, no. 2, spring 1991.

LEROI, P., 'Salon de 1875: XV', *L'Art*, vol. 2, 1875.

LIFTON, N., 'Thomas Eakins and S. Weir Mitchell: Images and Cures in Nineteenth Century Philadelphia', in vol. 2, M. Gedo (ed.), *Psychoanalytic Perspective on Art*, Hillsdale, 1987.

LONG, D.E., 'The Medical World of *The Agnew Clinic*: A World We Have Lost?', *Prospects*, vol. 11 (1987), pp. 185–98.

'Looking at Paintings with Bernard Dunston', *American Artist*, vol. 44, February 1980.

LUBIN, David, *Act of Portrayal: Eakins, Sargent, James*, New Haven, 1985.

LYNES, R., *The Art Makers of the Nineteenth Century*, New York, 1970.

MARCEAU, H.G., 'Catalogue of the Works of Thomas Eakins', *Pennsylvania Museum Bulletin*, vol. 25, March 1930.

MARCEAU, H.G., 'The Fairman Rogers Four-in-Hand', *Pennsylvania Museum Bulletin*, vol. 26, January 1931.

MARZIO, P., *The Art Crusade: An Analysis of American Drawing Manuals, 1820–1860*, Washington, 1976.

MATHER Jr., Frank Jewett, 'Thomas Eakins's Art in Retrospect', *International Studio*, vol. 95, no. 392, January 1930.

MATHER, Jr., Frank Jewett, *Estimates in Art*, vol. 2, 1931.

MATHER Jr., Frank Jewett, MOREY, Charles Rufus and HENDERSON, William James, *The Pageant of America*, vol. 12, *The American Spirit in Art*, ed. R.H. Gabriel, New Haven, 1927.

MATHEWS, Marcia, *Henry Ossawa Tanner, American Artist*, Chicago, 1969.

MATTHIESSEN, F.O., *American Renaissance: Art and Expression in the Age of Emerson and Whitman*, New York, 1941.

MCBRIDE, H., 'Exhibitions at New York Galleries', *Fine Arts Journal* (Chicago), vol. 35, December 1917.

MCBRIDE, H., *The Flow of Art*, New York, 1975.

MCCAUGHEY, P., 'Thomas Eakins and the Power of Seeing', *Artforum*, vol. 9, December 1970.

MCCURDY, C., (ed.), *Modern Art, a Pictorial Anthology*, New York, 1958.

MCDANNALD, A.H. (ed.), *The Encyclopedia Americana*, New York, 1941.

MCELROY, Guy C., *Facing History: The Black Image in American Art 1710–1940*, exh. cat., Corcoran Gallery of Art, Washington, DC, 1990.

MCHENRY, Margaret, *Thomas Eakins Who Painted*, Oreland, Pennsylvania, 1946.

MCKINNEY, R., *Thomas Eakins*, New York, 1942.

MCLANATHAN, R., *The American Tradition in the Arts*, New York, 1968.

Memorial Exhibition of the Works of the Late Thomas Eakins, exh. cat., Pennsylvania Academy of the Fine Arts, Philadelphia, 1917.

Metropolitan Museum of Art Bulletin, vol. 33, winter 1975–1976.

MILLER, Edwin Haviland (ed.), *Walt Whitman: The Correspondence 1842–1892*, 6 vols., (vols 1 and 2 [1842–1875] 1961; vol. 3 [1876–1885] 1964; vols 4 and 5 [1886–1892] 1969; vol. 6 [index and supplement] 1977), New York, 1961–1977.

MILLET, J.B., 'Boston Art Club, Twenty-Third Exhibition', *American Art Review*, vol. 2, part 1, 1881.

MILROY, Elizabeth, 'Thomas Eakins's Artistic Training 1860–1870', unpublished Ph.D. thesis, University of Pennsylvania, 1986.

MILROY, Elizabeth, ' "Consummatum Est" ': A Reassessment of Thomas Eakins' *Crucifixion* of 1880', *Art Bulletin*, vol. 71, no. 2, June 1989.

MOORE, A.D., 'Henry Rowland', *Scientific American*, 246, February 1982.

MORGAN, H.Wayne, *Keepers of Culture: The Art-Thought of Kenyon Cox, Royal Cortissoz, and Frank Jewett Mather, Jr.*, Kent, Ohio, 1989.

MORRIS, H.S., *Century*, no. 47, March 1905.

MORTIMER, K.A., *Harvard University Art Museums: A Guide to the Collections*, New York, 1985.

MOSBY, Dewey F. and SEWELL, Darrel, *Henry Ossawa Tanner*, Philadelphia, 1991.

MUMFORD, L., *The Brown Decades: A Study of the Arts of America 1865–1895*, 1931.

Nation, vol. 106, 21 February 1918.

NEVIN, Thomas R., *Irving Babbitt: An Intellectual Study*, Chapel Hill, 1984.

'Noted Picture and Its Maker', *Philadelphia Record Magazine*, 29 March 1914.

NOVAK, B., *American Painting of the Nineteenth Century: Realism, Idealism, and the American Experience*, New York, 1969.

O'CONNOR Jr., J., *Carnegie Magazine*, vol.19, May 1945

ORMSBEE, T.E., 'Thomas Eakins, American Realist Painter', *American Collector*, vol. 13, July 1944.

Outlook, vol. 117, 21 November 1917

PACH, Walter, 'American Art in the Louvre', *Fine Arts* (New York), vol. 20, no. 1, May 1933.

PACH, Walter, 'A First Portfolio of American Art', *Art News*, vol. 35, 3 October 1936.

PANZER, M., *Philadelphia Naturalistic Photography, 1865–1906*, New Haven, 1982.

PARRY III, Ellwood C., 'Thomas Eakins and *The Gross Clinic*', *Jefferson Medical College Alumni Bulletin*, vol. 16, summer 1967.

PARRY III, Ellwood C., '*The Gross Clinic* as Anatomy Lesson and Memorial Portrait', *Art Quarterly*, vol. 32, no. 4, winter 1969.

PARRY III, Ellwood C., *The Image of the Indian and the Black Man in American Art, 1590–1900*, New York, 1974.

PARRY III, Ellwood C., 'Thomas Eakins and the Everpresence of Photography', *Arts Magazine*, vol. 51, June 1977.

PARRY III, Ellwood C., 'The Thomas Eakins Portrait of Sue and Harry; or, When Did the Artist Change His Mind?', *Arts Magazine*, vol. 53, no. 9, May 1979.

PARRY III, Ellwood C., *Photographer Thomas Eakins*, Philadelphia, 1980.

PARRY III, Ellwood C., 'Some Distant Relatives and American Cousins of Thomas Eakins's Children at Play', *American Art Journal*, vol. 18, no. 1, 1986.

PARRY III, Ellwood C. and CHAMBERLIN-HELLMAN, Maria, 'Thomas Eakins as an Illustrator, 1878–1881', *American Art Journal*, vol. 5, May 1973.

PEALE, Rembrandt, *Graphics: A Manual of Drawing and Writing*, 1834.

PENNELL, J., 'Photography as a Hindrance and a Help to Art', *British Journal of Photography*, vol. 38, 8 May 1891.

PETERSON, M., 'Elizabeth with a Dog by Thomas Eakins', in *San Diego Fine Arts Gallery Report*, San Diego, 1971.

PHELPS, Mrs Lincoln, *The Educator: or Hours With My Pupils*, New York, 1868.

Philadelphia Inquirer, 8 February 1914.

Philadelphia Ledger, 23 December 1895.

'Philadelphia Society of Artists, Second Annual Exhibition', Philadelphia *Evening Bulletin*, 28 October 1880.

'Philadelphia Society of Artists, Second Annual Exhibition', Philadelphia *Evening Telegraph*, 4 November 1880.

'Philadelphia Society of Artists, Second Annual Exhibition', Philadelphia *Daily Times*, 24 November 1880.

PISANO, R.G., *A Leading Spirit in American Art: William Merritt Chase 1849–1961*, exh. cat., Henry Art Gallery, University of Washington, Seattle, 1983.

PORTER, F., *Thomas Eakins*, New York, 1959.

The Portrayal of the Negro in American Painting 1710–1963, exh. cat., Bowdoin College Museum of Art, Maine, 1964.

PROWN, Jules David, *American Painting from its Beginnings to the Armory Show*, 1969.

PROWN, Jules David, 'Thomas Eakins' *Baby at Play*', *Studies in the History of Art*, vol. 18, National Gallery of Art, Washington, DC, 1985.

RATCLIFF, C., *Art International*, vol. 14, Christmas 1970.

RENNIE, D.B., 'The Portraiture of Thomas Eakins', *North Carolina Museum of Art Bulletin*, vol. 8, December 1968.

REWALD, John, *The John Hay Whitney Collection*, exh. cat., Tate Gallery, London, 1961 and National Gallery of Art, Washington, DC, 1983.

RHODES, R., *Sport in Art from American Museums*, New York, 1990.

RICHARDSON, E.P., *American Romantic Painting*, exh. cat., Detroit Institute of Arts, Detroit, 1944.

RITCHIE, A.C. and NEILSON, K.B., *Selected Paintings and Sculpture from the Yale University Art Gallery*, New Haven, 1972.

ROBB, D.M. and GARRISON, J.J., *Art in the Western World*, New York, 1932, 1955.

ROBB, D. M., *The Harper History of Painting*, New York, 1951.

ROBINSON, Franklin W., *One Hundred Master Drawings from New England Private Collections*, exh. cat., Wadsworth Atheneum, Hartford, 1973.

ROGERS, Fairman, 'The Zoötrope', *Art Interchange*, no. 3, July 1879.

ROOF, K.M., *The Life and Art of William Merritt Chase*, New York, 1917.

ROOT, Marcus Aurelius, *The Pencil and the Camera, or, the Heliographic Art*, Philadelphia, 1864.

ROSENBERG, H., *Art News*, vol. 52, January 1954

ROSENZWEIG, Phyllis D., *The Thomas Eakins Collection of the Hirshhorn Museum and Sculpture Garden*, Washington, DC, 1977.

ROTH, G.B., 'An Early American Pharmacologist: Horatio C Wood', *Isis*, vol. 30, 1939.

ROTH, R., 'The New England or "Olde Tyme", Kitchen Exhibit at Nineteenth-Century Fairs', in A. Axelrod (ed.), *The Colonial Revival in America*, New York, 1985.

RULE, H.B., 'Walt Whitman and Thomas Eakins: Variations on Some Common Themes', *Texas Quarterly*, 17, winter 1974.

SANDWEISS, M. (ed.), *Photography in Nineteenth-Century America*, Fort Worth, Texas, 1991.

'Sartain Papers', Archives of American Art, Smithsonian Institution, Washington, DC.

SCHENDLER, Sylvan, *Eakins*, Boston and Toronto, 1967.

SCHLAPEIT-BECK, D., 'Frauenarbeit und Stand der Technologie als Thema der Malerei: Das Motiv der Spinnenden Frau', *Kritische Berichte*, vol. 15, 1987.

SEIBERLING, G. and BLOORE, C., *Amateurs, Photography and the Mid-Victorian Imagination*, Chicago, 1986.

SELLIN, D., *The First Pose, 1876: Turning Point in American Art. Howard Roberts, Thomas Eakins, and a Century of Philadelphia Nudes*, New York, 1976.

SELLIN, D., *Thomas Eakins, Susan Macdowell Eakins, Elizabeth Macdowell Kenton: An Exhibition of Paintings, Photographs and Artifacts*, exh. cat., Roanoke, Virginia, 1977.

SEWELL, Darrel, *Thomas Eakins, Artist of Philadelphia*, exh. cat., Philadelphia Museum of Art, Philadelphia, 1982.

SHERRILL, S.B., *Antiques*, vol. 98, October 1970.

SHESTACK, A. (ed.), *Yale University Art Gallery; Selections*, New Haven, 1983.

SHINN, E., in *Nation*, vol. 26, no. 66, 28 February 1878.

[SHINN, E.], 'Fine Arts: The Lessons of a Late Exhibition', *Nation*, vol. 26, 11 April 1878.

SHOOLMAN, R.L. and SLATKIN, C.E., *The Enjoyment of Art in America*, Philadelphia, 1942.

SIEGL, T., *Philadelphia Museum of Art Bulletin*, vol. 65, no. 304, 1969.

SIEGL, T., 'Perspective Drawing for *The Pair-Oared Shell* (I) and (II)' in *Philadelphia: Three Centuries of American Art*, Philadelphia, 1978.

SIEGL, T., *The Thomas Eakins Collection*, Philadelphia, 1978.

SILL, Geoffrey M., and TARBELL, Roberta K. (eds.), *Walt Whitman and the Visual Arts*, New Brunswick, 1992.

SIMPSON, Marc, 'Thomas Eakins and His Arcadian Works', *Smithsonian Studies in American Art*, vol. 1, no. 2, fall 1987.

Sixth Loan Exhibition: Winslow Homer, Albert P. Ryder, Thomas Eakins, exh. cat., Museum of Modern Art, New York, 1930.

SIZER, T., 'Eakins's *John Biglen*', *Yale University Associates in Fine Arts Bulletin*, vol.8, February 1938.

SMITH, J.G., 'The Enigma of Thomas Eakins', *American Artist*, vol. 20, November 1956.

SMITH, M.S., '*The Agnew Clinic*: "Not Cheerful for Ladies to Look at"', *Prospects*, vol. 11, 1987.

'The Society of American Artist's Exhibition', *Art Age*, vol. 5, June 1887.

'The Society of American Artists', *Art Interchange*, vol. 2, no. 6, 19 March 1879.

SONNEDECKER, G., 'Horatio C Wood' in *Dictionary of Scientific Biography*, New York, 1976, p. 496.

SPASSKY, Natalie, *et al.*, *American Paintings in the Metropolitan Museum of Art*, vol. II, *A Catalogue of Works by Artists between 1816 and 1845*, New York, 1985.

SPASSKY, Natalie, *American Paintings in the Metropolitan Museum*, vol. III, New York, 1985.

STAVITSKY, Gail, 'John Weichsel and the People's Art Guild', *Archives of American Art Journal*, vol. 31, no. 4, 1991.

STEBBINS Jr., T., *American Master Drawings and Watercolors*, exh. cat., New York, 1976.

STEBBINS, T.E. and GOROKHOFF, G., *A Checklist of American Paintings at Yale University*, New Haven, 1982.

STRAHAN, E. [Earl Shinn], 'The Metropolitan Museum of Art', *The Art Amateur*, vol. 2, no. 6, May 1880.

STRAHAN, E. [Earl Shinn], 'Exhibition of the Philadelphia Society of Artists', *Art Amateur*, vol. 4, December 1880.

STUART, E., 'Memories of Thomas Eakins', *Harper's Bazaar*, vol. 81, no. 2828, August 1947.

TANNER, Benjamin Tucker, *The Color of Solomon – What? 'My Beloved is White and Ruddy'. A Monograph*, introduction by William Scarborough, Philadelphia, 1895.

Thomas Eakins 1844–1916. Exhibition of Painting and Sculpture, exh. cat., The American Academy of Arts and Letters and the National Institute of Arts and Letters, New York, 1958.

THURSTON, R.H., 'Rear-Admiral G.W. Melville, U.S.N., and Applied Science in Construction of the New Fleet', *The Popular Science Monthly*, vol. 64, December 1903.

TOMKO, G., *Catalog of the Roland P. Murdock Collection*, Wichita, 1972.

TRAUBEL, Horace, *With Walt Whitman in Camden*: vol. 1, New York, 1905, (reprinted New York, 1961); vol.2, New York, 1907 (reprinted New York, 1961); vol. 3, New York, 1912 (reprinted New York, 1961); vol. 4, S. Bradley (ed.), Philadelphia, 1953; vol. 5, G. Traubel (ed.), Carbondale, Illinois, 1964; vol.6, G. Traubel and W. White (eds.), Carbondale, Illinois, 1982; vol. 7, J. Chapman and R. Macisaac (eds.), Carbondale, Illinois, 1992.

TRENT, Josiah C., MD, 'Walt Whitman – A Case History', *Surgery, Gynecology and Obstetrics*, vol. 87, July 1948.

TRUETTNER, W., 'Dressing the Part: Thomas Eakins's Portrait of Frank Hamilton Cushing', *American Art Journal*, vol. 17, spring 1985.

TURNER, Evan H., 'Thomas Eakins at Overbrook', *Records of the American Catholic Historical Society of Philadelphia*, vol. 81, no. 4, December 1970.

TURNER, E., 'Thomas Eakins: The Earle Galleries' Exhibition of 1896', *Arts Magazine*, vol. 53, no. 9, May 1979.

URDANG, L., (ed.), *The Timetables of American History*, New York, 1981.

VALECCHI, M., *Landscape Painting of the Nineteenth Century*, Greenwich, 1971.

VAN RENSSELAER, Mariana Griswold, 'The Philadelphia Exhibition, II', *American Architect and Building News*, vol. 8, no. 261, 25 December 1880.

VAN RENSSELAER, Mariana Griswold, 'Picture Exhibitions in Philadelphia – II', *American Architect and Building News*, vol. 10, no. 314, 31 December 1881.

VAN RENSSELAER, Mariana Griswold, 'The Society of American Artists, New York, II', *American Architect and Building News*, 20 May 1882.

VAN RENSSELAER, Mariana Griswold, *The Book of American Figure Painters*, 1886.

VARNEDOE, J.K.T. and LEE, T.P., *Gustave Caillebotte, A Retrospective Exhibition*, exh. cat., Museum of Fine Arts, Houston, and the Brooklyn Museum, New York, 1976.

VOGEL, Hermann, 'Photographic Sketches from the Centennial Grounds', *Philadelphia Photographer*, vol. 8, September 1876.

WALKER, J., *Paintings from America*, Baltimore, 1951.

WASHINGTON, Booker T., *Up From Slavery: An Autobiography*, Garden City, New York, 1963.

[WATSON, F.], 'Comment', *Arts*, vol. 3, no. 3, March 1923.

WATSON, F., 'Exhibitions in New York', *Arts*, vol. 12, no. 6, December 1927.

WATSON, F., 'In the Galleries: Ryder, Eakins, Homer', *Arts*, vol. 16, May 1930.

WATSON, J., 'News and Comment', *Magazine of Art*, vol. 33, December 1940.

WEAVER, Jane Calhoun (ed.), *Sadakichi Hartmann, Critical Modernist: Collected Art Writings*, Berkeley, California, 1991.

WEAVER, M. (ed.), *British Photography in the Nineteenth Century: The Fine Art Tradition*, Cambridge, 1989.

WEINBERG, H. Barbara, *The American Pupils of Jean-Léon Gérôme*, Fort Worth, Texas, 1984.

WEINBERG, H. Barbara, *The Lure of Paris*, New York, 1991.

WEISS, J.A.W., 'Clarence Cook: His Critical Writings', unpublished Ph.D. dissertation, The Johns Hopkins University, Baltimore, 1976.

WELLING, W., *Photography in America: The Formative Years, 1839–1900*, New York, 1978.

WELLS, H.G., 'The Future in America: A Search After Realities', *Harper's Weekly*, no. 50, 15 September 1906, p. 1317.

WHITMAN. W., *Leaves of Grass the First* (1855), M. Crowley (ed.), London, 1986.

WHITMAN, W., *Leaves of Grass*, Library of America edn, New York, 1982.

WILLIAMS, Jr., H.M., *Mirror to the American Past: A Survey of American Genre Painting: 1750–1900*, New York, 1973.

WILLIAMS, T.C., 'Thomas Eakins: Artist and Teacher for All Seasons', *American Artist*, vol. 39, March 1975.

WILMERDING, John, *A History of American Marine Painting*, Boston, 1968.

WILMERDING, John, *American Art*, 1976.

WILMERDING, John, 'Harvard and American Art', Fogg Art Museum bound reprint of *Apollo*, May–June 1978.

WILMERDING, John, 'Thomas Eakins' Late Portraits', *Arts Magazine*, vol. 53, no. 9, May 1979.

WILMERDING, John, 'Walt Whitman and American Painting', *Antiques*, vol. 128, no.5, November 1985.

WILMERDING, John, *American Masterpieces from the National Gallery of Art*, rev. edn, New York, 1988.

WILMERDING, John, *American Light: The Luminist Movement, 1850–1875*, Princeton, 1989.

WILMERDING, John, *American Views: Essays on American Art*, Princeton, 1991.

WOOD, Horatio C, *Brain-work and Overwork*, Philadelphia, 1880.

WRIGHT, M.E., *Brush and Pencil*, vol. 7, February 1901.

YOUNG, M., *American Realists, Homer to Hopper*, New York, 1977.

ZEIGLER, F., 'Eakins Memorial Exhibition in New York', *Record* (Philadelphia), 11 November 1917.

List of Exhibitions

Exhibitions are listed in chronological order

Boston, Boston Art Club, *First Exhibition for 1878*, 1878.

New York, Brooklyn Art Association, *Spring Exhibition*, 1878.

New York, Kurtz Gallery, *Society of American Artists First Anniversary Exhibition*, 1878.

Philadelphia, Pennsylvania Academy of the Fine Arts, *Philadelphia Society of Artists Second Annual Exhibition*, 1880.

Boston, Boston Art Club, *Twenty-third Exhibition*, 1881.

New York, National Academy of Design, *Fifty-sixth Annual Exhibition*, 1881.

New York, Society of American Artists, *Fourth Annual Exhibition*, 1881.

Philadelphia, Pennsylvania Academy of the Fine Arts, *Special Exhibition of Paintings by American Artists at Home and in Europe*, 1881.

Chicago, Inter-State Industrial Exposition, *Tenth Annual Exhibition*, 1882.

Philadelphia, Pennsylvania Academy of the Fine Arts, *Fifty-fourth Annual Exhibition*, 1883.

New York, American Art Association, *A Special Exhibition of American Paintings*, 1884.

Toronto, Ontario Society of Artists, *Loan Exhibition*, 1885.

Philadelphia, College of Physicians of Philadelphia, *College of Physicians of Philadelphia Centennial Celebration: Loan Collection of Portraits*, 1887.

Chicago, Art Institute, *Second Annual Exhibition, American Oil Paintings*, 1889.

Philadelphia, Pennsylvania Academy of the Fine Arts, *Academy Annual*, winter 1891.

New York, Society of American Artists, *Retrospective Exhibition*, 1892.

Chicago, State Building, Art Gallery and Women's Building, Pennsylvania Art Contributions to *World's Columbian Exposition*, 1893.

Philadelphia, Art Club of Philadelphia, *Sixth Annual Exhibition*, 1894.

New York, National Academy of Design, *Seventieth Annual Exhibition*, 1895.

Philadelphia, Earle Galleries, *Eakins Exhibition*, 1896.

Pittsburgh, Carnegie Institute, *Fourth Annual Exhibition*, 1899–1900.

Philadelphia, Pennsylvania Academy of the Fine Arts, *The Sixty-ninth Annual Exhibition*, 1900.

Buffalo, *Pan-American Exposition*, 1901.

Boston, Copley Hall, *The Copley Society Second Annual Exhibition of Contemporary Art*, 1902.

New York, American Fine Arts Society, *Twenty-fifth Annual Exhibition of the Society of American Artists*, 1903.

St Louis, *Universal Exhibition*, 1904.

Pittsburgh, Carnegie Institute, *Tenth Annual Exhibition*, 1905.

Detroit, Museum of Art, *Annual Exhibition of American Artists*, 1906.

Washington, DC, Corcoran Gallery of Art, *First Annual Exhibition of Oil Paintings by Contemporary American Artists*, 1907.

New York, National Academy of Design, *Eighty-third Annual Exhibition*, 1908.

Philadelphia, Pennsylvania Academy of the Fine Arts, *One Hundred and Seventh Annual Exhibition*, 1912.

New York, National Academy of Design, *Eighty-eighth Annual Exhibition*, 1913.

New York, Brooklyn Museum, *Contemporary American Painting*, 1914.

Philadelphia, Pennsylvania Academy of the Fine Arts, *One Hundred and Ninth Exhibition*, 1914.

Washington, DC, Corcoran Gallery of Art, *Fifth Annual Exhibition of Oil Paintings by Contemporary American Artists*, 1914.

San Francisco, Fine Arts Section, *Panama-Pacific International Exposition*, 1915.

Chicago, Art Institute, *Twenty-ninth Annual Exhibition*, 1916.

New York, National Academy of Design, *Ninety-first Annual Exhibition*, 1916.

New York, Metropolitan Museum of Art, *Thomas Eakins Memorial Exhibition*, 5 November–3 December 1917.

Philadelphia, Pennsylvania Academy of the Fine Arts, *Memorial Exhibition of the Works of the Late Thomas Eakins*, 1917.

New York, Whitney Studio Club (and tour to Venice, London, Sheffield and Paris), *Overseas Exhibition of American Paintings*, 1921.

Minneapolis, Minneapolis Institute, *Thomas Eakins*, 1923.

New York, Joseph Brummer Galleries, *Exhibition of Paintings and Watercolors by Thomas Eakins*, 1923.

Washington, DC, Corcoran Gallery of Art, and New York, Grand Central Art Galleries, *Commemorative Exhibition by Members of the National Academy of Design*, 1925–1926.

Philadelphia, Department of Fine Arts, *Sesqui-Centennial International Exposition*, 1926.

Portland, Oregon, Portland Art Museum, January 1927.

Washington, DC, Phillips Memorial Gallery, *A Period in Art: Portraits, Ideal Heads and Figures in Praise of Girls and Women*, February-March 1927.

Cleveland, Museum of Art, *Memorial Exhibition of Paintings by Thomas Eakins, Albert P. Ryder and J. Alden Weir*, 1928.

Washington, DC, Phillips Memorial Gallery, *American Old Masters*, February-May 1928.

Los Angeles, California, Los Angeles Museum Exposition Park, *Paintings from the Phillips Memorial Gallery*, 21 July–31 August 1930.

New York, Museum of Modern Art, *Sixth Loan Exhibition: Winslow Homer, Albert P. Ryder, Thomas Eakins*, 1930.

Philadelphia, Pennsylvania (now Philadelphia) Museum of Art, *Thomas Eakins, 1844–1916*, 1930.

Hanover, New Hampshire, Carpenter Hall, Dartmouth College, *An Exhibition of Sixteen Paintings by Contemporary Modernists from the Phillips Memorial Gallery*, 1–14 February 1931.

New York, The Century Association, *Exhibition of Portraits*, March 1931.

Pittsburgh, Carnegie Institute, *Special Exhibition of American Genre Painting*, 1931.

Los Angeles, Los Angeles Museum, *Tenth Olympiad: Olympic Competition and Exhibition of Art*, 1932.

New York, Metropolitan Museum of Art, *The Taste of Today in Masterpieces of Painting Before 1900*, 10 July–2 October 1932.

New York, Whitney Museum of American Art, *Thomas Eakins*, 1933.

Chicago, Art Institute, *A Century of Progress: Exhibition of Paintings and Sculpture*, 1934.

Washington, DC, Phillips Memorial Gallery, *Pictures of People*, 5 November 1933–15 February 1934.

New York, Whitney Museum of Art, *American Genre Painting: The Social Scene in Painting and Prints*, 1935.

San Francisco, M.H. de Young Memorial Museum and California Palace of the Legion of Honor, *American Painting*, 1935.

Baltimore, Museum of Art, *Thomas Eakins: A Retrospective Exhibition of His Paintings*, 1936.

Cleveland, Museum of Art, *Exhibition of American Paintings from 1860 until Today*, 1937.

Detroit, Institute of Arts, *Eighteenth Annual Exhibition of American Art*, 1937.

Minneapolis, University of Minnesota Art Gallery, *A Survey of Colonial and Provincial Painting*, 1937.

Philadelphia, Museum of Art (and tour), *Problems of Portraiture*, 1937.

Baltimore, Museum of Art, *Two Hundred Years of American Painting*, 1938.

Paris, Jeu de Paume, *Trois Siècles d'Art aux Etats-Unis: Exposition en Collaboration avec le Museum of Modern Art, New York*, 1938.

Chicago, Art Institute, *Half a Century of American Art*, 1939.

New York, Kleeman Galleries, *Exhibition of Paintings by Thomas Eakins*, 1939.

New York, Metropolitan Museum of Art, *Life in America: A Special Loan Exhibition of Paintings held during the Period of the New York World's Fair*, 1939.

New York, Museum of Modern Art, *Art in Our Time*, 1939.

New York, National Academy of Design, *Special Exhibition*, 1939.

New York, World's Fair, *Masterpieces of Art, 1500–1900*, 1940.

Philadelphia, Museum of Art, *Life in Philadelphia: An Exhibition in Conjunction with the Bicentennial of the University of Pennsylvania*, 1940.

San Francisco, *Golden Gate International Exposition*, 1940.

Toronto, Art Gallery of Toronto, November-December 1940.

Washington, DC, Phillips Memorial Gallery, *Emotional Design in Painting*, 7 April–5 May 1940.

Washington, DC, Phillips Memorial Gallery, *The Functions of Color in Painting: An Educational Loan Exhibition*, 16 February–23 March 1941.

Washington, DC, Howard University, *The Negro in American Art*, 1942.

New York, Museum of Modern Art, *Romantic Painting in America*, 15 November 1943–6 February 1944.

Boston, Museum of Fine Arts, *Sport in American Art*, 1944

Detroit, Institute of Arts, *The World of the Romantic Artist: A Survey of American Culture from 1800–1875*, 28 December 1944–28 January 1945.

New York, M. Knoedler & Co., *Loan Exhibition of the Works of Thomas Eakins, 1844–1944, Commemorating the Centennial of his Birth*, 5 June–31 July 1944

Philadelphia, Museum of Art, *Thomas Eakins Centennial Exhibition, 1844–1944*, 1944.

Washington, DC, Phillips Memorial Gallery, *The American Paintings of the Phillips Collection*, 9 April–30 May 1944.

Wilmington, Delaware, The Wilmington Society of Fine Arts, *Thomas Eakins*, October 1944.

Philadelphia, The Philadelphia Art Alliance, *Memorial Exhibition of the Paintings by Henry O. Tanner*, October-November 1945.

Pittsburgh, Carnegie Institute, *Thomas Eakins Centennial Exhibition 1844–1944*, 26 April–1 June 1945.

Boston, Boston Symphony Orchestra, Symphony Hall, *Exhibition of Musical Instrument Paintings*, 29 January–12 February 1946.

London, Tate Gallery, *American Paintings from the Eighteenth Century to the Present Day*, 1946.

New Jersey, Newark Museum, *Nineteenth Century French and American Paintings from the Collection of the Metropolitan Museum of Art*, 1946.

Colorado Springs, Fine Arts Center, *Twenty-one Great Paintings*, summer 1947.

Milwaukee, Milwaukee Art Institute, *Sport and Adventure in American Art*, 1947.

Columbus, Ohio, Columbus Museum of Fine Arts, *American Heritage Series*, 1948.

New York, Brooklyn Museum, *The Coast and the Sea: A Survey of American Marine Painting*, 1948.

Dallas, Museum of Fine Arts, *Exhibition at the Texas State Fair: Famous American Paintings*, 1948.

Des Moines, Iowa, Des Moines Art Center, *Nineteenth and Twentieth Century European and American Art*, 1948.

Cambridge, Massachusetts, Fogg Art Museum, *Semi-centennial Meeting of the American Physical Society*, 1949.

Fort Worth, Texas, Fort Worth Art Association, *Fort Worth Centennial 1849–1949*, April 1949.

New York, The Century Association, *Aspects of New York City Life*, 1950.

New York, Metropolitan Museum of Art, *Twentieth Century Painters*, 1950.

Philadelphia, Museum of Art, *Diamond Jubilee Exhibition: Masterpieces of Painting*, 1950.

Toronto, Art Gallery, *Old Masters Exhibition*, 1950.

Washington, DC, Corcoran Gallery of Art, *American Processional*, 1950.

Washington, DC, National Gallery of Art, *Makers of History in Washington*, 1950.

Washington, DC, The Phillips Gallery, *Selected American Paintings from the Collection*, summer 1950.

New York, The Century Association, *Eakins-Homer Exhibition*, 1951.

New York, Metropolitan Museum of Art, *The Seventy-fifth Anniversary Exhibition of Paintings and Sculpture by Seventy-five Artists Associated with the Art Students' League of New York*, 1951.

New York, National Academy of Design, *The American Tradition 1800–1900*, 1951.

Pomona, California, Los Angeles County Fair, *One World of Art*, 1951.

Frankfurt, American Federation of the Arts and United States Information Agency, *American Paintings in the Nineteenth Century*, 1953.

New York, Metropolitan Museum of Art, *American Painting 1754–1955*, 1953.

Philadelphia, Museum of Art, *Homer, Eakins, Cassatt*, 1953.

Baltimore, Museum of Art, *Man and His Years*, 1954.

New York, American Academy of Arts and Letters, *The Great Decade in American Writing with Paintings by Friends and Acquaintances of the Authors*, 1954.

New York, Cooper Union Museum, *An Exhibition of American Drawings*, 1954.

Madrid, National Library (and tour), *Pennsylvania Academy's One Hundred and Fiftieth Anniversary Exhibition*, 1955.

New York, Museum of Modern Art, *Paintings from Private Collections*, 1955.

Philadelphia, The Pennsylvania Academy of the Fine Arts, *One Hundred and Fiftieth Anniversary Exhibition*, 1955.

State College, Pennsylvania State University, *Centennial Exhibition: Pennsylvania Painters*, 1955.

Wilmington, Society of the Fine Arts, *Twenty-Three American Painters: Their Portraits and Their Work, 1815–1945*, 1956.

New York, Brooklyn Museum, *Face of America: The History of Portraiture in the United States*, 14 November 1957–26 January 1958.

Pittsburgh, Carnegie Institute, *American Classics of the Nineteenth Century*, 1957–1958.

Washington, DC, Corcoran Gallery of Art, *The Twenty-fifth Biennial Exhibition of Contemporary American Oil Paintings*, 1957–1958.

Dallas, Texas, Museum of Fine Arts, *Famous Paintings and Famous Painters*, 1958.

New York, American Academy of Arts and Letters and National Institute of Arts and Letters, *Thomas Eakins 1844–1916: Exhibition of Paintings and Sculpture*, 1 January–16 February 1958.

New York, Metropolitan Museum of Art, *Fourteen American Masters*, 1958.

Washington, DC, Corcoran Gallery of Art, *The American Muse: Parallel Trends in Literature and Art*, 4 April–17 May 1959.

Westmorland County, Museum of Art, *Two Hundred and Fifty Years of Art in Pennsylvania*, 1959.

New Haven, Yale University Art Gallery, *Paintings, Drawings, and Sculpture Collected by Yale Alumni*, 1960.

London, Tate Gallery, *The John Hay Whitney Collection*, 1961.

Richmond, Virginia Museum of Fine Arts, *Treasures in America*, 1961.

Toronto, Art Gallery of Toronto; Winnipeg, Art Gallery Association; Vancouver, Art Gallery; New York, Whitney Museum of American Art, *American Painting, 1865–1905*, 1961.

Washington, DC, National Gallery of Art (and tour), *Thomas Eakins: A Retrospective Exhibition*, 1961.

Philadelphia, Museum of Art, *Eakins in Perspective*, 1962.

Bowdoin, Maine, Bowdoin College Museum of Art, *The Portrayal of the Negro in American Painting*, 1964.

New York, Arts Students' League, *American Masters From Eakins to Pollock*, 1964.

New York, Brooklyn Museum, *The Triumph of Realism*, 1964.

New York, Metropolitan Museum of Art, *Three Centuries of American Painting*, 1965.

Philadelphia, Museum of Art, *The Art of Philadelphia Medicine*, 1965.

Trenton, New Jersey State Museum, *New Jersey and the Artist*, 1965.

New York, Whitney Museum of American Art, *Art of the United States: 1670–1966*, 1966.

New York, Art Students' League, *American Masters: Art Students' League*, 1967.

New York, Center for Inter-American Relations, *Precursors of Modernism in Western Hemisphere Art, 1860–1930*, 1967.

New York, Forum Gallery, *The Portrayal of Negroes in American Art*, 1967.

New York, Hirschl and Adler Galleries, *The American Vision: Genre Paintings, 1825–1875*, 1968.

New York, National Art Museum of Sport, *The Artist and the Sportsman*, 1968.

Washington, DC, Smithsonian Institution, National Portrait Gallery, *This New Man: A Discourse in Portraits*, 1968.

Tulsa, Oklahoma, The Phillbrook Art Center, *The American Sense of Reality*, 1969.

Washington, DC, Corcoran Gallery of Art, *The Sculpture of Thomas Eakins*, 1969.

Washington, DC, Smithsonian Institution, National Collection of Fine Arts; Cleveland, Museum of Art; New Orleans, McNay Museum of Art; Pittsburgh, Carnegie Institute; Waltham, Massachusetts, Rose Art Museum; Brandeis University, *The Art of Henry O. Tanner*, 1969.

Waterville, Maine, Colby College (and tour), *Nineteenth and Twentieth Century Paintings from the Collection of the Smith College Museum of Art*, 1969–1972 (organized by Smith College of Art, circulated by American Federation of the Arts).

Bloomington, Indiana University Art Museum, *The American Scene, 1820–1900*, 1970.

New York, Binghampton, State University of New York, University Art Gallery (and tour), *Selections from the Drawing Collection of Mr and Mrs Julius S. Held*, 1970.

New York, Metropolitan Museum of Art, *Nineteenth-century America, Paintings and Sculpture*, 16 April–7 September 1970.

New York, Whitney Museum of American Art, *Thomas Eakins Retrospective Exhibition*, 1970.

Overbrook, Pennsylvania, St Charles Borromeo Seminary, *Yours Truly Thomas Eakins*, 1970.

New York, M. Knoedler & Co., *What is American in American Art?*, 1971.

Oakland, California, Oakland Museum, *Thomas Eakins: His Photographic Works*, 1971.

Washington, DC, National Gallery of Art, *Great American Paintings from the Boston and Metropolitan Museums*, 1971.

Glens Falls, New York, The Hyde Collection, *The Art of Henry Ossawa Tanner*, 1972.

Hartford, Connecticut, Wadsworth Atheneum, *One Hundred Master Drawings from New England Private Collections*, 1973.

New York, Whitney Museum of American Art, *The Painter's America: Rural and Urban Life 1810–1910*, 1974.

London, Embassy of the United States, *A Portrait of Young America*, 1975–1976.

San Jose, California, San Jose Museum of Art, *Americans Abroad; Painters of the Victorian Era*, 1975–1976.

Washington, DC, Hirshhorn Museum and Sculpture Garden, *Inaugural Exhibition*, 1 October–15 September 1975.

Washington, DC, Smithsonian Institution, *Artists and Models: An Exhibition of Photographs, Letters, and Other Documents of the Archives of American Art*, 1975.

Minneapolis, Minneapolis Institute of Arts, 23 November 1976–23 January 1977.

New York, Metropolitan Museum of Art, *A Bicentennial Treasury*, 1976 (1).

New York, Metropolitan Museum of Art, *Selections of Nineteenth-Century Afro-American Art*, 1976 (2).

New York, Whitney Museum of American Art, *American Master Drawings and Watercolors: Works on Paper from Colonial Times to the Present*, 23 November 1976–23 January 1977.

Philadelphia, Museum of Art, *Philadelphia: Three Centuries of American Art*, 1976.

Philadelphia, Pennsylvania Academy of the Fine Arts, *In This Academy: A Special Bicentennial Exhibition*, 1976.

Providence, Rhode Island, Bell Gallery, Brown University, *The Classical Spirit in American Portraiture*, 6–29 February 1976.

Washington, DC, The Phillips Collection, *American Art From the Phillips Collection, Part 1*, 29 May–21 August 1976 (1).

Washington, DC, The Phillips Collection, *American Art From the Phillips Collection, Part 2*, 4 September–24 October 1976 (2).

Worcester, Massachusetts, Worcester Art Museum, *The Second Fifty Years: American Art 1826–1876*, 1976.

Cambridge, Massachusetts, Fogg Art Museum, *Master Paintings from the Fogg Collection*, April-August 1977.

Moscow, Pushkin Museum, Leningrad, Hermitage, and Minsk, Palace of Art, *Representation of America*, 1977–1978.

New York, Whitney Museum of American Art, *Turn of the Century America: Paintings, Graphics, Photographs 1890–1910*, 1977.

San Francisco, Fine Arts Museums of San Francisco, *American Master Drawings and Watercolors: Works on Paper from Colonial Times to the Present*, 20 February–17 April 1977.

Washington, DC, Hirshhorn Museum and Sculpture Garden, *The Thomas Eakins Collection of the Hirshhorn Museum and Sculpture Garden*, 1977.

Williamstown, Massachusetts, Clark Art Institute (and tour), *Master Drawings from the Collection of Ingrid and Julius S. Held*, 1979.

Chadds Ford, Pennsylvania, Brandywine River Museum, *Eakins at Avondale and Thomas Eakins: A Personal Collection*, 15 March–18 May 1980.

Houston, Meredith Long & Co., *Americans at Work and Play*, March 1980.

Washington, DC, National Gallery of Art, *Post-Impressionism: Cross-Currents in European and American Painting 1880–1906*, 25 May–1 September 1980.

Birmingham, Alabama, Birmingham Museum of Art, *The Art of Healing: Medicine and Science in American Art*, 1981.

San Francisco, California, the California Palace of the Legion of Honor, The Fine Arts Museums of San Francisco, *Impressionism and the Modern Vision: Master Paintings from The Phillips Collection*, 4 July–1 November 1981.

Washington, DC, Corcoran Gallery of Art, *Of Time and Place: American Figurative Art from the Corcoran Gallery of Art*, 1981.

Philadelphia, Museum of Art, *Thomas Eakins: Artist of Philadelphia*, 29 May–4 August 1982 (1).

Philadelphia, Museum of Art, *Thomas Eakins: Themes and Studies*, 1982 (2).

Boston, Museum of Fine Arts, *A New World: Masterpieces of American Painting 1760–1910*, 7 September–13 November 1983.

Washington, DC, National Gallery of Art, *The John Hay Whitney Collection*, 1983.

Williamstown, Massachusetts, Williams College Museum of Art, *The New England Eye: Master American Paintings from New England School, College, and University Collections*, 11 September–16 November 1983.

Clinton, New York, Fred L. Emerson Gallery, Hamilton College (and tour), *The Art of Music: American Paintings and Musical Instruments 1770–1910*, 7 April–3 June 1984.

Paris, Palais du Louvre, *A New World: American Painting, 1760–1900*, 1984.

Collegeville, Pennsylvania, Fetterolf House at Ursinus College, *Inaugural Exhibit: A Selection of American Art*, 26 September–5 October 1986.

Chicago, Terra Museum of American Art, *A Proud Heritage: Two Centuries of American Art*, 1987.

Washington, DC, The Phillips Collection, *The Return of the Master Painting*, 22 April–27 August 1989.

Andover, Massachusetts, Addison Gallery of American Art, *American Masterworks*, 5 October–16 December 1990.

Southampton, The Parish Art Museum, *A Celebration of American Ideals: Paintings from the Brooklyn Museum*, May-July 1990.

Washington, DC, Corcoran Museum of Art, *Facing History, The Black Image in American Art 1710–1940*, 1990.

Buffalo, Albright-Knox Art Gallery, *A Celebration of American Ideals: Paintings from the Brooklyn Museum*, November 1991–January 1992.

Philadelphia, Pennsylvania Academy of Fine Arts, *Thomas Eakins Rediscovered*, 26 September 1991–5 April 1992.

Washington, DC, National Gallery of Art, *Art for the Nation: Gifts in Honor of the Fiftieth Anniversary of the National Gallery of Art*, 1991.

Washington, DC, Smithsonian Institution, National Portrait Gallery and National Museum of American Art, *World Columbian Exposition*, April-August 1993.

Index

Page numbers in bold refer to catalogue entries of works exhibited.
Numbers in italics refer to illustrations.